How to Stop Your Kids Watching Too Much TV, Spending Hours on the Computer, Wasting Days on the Game Boy™ and Endlessly Texting Friends, etc...

How to Stop Your Kids Watching Too Much TV, Spending Hours on the Computer, Wasting Days on the Game Boy™ and Endlessly Texting Friends, etc…

649. 5

Top Tips for Every Parent

Teresa Orange & Louise O'Flynn

HAY HOUSE

HAY HOUSE

Australia • Canada • Hong Kong
South Africa • United Kingdom • United States

First published and distributed in the United Kingdom by:
Hay House UK Ltd, 292B Kensal Rd, London W10 5BE.
Tel.: (44) 20 8962 1230; Fax: (44) 20 8962 1239. www.hayhouse.co.uk

Published and distributed in the United States of America by:
Hay House, Inc., PO Box 5100, Carlsbad, CA 92018-5100.
Tel.: (1) 760 431 7695 or (800) 654 5126; Fax (1) 760 431 6948 or (800) 650 5115.
www.hayhouse.com

Published and distributed in Australia by:
Hay House Australia Ltd, 18/36 Ralph St, Alexandria NSW 2015.
Tel.: (61) 2 9669 4299; Fax: (61) 2 9669 4144. www.hayhouse.com.au

Published and distributed in the Republic of South Africa by:
Hay House SA (Pty), Ltd, PO Box 990, Witkoppen 2068.
Tel./Fax: (27) 11 706 6612. orders@psdprom.co.za

Published and distributed in India by:
Hay House Publishers India, Muskaan Complex, Plot No.3,
B-2, Vasant Kunj, New Delhi – 110 070.
Tel.: (91) 11 41761620; Fax: (91) 11 41761630. contact@hayhouseindia.co.in

Distributed in Canada by:
Raincoast, 9050 Shaughnessy St, Vancouver, BC V6P 6E5.
Tel.: (1) 604 323 7100; Fax: (1) 604 323 2600

A catalogue record for this book is available from the British Library.

Extended version previously published as *The Media Diet for Kids* by Hay House, 2005,
ISBN 978-1-4019-0768-6

ISBN 978-1-4019-1547-6

Printed and bound in Great Britain by TJ International, Padstow, Cornwall.

To Mum and Dad

About the authors

Teresa Orange and Louise O'Flynn were described by The Observer newspaper in 2005 as 'two mothers on a mission to save children from television', after they sparked off a national debate about the role of the media in children's lives today.

At the time a lot of people were still in denial about the harmful effects of too much time spent in front of the television or computer. Thanks to the media coverage, and the support of figures like Michael Morpurgo, there has been a sea change in public opinion.

Over the past two years Teresa and Louise have appeared frequently on national and regional TV and radio talking about the dangers of 'screen bingeing' and what practical steps parents can take to bring up a well-balanced media child. They have also worked closely with teachers and schools advising on media parenting issues.

Teresa Orange has a degree in psychology and was the children's expert at the advertising giant, J Walter Thompson. She is an industry spokesperson on advertising and marketing to children. She is an expert qualitative researcher with an in-depth understanding of childhood development, childhood emotions and the relationship children have with brands and advertising.

Louise has worked with the media for the last twenty-five years. As director of communications at Camelot, she was responsible for promoting the UK's biggest consumer brand – The National Lottery. She is currently a freelance writer and media consultant.

They are both mums with children ranging between 5 and 14 years old.

Contents

PART 2: ENSURING THAT SCREEN TIME IS QUALITY TIME

Tips on ...

Foreword by Michael Morpurgo

You hear it all the time, don't you? 'Children these days have so much choice.' And they have too, and that's fine. Choice can be hugely enriching, but it can be overwhelming.

Thinking back to my own childhood, we could either listen to the radio (one programme), read books (Blyton mostly) or play out. That was it. Now children have in-house entertainment of every conceivable variety, and all instantly available, instantly stimulating. Like fast food, it is seductive and compelling, and can become deeply habit-forming. Like fast food, too much of it is seriously bad for you. We know that.

The question is then how you as a parent can find the positive in all this, so that your child can benefit from the best of it rather than suffer from the worst of it, or from simple overindulgence.

Never has parenting been as complex as it is now. This much-needed book helps parents to unravel these complexities, giving so much confidence to them in their efforts to ration and select, in their attempts to help children towards making sensible choices for themselves.

Once the new habits have been inculcated and accepted, the need and the appetite diminish, and it all becomes so much easier and happier for child and parent alike.

Michael Morpurgo
Children's Laureate 2003-2005

What this book promises

Most parents no longer need convincing: they know that too much screen time is bad for their kids. Now they want practical tips on how to cut down.

Time and time again over the last couple of years we have been asked for tips on how to limit the amount of time children spend in front of the television and computer. And often it's been a two-way process: parents, grandparents, carers and teachers have been keen to share their tips with us too.

This book is full of practical tips to stop your kids watching too much TV, spending hours on the computer, wasting days on their consoles and endlessly texting friends, etc. In short, it will help you bring up a well-balanced media child who is then able to control the role of the screen in his or her teenage years and beyond.

Some of the tips are more obvious than others. Some require radical action. Others a little tweak here or there.

The great thing is that you can pick and choose what tips to follow according to what feels right for you and your child. There is something for everyone and – remember – it often only takes a tiny change in what we do as parents, to make a huge change in the media habits of our kids.

Introduction

It's all about balance ...

Most parents will be familiar with the situation ... the kids are glued to the telly or gripped by some new computer game. There's homework to be done and it's time for bed. But they're there. In front of *that* screen.

'Turn *that* thing off!' you shout.

'Just five more minutes, pleeese!' they reply.

You reluctantly give way ... and before you know it, another half an hour has passed. As parents, most of us have firm views about bringing up our children. We naturally want the best for them. We care about the food they eat, the friends they make, how they behave and what they're taught at school.

Why is it, then, that we don't have a clearer idea about how to deal with two of the biggest single influences in our children's lives – the TV and computer? Perhaps it's because we don't appreciate just how much time kids do spend watching TV or playing on the computer, and exactly what harm it might be doing them.

Believe it or not, eleven- to fifteen-year-olds spend on average 52 hours a week in front of the screen – whether it's watching

TV, videos or DVDs, playing computer games or just being online. This compares with 38 hours a week in 1994. It means that many kids are now spending more than seven hours in front of the screen every day. And the majority of children spend more time watching TV than actually learning at school. [1]

Most people would agree this can't be a good thing. And nowadays there is an abundance of evidence to prove it isn't. How to control the TV and the computer has become a major challenge of parenting today. Even those parents who are coping seem to find it increasingly difficult.

INCREASING SCREEN CONSUMPTION

Average number of hours per week* amongst 11-15 year olds

	1994	1996	2000	2006**
TV	26.6	28.8	33.5	30.7
Videos/DVDs	5.9	5.8	5.8	5.0
Computer Games	5.8	5.6	7.3	7.3
Internet			5.2	8.8
Total 'Screen Time'	38.3	40.2	51.8	51.8

*Averages per week include time spent in school holidays and at school
**2006 average Internet usage comprises 5.4 hours at home, 2.0 hours at school, 1.4 hours elsewhere
Source: Youth TGI, Copyright BMRB International 1994-2006

We're two mums with screen-hungry kids and we know just how difficult it is to control the screen, not only at home but also away from home too. Some time ago we started to worry that things weren't quite right. We were concerned about the balance in our children's lives.

We also became aware of the growing number of research studies that show that children suffer long-term problems if they spend too much time in front of the TV, or computer screen, in their formative years.

Obviously we're not the only mums like us around. Lots of us – and dads, of course – have children with big screen appetites. That's modern living. But that's no reason to sit back and feel defeated as modern media threatens to take charge of family life.

As media professionals we're familiar with the tricks of the trade and wanted to put this expertise to good use. So we decided to use what we had learnt in our media lives to explore how parents could control, and make the most of, the media when bringing up children.

We did our own research talking to parents, grandparents, carers and teachers. We asked them questions:

- What role should the TV and computer play in children's lives?

- How much time should our children be spending in front of the screen?

- What's the best way of controlling their media consumption?

- What other things should we be encouraging them to do?

Everyone we spoke to was quick to point out that children benefit in all sorts of ways from modern media. So let's remind ourselves of some of the positives.

For kids the best thing about the screen is that 'it's a boredom buster' - in other words, it's great entertainment. It also allows them to relax and chill out, and thanks to the Internet and mobile phones there are loads of social opportunities for kids to stay in contact with friends and family.

And, whomever you speak to, everybody agrees that modern media is great for learning. Whether at home or at school, the screen has revolutionised what and how children are taught. The interactive experience helps make learning fun and encourages new interests and creativity. Certainly, the more competent children are with the screen, the easier they'll find the transition into a working environment.

So, the message is clear. Modern media is great for children but it needs to be consumed in moderation because too much screen time is clearly damaging. That's why this book is all about balance. We're not advocating media starvation but a balanced approach which gives your child the best of all worlds.

So in this book we start off by highlighting some of the dangers of media bingeing and why it's right to find media balance in your child's life. We then look at how to limit your child's time in front of the screen and suggest alternative activities to fill the void. And finally, we look at how to ensure your child's screen time is also quality time so that you can make the most of everything that modern media has to offer.

>TOP TIPS<

- Be positive from the start. It's very difficult to stop your kids watching too much TV if they think you're a negative old busybody.

- Let your kids know why you value the screen. If they sense your appreciation, they will be more prone to listen when you try and enforce limits.

- A good way of showing your appreciation is to sit at the screen with your children. Admire your son's gaming skills, or get your daughter to show you her creative designs on Bebo.

- It's always good to show a few screen initiatives of your own: for instance, developing the family website, or simply using Sky+ to arrange the weekly TV schedule.

Why too much screen time is bad for your kids

This section provides any parent unsure about the need to take action with the reasons why it's so important not to let kids binge on the screen.

Media dangers – what we all know for sure

There has been a huge amount of research in recent years that shows the range of physical, social and mental conditions that millions of children are suffering, simply because they're spending so much time watching TV or playing on the computer. And most children – whether their parents realise it or not – are affected.

Research shows that more than two hours a day in front of the television can cause long-term damage. So it's no longer just a gut feeling we might have. Now there is no debating – too much screen time is bad for your kids.

We have outlined five areas where the dangers of too much screen exposure are most evident:

1. Behaviour
2. Physical wellbeing
3. Education
4. Relationships
5. World outlook.

We're not scientists ourselves and don't pretend to be. A lot of what follows is what we have gathered from talking to people with first-hand experience of kids – and from kids themselves. We've also been monitoring studies published in recent years and have included some of the facts which impressed us the most.

YES, TOO MUCH IS DAMAGING ... and there's plenty of evidence to prove it.

1. Behaviour

By the age of 18 the average child in the US has witnessed 200,000 acts of violence on the TV.[2] And that's even before you add up all the hours of shooting and fighting on their PlayStations and computers. You don't need to be a scientist to work out that kids mimic what they see. It's natural.

The advertising world knows only too well about the 'mimicking power' of the screen. In fact they positively exploit it. Even film people agree that too much violence on the TV isn't a good thing – 80 per cent of Hollywood executives believe there is a link between TV violence and the real thing.[3] And in 2005, parents took a media company to court because they believed that a violent computer game led to the murder of their son.

Specific media dangers associated with behaviour are: anti-social behaviour; impulsive outbursts; play apathy; depression and premature adulthood. For the Media Dangers Checklist go to page 173.

>TOP TIPS<

- If you're suspicious that a particular TV programme or computer game is having a bad effect on your child, why not conduct your own experiment? You could enforce a complete ban of the offending programme or game-screen activity for a set period of time, for instance a week. At the end of the week, take note of how your child has changed. We found that parents are often amazed by the results.

- Alternatively, quietly remove the screen activity from your child's agenda. You may need to be a little devious. For instance, you could try 'losing' the disc during a major tidy-up, or removing the fuse from the plug of the offending screen.

- If things change for the better, share the results with your child. Kids often don't realise how the screen is affecting their behaviour, and if you can help them understand, it makes it easier to eliminate the offending TV programme or game for good.

2. Physical wellbeing

The biggest health hazard of sitting for hours in front of a screen is simply that you're inactive. Kids need active bodies to have healthy bodies. The World Health Organization has reported that physical inactivity is one of the ten leading causes of death in developed countries, producing around 2 million deaths worldwide per year.[4]

Childhood obesity and diabetes have become major concerns across the world – 16% of children in the US are obese. Europe's children are fast catching up and some are even overtaking. For instance, in Scotland, a third of 12-year-olds are overweight and a fifth are obese, while it is estimated that 50% of British children could be obese by 2020.[5] As obesity levels rise, more young people are affected by type II diabetes, and it is estimated that the UK could witness a health crisis within six years with 3m sufferers.[6]

These are appalling figures – representing a modern-day health crisis. A sedentary life – often caused by too much screen time – is a major contributing factor.

Specific media dangers associated with physical wellbeing are: obesity, diabetes and other health problems; poor coordination; energy imbalance; screen strain and mobile radiation. For the Media Dangers Checklist go to page 173.

>TOP TIPS<

- You may be bored by all the press coverage about 'couch-potato syndrome', but don't turn off as a result. We all need to recognise that screen bingeing does influence a child's physical shape.

- It's easy to blame everybody else for the world's obesity epidemic, for instance the junk food advertisers and the school dinner ladies. But don't forget that your child's lifestyle is in your hands.

- Children need educating too and you must encourage them to take responsibility for their own physical wellbeing. Most older children understand the concept of 'you are what you eat', so encourage them to believe that 'they are what they DO'.

3. Education

More and more research is proving that too much screen time can be bad for education. It can put pressure on your children's schedule and affect the way they develop intellectually. In the US, for instance, a study found that over ten hours a week of TV viewing has a negative influence on a child's academic performance, while other research shows that too much TV as a young child can lead to attention problems when you are older.[7] If you ask any teacher how children have changed over the last few years, one of the things they often mention is that children have shorter attention spans than before. It's not surprising. Kids have got used to screen communication that bombards them with constant visual and audio stimulation.

Specific media dangers associated with education are: attention problems; poor speech development; literacy retarded; spoon-fed minds and sleep deprivation. For the Media Dangers Checklist go to page 173.

>TOP TIPS<

- If you need convincing about the educational dangers, just talk to some teachers. We were struck by how concerned they are about the dangers of screen bingeing.

- And if your child is a real screen addict, a few words with their form teacher can be extremely helpful. Find out what they think, or ask them for advice, and then you will have extra resolve (and authority!) to take action.

- You might be surprised at what children think about screen bingeing and education – they told us that as grown-ups they would be stricter with their kids. 'Why?' we asked. 'So they do well in life,' they replied. Why not find out what your child thinks?

4. Relationships

Developing happy and stable relationships is an important part of growing up. In many ways modern media can be a great 'socialising' force. But it can also cause problems when it comes to relationships. Close relationships that deteriorate, or are lost altogether, are the biggest concern for parents with kids who binge on TV and computer games. These children appear to value the screen above anything else and are at risk of becoming loners – or modern-day hermits. We found that it was this loss of social interaction that often prompted parents to take action and cut back on their kids' media consumption.

Specific media dangers associated with relationships are: turning into modern-day hermits; parents being in the dark; social overload and Internet grooming. For the Media Dangers Checklist go to page 173.

>TOP TIPS<

• As you watch a gang of kids play on the computer you may conclude that the screen is great for social interaction and bonding. In many ways you would be right. But beware, all too easily a child's relationship with a screen can become addictive.[8]

• So what are the signs of screen addiction? As with other addictions the screen becomes all-consuming – for instance, watch out for kids who simply think of the screen as soon as they wake up. See page 22 for our Media Addiction Checklist.

• It is devastating to watch a child turn into a social hermit. We found that when this happens, setting screen limits often becomes a non-negotiable family policy. So don't be afraid to be firm.

5. World outlook

The media for many children is their window on the world. They see life through it and form their own judgements and values from it. The real world becomes boring because the media world seems so much more exciting. There is a risk that kids become emotionally numb. They lose the ability to enjoy simple pleasures because they are so used to the fast-moving pace of the virtual world. There is also a risk that kids acquire a distorted view of the world. They can develop perceptions of life which are at odds with reality. So, for example, they develop unfounded fears, have an upside-down sense of value, and are quick to stereotype people and emotions.

Specific media dangers associated with world outlook are: becoming an earth alien; bunker mentality; realism deficiency; dumbed-down values and an 'I want culture'. For the Media Dangers Checklist go to page 173.

>TOP TIPS<

- Don't underestimate the power of the screen and the fact that it has become the single biggest influence in many children's lives. Ensure that it is you, not the media, that nurtures the 'out-look' of your children.

- Have the courage to play a more proactive role as 'screen monitor'. If you let your children spend hours in front of violent computer games, don't be surprised if they develop aggressive tendencies.[9] Similarly, hours in front of offensive reality shows may well contribute to cultural and racial mis-understandings.

- You're entitled to feel daunted by your responsibilities – in this digital world controlling what your children view can seem impossible. So don't make life harder for yourself ... for instance, by letting your kids have TVs in their bedrooms (see Golden Rules, page 38).

So ... yes, too much is damaging

All the research just confirms what we as parents instinctively know. Too much time sitting alone in front of a screen can't be a good thing for anyone. Or as one grandmother put it: 'Life isn't just about sitting in front of the box. If you spend hours and hours watching TV or playing on the computer, there's less time for other things.'

>TOP TIPS<

- Check that the whole family is aware of the lasting dangers of the screen. Yes, screen bingeing today will influence a child's life as an adult, and this must be made clear.

- Scientific gobbledegook can do wonders with husbands who need convincing: 'Darling, did you know that too much TV can jeopardise the synaptic pathways of the brain?'[10] If you need more scientific talk, look up the references throughout this section.

- True horror stories are great for the kids: for instance, the story about the young boy who tried to kill his mum after she took away the TV, or the girl who hanged herself after watching an 18-rated film.[11] Look out for more real-life stories in the press.

 **PART I**

LIMITING SCREEN TIME AND FINDING OTHER THINGS TO DO

Time counting
Understanding your starting point

The first step in reducing your child's screen time is to understand your starting point:

'How much time is your child spending watching TV or playing computer games?'

An easy way of recording your child's screen time is to keep a Media Diary. You only need to do it for a week and it only takes a couple of minutes a day, but you must be honest with yourself – every five minutes count. It's also a good idea to make a separate note of TV and computer time so that you have some idea of what the balance is.

We found from our research that the process of just completing the Media Diary was quite an eye opener for some parents. Time and time again parents were under-estimating the time their children were spending in front of the TV or computer. In fact, the two of us were guilty of doing this too. It wasn't until we kept a careful note that we had a clear idea of what was going on. The five minutes here and there were all adding up.

THE MEDIA DIARY

DAY OF WEEK	TIME SPENT WATCHING TV	TIME SPENT PLAYING COMPUTER GAMES	TOTAL SCREEN TIME
MONDAY			
TUESDAY			
WEDNESDAY			
THURSDAY			
FRIDAY			
SATURDAY			
SUNDAY			
TOTAL			

Have a go at filling in the diary yourself. You can print off copies of the Media Diary from www.mediadietforkids.com.

>TOP TIPS<

- The focus mustn't just be on the kids, otherwise they'll start to feel victimised. So check that all the family get involved from the start – cutting back on screen time is as important for goggle-eyed parents as it is for the kids.

- When you are filling in your diaries don't forget to make a 'guesstimate' of all those odd five minutes here and there – you'll be amazed at how they all add up.

- Get everyone to play a guessing game at the beginning of the week: for instance, guessing their own screen time totals, as well as guessing the times for other members of the family.

How can I tell if my child is addicted to the screen?

There's no scientific formula to tell whether or not your child is, or isn't, a 'media addict'.

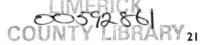

But there are questions which you can ask yourself if you're worried your child is becoming too dependent on the screen. We've compiled a Media Addiction Checklist. If you find that most answers to these questions are 'yes', your child isn't necessarily addicted but you should certainly watch the situation closely.

MEDIA ADDICTION CHECKLIST

Fill in the chart, or get a copy from www.mediadiet forkids.com.

Six Key Questions for Parents to ask:	Yes	No
1. Is watching the TV or playing the computer the first thing your child wants to do in the morning?		
2. Would your child generally prefer to be alone in front of the screen rather than doing things with friends or family?		
3. Is your child particularly depressed when he or she comes away from the screen?		
4. Does your child seem to be thinking of the screen most of the time?		
5. Is your child 'screen-blinkered' – in other words, does he or she have difficulty completing any non-screen-based activity?		
6. Does your child need the television or computer before going to sleep at night?		

Remember, if most of the answers are 'yes', your child is not necessarily addicted but you should watch the situation carefully.

How to set limits for TV and computer games

Now you know your starting point, you can set screen time limits. But how much time is too much time? Although there is general agreement that our children are overdosing on too much screen media, few people are prepared to say what the limit should be.

We recommend that you aim for less than 2 hours as your child's daily limit for 'screen entertainment'. We propose the figure of 2 as an average across the year because your child's needs will differ from day to day.

Think of the figure 2 as a rule of thumb – your child may come in well below it, or even above it. The most important thing is that you think time and decide on a figure to aim for.

Now, before we explain why we believe that the figure 2 is so important, we'd like to explain what we mean by 'screen entertainment'.

What is 'screen entertainment'?

First of all, what do we mean by the 'screen'?

In the majority of homes the television and computer are treated as two different types of activity. Children start off the evening watching telly, and then migrate seamlessly from it to the computer and back to the telly again. As far as their parents are concerned, it's a separate thing. So it's either telly time or computer time.

We believe that it's time to treat the television and computer screen as one activity, and there are a number of reasons why we believe this is important:

1. The merging together of computer and television technology means that they share more and more of the same characteristics. And this trend will continue in the future.

2. People may describe the TV as passive and the computer as interactive, but the similarities are great. Both tend to be sedentary activities and, most importantly, a child's fantasies and imagination are constrained by the images on the screen.

3. Time spent on the computer or watching television means time not spent doing other things. If you want a healthy balance in your child's life there needs to be a good mixture of screen and non-screen activity.

So that's what we mean by the 'screen'. What then do we mean by 'screen entertainment'?

When we say screen entertainment, we mean 'entertainment'. We do not, for example, mean to limit your child from using the computer for educational and creative purposes. It is the screen as entertainer that has become so addictive – and it is this entertainment, be it passive TV or interactive games, that needs controlling.

More specifically, 'screen entertainment' does not include any activity where your child is:

Doing research
Taking the initiative and using media for specific research tasks, such as using the Internet to investigate a specific subject for pleasure or for homework. Internet research has become an important part of the National Curriculum, and it is important that kids develop these research skills for adult life.

Being creative
Using the computer as a medium for creativity – just as a writer or an artist uses a blank sheet of paper. In these situations children have to dig deep into their own creative resources. Children are initiating the ideas and simply using the computer as a word or creative processor.

Contacting friends
Making contact with friends. This is territory where a parent needs to keep a close eye on their child. We believe

that it is good to encourage children to use email, texting and social networking sites in moderation. However, if a child shows signs of spending obsessive lengths of time on them, then we suggest that parents should set limits.

Learning and exercise

Using the screen for specific educational or exercise roles, such as educational games, language learning or dancing. When a child is using the screen as a means of independent learning – as support for school work or simply for pleasure – this is obviously an activity that should be valued and encouraged.

The 2-hour time limit

As we said at the start of the chapter, we recommend that you aim for less than 2 hours as your child's average daily limit for 'screen entertainment'. The limit of 2 hours is a figure we chose for a number of reasons.

As one of the country's leading children's researchers, Teresa has been studying the impact of modern media on children for the last twenty years. In particular, she has followed the effects that too much media exposure can have on a child's development. She believes the limit of 2 is the right figure.

Her views are supported by a new wave of research studies which confirm that too much screen time is a real threat – and that over 2 hours' TV a day can damage a child for life. The figure of 2 is in line with leading children's and health experts. The American Academy of Pediatrics, for instance, recommends that children should watch no more than 2 hours of television a day.[12]

And – very importantly – it's a figure that felt right to mums. As two mums ourselves we felt we could live with it and keep to it. And when we tried it out on other mums and dads they felt the same. It's low enough to protect children from the dangers of too much media exposure. But it's not high enough to stop kids benefiting from everything that the modern media world has to offer.

Don't panic if 2 seems impossible. If your child's current media consumption is considerably more than 2 hours a day, and you feel uncomfortable about aiming for 2 straightaway, there are a number of options to consider.

1. Stagger your approach

It's important to set yourself realistic targets. So decide what time limit feels comfortable for you and your child. If, for instance, your child is currently spending five hours a day in front of the screen, you might decide to aim for four hours in the first month, three in the second and two in the third.

2. Wait for the right moment – if now's not a good time

A good time to start cutting down on your child's screen consumption is when there's a natural change in circumstances or routine. So you might want, for instance, to wait until the beginning of the school holidays, or the start of a new term, to take action.

3. Go 'Cold Turkey'

Some parents find the easiest way of regaining control is to take drastic action. They get rid of the TV and computer altogether and then have a fresh start. This approach is particularly popular with parents of children who were spending excessive amounts of time in front of the screen. If you decide to go down this route, make sure that your child understands that it is only for a limited period. You also need to have plenty of ideas and activities lined up for your child to fill the void once the TV and computer are switched off. And once you do bring the TV and computer back, make sure this is done on your own terms.

What do we mean by 'a daily average'?

Your children's needs differ from day to day, and from week to week. Not every day is the same.

The figure of 2 hours, therefore, is an average across the year. How does this work in practice? Well, take a school day, for instance. If you're anything like us, there's never enough time to cram everything in. The kids get back from school. They've got to be fed. They need to relax. They want to play. There's homework to be done. And before you know it, it's time for bed.

The weekend is a different ball game altogether. There's lots of time to fill. It's also a time to relax and chill out. So you might decide to aim for 1 hour screen time on a school day, and 3 for a home day. It will average out roughly, so you're still achieving that magic 2.

Likewise, the weather is an important factor. If it's pouring with rain and you've nowhere to go, some extra screen time is probably going to keep the whole family sane. But if it's a beautiful day, don't waste it! Save up those 'media hours' for another day. Get the kids outside enjoying the weather. Again, just make sure that it averages out roughly at no more than 2 hours screen time a day.

THE MEDIA CLOCK

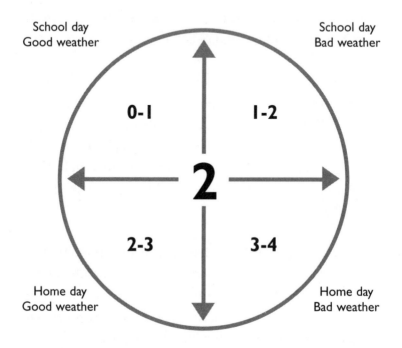

School day
Good weather

School day
Bad weather

0-1

1-2

2

2-3

3-4

Home day
Good weather

Home day
Bad weather

Here's a blank Media Clock to fill in. Decide with your child what figures to aim for. For more copies of The Media Clock, go to www.mediadietforkids.com.

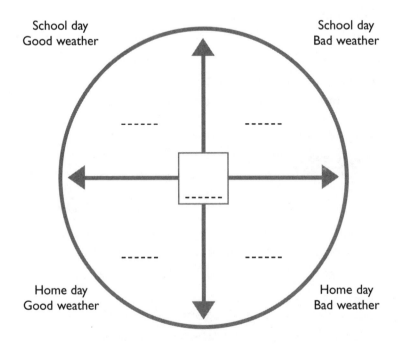

School day
Good weather

School day
Bad weather

Home day
Good weather

Home day
Bad weather

Does the 2-hour limit apply to all ages?

The 2-hour limit is aimed at children between the ages of 2 and 12 years old. But a certain degree of flexibility is also important. The demands and needs of a two-year-old are – of course – very different to those of a twelve-year - old. So at times you might find yourself being more indulgent to a particular child because of their age and stage in life. That's fine. Go with it. Be sensitive to your child and where they're coming from ... while trying to keep half an eye on their Media Clock. And remember that kids look to you as their role model. So if you're spending lots of time in front of the screen, you may want to try and keep an eye on your Media Clock too.

>TOP TIPS<

- Decide on screen time limits with your child. Don't think that children want it all their own way – deep down they want adults to tell them when enough is enough.

- Agree limits that reflect your child's starting point. If they're used to 5 hours screen time in a day, first reduce it to 4 hours and then gradually to 2. Step-by -step goal setting makes life smoother for everybody.

- If you are having difficulty getting through to your child, consider shocking them into action, for instance by getting rid of the screen completely for a set period of time – and then bringing it back with new rules.

To help you along, here are a few thoughts about the different ages and what you can expect from a media perspective.

2- to 5-year-olds

Enjoy it while it lasts. These children can still be easily distracted with games or other activities away from the screen. And the problem of peer pressure hasn't yet properly kicked in. Make the most of these early years to protect your child from too much screen time.

Kids of this age group are growing fast and so it's important that they are given plenty of opportunities to develop basic skills like talking, interacting with others, learning how to think and solve problems. Also, if you establish good habits early on, the next stage will be that much easier.

6- to 9-year-olds

This is when it starts to get trickier and your media parenting skills will begin to be put to the test. Just when you thought you had everything under control, things change. Children are at primary school and television and computer games become the topic of playground chatter. Kids are also discovering for themselves what the media world has to offer. Kids in this age group often benefit from some time in front of the screen just to chill out. But it's important that guidelines are set and kept to.

10- to 12-year-olds

It's pressure all round – the kids have 101 things to do and they're asking you for yet more time in front of the screen. Computer game usage normally peaks amongst children aged 9 to 14 years old. Schoolwork becomes more important and homework eats into more of the evening. Kids are also often being encouraged to do lots of other activities and hobbies. Your child is changing too. He or she has become more independent and probably more difficult to control. You have to be firm about how the TV and computer can be used, but you also need to encourage your child to start taking some responsibility for their own media time.

Understanding why '2' is right for you

It's important that your child understands and believes in the 2-hour limit. We recommend one way of doing this, which is to do a 'Time Check'. To do this, all you have to do is prioritise the things that need to be fitted into your child's day – for example, homework, a hobby, some exercise outside and a family meal. Once you've done this you can work out how much time is left for your child to spend in front of the TV or computer. You then allocate your child's 'media time' accordingly.

The Time Check is useful because it illustrates clearly why the 2-hour limit is so important. By focusing on what ideally needs to be done in a day – and the limited hours available – you can appreciate the importance of controlling your children's media time.

MEDIA TIME CHECK – SCHOOL DAY

4.00–4.30 pm	TV
4.30–5.00 pm	Outdoors
5.00–5.30 pm	Homework
5.30–6.00 pm	Eating/chat
6.00–6.30 pm	Non-screen play
6.30 –7.00 pm	Computer
7.00–7.30 pm	Bath
7.30–8.00 pm	Bedtime reading

Total = 8 half-hour units.
Agree your own family priorities and see what screen limit feels right for you.

Fill in the chart on the next page or to get a copy of the chart to fill in, go to www.mediadietforkids.com.

MEDIA TIME CHECK – SCHOOL DAY

4.00–4.30 pm	
4.30–5.00 pm	
5.00–5.30 pm	
5.30–6.00 pm	
6.00–6.30 pm	
6.30 –7.00 pm	
7.00–7.30 pm	
7.30–8.00 pm	

Holiday guidelines

During the holidays there's no need to be too clock-bound. Just think of the day in terms of slugs of time, e.g. before breakfast, first half of morning and so forth. Now think roughly how much screen time seems right, e.g. four half-hour units for a sunny out-and-about day, or eight half-hour units for a wet, home day.

Let your child decide where he/she spends those units of screen time.

KIDS' TRICKS TO KEEP SWITCHED ON – TAKE NOTE!

We asked children to admit to some of the ploys they use to grab more screen time:

'I wake up really early and I creep down and play on Sims. I'll play from 7.30 for about an hour.' *11-year-old girl*

'I say I've worked so hard today. I really deserve it.' *11-year-old girl*

'My mum sometimes takes the keyboard away. Except my brother gets around that because he has found an on-screen keyboard. Mum doesn't know.' *10-year-old boy*

'My mum says stop playing and go off and do something else. But I stop and go off and play on my MP3. She means go off and do some drawing.' *8-year-old girl*

'I take my Game Boy and hide in a cupboard and play it. I lock the door with a ruler so she doesn't know I'm there.' *9-year-old girl*

'I just wind up my mum, "Please, please, please".' *9-year -old girl*

How to keep to the limit – the Seven Golden Rules

Of course, children will always try and find ways of getting what they want, but we believe these tried and tested rules will get you on the right track.

 Golden Rule 1:
Parents stay in control of TV and computers

With most games it's OK for children to play with them when and where they want. But TV and computers aren't like any other game. They need to be controlled and so should be treated very differently from anything else in the toy cupboard.

It's important that you try and keep your child asking permission to switch on the TV or computer for as long as possible, preferably up to the age of 12. Once they're out of the habit it's hard to reinstate the rule. If your child has to ask permission, they are more likely to recognise and value media time as different from any other time. It will also make the job of controlling your child's media consumption a lot easier for you.

It's important also that you have a set of ground rules for using the TV and computer, and that your child is fully aware of what they are. It's easier if you establish ground rules right from the start. So, before you buy your child a new computer or computer game, sit down with them and decide what the rules are.

Golden Rule 2:
When it comes to media time – think in half-hour units of time

The longer you leave a child in front of the screen, the more difficult it becomes to drag him or her away. Many children's television programmes are half an hour long, which is plenty of time for a child to chill out or relax before going off to do something else. Likewise, half an hour on the computer is plenty of time to complete a game or try and move up to the next level. A child also shouldn't stay too long in one position because it's better for the body to move around at regular intervals.

Golden Rule 3:

Don't allow televisions in bedrooms of under-12-year-olds

TVs in the bedroom was one of the most emotive areas touched on in our research. For some families it has become part of a way of life. For other parents TV in a child's bedroom is a definite 'no'. Around 80 per cent of children aged 11 to 15 have a TV in their bedroom, although most parents don't think it's a good idea. [1]

Once you allow the TV in your child's bedroom you risk letting go of some of your control. Ideally, there should be areas of the home which are 'TV-free' zones. Children's bedrooms are one such area. Children need somewhere to retreat to where they can enjoy some peace and quiet. And, once the TV is introduced into the bedroom, the bedtime story risks being dropped altogether.

Ideally, the TV should be in communal areas where you can keep an eye on who's watching what, and where the programme can be enjoyed by the whole family together. A lot of televisions find their way into kids' bedrooms because of TV games consoles, such as the PlayStation. Try and resist putting the PlayStation in your child's bedroom, but if you do, there's a simple answer – don't aerial up the TV facility. This will ensure the TV is just being used as a games console screen and nothing else. Don't be afraid of confiscating any portable screens if they're being used after lights-out.

Golden Rule 4:
Watching the TV during meal times should be a treat – not the norm

In many families, having the television on during meal times has become the normal way of doing things. Other families try to ensure that at least some meals are telly-free. The TV at meal times kills conversation and distracts children from eating.

Meal times are special family times. It's often the only time when the family is all together and can catch up on the day's events. Children develop their conversational skills while chatting over their tea. They also learn to listen and take an interest in others and, crucially, develop a sense of being part of a family unit.

Try and make meals a family event. Even if you're not eating at the same time, sit down with your children and have a cup of tea. Use it as catch-up time and don't let the TV invade family moments.

Golden Rule 5:

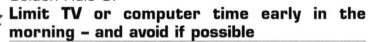

Limit TV or computer time early in the morning – and avoid if possible

Starting the day in front of the TV or computer screen can get it off to a bad start. If children are watching TV or play-ing on the computer first thing in the morning, it's often harder to get them on to other activities. And on school days it can be particularly distracting when you are trying to get them out of the house. Parents we interviewed found that once they had allowed early-morning TV or computer time, children were getting up earlier and earlier.

Parents also pointed out the problem of not being able to supervise what their children watch or play very early in the morning. For example, young kids end up watching news bulletins that can be disturbing. Parents also mentioned the issue of bad behaviour. A lot of parents found that long bouts of early-morning television left children in particularly bad moods – either over-agitated or too soporific.

It's understandable that some parents – particularly those with toddlers and young children – may want to stick to some early-morning TV. If kids get up early, the TV often gives parents some much-needed extra time in bed.

If so, it's not a problem. Just make sure you limit it and put in some controls. One mum we spoke to kept the remote control by her bedside so she knew her child couldn't watch any TV unless he came and asked her.

If your child is going to school you need to be very strict with the limit – ideally no TV in the morning, but certainly no more than 20 minutes. Interestingly, from our research we found a lot of parents use early-morning TV tactically – to get kids dressed, or even out of bed. So, if your kids are into early-morning viewing, try and get something positive out of it.

Golden Rule 6:
Don't allow any screen activity in the run up to – or after – bedtime

A big concern amongst teachers – as well as parents – is that children are often exhausted and tired at school. One of the main reasons is that bedtime isn't what it used to be. Instead of quiet bedtime stories, kids are enjoying computer games or exciting videos just before going to bed. Screen activity before bedtime stimulates the brain and makes it more difficult for a child to go to sleep. And then there are too many distractions in the bedroom. So after bedtime children are still playing on the computer, watching videos and TV – and even emailing and texting friends. No wonder our kids are all exhausted. If need be, ban mobile phones from the bedroom after lights-out, and unplug any media equipment. Make time for a calm period immediately before putting your children to bed.

Try not to lurch from the screen to bed. Children need time to unwind. The best way of doing this is reading a bedtime story. It offers a moment of calm and the chance to have a final catch-up with Mum or Dad.

Golden Rule 7:

 Create periods of time without the computer or television

TV isn't like music, which you can easily have on in the background while doing other things. It dominates a room and can be extremely distracting. But in many homes the TV is put on first thing in the morning and stays on until last thing at night. Children get used to it and find it hard to imagine being without it. If the television is constantly on it becomes difficult for everyone to focus on other things. It also becomes hard for a family to communicate properly with each other. Clearly differentiate between television and non-television time. When it's not television time switch it off. Don't let your child, for instance, do homework in front of the TV.

A good way of doing this is to introduce the concept of TV planning. Encourage your child to plan their TV viewing so that they know what they're going to watch before they turn it on (see page 111). Once the programme is finished, the TV should be switched off.

The position of screens in your home can also be important. As one mum said to us, 'It's all about where you put the screens. That's the number-one consideration.' Try and make sure that the TV doesn't totally dominate the main living area so that when it's on, it's difficult to get away from.

>**TOP TIPS**<

• Be firm – that's what kids respect. So when you say 'Off', you must mean it.

• Keep a clock by your screens so timekeeping becomes more automatic, or consider buying a half-hour egg timer to encourage kids to stick to half-hour media units.

• Develop your own family rules. For example, here are some rules that other parents have used with success: no TV in the morning, no TV until they have dressed and had breakfast, no PlayStation on weekdays, etc.

• If your children are looked after by different adults, for instance by child carers or separated parents, check that everybody is working to the same rules. It's easy for kids to play one lot of adults off against another, so it's so important to synchronise on screen-time rules.

• Finally, remember that it's so important that you set a good example yourself. Show the kids that you are cutting down as well, and when they see that you can do it, they will be more inclined to follow your lead.

TIPS ON ... WHERE TO PUT SCREENS IN THE HOME

- Limit the number of screens – don't give each child a PlayStation, for instance.

- Don't let the TV totally dominate your main living area.

- Keep the TV out of children's bedrooms.

- Check there is screen-free space in the home.

- Screens with Internet access should be placed where you can keep an eye on them.

- Hide the DVDs and computer games, so they're not the first thing the children see as they walk in the room.

More Top Tips

TIPS ON ... **A SMOOTH SWITCH-OFF**

A few parents we spoke to – most of them dads – couldn't see what the fuss was about. 'It's easy,' they said, 'You just switch it off. Don't worry about the grief, they soon forget about it.' To a certain extent, they're right. But for most of us – particularly anyone faced with the problem every day – a 'smooth' switch-off is important. If handled well, switching-off shouldn't result in tantrums or be a moment we all dread as parents.

- Agree how long children are going to be in front of the screen at the moment they switch on. You may decide to put a time limit on it, or to switch it off after a specific programme.

- Watch out for computer games where there's always another level of a game to achieve. With games where there is no clear cut-off point it's best to set a time limit.

- Let your child wrap up a computer game in a way that makes them feel good about what they've done. You may need to allow them, for instance, to save where they are so they can go back to it later.

- Get your child to keep a check on the time. A good way of doing this is to put a clock or timer right next to the television or computer.

- Give them a warning before switching off – for example, 'Just five more minutes.'

- Try to make the 'switching-off' their responsibility. If they have to switch off the button, they often feel much better about it.

- Stick to what you've agreed – say no to, 'Just five more minutes pleeese!' This is where you may need to be resilient. Take a deep breath and wait for the moment of confrontation to pass.

- Be sympathetic with your child during the 'cold turkey moment'. As the screen is switched off they'll probably experience a period of inertia and frustration and take it out on you.

- Get them to focus on what's next – the screen alternatives. Often a good way of doing this is to change their environment. Get them into another room or go outside.

- Don't be afraid of letting them get bored. Children are often at their most creative when they're bored and looking for things to do.

• If you get faced with a tantrum, stick with it and after five minutes it should be fine.

How kids get round the switch-off

'My computer has this button on the remote that changes it on to TV. She says, "Get off the Sims now and watch some TV," but I keep the Sims there, and when she's out of the room I switch.' *11-year-old girl*

'I say it's almost the end of the programme, when it's just started, and then just five more minutes, until the end.' *12 -year-old boy*

'Mum says, "Better get your homework done." I say, "In a minute." She comes back, says, "Get your homework done." I say, "In a minute." It goes on like that for about 2 hours.' *8-year-old girl*

'I just keep on going, "Please can I go on the computer?" every five minutes, until she gives up.' *9-year-old boy*

'I quickly set up another match.' *11-year-old boy*

'I just say I'm finishing off the level.' *11-year-old boy*

TIPS ON ... **JUGGLING KIDS OF DIFFERENT AGES AND SEXES**

- Personalise media time so there isn't the assumption that when the TV is on it's there for everyone to watch. Create the feeling that each child has his or her special time in front of the TV – sometimes with other members of the family, sometimes on their own.

- When the time's up for one child to stop watching TV, you may need to draw them away from the screen by enticing them into another room – or into another corner of the room – to do a specific activity. It's good to have something in mind to fill the void: homework, a play activity or simply helping you prepare tea in the kitchen.

- Try and make sure that the TV doesn't dominate the main family room so that it's impossible to do anything else in the room when it's on. Even in a small room you can arrange things to create a more focused TV area and a non-TV area.

TIPS ON ... **STOPPING KIDS SQUABBLING**

- Try and establish a sense of 'screen sharing'. Don't solve the problem of kids fighting over TV programmes or computer games by getting everyone their own screen. It's good for children to share. Get them to agree between themselves, and with you, who's going to use what when. This will also help them think carefully about how to allocate their own media time.

- One mum told us how she had introduced the idea of sharing the screen according to the days of the week. As a result her two children have the use of the PlayStation on alternate days.

- In another home we found the PlayStation was rotated around the home so that every two months it would move to the next child's room.

TIPS ON ... COPING WITH PEER PRESSURE

- Try and get your child used to the concept of not having everything. Just because a friend has the latest computer game doesn't automatically mean that they should get it too.

- Do the time test. If after a certain period your child is still wanting something, you can start taking the request more seriously. Never give in straightaway.

Peer pressure is all about buying the talk of the town. Before you know it, things have moved on and another fad has appeared.

- Point out that it's good that different homes have different things. You don't always have to replicate what friends have got, and it's fun to enjoy games in different environments.

- Get your child to buy computer games out of their own pocket money. If they've had to save up for something, they're likely to value it more.

- And don't be afraid to chat with other parents. Check out whether what your child's saying is totally accurate. You may find, for instance, that it's not your son's friend who has the computer game, but his older brother. It's also good to share your experiences with other mums and dads.

TIPS ON ... MANAGING PLAY DATES

- Make sure that when friends come round they start off with some 'screen-free' time. They can always move on to the screen once they've had some time playing together.

- Try and encourage media activity which is social. For instance, encourage two-player games rather than having one child playing on the computer and the other just looking on.

TIPS ON ... HOLIDAYS

- Ideally, try and resist your children taking TV consoles, such as PlayStations, on holiday. Holidays are a great opportunity to broaden children's horizons, so try and get them to leave screen distractions at home. It's good to have some time without them.

- If you want your child to break any bad media habits, holidays are also a good time to do it. If you leave the PlayStation at home, it'll give them a clean break and make it easier to start afresh back home.

- On the other hand, mobile consoles can be useful during long journeys. But beware. Once the travelling is done, try and get your child to pack the console away so that they get a break.

- We found that several parents had specific rules for holiday screen activity. Some parents, for instance, say no TV before an outside activity, and others restrict when and for how long the TV or computer can be turned on.

TIPS ON ... SCREEN MEDIA USED FOR INCENTIVES OR REWARDS

• There are some people who believe that using rewards isn't a good idea because it sends out the wrong messages to your child. From our research we found that parents were successfully using the TV and computer as rewards or incentives for doing things – for instance, getting dressed and having breakfast in the morning, or finishing home-work in the evening.

• So, yes, use them as a reward if it helps you. But don't do it the whole time. Don't let yourself become too dependent on the TV or computer for getting things done.

TOP TIPS **FROM PARENTS AND CARERS**

'I always get anger confrontation. You've got to stick with it and then it'll be OK.' *Felicity, mum with a strong-minded boy.*

'He's very angry when I say, "Right, turn the TV off." Very, very cross. It takes him about 5 minutes to calm down.' *Rosie, mum who dreads the switch-off*

'We've made a game of turning the TV off. My two girls take it in turns and when we can't remember whose turn it is, they race to turn off the button.' *Loulou, mum with two girls aged 2 and 4*

'I'll try and get them to focus on what they're going to do next.' *Jo, carer of three families*

'I tell them I'm going to do the washing up and when I've finished I'll say, "Sizzling sausages," and then we'll turn it off.' *Emma, nanny of two boys and a girl*

'The important thing is to have a definite routine for turning it off.' *Susan, mum with two toddlers*

'The easiest thing is to go outside and away from that room.' *Julie, nanny of three kids*

'Agree a time as they sit down. It creates the right expec-tations and also makes them part of the process.' *Liz, mum of two girls and a boy*

'There's always a five-minute period when it's, "Oh, Mum ...!" They don't quite know what to do. But if you let them fester long enough, they come up with an alter-native. You need grit to get through that resistance period.' *Sarah-Jane, mum of two boys*

'It's saying "no" when you mean it. Parents make it hard for themselves if they say "no" and don't mean it.' *June, grandmum with three grandchildren*

TOP TIPS FROM KIDS TO PARENTS!

'Suggest rather than being too bossy. If things aren't allowed the child rebels. Do things gently, and suggest things.' *12-year-old girl*

'Say: "You've got five more minutes, and if you don't come off, no TV tomorrow."' *12-year-old girl*

'You need to reward them with pocket money.' *11-year-old girl*

'Put a timetable up on the wall.' *11-year-old girl*

'You have to trust your child!' *12-year-old girl*

'If they've had their TV time for the day, record it so they can watch it tomorrow.' *11-year-old girl*

'Don't give in, it shows you're weak.' *12-year-old girl*

'Make sure they don't go back on and ban them from it if they do.' *10-year-old boy*

'Don't shout too much. Say, "It's my turn." Teach them what they can do instead.' *8-year-old boy*

'Say, "Your next door neighbour is outside, why don't you go and play?"' *8-year-old boy*

'Pull the plug out.' *12-year-old boy*

'Get a little man on the screen who bleeps when you need to get off. And then if you don't, everything explodes.' *11 -year-old boy*

'Stand there and watch them turn it off.' *11-year-old girl*

Time counting – Summary

- The first step in reducing your child's screen time is about knowing your starting point. You can then set limits for the amount of time your child is entertained in front of the TV or computer screen.

- We recommend 2 hours of screen entertainment time as the upper limit for a daily average across the year.

- The 2-hour limit should be used as a rule of thumb. The important thing is that you become conscious of how much time your child is spending in front of the screen and that you have a figure to aim for which feels right to you.

- There is help on planning your own family schedule, a set of seven Golden Rules.

- There are loads of practical tips to help you on your way.

Alternatives to the screen

To cut down on your child's media consumption, you need to get them away from the screen. And that means finding good substitutes to fill the void once the switch is turned off. If you can do this, you'll also help prevent the whole 'switching-off' experience becoming a negative one.

Encouraging activity away from the screen

So what non-screen activities should you be encouraging? And how can you do this in a way that isn't too time-consuming for you? To come up with the answers we asked our research group of over 100 parents, kids, grandparents, carers, teachers and children's experts. We asked them their views and tips on the subject. Many of the mums had interesting and useful things to say. But we found, in this particular area, that it was the grannies and carers who had some of the best advice to give.

We also tapped into Teresa's experience of the toy market. Once you know what makes a good toy, you have a pretty good understanding of what motivates children to play at home. And motivation is often the name of the game.

To start with, here is a bunch of general tips about encouraging kids' activity away from the screen.

Become more time-smart

The grannies and carers particularly noticed how time-pressed mums have difficulty in setting time priorities. They recognised that mums today are very busy, but there was a general feeling that mums aren't always as time-efficient as they could be. So, as mums, maybe we need to make sure we're more time-smart. This doesn't necessarily mean spending more time on our children, but being more effective with how we use our time.

First of all, there's 'starter time'

If you want your child to get going on an activity they often need encouragement and – more often than not – your attention. It's worthwhile investing properly in 'starter time' at the beginning of any new activity.

So, rather than setting something up and then quickly leaving your child to get on with it, stop. Take some time out from what you're doing to get involved in the activity too. An extra five minutes of your time at the start will help make the activity a success. Your child will play longer and you'll end up having more time to yourself.

And then there's 'nurture time'

You need to invest in a bit of nurture time too. Once your child's properly set up doing an activity, you can get on with something else. But keep popping back for another five minutes here or there to see how they're doing. Children often just need little bits of encouragement to keep them going. Once they've decided that they're bored with a game, that's it. It's difficult to drum up enthusiasm again. And if that happens, you'll then have to spend more time getting them started on something else.

Being 'time-smart' is about being flexible

If your child is happily playing or doing something, don't interrupt them if you don't have to. Go with the flow. Let whatever they're doing come to a natural end and make the most of the extra little bit of time you now have.

>TOP TIPS<

- Never forget that your child longs for more time with you. They may ask for the latest thingamajig or a holiday in Barbados, but we found that, above all else, children want more quality time with Mum or Dad.

- So don't underestimate the value of time spent with them. With all the demands of home and work, you might think you don't have time for building Lego castles. But just remember that five minutes on the floor with the kids are five minutes very well spent.

Seed ideas – don't impose them!

Become a good 'seeder' of ideas, rather than always imposing ideas on your children. Children are the same as adults. They'll pursue an idea better if they think that it's their own. So don't be proud. Encourage your child to take ownership of your ideas. Give your child activity options and then let them take it from there. Things may not develop quite how you imagined – in fact they probably won't. But then it doesn't really matter. Be prepared for some of your ideas to fall on deaf ears.

Sometimes ideas quickly take root, and on other occasions children just aren't in the mood. One day they'll be mad on doing one thing, and the next they'll reject it just like that. So don't be dogged with ideas that haven't inspired your child. Just drop them and keep them up your sleeve for another day. But above all, listen out for their ideas and only suggest things to do if you need to. Kids often come up with the best ideas.

Develop 'themes'

In the mid eighties the big talk in children's marketing was all about 'concept marketing' and 'multi-media' strategies. It sounds like a whole lot of jargon but the ideas were simple. Instead of selling 'one-off' toys you developed 'a concept' which was often based on a character in a film. You then flogged it across as many different markets as you could.

Now, turning to our families – how can we put the tricks of concept marketing to good effect? The first thing is to identify a theme which is captivating your child. This might be a film, TV show, song, story from a book or a family big event. Then have fun thinking how you can develop the theme. We found that carers were instinctively doing this.

One carer described how she and her children had all been singing 'The Toothbrush' song on the way home. Once inside, they painted a picture of a toothbrush and then made a giant toothbrush to play with. It might have been a mad song but it provided a great theme for an afternoon's activity. Other themes we came across that fuelled play and creativity were princes and princesses, weddings, going on holiday and favourite films. The list could go on and on because there's no end to what children find captivating. TV and computer games are a rich source of inspiration for activity themes. Make the most of them.

Encourage hobbies and interests

We noticed in our research that it was often children with interests or hobbies who had the most balanced approach to watching the TV and playing on the computer. These children often speak with pride about what they do away from the screen. We also came across several cases where a child had become addicted to the screen, and the parents had managed to solve the problem by finding something else to interest them.

There was an example of a single mum who was worried her daughter was spending too much time on the Internet and computer. She encouraged her daughter to get a hobby. Eventually she started working for a local riding stables in her spare time. Looking after the horses gave the girl a great sense of purpose. It also made her feel part of a local community.

Six simple ideas for time away from the screen

We asked our research groups what activities they would encourage children to do away from the screen. We wanted them to come up with activity areas which would provide a healthy balance in a child's life.

They identified six key activity areas:

- Chat
- Reading
- Creativity and music
- Exercise
- Helping around the home
- Play.

And, when you think about it, it makes total sense. Between them, these six activity areas provide some of the essential ingredients for creating a happy and healthy child. They also give your child a useful jumping-off point for the future. If they're used to this mixture of activities in the early years, they'll be more likely to get the balance right as an adult. Encouraging your child to love exercise isn't, for instance, just about controlling their current waistline. It's about giving them a love for exercise and a habit that they can take on into adulthood. Likewise, play isn't just about entertaining a child now. It will encourage them to interact with others, and help them tap into their inner initiative and resourcefulness.

So focus on encouraging these six activity areas. Think of them as essential components for your child's healthy lifestyle. Try and ensure that your child gets a good all-round balance.

The six key activity areas

Here are some specific tips on how to encourage children to become involved in the six activity areas. Think of them as a bundle of ideas. You'll probably have loads more yourself, but these were the ones which our research team thought were the most important and helpful. And, because this is above all a media book and we're two media enthusiasts, we've included lots of ways of using the media itself to encourage each activity area.

1. Chat

It's important for all sorts of reasons that children learn to talk and have proper conversations. It helps them socially because they can articulate their own feelings and views, and interact with others.

If a child is articulate, it also helps them academically

because they're able to take a full part in the learning experience. They can ask and answer questions and follow a line of debate. Being a good talker also gives any child a much-needed boost in confidence. So the more we talk and chatter to our kids, the better. It doesn't matter if we don't have something important to say. We should be talking to them about anything and everything – the weather, what we're doing, what they've done or simply how they're feeling.

It is also important not to rush children if you want a proper chat. Children often just need time to respond and will give their best responses after a moment of reflection. So try not to hurry them.

TIPS ON ... CHATTING

Establish a 'catch-up' routine
Make 'catch-up moments' part of your daily routine. Let your child know that at certain times of day – on the way back from school, at tea or after the bedtime story – they'll have your undivided attention. Use this time to chat and find out what they've been doing and how they're feeling. Don't worry if it's only five minutes here or there – it's better than nothing.

Don't be put off by a 'grunt'
A lot of parents talked to us about 'grunting' kids who

were difficult to communicate with. If you get a grunt from your child, or a monosyllabic yes or no, it's probably because they don't feel you're on their wavelength. Think carefully about how you phrase questions. If one approach doesn't work, try a different way of asking the same question.

Question and imagine

Children like to be asked about themselves, so ask them questions even if you know the answers. Sometimes their responses and comments won't make total sense. Be patient and use your imagination to find out what they're really trying to tell you.

Make meal times, chat times

In many homes the family meal is under threat because of the TV. As a result, parents and children don't regularly sit around the table and talk to one another. Try and use meal times as an opportunity for everyone in the family to catch up on the day's events. It should be a relaxing moment when you can all enjoy a good chat. And even if you don't eat with your children, get a cup of tea and sit down with them.

If need be, you can use recording services like Sky+ to pause a programme during meal times. It can be difficult to get the family to come away from something good on TV when you're ready to serve up – but with the help of the digital pause facilities, TV needn't dominate meal times any more.

Use songs

Songs are a great way of getting kids to be expressive and remember words. Sing along with your children whenever you can – doing the cooking, at bath time or walking to school.

Consider getting a pet

Pets can encourage kids to develop strong relationships in their lives. Children will often talk to their pets, even when they don't seem in the mood to talk to anyone else.

Pets are a great asset to a child as they are often someone to ...

... talk to ("when I'm fed up with everyone else")
... play with ("he gets me outside")
... care for ("with a little help from mum")
... indulge ("if he does a trick for me")
... be quiet with ("he shares my thoughts").

USE THE MEDIA

Chatter about the TV and computer games

Modern media provides loads of things for you to chat

about. So, for instance, discuss the story lines of the soaps with your child, the characters of a film or even the best ways of playing a particular computer game.

Debate moral and social issues

Use what your child has seen in the soaps, or on the news, as a stimulus for discussion. Listen to their views and encourage them to develop their own thoughts.

Build friendships

It goes without saying that encouraging friendships is an important way of getting kids to talk, and modern media has so much to offer when it comes to social networks. Encourage children from the age of about nine to use email, MSN and texting as a way of keeping in contact with friends and family. Make the most of the social networking sites to keep up with friends.

Encourage family viewing

Even if you all have TVs in your separate bedrooms, try and watch programmes together rather than allowing 'satellite' viewing – where everybody watches in their own personal space. We spoke to one mum who made it a rule that no one could watch TV in their room if they were all watching the same thing. It's more social because you can then talk about what you've all watched.

2. Reading

Learning to read takes time and it often requires a lot of patience from parents to inspire children with a love of reading. But it's worth the effort. If a child gets behind in reading they quickly get behind in their schoolwork. And if a child enjoys reading, they find a whole new world opening up before them. The teachers we spoke to stressed the importance of making reading something fun to do, rather than something which is just done at school or as part of homework. And if your child is a reluctant reader, the advice from the teachers is that some reading is better than no reading at all. So let them read *The Beano*, *Girl Talk* or the sports pages of the newspapers – if that's what they want. At least your child's reading.

TIPS ON ... READING

Read with your children – whatever their age
Start reading with your children at an early age to encourage a love of books and stories. And don't presume it's only the little ones who enjoy being read to. The older ones do as well. So, for example, try reading spy stories to a nine-year-old boy, or fashion magazines to a twelve-year-old girl. A good way of encouraging children to read is to share the reading. Take it in turns to read different bits. You can read one page – or even one sentence – and

your child can read the next. Or make it fun, with you being one character and your child being another.

Have a good selection of reading material

Build up a love of reading by having a good choice of books for your children to dip into and out of. Encourage your child to pick and choose the books they want. Having a good selection of books needn't cost money. Make the most of your local library and any school books. Try and involve your child in choosing which books to have. Libraries and bookshops can be inspiring for kids and great places to entertain them for the odd hour or so.

If you need advice about what good books to get, ask other parents or teachers at school, and staff at your local library or bookshop. There are also a number of good book guides – for example, *The Ultimate Book Guide* by Anne Fine and *The Rough Guide to Children's Books* by Nicholas Tucker – as well as organisations such as The Book Trust (www.booktrust.org.uk), which provide lists of popular books.

End the day with a bedtime story

Try and read to your child last thing at night. This is where dads in particular can play an important role. A lot of families make bedtime stories Dad's special time. If Dad has been out at work it's something easy and enjoyable he can do with the kids before they go to bed. But remember, reading isn't just for bedtime. Encourage your child to read five minutes here, and five minutes there, throughout the day.

Make the most of interests and hobbies

Sometimes kids get bored with reading because they're simply not interested in what they're reading. Get books and reading material connected with hobbies and things that interest your child. This is particularly important with boys, who aren't always natural readers. They often find non-fiction reading matter more interesting than fiction. Football and science magazines, for example, are great because they grab their attention and get them reading.

Start a family 'book club'

If you've got an 11- or 12-year-old, suggest to them that they choose a book for you both to read. You can then have fun discussing it, and the characters, with them.

USE THE MEDIA

Learn to read

There are great computer programmes that help kids develop their reading skills (see Educational Games section, page 139), and reading on-screen can offer kids a welcome break from school reading books.

Read around a favourite media theme

Make use of supporting comics, books and websites for television or computer programmes.

Read around factual TV programmes and series

Factual programmes often inspire a sudden interest and enthusiasm for a particular subject. Make the most of the moment. Encourage reading around the subject – either by visiting any supporting website, or getting books on the subject from the library.

Get reading on the Internet

Surfing the Internet involves reading all the time, and it can be a great way of encouraging a lazy reader to get motivated. Visiting sites about their favourite passions and interests makes them want to read – suddenly they realize that being able to read can be really useful.

Read the book of the film

Films are often good ways of inspiring interest in particular books, such as the Harry Potter books and *Lord of the Rings*. Make the most of your child's interest in a film by encouraging them to read the book.

Read newspapers to complement what's been on TV

It's often more interesting reading about things if they're topical. Encourage your child to read the newspaper to find out more about what they've seen on TV – for instance, football reports or news items. Foreign news-papers can be a good source for encouraging language learning. Explore the news options on the Internet with your child and get in the habit of printing off features that might be of interest: for instance, football articles for the boys and music features for the girls.

Visit the great selection of book-related sites on the Internet

There are lots of sites which are reading-related, such as www.bbc.co.uk/arts/books. Encourage your child to visit these sites to find out about authors and books.

3. Creativity and music

Try and seek out and encourage your child's creative strengths. If your child finds they're particularly good at something, the likelihood is that they'll become passionate about it too. You might be surprised by what you find. Just because you're no good at music, for instance, doesn't necessarily mean your child won't be either.

A lot of the teachers we spoke to commented that parents often stifle any potential creativity in their children by not giving them enough time and space. We try and cram too much into a day, rushing from one planned activity to another. As one teacher said, it's good for children occasionally to be left to their own devices because that's when they start to become very creative.

TIPS ON ... CREATIVITY

Explore different forms of creativity

Help your child explore their own creative potential by trying out different things. Look carefully, for instance, at what inspires your child to pick up a pencil and draw a picture, or start practising the guitar. Find an instrument or artistic outlet that inspires them, rather than imposing on them what you want them to do.

Expose kids to different types of instruments and music – classical, pop, bagpipes, jazz, army bands, African, Indian and Chinese. And show your child a variety of forms of art and styles – painting, sculpture, etching and mosaic, for instance.

Be spontaneous

Creativity should be spontaneous – don't just leave it for rainy days. So make sure your child has easy access to any art material – pens, papers, paints – or musical instruments. Your child can then easily, for example, start painting or making music. If everything is hidden away in cupboards and difficult to get to, the moment will pass and they'll be on to something else.

Be an audience for your child's talents

If kids feel their work is being appreciated, they'll want to do more. Create a display area for art at home. Consider, for instance, laminating pictures and sticking them up on the kitchen wall. It's a cheap way to protect them and makes them look good too.

Encourage your child, when they're ready, to play their latest pieces of music to the family and friends. Get them to put together little plays, and check you put time aside to come and watch.

Get your child to think visually

When asked how to encourage artistic creativity in children, one art teacher immediately replied, 'Open their eyes.' She went on to explain how important it is that children learn how to look at the world around them. Another teacher stressed the importance of art appreciation – discuss art in the world around you with your child, how it looks, how it makes them feel, how they would have done it.

Make use of the different times of year

The different seasons of the year provide great opportunities to be creative. Encourage your child to make cards and decorations at Christmas or Chinese New Year; decorate pumpkins or cut out witches at Halloween and paint eggs and bunnies at Easter. Prepare lamps in the home for the

Hindu festival of Diwali, the festival of light, or celebrations for the end of Ramadan.

Have fun with different materials

Put away the toys and leave your child with a large box of interesting items – old bits of material, shoes or whatever – and see what they do. Get them to look out for interesting boxes and packages that can be used to make things. Do collages and junk modelling with sweet wrappers, autumn leaves or old bits of newspaper. Make exotic jewellery with pasta or buttons, and try out old saucepans and spoons for musical instruments.

Make music practice part of the daily routine

One music teacher we spoke to said that music practice should be like brushing your teeth – in other words, doing it regularly is really what counts. So five minutes a day is better than 20 minutes just before the next lesson.

Encourage art and music as a form of escapism

As kids get older, art and music can increasingly provide them with light relief from the stresses and strains of the real world. This is something which should be encouraged. Remember, you are encouraging a hobby for life. It should be a pleasure rather than a chore. Don't let the pressures of exams spoil your child's love of music or art.

USE THE MEDIA

Get ideas and inspiration
There are some great TV programmes that encourage children to be creative – for example, *Art Attack* and *Blue Peter*. Visit the websites of these creative shows to get details of what's been shown on the screen. Popular light entertainment shows can be a great source of inspiration for getting the kids themselves to perform.

Get practical help and useful tools
The computer can provide a rich source of inspiration for writing, music, painting, arts and crafts. Explore software packages like Storyteller to help you become a film or cartoon producer, or Creative Writer to try your hand at being an author. If your child is artistically inclined they can have fun with Adobe Photoshop, creating work a professional designer would be proud of. Or they can go and be inspired by visiting the art galleries of the world – The Metropolitan, The National Gallery or The Louvre – all on the Internet. For musicians bored with practising their grade pieces, there's a site called www.musicroom.com where you can download popular sheet music that is fun to play. Or you can develop your skills as a DJ by creating your own music compilation using an iPod or other MP3 player.

Encourage kids to enter competitions

There are lots of competitions on TV. These can often be a useful focus and incentive for kids to get creative. There are also Internet sites where kids are encouraged to send in work and again this can inspire them into action.

4. Exercise

We all know exercise is vital for a child's healthy development. Children and young people should do a minimum of 60 minutes of physical activity a day, and at least twice a week this should include more vigorous exercise to develop bone health and muscle strength.[13] But kids today aren't exercising enough. In England and Scotland about 30 per cent of boys and 40 per cent of girls are not meeting the recommended activity guidelines.[14] One of the problems about modern living is our sedentary lifestyle. We drive or take the bus everywhere rather than walk. And a lot of sport is football-focused. So if you're not good at football, people often presume you're not good at sports. If your child shows no interest in football, don't give up. Explore other sports or exercise routines to get them interested and motivated.

TIPS ON ... **EXERCISE**

Get your child walking

The simplest way to get more exercise is to start walking more. If you can get somewhere on foot with your child, go there on foot. The more walking a child does, the better he or she will get at it – so get rid of the buggy as soon as you can. Walking can be an entertaining activity in itself. So if you're walking to the shops, enjoy doing other things along the way – kicking the leaves, playing 'I spy', counting the yellow cars, or getting them to play your own fantasy game.

With older children, let them lead the way and break up the journey by looking at things of interest. But remember, what you find interesting may not be the same as what interests them. You may want to stop to admire the view, while they may be interested in following a trail of ants.

Take your kids to the park or outside as much as possible

Children naturally want to run around and get outside. If there isn't a park nearby, still try and give your child as much outside time as possible. Traffic permitting, let them enjoy some 'supervised' street life. You can keep an eye on them from the door or out of the window, as they ride their bike or go on their rollerblades.

Don't feel you have to play with your child all the time when you're outside. Look at your watch and divide your time ... half for them and half for yourself with a good book or newspaper.

Exercise with your children

One of the biggest incentives for any child to take exercise is to see their parents taking some form of exercise too. Use their exercise time as an opportunity for you to get some exercise too. As they change into their football shorts, put on your tracksuit and either join them in a game or go off and jog round the pitch. Likewise, if you take your kids swimming, grab the opportunity to do a few lengths yourself.

And don't let the weather stop all exercise. There are plenty of things that can be done inside – jumping around to children's exercise tapes, or visiting the local swimming pool.

Encourage your children to join an after-school or weekend sports club

These are a great and easy way for children to get exercise – particularly if you don't have very accessible outside space. And children – particularly the boys – love them because they turn sport into a social and competitive event. Playing for a team is fun, as well as giving kids an extra incentive to do well.

Encourage the competitive spirit

We asked a cricket coach to describe how he encouraged children's enthusiasm for the game. He believed that encouraging children to be competitive is a great way to get them motivated. Children enjoy being competitive – and it's easy for an adult to ensure that everybody feels a winner. What's more, competitiveness isn't just about competing against other people. It's also about personal goal setting – and this is more important than anything.

Be an audience for kids as they play

Kids love an audience. Take time out to watch them do their sport. Comment on their new skills or tactics and give them the confidence to keep on going at it.

Involve Dad as much as possible

A lot of dads particularly love sports – either watching them or doing them. Make the most of this natural enthusiasm and competitiveness to encourage a love of exercise in your kids.

USE THE MEDIA

Play football after watching a match on TV

While they're still gripped by the excitement of the game, make the most of it. As soon as the match is finished, get them outside re-enacting bits of the game or just playing out their own fantasies.

Use big sporting events to inspire an interest in sport

Events like the Olympics or Commonwealth Games, which are broadcast on TV, or made into a computer game, are great opportunities to inspire an interest in a new sport. Use them as much as you can. See which sport takes your child's fancy and then investigate the best ways of trying it out.

Encourage fantasy games

If your child is keen on a particular sport, try and get them to build fantasy worlds around it. This might involve becoming a commentator of a pretend football match, building pretend stadiums or practising penalty shoot-outs.

Find out more about sports

There are lots of good sites on the Internet – such as www.bbc.co.uk/sportacademy – which can fuel an interest in a particular sport. The Internet can also put you in touch with local or specialist communities following a particular sport. The football club sites are classic examples.

Get dancing

You don't have to just sit in front of the screen. A lot of parents find products such as dance mats and EyeToys are great examples of how the screen can get kids to get up and exercise.

5. Helping around the home

Most of us mums complain that children don't help enough around the home. Maybe, however, it's often our own fault for not encouraging them to do more. When we're short of time we often think it's easier and quicker to do the job ourselves. It would certainly save us time in the long term if we got better at delegating. It would also help give our children a sense of belonging to a family unit. Helping around the home can create a moment of togetherness and a good opportunity to chat. It also encourages kids to take on responsibility. If, for instance, they have to tidy up after a play, it makes them more conscious of the mess they're making.

Interestingly, it was single mums and mums with an only child who had the best tips to pass on in this area. If you're a single mum it's particularly important that you work as a team with your children so you can share the responsibilities with them. And an only child will often enjoy the companionship of being with Mum or Dad as they share a task together. Taking responsibility for particular jobs can also give children a sense of pride and confidence as they become part of the adult world.

TIPS ON ... **HELPING AROUND THE HOME**

Make it fun
Try and make household tasks fun activities that you all do together, rather than just a chore. So, for instance, have a good chat or sing-song while you're making the beds, or run competitions to see who can finish their task first or do theirs best.

Allocate ownership
Give specific household responsibilities to your child so that they feel a sense of ownership and pride. Make them, for instance, in charge of sweeping the floor after tea, laying the table, washing up ... and, of course, tidying up their own mess. If there are particularly unpopular jobs, consider introducing rotas for them.

Resist giving rewards
Try not to give rewards for little jobs around the house. Ideally, your child should do them as a matter of habit. The big jobs – like washing the car – are a different matter, however. If appropriate, give your child a bit of extra pocket money for helping out on these jobs.

Appreciate and admire
Don't take your child's help for granted. Make sure you stop and admire what they've done.

USE THE MEDIA

There are lots of TV programmes about household things – cooking, DIY and gardening, for instance. Watch them with your child and have fun seeing how the celebrity chefs and gardeners go about their tasks.

6. Play

Play is a critical part of childhood. Through play children discover themselves, their friends and the world. So it's important that as parents we give our kids the space and time to play. We don't need to be there as a constant entertainer. We should occasionally just sit back and let them get on with it. The earlier children start playing by themselves, the better they'll get at it.

Toy manufacturers often use 'enduring play themes' when they're developing new toy concepts. These themes include caring, role play, good versus bad, construction, wheels and my little world. The reason they're called 'enduring' is that they represent the psychological motivations that are at the heart of play. These are fundamental play characteristics that endure from one generation to the next, and that attract children to the most successful toys.

As a parent it's useful to be aware of these different themes because this can help you understand what inspires a child to play. Try and ensure that your child has toys with a selection of different themes. And when you're putting toys away, think themes again. If the toys are in a muddle it makes it harder for a child to focus on any one activity.

ENDURING PLAY THEMES

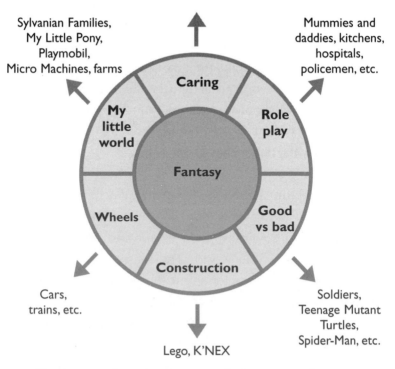

Teddies and dolls, e.g. Cabbage Patch, Barbie, Bratz, etc.

Sylvanian Families, My Little Pony, Playmobil, Micro Machines, farms

Mummies and daddies, kitchens, hospitals, policemen, etc.

Caring

My little world

Role play

Fantasy

Wheels

Good vs bad

Construction

Cars, trains, etc.

Soldiers, Teenage Mutant Turtles, Spider-Man, etc.

Lego, K'NEX

Fundamental motivations > enduring toys and games

TIPS ON ... PLAY

Develop play themes that can last for a couple of days
Encourage your kids to develop a theme that can act as a focus for a couple of days. This could involve building a setting for imaginative play, for instance, a Lego football pitch or a make-believe stadium for a pop concert. Forget about clearing up for a couple of days, and make the most of the centrepiece for all sorts of imaginary games.

Get your kid to improvise
Improvisation can be much more fun than ready-bought toys. It also spurs on your child's powers of initiative. So, for example, help them make a cot for their favourite dolly out of a shoebox; use kitchen pans as musical instruments; build dens and camps in cupboards, and set up table tennis on the kitchen table.

Let them be noisy from time to time
Don't throw the drum away that Granny gave them for Christmas. The occasional noisy game is good for them as it allows them to let off steam.

Don't forget the classic games
A lot of classic games like Snakes and Ladders, Monopoly, Battle Ships, Noughts and Crosses and Tiddly Winks have stood the test of time. Introduce your kids to them as well as trying out new ones.

USE THE MEDIA

Inspire imaginative play themes

So, for instance, get your child to dress up as Sleeping Beauty after watching the DVD, play pirates after watching *Pirates of the Caribbean*, or start dancing after seeing *Bombay Dreams*.

Inspire real action play

Game shows and big events can be an inspiration for real action. We came across a mum, for instance, who had created a challenge game after watching *Raven*.

Inspire kids to perform

Use films and musicals as a source of ideas for kids to do their own performances. Agree a theme with the kids and help them find the appropriate costumes. Then leave them to it – but agree a time when you will come back to view the production.

Find inspiration on the internet

For some great play ideas go to www.elc.co.uk.

Alternatives to the screen
– summary

- It's all very well limiting screen entertainment time, but something positive needs to fill the void. We have all experienced that empty feeling after a period of media bingeing – some parents describe it as the 'cold turkey' moment.

- We believe that there are six key areas of activity that a parent should encourage when it's time to look beyond the screen – chat, reading, creativity and music, exercise, helping around the home ... and above all, play.

>>> PART 2

ENSURING THAT SCREEN TIME IS QUALITY TIME

How to become a media-savvy parent

- **Understanding how your child responds to media**
- **The response check**

Now that you have your child's screen time under control, it's time to make sure that your child's media time is quality time. Part of this means becoming a media-savvy parent. 'What's that?' you're probably asking yourself. It's simple. You need to be able to tell whether a TV or computer programme is good or bad for your child. But here's where it's slightly more tricky. You don't just look at the programme and decide whether you like the look of it or not. A media-savvy parent also observes his or her child to see how they're responding to what they see on the screen. It's the response from the child – not just the programme content – which is the thing to look out for. A positive response means quality media time. No two children are the same and that's why it's important that you develop your own media antennae. What's good for one child might be bad for another. One child might mimic the actions of Power Rangers, while another one won't. Some children may pick up the bad language of The Simpsons, while others just sit back and enjoy a good belly laugh.

This book is not prescriptive. It doesn't recommend some content being good for children and some being bad. It will help you make your own judgements about how television and computer programmes affect your child. And to help you do this, we're going to share with you some of the tricks of the media trade. If you're going to be media-savvy, you need to know how the media works and why.

As media professionals we both have extensive experience of trying to manipulate the media to influence people's thoughts and lives. A simple technique in advertising, for instance, is to get people to think of brands as people. So if you're trying to promote a car you might give it the personality and characteristics of a reliable friend, or a fast sexy lady.

Understanding how your child responds to media

As parents we should look at the television and computer in the same way – as a person. Just as advertisers look out for the response that their brands have on consumers, we should look more closely at how our children respond to different aspects of the screen. So looking at how your child responds to an individual programme is *as important* as keeping in touch with programme content. Make sure you don't just switch on the TV or computer and walk away. Take a little time out to sit down with the child and simply observe how they respond.

Checking out the response

Once you start thinking of the television or computer as a person, you naturally start asking yourself some questions.

- Do I like this person and am I happy for him to be my child's playmate?

- Do I like the influence he has on my child or the mood he leaves them in?

- Is my child learning useful things from him, or does he leave them with no motivation or energy to do anything?

We have identified Seven Responses which are fundamental to how children relate to a TV or computer programme.

They are:

1. **Learning** – what learning does my child take out of the programme?
2. **Motivation** – what does the programme motivate my child to do?
3. **Energy** – how does the programme influence my child's energy levels?
4. **Language** – what language does my child adopt as a result of the programme?
5. **Role models** – what role models does the programme give my child?
6. **Emotions** – how does the programme influence the mood of my child?
7. **Relationships** – does the programme encourage my child to be social, and if so, in what way?

The Seven Responses offer parents a framework for questioning. A parent can focus on each area and consider – is my child responding to a specific TV programme or computer game in a positive or negative way? This questioning will automatically help parents decide whether a programme should, or shouldn't, be included in a child's media schedule.

THE RESPONSE CHECK

+ Positive responses   - Negative responses

	< **Learning** >	
Is my child getting valuable information, e.g. educational, world issues, street news?		Is my child exposed to unsuitable information, e.g. violence, sex, disturbing news?

	< **Motivation** >	
Is my child motivated to do something positive, e.g. a new subject, help others?		Is my child left demotivated to do anything positive, e.g. play apathy, bored, no interest in life?

	< **Energy** >	
Does it leave my child with an appropriate energy level, e.g. restored after school, calm before bed?		Does it leave my child with an inappropriate energy level, e.g. lethargic after breakfast, hyper before bed?

	< **Language** >	
Will my child's language improve as a result of it, e.g. new vocabulary, positive tone of voice?		Is it bad for the development of my child's language, e.g. limited vocabulary, bad words, aggressive tone of voice?

	< **Role models** >	
Does it contain positive role models, e.g. do I respect their values, outlook on life, priorities?		Does it contain negative role models, e.g. people and behaviour I don't respect, violent, anti-social behaviour?

	< **Emotions** >	
Do I like the emotional state it leaves my child in, e.g. happy, fulfilled, content?		Am I concerned about my child's emotional state after they switch off, e.g. sad, frightened, disturbed behaviour?

	< **Relationships** >	
Does it encourage good relationships between siblings and/or with friends?		Is my child turning into a loner as a result of it?

| **IfYES...** it's a reason to stay tuned | < > | **IfYES...** it's a reason to switch off |

97

Now you know what questions to ask, it's important that you're sensitive to your children's reactions. Tune into their body language and watch out for swings in mood. Be sensitive to how they anticipate and remember a particular programme. Do they really hanker after it? And what do they hang on to once the screen is switched off?

Putting the Response Check into action

To help get you thinking about what to look out for, here are some positive and negative responses from parents to modern media.

Response 1 – Learning
TV and computer games ... make it fun and easy to learn things ...
... Or ... they're full of stuff we'd prefer they didn't know about.

Response 2 – Motivation
TV and computer games ... encourage kids to do all sorts of things ...
... Or ... they leave kids feeling empty – not knowing what to do.

Response 3 – Energy
TV and computer games ... recharge the batteries after a

day at school or relax them after lunch ...

... *Or* ... make them totally hyper.

Response 4 – Language

TV and computer games ... encourage them to develop their language skills ...

... *Or* ... they soak up bad language.

Response 5 – Role models

TV and computer games ... introduce them to good role models ...

... *Or* ... bad ones.

Response 6 – Emotions

TV and computer games ... help them become more in touch with their emotions and put them in a good mood ...

... *Or* ... put them in a bad mood.

Response 7 – Relationships

TV and computer games ... help bring friends and family together ...

... *Or* ... pull them apart.

Now think about how your child responds to individual TV programmes and computer games.

Here's a Response Check for you to fill in, or get a copy from www.mediadietforkids.com.

THE RESPONSE CHECK

+ Positive responses   - Negative responses

	< Learning >	
	< Motivation >	
	< Energy >	
	< Language >	
	< Role models >	
	< Emotions >	
	< Relationships >	

If YES...
it's a reason
to stay tuned

<   >

If YES...
it's a reason
to switch off

How to raise a media-savvy child

- **Distinguishing reality from fantasy**
- **Putting the news into perspective**
- **Coping in a commercial world**

It's no use just you being media-savvy, your child needs to be media-savvy too. In the early years, when your child is still relatively young, you're the one in control. As your child grows up, however, they become more independent. You're not always going to be there to help them choose which TV programmes to watch, or which computer games to play. And you won't always be able to see how they're coping with, and reacting to, what they see on the screen. Your child needs to take on his or her own media responsibility. They need to understand the role media plays in their lives, how to make the most of it, and the best ways of protecting themselves from some of its hazards. If you're media-savvy as a parent, you can help your child become media-savvy too.

The best way of doing this is to sit down with your child in front of the screen and help them understand what they need to know. It may be explaining to them that advertisements try to tempt us to buy things we don't need, or that horrific murders seen on the news don't happen every day – or simply that witches don't exist.

Distinguishing reality from fantasy

Children's understanding of reality and fantasy evolves as they grow up. As parents, if we understand this evolution we can help our children when they have moments of concern or anxiety caused by the screen. Once we appreciate their understanding of what's really happening on the screen, we're in a better position to be of proper help. Do they, for instance, believe that a certain character is real or not? How much are they aware that the behaviour and action of actors in the soaps and dramas are exaggerated for effect?

The reality versus fantasy evolution

Outlined below are the different steps in a child's 'fantasy-versus-reality evolution'. As well as noting down what you as a parent should look out for, we've given some tips on how best to handle your child at each of the different stages. The most important thing is to keep on discussing TV and computer content with your child, so that you have a constant reality check.

2- to 3-year-olds

Children in this age group accept fantasy for what it is. They've got no reason or inclination to question it in any way. They understand the concept of 'make believe' and 'let's pretend'. They'll happily let the media pull them into a fantasy world, and don't have any real desire to understand whether media characters are real or not. To them, the television is a box full of things. If you lifted the lid there would simply be TV objects and people within it. They actually believe what they see.

>TOP TIPS<

- Let them enjoy their fantasy world during these years.

- The ideas that some things are 'pretend' and some things are 'real' can be introduced to a child – but do it gently.

- Get to know how your child reacts, so you can watch out for the moments in cartoons or videos that they're likely to find scary. Be ready to reassure them that it's 'just pretend'.

4- to 6-year-olds

Children start wanting to sort out what's real and what's not. One teacher told us of a four-year-old girl who had been taken to a film premiere with her grandfather who's an actor. When they got there she asked him why he was sitting down next to her – surely he had to go off onto the screen. For this particular child, the screen was the real world. The first thing children of this age group do is focus on the characters which are obviously not real – the cartoon characters, or characters in fantasy dramas. It becomes very important to children to be able to distinguish between fantasy and reality – and they're proud if they're able to do so.

There's a lot of questioning at this stage and children still turn to their parents for the final word. This makes it possible for parents to extend the 'make believe' if they want to. For instance, most six-year-olds still believe in Father Christmas. The television is perceived as a magical spyglass – something which lets you see into a world beyond your home and the sitting room.

>TOP TIPS<

- Kids of this age seem so grown-up, but beware. Don't underestimate what they might find frightening. It is often the tone or feel of a programme, rather than the content, which makes the most impression.

- Watch out for mimicking. At this age anything on the screen is there to be copied and becomes an inspiration for real-life play.

7- to 12-year-olds

By the time children reach the age of seven, they have developed their own framework for interpreting reality versus fantasy. They also understand the basic principles of the television, DVD or computer. However, this interpretation system isn't always as sophisticated as it might seem. In particular, children find themselves in difficulty where the reality versus fantasy distinction is blurred.

Good examples of these areas of confusion are the television soaps and virtual-reality games. Here, it all seems real enough – but of course, it isn't.

>TOP TIPS<

- Help your child interpret situations when the reality-versus-fantasy distinction becomes blurred.

- Explain to them that behaviour on reality shows is far from real and families portrayed in television soaps are not like the majority of us. So what's happening in *EastEnders* and *Neighbours* isn't necessarily going on in most homes across the country. Normal and happy family situations don't make good television.

- Keep a close eye on the use of violent games which feel too real. If the imagery looks too realistic, there is a danger that your child will become desensitised to the situation, and be more likely to emulate it in real life.[15]

Putting the news into perspective

And what about the news? On the one hand, the access to 24-hour global news is great. It means that we and our children know about world affairs. But on the other hand, it can give a very distorted view of life. When we were doing our research, one granny gave us a good example of how the news can distort a child's perception of reality. Her grandson had seen on the news the flooding of the Cornish village of Boscastle. Every time it rained in the weeks following the disaster, he was visibly distraught. He presumed that what he had seen on the television was a normal event. He was frightened that his home would also be washed away. In the boy's mind his perception of reality, as seen on the news, had become blurred with reality itself. As parents, it's very important that we put news into proper perspective for our children. Make sure you discuss news items with your child and explain the circumstances to them.

Here are a few things to consider:

News is always bad news ... and if there's sex, so much the better

So you just need to help your child put things into perspective. Get them to see things through the eyes of a news editor. For example, given the choice of headlines between 'Lottery winner gives money to charity and goes home to wife' and 'Lottery winner rats on girlfriend and gets convicted for fraud', which is the editor going to print?

The world in our sitting rooms

Thanks to the technology of modern media the world suddenly seems a much smaller place. So we can be watching recent world events on our screen – the fighting in Iraq or natural catastrophes – and it all seems so near and close to home. Children need to know that all these events aren't happening right on their doorstep. If they go outside the front door they're not going to be mowed down by an army tank, or washed away by a gigantic wave. Make sure, therefore, you differentiate clearly between local and international news.

News saturation

The media can latch on to one particular story and stay with it for weeks and weeks. This often happens in the summer when there's not much news . If it's a bad news story – which inevitably it is – then it can start to get depressing for children.

Coping in a commercial world

Modern media offers businesses a wealth of commercial opportunities. Companies can reach their customers – and target markets – quickly and relatively cheaply. The constant pressure of companies wanting to advertise this, or sell that, can put parents under considerable strain. Kids are deluged with information and images of exciting new products. They start wanting everything they see and pestering their parents for this and that.

As parents we have to learn to say 'no'... and mean it. We also need to manage our children's expectations. They can't – and shouldn't – have everything they want.

Advertising

One of the most powerful means of trying to influence children to want or do certain things is advertising. As a parent it's useful to understand what advertisers are trying to do, the techniques they use and the likely effect they will have on your child. If you understand all that, you'll be in a good position to help your child take advertising in his or her stride. So here are some tips about what to look out for at the various stages.

2- to 3-year-olds

Kids of this age enjoy recognising their favourite brands

on the TV, but they have little understanding of what an advertisement is. It's good to introduce the idea of advertising as early as possible to children. All you need to say at this point is that advertisements are there to tell us about a toy, or whatever, and make us want it.

Advertisers targeting this age group will be trying to establish their brand name in your child's early language repertoire, for example through sing-along songs. But most of the advertising will be targeted at the mums.

4- to 6-year-olds

At the age of four, many kids still don't realise the point of advertisements. They just think of them as mini programmes or stories. But by the age of six most of them understand that advertising is making them want this or that. Advertisements start becoming useful to kids because they use them to discover new brands, and to point out what they want. Check your child understands what advertisements are about. Advertisers will be targeting your child directly, although they still want the advertising to appeal to you. Advertisements will be designed to fuel fantasy and excitement. Advertisers will think of clever devices that a child might take on after the ads have finished, such as funny lines or actions to mimic. This is an effective way of prolonging the power of advertising beyond the commercial break.

7- to 12-year-olds

By the age of seven kids are wised-up to advertisements. They know exactly what they are about and gobble them up with interest. They enjoy adults' advertisements as much as kids' ones, and start to influence what adult brands their parents buy. The family car is a classic example. With kids' brands advertisers pitch their advertisements at kids just that little bit older than their prime target, because kids of this age group always look up to the kids above them. It's the kiss of death to talk down to these kids. Advertisers tend to use a lot of boy imagery because girls are more accepting of it. This means that ads can be very male-dominated. Mums are now out of the equation altogether. Advertisers aren't looking to appeal to them.

What the advertisers are doing

2-3 years old – establishing the brand name in early vocabulary

4-6 years old – giving the brand fantasy and excitement

7-12 years old – creating a brand's aspirational credentials

A good advertisement normally works at a number of different levels – performing different roles for kids of different ages

24-hours-a-day shopping

The Internet is creating an environment of buying 24 hours a day which encourages kids to want to buy, buy, buy. A lot of parents talk in despair about the pressure this causes. Previously parents had the power. If you didn't want your kid to have something, you didn't take them shopping; and if you did, you decided which shops to visit. Now things have changed. The shops have come to our sitting rooms and kids are more empowered to make things happen.

And then once your child has decided to buy something, there can be other problems. It's easy to get conned or be the victim of fraud on the net.

TIPS ON ... COPING IN A COMMERCIAL WORLD

• Get used to saying 'no' and meaning it - children should never assume they have control of the family purse.

• Make sure you give them more to think about than having this or that. If children are brought up in a family where shopping has become the number-one leisure pursuit, then it's not surprising that they turn into avid consumers.

- Encourage them to save up money themselves for things they want. This will teach them to appreciate the value of things.

- Help your child to properly check out what they're planning to buy and whom they're buying from. If there are terms and conditions, read them through with your child very carefully.

- Never give your child your credit card to buy things. Once they've decided what they want and you're happy with the decision, do the transaction yourself.

- Keep your kid away from any auctions on the net. It's very easy to get carried away and spend more than they can afford.

How to take charge of the schedule

- TV planning
- Buying computer games
- Using the Internet

TV planning

With such a wide choice of TV channels now available, it's a good idea to plan your child's TV viewing in advance. Getting into the routine of advanced planning gives you better control over the amount of time your child spends in front of the TV, and what they watch. It also encourages your child to start taking on their own screen responsibility. They have to be selective and make choices for themselves.

So if your child is old enough, it's important that they're involved in any planning too. This gets them to think about what they really enjoy, and appreciate more what they watch.

And if programmes are on at inappropriate times, record them. It's much better that children watch programmes at times that suit their schedule, rather than letting them disrupt the family routine. Digital services such as Sky+ and TiVo make the job of recording so much easier. These services allow you to select programmes in advance, and the recording is done automatically for you.

Don't be afraid of trying out new programmes, or insisting on programmes that sound worthwhile. Read the reviews of programmes coming up and see if anything sounds as though it might interest your child. TV documentaries can be a wonderful source of inspiration and a great way to learn things as a family.

And remember, if you can sit down for five minutes, watch the TV with your child. The more you can keep in touch with what they're watching, and see how they're reacting, the better.

Film ratings

When it comes to planning what films to watch at home (TV, video and DVD), or at the cinema, it is important for parents to be up-to-date with the subtleties of the ratings systems. For instance, do you know the differences between a PG-and a 12-rated video/DVD? The PG rating tells you that the content is suitable for children aged 8 years and over, while the 12 rating tells you that the content is suitable for children aged 12 years and older. The 12A category is a cinema category that allows younger children to go to 12-rated films with an accompanying adult, but it is important to note that the material in any 12 or 12A film is not always suitable for them.

The British Board of Film Classification (see separate box) classifies films in the UK, and their website (www.bbfc.co.uk) is well worth a visit. For instance, they give a short description of recent films and explanations of why they have been given a particular rating. There is also a children's section that explains how the ratings are decided. Ratings are important and if your child has an appreciation of the system, and knows that you believe in it, it will make it easier to monitor what they view.

TIPS ON ... AGE-APPROPRIATE VIEWING

• Children shouldn't just watch programming that is targeted at older children and adults. A review commissioned by The Literary Trust shows that children can suffer as a result of watching too much programming that goes over their heads.[16] There is so much good programming specially targeted at younger children – check that you allow your little ones to benefit from it.

BBFC – WHAT IS THE BRITISH BOARD OF FILM CLASSIFICATION?

The British Board of Film Classification is an independent organisation that exists to regulate and classify the content of films shown in cinemas and released on video and DVD.

While the BBFC's classifications remain advisory with regard to cinema releases, the 1984 Video Recordings Act gave it statutory powers for the first time. Almost all UK video/DVD releases have to be examined and classified by the BBFC.

At the same time the BBFC was also made responsible for classifying the more risky computer games. These are the games that are considered by law to need classification – you can spot them because they will have a BBFC 12, 15 or 18 classification sign – rather than the voluntary PEGI or ELSPA classification sign.

The BBFC awards its classifications based on what it considers to be the appropriate age limits for the film in question – and, if deemed necessary, by requesting that the distributor makes changes to the film or game, usually in the form of cuts.

There is often a short description on the back cover of a video, DVD or game that gives a flavour of why the content was given the particular age rating.

For more information: www.bbfc.co.uk, www.cbbfc.co.uk and www.bfi.org.uk.

The BBFC classifications currently in use are:

Uc - This denotes video releases deemed particularly suitable for preschool children.

U - This stands for 'Universal' and denotes that a film is suitable for everyone.

PG - This stands for 'Parental Guidance'. Although anyone can be admitted, PG certificate films contain an implicit warning that the film might contain material unsuitable for very young children.

12A – Replaced 12 at the cinema. Suitable for children of 12 and over, but children under 12 permitted if accompanied by a responsible adult.

12 – This covers videos and DVDs considered appropriate for 12-year-olds and upwards. No one under 12 can buy or rent them.

15 - This denotes that the film is unsuitable for children under the age of 15, and limits cinema viewing and video/DVD purchasing and rental to people 15 years and over.

18 - This denotes that the film is unsuitable for people under the age of 18, and limits cinema viewing and video/DVD purchasing and rental to people 18 years and over.

R18 - This classification was exclusively intended for videos that could only be sold in licensed sex shops. In other words, pornography.

The BBFC logo and symbols are the property of the BBFC and they are both copyright and trademark-protected.

TIPS ON ... **SUBSCRIBING TO DIGITAL SERVICES**

- In this digital world with so many channels on offer it is very easy for children to become overwhelmed by so much choice. So when you're new to a multi-channel service it's important to keep a close eye on how the kids use it. It's also important to set any ground rules firmly at the beginning.

- Overall, the multi-channel services can bring enormous benefits to the home – it's just a question of keeping things in control. There are fantastic channels specifically aimed at younger children. CBeebies and The Disney Channel, for instance, are particularly good for pre-school kids.

- Services like Sky+ and TiVo allow parents to be more selective in what they watch. Sky+ allows parents to select programmes to be videoed at the beginning of the week, so that parents and kids together can devise their own personal schedule.

- Parents with 5- to 9-year-olds need to watch out for the cartoon channels. These can be a terrific draw in homes that have just gone digital, and not surprisingly cartoon consumption amongst this age group tends to go up.

- With older children it's obviously important to keep them away from the adult channels, and several parents told us how they particularly objected to some of the content on the music channels. They thought that the language and images of contemporary music culture can often be too aggressive and sexually explicit for young children.

- But the biggest temptation for adults and kids on the multi-channels is sport. In fact nine out of the top ten programmes in multi-channel homes are football-based programmes. This is territory that can be difficult for parents to control, so when it comes to football it is particularly important to set out the ground rules early on.

TIPS ON ... SPORT ON TV

- Get your partner or husband to be supportive of what you're doing – it's essential that you work as a team.

- Set firm sports rules and limits. So, for instance, during the week you might decide your child can only watch matches if their home team is playing. Or at weekends you might allow them to watch the first and last twenty minutes of a game – making sure you record the whole thing so any goals missed can be replayed.

- To stop the problem of late-night sports watching, you might allow your children to watch the first half of any match, and record the second half to see the following day.

- Consider using the radio to get your children away from the screen. We spoke to one mum who allows her son to watch the first half of a football match in front of the TV. He then has to turn it off for the second half, but can listen to it on the radio. So, often he'll play carpet football as he's still following the match on the radio.

TIPS ON ... WATCHING FAVOURITE VIDEOS/DVDS

- There are many parents who are happier for their young children to watch favourite videos and DVDs time and time again, rather than watching programmes that they feel uncertain about. To a certain extent, there is no harm in this, as long as you are happy with the quality of the video.

• Research shows that repeat viewing of quality videos can help a child's language development.[17] 'Quality' might mean videos that have an educational element to them, or videos that have simple story lines that introduce the child to new vocabulary. According to research, young children benefit more from direct 'one to one' communication styles, rather than programming that floods them with information from lots of different directions.[17]

TIPS ON ... FILMS AND BOOKS – WHICH TO ENCOURAGE FIRST?

• It's often a good incentive for a child to read if you say that you'll take them to see a film once they've finished the book. It also ensures that your child puts their own imagination to work, rather than just being presented with all the fantasy and images on a plate. They then have the fun of either agreeing or disagreeing with the way things are shown in the film.

• But if your child can't read the book first, try and use the film itself as an incentive to read the book. They can still have fun discussing with you what they think worked, or didn't, in the film.

TIPS ON ... **VIEWING AT A FRIEND'S HOME**

- If you're worried about your child being exposed to inappropriate screen content at a friend's home, you should try and talk to the friend's parents about your concerns and see whether they're happy to keep some control on the situation when your child goes round.

- If you're still unhappy, try and get the children to play at your home as much as possible so that you can have more control.

- Try and encourage your child to monitor their own media activity, and give them the confidence to tell their friend that they'd prefer to do something else.

- Keep the lines of communications with your child open. So don't go beserk if they tell you they saw something inappropriate. Instead, explain why you think it is inappropriate for them.

TIPS ON ... HANDLING DISTURBING MATERIAL

- If your child is disturbed about something they have seen, first of all try and get a clear picture of what exactly is upsetting them. Don't be afraid to ask them specific questions about it.

- Then try and get your child to feel more comfortable with the bad thoughts. You can do this in a number of ways, for instance by explaining why the situation is so unreal, or why it is most unlikely to happen.

- Finally, try and get your kid to forget the vision altogether. Encourage them to dump their thoughts in an imaginary dustbin, or simply get your kid thinking about other things. One mum told us how her daughter has a little book by her bed. If she has something on her mind they'll write it down in the book together. This acted as an effective debriefing exercise, or in other words it was her daughter's 'scary-thought dustbin'.

TOP TIPS ON TV PLANNING

- Plan ahead using TV guides and listings and read the reviews carefully.

- Involve your child in making the choices – keep the TV guide where they can find it.

- Don't be put off by awkward timings – you can video programmes, if need be. This is now so quick and easy to do with recording services like Sky+.

- Sky + is also great for ensuring that children don't watch too much TV at any one time. If the broadcast schedule is playing two favourite programmes one after the other, record the second one and insist your child plays outside for 20 minutes before they come in and watch it.

- Try and choose a mix of programmes – don't be afraid of saying it's your turn to choose.

- Be in touch with the ratings system and use it.

- Switch off once the programme is finished!

Buying computer games

Once you've bought the computer or games console for your child the next decision is what games to buy. Think of computer games in terms of:

What they get your child to do, and ...
What kind of world they encourage your child to step into.

So, for instance, start distinguishing between games that are all about fast action and eye-and-hand coordination, and games that are designed to get your child thinking. Some games are great at making children process information and take decisions, others are good at encouraging speedy reactions.

Notice the difference also between games where kids step into a fun fantasy world, and games where they enter a world of violence and aggression. And look at how true to life the different worlds seem.

Below we've created four key groups of computer games. There are lots of ways that computer games can be categorised, but when we talked to parents we found that these distinctions were the important ones.

For each group of games, we've included some points to consider if you're looking to buy a particular game. Ideally you want your child to have a healthy mix of different games. It's the overdosing on too much of the same thing that often leads to problems.

Then we've taken a separate look at educational games and software (see page 139). These are games that are more about learning than entertainment, and it is territory where parents need to take the initiative. There are some fantastic programmes about, and although your child won't be pestering you for them, they are well worth looking at.

When buying a computer game, make sure you do your research. Check the age rating and any information given out on the game, either from the manufacturer or independent reviews. A good source of advice and information can be other parents. Find out if they have views on a particular game, and even get their kids to give you a demonstration of the game in action. Computer magazines also provide game demos.

Alternatively, you can borrow games from the local library to help you decide whether or not to buy them. We came across one mum who bought her computer games from a shop where they have a return policy within 10 days if you don't like the game.

Finally, don't forget that computer games can be down-loaded from the Internet and can often come as part of your computer hardware package. If this is the case, you need to check that you're happy with them. If not, you can ask the hardware provider not to load the games on to the hardware drive, but to supply them on discs which will give you more control.

The four groupings of games which we have identified are:

1. Fast-action games

These are good for hand-and-eye coordination, but they can be intellectually limiting if your kid spends too long on them. This is the territory of sporting and racing games, and the fantasy the child enters can be very real to life. So you can believe you're driving a Formula 1 racing car at the Grand Prix, or playing football in the Premier League. Examples of these types of games are FIFA, TT SuperBikes and Gran Turismo.

2. Strategy and creative games

Parents can buy these games with confidence because they're designed to get kids thinking. They include family quizzes, the creation of virtual worlds, strategic war games, sports management, flight simulation and educational games. Examples of these types of games are Sims and Roller Coaster/Zoo Tycoon.

3. Adventure games

Games of this type will often involve a voyage or mission, with tasks and obstacles along the way. The fantasy is often from a film or favourite TV programme. These games are good for decision-making skills, but as a parent you need to check you're happy with the imagery. Examples here include many classics such as Lord of the Rings, James Bond, Tomb Raider, Doom and Sonic, and The Simpsons: Hit & Run.

4. Fighting and war games

These include beat 'em ups and bash 'em ups, combatitive war games, wrestling and murder games. As in adventure games the player may be challenged to complete a number of missions – but in this territory the heart of the experience is about the fighting and destruction. The suitability of these games for children can be a concern for parents. Some are pure good fun, while others are OK in moderation. But many of these games are not suitable for young children and you will find they are rated 15 or 18. It's important for parents to follow the advice of ratings and stick to their instincts – particularly when imagery and graphics become too realistic.

Violence in computer games

The biggest concern for most parents is the level of violence introduced into some computer games. There are a number of questions to ask yourself, in order to decide whether or not a game is too violent for your child.

1. Is the killing of people the sole purpose of the game?

If you look at the computer game Manhunt, for instance, the objective of the game is to murder people. It is about the thrill of taking life away. There are other war games, however, where there is a specific mission – for instance, to capture a bridge or gain a territory – and people get killed along the way. The objective isn't to kill, but it becomes necessary as part of the mission. We believe that this is an important distinction.

2. Are you worried that there's no respect for human dignity in the game?

Look at how the game manipulates the player's emotions. Is death or the harming of people glorified? Are you, for example, encouraged to gloat over any killings you carry out or any harm you cause?

3. How realistic does the violence appear?

When screen violence is portrayed in a fantasy world it's easy for a child to understand that it has nothing to do with real life. However, the distinction between reality and fantasy can become blurred as violent games become more true to life. One of the big advances in computer games over the last decade has been the improvement of computer graphics. As computer games become more like films, it becomes all the more important for parents to take a good look at the character of a game. A child is in no doubt that the violence in Star Wars is fantasy, while a child playing a game in an urban world of crime and street violence may not be so sure.

4. Does the age rating, or what you have heard from other sources, warn you against the game?

We noticed that parents appear to be more cautious about film ratings than computer game ratings. It's as though parents think of game ratings like the age symbol on toys – a vague guideline that's often wrong anyway. This relaxed attitude was confirmed when we spoke to a ratings officer. He thought that the problem lies with the word 'game', because it suggests playful territory that doesn't need to be taken too seriously.

Children naturally put parents under pressure to buy things that are out of bounds age-wise. Playing an 18, after all, has more playground credibility than playing Sonic. We found plenty of nine-year-olds playing 18s. We do believe it's important for parents to be more vigilant about ratings. The ratings are there to help us, and we should use them to control the quality of our children's screen time.

5. Do you feel comfortable about the game?

Above everything else, you need to listen to your instincts. You're the best judge of what is or isn't good for your child. So finally, the most important question to ask yourself is whether you're happy with the level of violence or not? Think back to The seven-point Response Check (page 97) – how will your child respond to the content of the game? Will your child learn about things you would prefer they didn't know – for example, the tactics of the drug barons in a corrupt underground world? Will they want to copy bad role models – for example, aggressive skateboarders who threaten the neighbourhood with their graffiti? Will they pick up bad language that you'd prefer them not to use? These are personal moral and family issues. Don't be tempted to dodge them just because your kids put you under pressure. So stay in tune with your own values and let them guide you when you're faced with a tricky decision.

Controlling violent computer games

If the answer is 'yes' to any of the five questions above, there are a number of options you've got if you want to control your child's use of violent computer games. It needn't just be a question of whether you buy a game or not.

Your options are:

Not to buy the computer game
The younger the child, the easier this is to do. But even with older children, try not to get pressurised to buy a game if you feel it's the wrong thing to do. If you decide not to buy, explain clearly to your child why you've taken this decision. Show them that you've taken their request seriously and done your research.

Be prepared for your child to play the game when he or she is visiting friends. It's impossible to control them all of the time; just make sure you keep the lines of communications open with your child so you know what's going on.

Hire the game from a video shop or borrow it from a friend
This can be a good option because it allows your child to see and experience the game, without being overexposed to it. They can then be part of the playground chatter because they've played it themselves – and that's often all that kids want. Getting a game on loan also gives you a chance to sit down with your child and actually show them what you don't like about the game – and explain the reasons why.

Buy it, but limit its usage

The real problem with violent computer games is kids being overexposed to them. Agree with your child before you buy the game what the rules about playing are – how long they can play it and when. If there are younger siblings, for instance, you might decide that the child can't play it when they're about. And make sure that your child doesn't just play violent computer games. Make sure they have a healthy mixture of different types of games.

WHEN DOES A GAME BECOME TOO VIOLENT?

- When killing becomes the sole purpose
- When human dignity is not respected
- When the game becomes too true to life
- When the age rating warns against it
- When you don't feel comfortable with it

HOW TO TELL WHAT YOU ARE BUYING

The game in pictures
These pictures are taken from the game and give you an indication of the graphic quality. Watch out for violence that looks too real

The game in words
This gives you a brief description of the game content. It will give you a sense of what the player does and what kind of world they enter. Check you feel comfortable with this description

The format
This is how you check whether the game is for a PC or a console – PlayStation, PlayStation 2, Nintendo GameCube, Game Boy, XBox

PC CD-ROM

COMPUTER
GAME
FRONT COVER

DIGITAL
PUBLICATIONS

STUDIO A

12+

COMPUTER GAME
(BACK COVER)

blah blah blah blah blah blah blah blah blah blah blah blah blah blah blah blah blah blah blah blah blah blah blah blah blah blah blah

12+

The descriptor
This icon lets you know the type of content in the game – violence, sex, drugs, fear, discrimination and bad language (see PEGI System)

Front cover design
Beware – we spoke to parents who had been fooled by childish cartoon designs, thinking they were buying a children's game, but in fact they were buying an 18

The publisher
The name of the company that publishes the game, similar to a record label

Technical specifications
These are the minimum technical parameters that your PC or console needs in order to play the game

The age rating
This tells you the minimum age the game is suitable for, based on the content of the game (see PEGI System). Beware – we spoke to one dad who had just bought an 18 for his 11-year-old son – his son had hidden the rating with his thumb

The developer
The name of the studio that created the game, similar to a movie production company label

Source: www.elspa.com and Teresa Orange Research.

WHAT IS PEGI?

The Pan European Games Information (PEGI) system is a new age rating system for interactive games. It is a voluntary system that is supported by the major console manufacturers, including PlayStation, Xbox and Nintendo, as well as by publishers and developers of interactive games throughout Europe.

Started in the early spring of 2003, PEGI replaces existing national age rating systems with a single system that is identical throughout most of Europe. In the UK it takes over from the Elspa rating system, which you will still see on games that were launched prior to 2003.

The age rating system comprises two separate but complementary elements. The first is an age rating, similar to some existing rating systems. The PEGI age bands are 3+, 7+, 12+, 16+, 18+. The second element of the new system is a number of game descriptors. These are icons, displayed on the back of the game box, that describe the type of content to be found in the game. Depending on the type of game, there may be up to six such descriptors.

The combination of age rating and game descriptors allows parents and those purchasing games for children to ensure that the game they purchase is appropriate to the age of the intended player. Some of the more risky games will have a compulsory BBFC rating, rather than a PEGI rating.

Before any game can be rated under the voluntary system it must be established that the game is exempt from legal classification in the UK, i.e., whether it needs a BBFC certificate (see separate note on BBFC).

 Game contains depictions of violence

 Game may be frightening or scary for young children

 Game depicts nudity and/or sexual behaviour or sexual references

 Game contains depiction of, or material which may encourage, discrimination

 Game refers to or depicts the use of drugs

 Game contains bad language

For more information visit: www.pegi.info (the Pan European system), www.videostandards.org.uk (the agents in the UK). PEGI symbols are the property of ISFE – Interactive Software Federation of Europe – and are copyright and trademark protected.

TIPS ON ... **LIMITING WHAT YOU BUY**

- Don't spoil your child with too many games. We spoke to one dad who proudly told us that he had bought his children 34 games over the last couple of years. He went on to describe how his youngest son had become addicted to computer gaming.

- Let your child get bored with existing games before introducing any new ones into the home. It'll give them a cooling-off period away from the computer when they can go off and do other things.

- Above all, don't use your children as an excuse to buy every new game. Dads are particularly prone to doing this. It's important to remember that some kids find it hard to cope when there's so much on offer.

TIPS ON ... **PORTABLE GAMES**

- It's very important that the mobility of mobile games doesn't mean that your child never gets away from them.

- As a rule of thumb, we suggest that kids are allowed to use mobile games away from the home if they're having to wait around or be patient. For instance, if a sibling is having a swimming lesson then let your other child play on their mobile game. But don't let mobile games intrude on other activities, or social occasions.

- Look out for the new generation of mobile games. With the bigger screens these hand-held consoles offer a game experience that is far closer to TV than the original Game Boys. This means that they are more compulsive and less of a second-best. So there will be more of a need to keep a check on how your child is using them.

- Remember that playing on a portable game, be it a mobile-phone game, or a hand-held console, counts as screen time. Just because your child is playing while they are out and about doesn't mean that you shouldn't keep an eye on how long they are playing. It should be counted as screen time and your child should understand that it is included in his or her daily quota.

TIPS ON ... SCREEN EXERCISE

- A number of computer companies are focusing on games that get children off the couch, for instance dance mats and most recently the Nintendo Wii. We found that there is great enthusiasm for these active games, and they certainly appear to be getting kids moving in some households.

• But do they really give you proper exercise? Well, that's up to your children – it's certainly possible to build up a sweat if you put your mind to it. But don't let it replace a walk down to the playground – there's no substitute for a bit of fresh air.

TIPS ON ... GAMES WITH CAMERAS

• There are a number of programmes that incorporate the player into the game on screen. In the case of the EyeToy the camera sits on top of the TV, and in other cases voice recordings are made directly into the computer.

• Does it matter that the distinction between reality and fantasy becomes too blurred? It really just depends on what the game involves. Think back to the key questions – what is the game getting my child to do, and what world do they enter? One father described an EyeToy game where his son had to pretend to be a window cleaner. The son had a laugh and totally exhausted himself washing the imaginary windows.

- With the fighting games, just look carefully at the imagery. Check you feel happy with it before you get it. And if you do get it, keep a close eye on how the game affects your child's behaviour.

Buying educational games and software

What age kids should I buy for?
Some parents start buying educational games and software for kids as young as two or three years old. There's nothing wrong with this as long as everyone understands that the computer isn't just like any other toy. It comes with certain rules. Educational games become particularly valuable when your children are aged between four and seven years old. This is the age when they're still happy to engage in 'learning fun' and enjoy doing things encouraged by mum and dad. Once kids reach the ages of between seven and twelve it becomes more difficult to maintain their interest in educational material, mainly because they've discovered the likes of the PlayStation. Keep buying for this age group, however, because there's lots of good material out there.

What subjects should I go for?
There are lots of excellent programmes to help build literacy and numeracy skills for the under-sevens. For the older kids the choice becomes more subject-specific: for

example, programmes which are designed to support schoolwork and revision. Alternatively there are creative and multi-activity programmes which have a wide age appeal, and are particularly popular with girls. Specific programmes are also available to improve IT literacy, typing skills and language learning.

What should I buy?

The best source of advice about what to buy will come from other parents. Try and get some advice as well from teachers at school. They should have a good idea about what's right for your child. But check you buy games which are fun to do at home. It's good also to shop around. Online brochures often have a bigger choice than the High Street stores, so explore sites such as www.brain-works.co.uk. Once you've identified a specific educational game or piece of software, you need to decide whether it would interest and motivate your child. To help you do this, we've listed ten key questions to ask yourself.

The ten questions to ask

1. How could the software help my child to learn?
2. Does it look and sound appealing?
3. What are the depth and range of content?
4. Will my child find it easy to use?
5. Would my child want to use it?
6. Is there any feedback on a child's progress?
7. Would my child want to return to it time and time again?
8. Does it support learning at home, or is it obviously aimed at classroom use?
9. Does it offer support for the school curriculum?
10. What support materials are there? (e.g. are there activity packs to stimulate projects away from the screen?)

Using the Internet

The Internet has opened a whole new world and, not surprisingly, kids have been quick to pick up on what it has to offer. This is great, but for those of us with kids it presents a whole new parenting challenge. With the arrival of the Internet has come a new responsibility to protect kids – not just when they're out on the street, but in our homes.

A lot of the parents we spoke to were struggling with how best to manage their kids' use of the Internet. On the one hand they want their children to benefit from this new phenomenon. But at the same time they're naturally worried – and the biggest worry of all is control. By allowing your child on to the Internet you're letting them loose into a world where it's difficult to keep track of where they go, whom they meet and what they do.

And if that wasn't enough, in most homes it's the kids that know more about the technology than the parents. Research shows that children usually consider themselves more of an Internet expert than their parents – 28 per cent of parents describe themselves as beginners on the Internet, compared with only 7% of children. No wonder a lot of us feel slightly helpless.[18]

The risks of the net

There are two main risks to kids using the internet – inappropriate content and contacts. Because of the vast amount of information on the web it's easy for children to come across material which is unsuitable for them – pornography or material which is obscene, racist or just offensive. The contacts children make on the net can also be inappropriate. If children meet strangers on the web – in a chat room, for instance – there's no way of knowing the true identity of whom they've come in contact with, or what their intentions are.

5 TOP TIPS FOR ... NET SAFETY

Talking to parents and experts, they identified five key actions for good internet parenting.

1. Make sure you're Internet-savvy

You don't have to be up-to-date with every bit of new technology, but if you want to control your child's use of the Internet it certainly helps if you know what's going on. It's essential to have some idea of what the technology is and what it can do. You may already be very conversant with the Internet. If so, that's great. But beware. Just because you know your way around doesn't mean you have a good idea of how children use the net and what they can get up to.

A good starting point, therefore, is to sit down with your child and ask them to show you how they use the net. You might want to ask them what they like doing best, which are their favourite sites, things they don't like about it and whether they've had any uncomfortable experiences.

There are also a lot of good sources of information and advice on net safety for parents. Make the most of them. They vary widely – some are clearly aimed just at parents and go into a great amount of detail, others are for kids and adults and are both informative and fun (see list on page 170).

2. Get your child Internet-savvy

In the same way that children know what might happen if they don't look before crossing the road, or if they go off with strangers, try and make them aware of the possible dangers of the net. If you share with them what your worries are, then they're more likely to be careful themselves. Sometimes kids listen more if it's somebody else giving them advice rather than their parents. So you might want to visit with your child some of the websites aimed at children that spell out what the dangers of the Internet are and the best precautions to take (see list on page 169). A good site to visit is www.chatdanger.com. This tells the story, for example, of one girl who ended up being hurt by a man she met in a chat room.

3. Control and monitor

There are things you can do to make your child's use of the net more safe. The most obvious thing is to install filtering software that blocks unsuitable content, as well as antivirus and firewall protection. But be careful, these blocking devices aren't perfect. Kids can resent being 'controlled' in this way, and so become motivated to beat the system. We came across lots of examples of children who had found ways around them. Parents can also often get fed up with filtering systems because they either let through stuff they don't think should get through, or block stuff that they regard as completely harmless.

Another way to control what's going on is to keep the Internet screen somewhere in the house where you can easily keep an eye on it, for instance in the living room or kitchen. And if you want to keep your kids away from harmful content, try and direct them towards content that is educational, entertaining and appropriate for children. Some parents use child-friendly sites like www.yahooligans.com or www.askjeevesforkids.com.

4. Encourage responsibility

Whatever you do, your kid's use of the Internet will always be difficult to control completely. And even if you can keep control of their home usage, you won't necessarily be able to control how they use it elsewhere. Your child, therefore, needs to share responsibility. A good way of doing this is to sit down with your child and agree a 'Family Web Code'. Ideally this should be done before you allow your child to start using the Internet, but whenever you do it, it's never too late. The key to making the code a success is to explain the reasons behind the different rules.

5. Keep talking

Above all, keep talking to your child so that they feel comfortable about coming to you if they have any problems. Make it part of the daily routine to ask them what they've been doing on the Internet. And do it in such a way that it doesn't sound as if you're snooping but are genuinely interested in what they've been up to. If they have done something they shouldn't have, or been exposed to something inappropriate, don't overreact. The most important thing is that you both keep talking and work together to solve any problems.

An example of a Family Web Code

Don't give out any personal information – for instance, your name, email address, postal address, phone number, photo, school address, or even your hobbies – without permission.
Reason: you don't know where this information will end up or how it will be used.

Be cautious with anyone you meet on the net.
Reason: they may not be who they say they are and their intentions may not be good.

Don't believe everything you read on the Internet.
Reason: there is a lot of unreliable information on the net. Children are very trusting of anything printed – so you need to explain that just because it's printed it doesn't mean that it's true. It's also important to explain to children that there are a lot of self-publicists and fraudsters about. A lot of Internet material is nothing more than cheap advertising, while other material may be deliberately trying to deceive the reader. Kids need to be taught how to check out sources – show them how to do a bit of detective work before accepting things as true.

Only respond to emails or instant messages from people – or addresses – you know.
Reason: they may contain viruses or horrible messages.

Let Mum or Dad know if you're concerned about anything or anyone that you've come across on the web.
Reason: it's better to share any problems because Mum and Dad might be able to help you.

Never arrange to meet anyone you've met on the web without talking to Mum or Dad first.

Reason: you might think you know them, but they are in fact complete strangers.

Don't step into territory that doesn't feel right. If you get sent an obscene message, for instance, don't be tempted to explore further. Or if you accidentally end up on a dodgy web site, take the exit rather than reading on.

Reason: using the Internet is all about trust. If Mum and Dad can't trust where you are going then they will stop you from using the Internet. And thanks to the history/memory facilities on the computer they can check up on where you are going.

But, most importantly, help your child understand why it is best not to dig into inappropriate territory. There is a lot of nasty stuff out there – put up by people who want to shock adults and kids alike. You let those people win the day if you delve into their worlds.

TIPS ON ... BLOCKING DEVICES

- If you're looking for a simple solution on how to block inappropriate content, be prepared – there isn't one. While filtering products can be good, they are not foolproof and there is no substitute for parental involvement.

- Choose your Internet Service Provider carefully. Some provide educational material, safety information or protective software. Others do very little.

- Think carefully about what you want any filtering software to do. There are lots of different safety features ranging from those which control content, contacts or shopping to those which ensure privacy, improve your computer's security or monitor, record and stop Internet activity.

- If you want detailed advice on what filtering product to get, visit www.getnetwise.org. The site lists what filtering products are available and allows you to search for whatever feature interests you. You may also want to check out the Childnet International site at www.childnet-int.org. They are a non-profit organisation working for children's safe use of the Internet.

- See also section on safe chat on page 156.

A note on social networking sites and services - the dangers of MSN, Bebo, Facebook, MySpace etc...

MSN (or Microsoft Network) has become one of the standard online meeting places for children aged ten and upwards. It allows them to access an instant messaging network, which is far more spontaneous than email. Kids define whom they want to talk to through the address book scheme. These are lists of contacts that individuals can set up through a mutual request system, and most of the children we spoke to had books with well over 50 contacts. Kids also have fun blocking people from their address books, for instance a friend who has become a bit of a pain, or simply a friend of a friend who can't be trusted.

MSN is a wonderful vehicle for building friendships and keeping in contact with old friends. It is particularly great for kids who live some distance from their school. What's more, MSN prepares kids for the adult world where corporate instant messaging systems are becoming the norm.

But watch out – it can become an obsession. We believe that MSN is a great networking tool for kids, but it does need to be monitored carefully. In some homes it has become an enormous drain on kids' time. Children become addicted to it and spend unhealthy amounts of time socialising on the Internet instead of forming social relationships with their peers offline.

This is also true of social networking sites such as Bebo, MySpace, Friendster, MyYearBook, Classmates, LiveJournal, Xanga, Facebook and hi5. These sites allow members to upload pictures, music, photos and videos and to customise their own page to reflect their personality, as well as comment on their friends' pages. Whilst these sites can be a great tool for self-expression (see tips on YouTube page 160), there is a big danger that they become the playground of paedophiles or adults who simply want to pry on young people.

Protecting children from sexual predators and scammers

It is important that your children understand who has access to their site – and to a certain extent they can control this by which network they choose. Entry to many of the services is limited to a specific group of individuals, for example young people who fall within a certain age band. But it is impossible to verify identification on the Internet, and consequently these safeguards are openly abused. Young children wanting access to teenage sites claim false dates of birth, and adults wanting access to young people do the same.

As part of the registration process new members are often given the choice of 'private' or 'public' settings. Private settings limit access to an approved list of friends, while public settings leave your site open to a wider audience. Children are often tempted to opt for the more public options so they can meet friends of friends – and for many that is the whole point of social networking. In all cases it is important that children realise that nothing is guaranteed – the Internet is a public place – and access safeguards can be easily bypassed. So children may think they know who is there, but in reality anybody may turn up.

Since access cannot be guaranteed it is important that parents stay aware and up-to-date with what sites their children are using, and keep their eyes open for anything untoward. Children should also be encouraged to look out for the signs of fraudsters (see tip section on page 154), and should be encouraged to report anything suspicious to the network's monitoring services. For instance, there may be a 'report abuse' icon that the children should be encouraged to use if necessary.

It is also important that children understand how unwelcome guests might use material on their sites. They should be told that paedophiles might use material to befriend and contact them. Consequently, children should never include any identifiable information or photos on their sites (see tip section on page 154). Similarly, they should know that pranksters may use the copy/paste facilities to manipulate photos – for instance, there is software that 'undresses' individuals and portrays them in the nude.

Bullying on social networks

Bullying through the social networks has become a very prevalent problem, and parents should not underestimate the disturbing effect it can have on their children. Bullies have been quick to use these sites to make life miserable for their victims, while other children inadvertently cause hurt by not thinking about the consequences of their actions.

Bullies have been known to organise leagues of the 'most hated' children in a school, or to conduct polls that are designed to humiliate – for instance, votes on whether a specific girl has Aids or not.[19] They can also assume a child's identity and create mischief – for instance, one boy discovered that he had been portrayed as the founding member of a 'H8 (Hate) Band' against his headmaster.

Children don't always think about the consequences of what they do, and it can be easy for children to forget whether they are in private or public territory. It is easy to be mean about a friend when you think you are engaged in private chitchat, but so often, children forget that the whole school has access to their hurtful gossip. Children should be reminded that what we say in private is different to what we say in public, and parents should ensure that they know where a public forum begins.

It's also easy for the networking sites to become a focus of unhealthy social competition. Children can monitor how many people visit their sites, and if you are unpopular at school, your low 'hit rate' can just add to your social agonies.

TIPS ON ... SOCIAL NETWORKING

- Enforce time limits if you need to – don't let the social networks be too much of a drain on your children's time.

- Don't be fooled by the 'minimise' facilities – children may pretend to being doing homework when they are really chatting with friends.

- When your children get started on Bebo or any of the other social network sites, discuss which access settings they are using. It is often possible to limit access to their page to an approved list of friends, but if they opt for the more public settings, check they understand the dangers.

- Explain that with whatever access level they choose, nothing is for sure – and they should anticipate that strangers may turn up on their site.

- Check that they don't put up any identifiable information that would help a stranger hunt them out: for instance, telephone numbers, home or email address, school name or a photo that could lead to their home being recognised.

- Discuss the character of the material they choose to put up – they must understand that each page can act like an advert to a paedophile. Bikini-clad girls with pouting lips are obviously to be avoided.

- Warn your children of the tricks that paedophiles and fraudsters might use on their web pages: for instance, using photos of stunning male models to tempt girls, copy-pasting team shots from school websites to appear sporty, etc.

- Look out for suspicious activity on strangers' sites: for instance, a guy who only has girls as friends, anyone who has no local friends, a guy who seems to be targeting girls at one school, etc.

- Prepare your children for bullying and check they know how to remove hurtful messages on their sites. Explain why they mustn't leave mean chitchat else-where, particularly when the whole world can see it.

- Help them use the 'report abuse' icons if they spot anything bad.

- Keep in touch with what your children are doing, and if you feel unhappy, don't be afraid to enforce a ban.

Software that protects children against dangerous chat

With increasing concerns about the safety of online chat, a number of software companies have created packages that are specifically designed to protect children.

In Loco Parentis (www.ilp4parents.com) allows you to monitor exactly where your child goes online, and you can build up a personalised library of words that you do not want your child to use or see online. It also provides parents with a list of acronyms that could be used as part of a grooming discussion. For instance, GNOC which stands for Get Naked on Cam, and MOS which stands for Mum Over Shoulder.

XGate (www.xgate.com) is an Internet security device that monitors your child's chat-room activities, and can, for instance, terminate your child's chat-room conversation via your mobile. Crisp Thinking (www.crispthinking.com) has developed a child-protection gateway and an anti-grooming device. This is territory that is developing fast, and if you are concerned about how your child is chatting online, it is certainly worth spending time to review the latest options.

The Childnet site is also useful in this instance – they have a specific area on their site about Blog Safety (www.childnet-int.org/blogsafety), where they try and keep you up-to-date with your child's online social life.

For further useful internet addresses see page 169.

TIPS ON ... SAFE CHAT

- Many of the social networks host separate chat rooms which are very popular with children. Encourage your child to use 'child-friendly' chat rooms. The good ones, for instance, will have a moderator to block any personal details being swapped and keep the chat suitable.

- If your child is visiting a chat-room, encourage them to keep to the public area where everyone can see the conversation, and they should be safe.

TIPS ON ... **VIDEO TELEPHONY, WEBCAMS AND MOBILE PHONES WITH CAMERAS**

- Be sure that you can trust your child before you install a webcam. Children love playing up to a camera – so it's not surprising that many parents are wary about giving children this facility. There have been a number of reports that young girls are being encouraged by friends and strangers to be sexually provocative in front of the camera.

- Mobile phone cameras have become a favourite tool for bullies and immature pranksters. We heard of a headmaster who had just told a group of parents that such phones had become his major concern. He described how bullies were using them to take demeaning pictures of other classmates. The pictures were then emailed to the rest of the school, or put up on a website for the world to see. Such cameras are also being used to send and create pornographic pictures.

- If you decide to give your child a mobile phone with a camera, keep in touch with how they are using it and ensure that they understand that you will take it away if they misuse it. It's easy to understand why these new phones are a threat as well as a wonderful opportunity for kids. They fit in your pocket, it doesn't cost anything to take a photo and then it's as easy as can be to post your photo to the world. It's important that parents and kids recognise the dangers.

Home videos on the Internet, YouTube, etc

At last video over the Internet has really taken off, and as a result the world of broadcasting has opened up to everyone. The phenomenal success of sites like YouTube demonstrates the appeal of this new medium, and there is no doubt that these Internet video sites offer young people a raft of new opportunities.

Young people can genuinely break into the music or film world through the creation of their own home-made material, and they have the power to fuel word-of-mouth success where they feel it is deserved. This empowerment poses an enormous threat to traditional broadcasters and the music industry. However, it also poses dangers for young people themselves.

The first danger to note is that video content is much harder for the sites to monitor than text. Predictably, much content is not suitable for children and of course this is fuelling children's interest in these sites. When children come across disturbing material they should be encouraged to share it with you, but above all they should be taught why it is wrong to hunt it out.

Children can spend hours watching these small video clips, and there is no doubt that there is an addictive character to this medium. It is the instant reward and the bite-sized character of the clips that children find so captivating.

TIPS ON ... YOUTUBE AND HOME VIDEOS

- Limit the time you allow your kids on sites like YouTube – a short burst of fun is plenty.

- Keep a close eye on children who start to prepare video material for the Internet. Let them have fun being creative and imagining themselves as real film directors. But, watch out for the daredevil stunts or the undercover filming that might be used to bully unsuspecting classmates.

TIPS ON ... GAMBLING

- Internet gambling and gambling on interactive TV services such as Sky Active have led to an all-time gambling boom, and it is important that children are protected from them. One of the main problems is that these services bring gambling into the home – this not only makes it more accessible but normalises it too.

- Make sure your kids are wised-up to the dangers of gambling. It's a loser's game – the odds will always be against you and the only real winners are the gaming companies.

- Check your children don't have your credit card details – and if they do, because of an iPod account, for instance – keep a close eye on how they are using it. Slot machine gambling amongst teenagers can lead to crime in and outside the home, and it is important that parents keep an eye on children who they suspect might be tempted by the easy access of gambling on the screen.

Spam

Spam has become a big problem for anyone using the Internet. Spam is any unsolicited material you receive – a phone call, text or email. It's annoying and can be offensive. Spam can also end up costing you money because you're often encouraged to phone premium-rate numbers. Spam can also contain viruses which may harm your computer. The thing that can make spam particularly difficult for kids to cope with is that it feels so personal. You receive messages on your personal computer or mobile phone. It's a good idea to check with your Internet Service Provider (ISP) to see what their anti-spam policies are. You might also consider installing a filter.

But the likelihood is that your child will receive spam and so here are some tips to share with them on how to deal with it.

TIPS ON ... DEALING WITH SPAM

- Be careful about whom you give your email address or mobile phone number to. The more people who have your details, the more risk there is of you being sent spam.

- Never open attachments from people you don't know – they may contain viruses.

- Don't respond to spam. It will encourage the sender to keep on contacting you because they'll know that your email address or phone number is a 'live' one.

- If you do respond, be wary. Check the identity of whom you're dealing with and don't be afraid of saying 'No thank you'.

- Don't click on any links in spam. You don't know where you might end up if you do.

- Don't forward spam to friends. If you do you're only passing on a problem.

TOP TIPS **FROM KIDS TO PARENTS!**

'Mum only lets me go on the CBeebies site. I wait for her to go into the dining room and then I go where she doesn't see me.' *9-year-old girl*

'I go to a teens site. It's just gossip about bands that aren't really suitable for younger kids. When there are swearing songs, my mum doesn't really like that – I just minimize the screen when she comes in the room.' *8-year-old girl*

'In chat rooms I'm allowed to type in fake stuff, but no real details.' *9-year-old girl*

'In the library you say how old you are. There are millions of websites that are blocked for your age, so I just give somebody else's library number.' *9-year-old girl*

'When I was at school I went on eBay by accident.' *11-year-old boy*

'We put sex and things on other people's memories.' *12-year-old boy*

'My friend nearly met up with a paedophile pretending to be a guy. He'd put a really hot photo on his page, which had to be a model. He claimed it was a holiday snap. He pretended to be at a school, but when we checked out the school yearbook, it turned out he didn't exist.' *13-year-old girl*

'It's like a war against the teacher, she's banned Bebo, but we're all using Facebook now.' *12-year-old girl*

Conclusion: Time to take action!

There has never been a better time to stop children watching too much TV, spending hours on the computer, wasting days on Game Boy and endlessly texting friends, etc…

For a start, there's no longer any doubt that too much time spent in front of the TV and computer can damage our children for life. It's a fact. It can. As parents, therefore, we should try and do what we can to limit and control our children's media consumption.

Once our children become teenagers we inevitably lose some control. We need, therefore, to establish good media habits in our kids at an early age, so that they can learn to take full responsibility for their own screen activity before their teenage years.

We need to take action before it's too late. The media revolution is just beginning. Each year our children are presented with more and more temptations. Large flat-screens are turning our sitting rooms into private cinemas. And small portable screens are enabling us to do just about anything, anywhere.

Just looking back over the last couple of years we can see how much our media choice has grown. Look at the iPod – offering children a choice of thousands of songs in the palms of their hands. It hasn't been around long and already Apple has become the world's favourite music store. And now Apple TV is set to do the same with video.

It's all great stuff, but the downside is that it makes it more difficult for us parents to control and monitor our children's screen consumption.

So don't delay in taking action. We all need to be more proactive in our roles as 'screen monitors', and take more control over the quantity and quality of what our children watch.

And, don't be put off from starting because you don't think you've got the time. It does require a little bit more time and effort from you as a parent, but probably not as much as you think. Once your child becomes less dependent on the screen, and better at entertaining himself or herself, you'll get more of your own time back again.

The success of any action to reduce screen time relies on you enthusing and involving your child right from the start. We have given you a bundle of tips, but in the end, how you do it is up to you.

We all know the importance of looking left and right before we cross a road. Similarly, we hope this book will help you instil good media habits – so that switching off becomes as easy as switching on. It has certainly helped our children.

We hope you have enjoyed the book – and good luck!

List of media websites

1. Appropriate content

www.bbfc.co.uk

The British Board of Film Classification classifies films in the UK.

www.cbbfc.co.uk

The BBFC's website for primary school children.

www.bfi.org.uk

The British Film Institute provides news and information on all types of films.

www.pegi.info

The Pan European Games Information (PEGI) system is a new pan-European age-rating system for interactive games.

www.videostandards.org.uk

The Videos Standards Council provides advice to parents on videos and computer games.

2. Choosing computer games

www.brainworks.co.uk

An online brochure for fun, educational CD-ROMs, science discovery products and games.

3. Child-friendly search engines

www.askjeevesforkids.com

www.yahooligans.com

4. Internet safety

www.getnetwise.org

Offers detailed and comprehensive advice on all aspects of Internet use, including information on filtering products. (Produced by Internet companies and public interest groups.)

www.chatdanger.com

Outlines potential dangers of Internet activity such as chat rooms and IM (instant messaging). Good site for parents to visit with kids. (Produced by Childnet International.)

www.parentscentre.gov.uk

Comprehensive advice for parents on Internet safety. (Produced by the Department of Education and Skills.)

www.thinkuknow.co.uk

Cartoon-based website with advice on safe Internet surfing. (Produced by The Home Office.)

www.ilp4parents.com

In Loco Parentis – allows you to monitor exactly where you child goes online, and you can build up a personalised library of words that you do not want your child to use or see online.

www.xgate.com

An Internet security device that monitors your child's chat-room activities.

www.crispthinking.com

A child-protection gateway and an anti-grooming device.

www.childnet-int.org/blogsafety

A non-profit organisation working for children's safe use of the Internet. They have a specific area on their site about Blog Safety.

5. Media complaints and education
www.ofcom.org.uk

The Office of Communications (OFCOM) considers complaints about any TV or radio programme.

www.asa.org.uk

The Advertising Standards Authority considers complaints about TV or radio advertisements.

www.iwf.org.uk

The Internet Watch Foundation offers an authorised hotline for anyone to report illegal content on the Internet.

www.mediasmart.org.uk

Media Smart helps kids understand and interpret advertising.

www.bbc.co.uk

The BBC runs an easy-to-follow Webwise Online Course. Great for parents who don't feel very Internet-literate.

For other media news and views, visit our website: www.mediadietforkids.com.

Media Dangers Checklist

BEHAVIOUR

	SYMPTOMS	MEDIA ALERTS
Anti-social behaviour	No respect for others, mimicking screen bad behaviour.	Screen behaviour becomes the norm. Bad role models. Violence glamorised.
Impulsive outbursts	Low level of tolerance/easily frustrated – leading to bad temper. Physical and verbal outbursts. Constant swearing becomes the norm. Not prepared to wait for anything.	Sedentary existence/ bottled-up energy. Instant gratification of TV and compulsive character of computer games. Inability to express self through language. Swearing on screen.
Play apathy	Difficulty playing away from the screen. Always turning to adults to be entertained. Easily bored.	Too much time in front of the TV and computer can hinder a child's ability to play imaginatively.
Depression	Sense of depression and low self-esteem.	Long periods in front of the screen leading to frustration.
Premature adulthood	Acting older than your age without maturity of that age. Superficially in the know about sex, but deep down confused about it all. Getting involved in under-age sex. Visiting sex and porn sites.	Over-exposure to adult viewing and material. Introduced to explicit character of sex before understanding role of different relationships. Easy to surf into dirty territory.

PHYSICAL WELLBEING

	SYMPTOMS	MEDIA ALERTS
Obesity, diabetes and other health problems	Being so overweight that a child's health is at risk from, for example, diabetes, heart disease, some cancers and musculoskeletal problems. Being physically unfit.	Too much time just sitting – and snacking – in front of the screen.[20]
Poor coordination	Clumsiness and lack of bodily coordination. This isn't just a physical problem but can lead to early learning problems: for example, recognising shapes and writing skills.	Being entertained in a sedentary way, rather than being active doing physical play. Too many armchair sportsmen.[21]
Energy imbalance	Either a surplus of energy (hyperactivity), or a lack of energy (inertia).	Long periods of time in front of the screen without physical activity.[22]
Screen strain	Repetitive Strain Injury (RSI), musculo-skeletal injuries, computer elbow, back-, neck- and eye-ache.	Constant repetitive movements and poor posture as a result of hours sitting in front of the screen. Kids are particularly vulnerable because their bones and muscles are still developing.[21]
Mobile radiation	Not yet fully known or proved. If there is a danger, children may be more at risk because their skulls are thinner than adults.	Young children's use of mobile phones.[23]

EDUCATION

	SYMPTOMS	MEDIA ALERTS
Attention problems	Difficulty in focusing on specific tasks ('attention deficit/hyperactivity disorder'). Child's mind darts around, unable to develop logical trains of thought.	Child's senses are bombarded by a constant stream of stimuli from the screen. Soundbite character of screen entertainment.[22]
Poor speech development	Slow to develop language and ability to communicate.	Not enough interaction/conversation with real people. Constant background noise of TV.[7,24]
Literacy-retarded	Slow in developing reading/writing skills.	Too much media time and no time for reading. Media overshadows fun of learning through books.
Spoon-fed minds	See everything through screen images. Not tapping into your own creative and imaginative resources. Avoiding tasks that challenge your own intellectual thought	Media that constantly force images on viewers can result in the loss of a child's internal space. So much comes on a plate – for example, being able to copy and paste from the Internet.[18]
Sleep deprivation	Too tired to concentrate on anything/nodding off in class.	Temptation to watch TV/ play computer games/text on the mobile after bedtime. Over-stimulation just before trying to get to sleep. TV in bedrooms.[27]

RELATIONSHIPS

	SYMPTOMS	MEDIA ALERTS
Modern-day hermits	Children going around in their own little world – 'virtual' friends become more important than family and friends. Selfish approach to life.	Portable, personal media. Satellite living where family members are living in their own media orbits. Bedroom culture – kids' bedrooms become a self-sufficient media centre. Few family meals together. [25]
Parents in the dark	Parents not in touch with their children's lives. Poor communication/inability to spot when things go wrong.	Technology whizz kids – out-of-touch parents. Parents lacking language and know-how of modern media. [18]
Social overload	Always wanting to be in touch with peers – fear of being left out.	The constant availability of communications, emailing, texting, instant messaging, social networking, etc. [26]
Internet grooming	When an adult develops a relationship with a child over the Internet – manipulating the child to trust and depend on them.	Unsupervised Internet chat rooms, Internet dating. Kids not being aware of the dangers of the Internet and being tempted by the excitement it offers. [18]

WORLD OUTLOOK

	SYMPTOMS	MEDIA ALERTS
Earth alien	Inability to experience pleasures of the real world – constantly needing the stimulation of the screen world. Emotionally numb when it comes to real events and relationships.	The media world can be so exciting – the real world can appear boring. Virtual experiences make fantasy seem like the real thing. Emotions are stretched by the TV/ computer. Events on television are exaggerated for effect.[22]
Bunker mentality	Feelings of anxiety about the world. Frightened about crime, preferring the haven/security of home.	Violent and distorted view of the world as portrayed on TV. Overdosing on news at an early age.[22]
Realism deficiency	Unable to grasp the real picture beyond the screen. Happy to live with the fantasy of an unreal world. Tendency to see things in black and white. Perceptual distortions can lead to depression, prejudice and violence.	Distorted view of life through programmes and constant exposure of celebrities. Simplistic view of the world as shown on TV/computers where people are either good or bad.[22]
Dumbed-down values	Kids taking on values and perceptions of society that are at odds with your own values as a parent.	The constant tide of programmes/games that dramatise bad behaviour, and that portray a cool culture where anything goes. Inappropriate role models.[22]
'I want' culture	Wanting the latest model of everything – collecting goods like trophies – being brand-obsessed.	Over-exposure to advertising. Popular culture that idolises material goods.[22]

References

1.   Youth TGI. Copyright BMRB International, 1994–2004.

2.   Senate Judiciary Committee Staff Report, *Children, Violence and the Media*, 1999 (cited by TV-Turnoff Network, June 2005 (www.tvturnoff.org)).

3.   US News and World Report, 8 Apr 1997 (cited by TV-Turnoff Network, June 2005 (www.tvturnoff.org)).

4.   World Health Organization, 'Sedentary lifestyle: a global public health problem', June 2005 (www.who.int).

5.   ISD / World Health Organisation December 2005.

6.   World Health Organisation / Diabetes UK / The Royal College of Physicans, October 2005.

7.   Christakis, D. Zimmerman, F. Di Giuseppe, D. and McCarty, C. 'Early Television Exposure and Subsequent Attentional Problems in Children', *Pediatrics*, vol. 113, Apr 2004.

8.   A study at Nottingham Trent University has shown that one in nine online gamers displayed at least three signs of addiction. Prof Mark Griffiths, November 2006.

9.   Browne, K. and Hamilton-Giachritsis, C. 'The influence of violent media on children and adolescents: a public health approach', *The Lancet*, vol. 365, 19 Feb 2005.

10. Christakis, op.cit.

11. Kyesha Freeman made a noose from her pyjamas after seeing the 1999 film *Girl, Interrupted*, starring Whoopi Goldberg. It is set in a psychiatric hospital and in it one patient commits suicide by hanging herself.

12. American Academy of Pediatrics (www.aap.org).

13. A report from the Chief Medical Officer, *At least five a week – evidence of the impact of physical activity and its relationship to health*, Apr 2004.

14. *Health Survey for England 2002 – The Health of Children and Young People. The Scottish Health Survey 1998.*

15. Research at the University of Missouri-Columbia demonstrates a causal link between computer games and violence, rather than a simple association. The research suggests that violent computer games trigger a mechanism in the brain that makes people behave more aggressively. The research suggests that game players are desensitised to violent images in the same way that soldiers are desensitised when they prepare for war. Bruce Batholow, January 2006.

16. South West Learning and Skills Council, Jan 2004 (cited by National Literacy Trust (www.literacytrust.org.uk)).

17. Close, R. *Television and language development in the early years: a review of the literature*, Mar 2004.

18. Livingstone, S. and Bober, M. *UK Children Go Online*, July 2004 (www.childrengo-online.net).

19. An investigation by *Computing Which?* found that two of the most popular websites are failing to guard against cyber-bullying and imposters posing as teenagers. September 2006.

20. Dr Faisel Khan, Dundee University (cited in 'One in five teenagers show signs of heart disease', *Daily Telegraph*, 7 Sept 2004).

21. The British Chiropractic Association, press release, 1 Sept 2004 (www.chiropractic-uk.co.uk).

22. Teresa Orange Research, Nov 2004.

23. 'Don't allow under-9s to use a mobile', *Daily Telegraph*, 12 Jan 2005.

24. www.literacytrust.org.uk/Researcherindex/SallyWard.html.

25. Mintel, *Marketing to 11-14-year-olds*, April 2004; *Toy retailing in the UK*, Apr 2004.

26. Haste, H. University of Bath/Mori/Nestle Social Research Programme (cited in 'Don't speak, text, says mobile generation', *Daily Telegraph*, 20 Dec 2004).

27. University of Oxford, (cited in 'Today's couch potatoes are tomorrow's insomniacs', *Daily Mail*, 14 June 2004).

We hope you enjoyed this Hay House book.
If you would like to receive a free catalogue featuring additional
Hay House books and products, or if you would like information
about the Hay Foundation, please contact:

Hay House UK Ltd
292B Kensal Rd • London W10 5BE
Tel: (44) 20 8962 1230; Fax: (44) 20 8962 1239
www.hayhouse.co.uk

***

Published and distributed in the United States of America by:
Hay House, Inc. • PO Box 5100 • Carlsbad, CA 92018-5100
Tel.: (1) 760 431 7695 or (1) 800 654 5126;
Fax: (1) 760 431 6948 or (1) 800 650 5115
www.hayhouse.com

Published and distributed in Australia by:
Hay House Australia Ltd • 18/36 Ralph St • Alexandria NSW 2015
Tel.: (61) 2 9669 4299; Fax: (61) 2 9669 4144
www.hayhouse.com.au

Published and distributed in the Republic of South Africa by:
Hay House SA (Pty) Ltd • PO Box 990 • Witkoppen 2068
Tel./Fax: (27) 11 706 6612 • orders@psdprom.co.za

Published and distributed in India by:
Hay House Publishers India • Muskaan Complex • Plot No.3
B-2 • Vasant Kunj • New Delhi – 110 070.
Tel.: (91) 11 41761620; Fax: (91) 11 41761630.
contact@hayhouseindia.co.in

Distributed in Canada by:
Raincoast • 9050 Shaughnessy St • Vancouver, BC V6P 6E5
Tel.: (1) 604 323 7100; Fax: (1) 604 323 2600

WITHDRAWN FROM STOCK

***

Sign up via the Hay House UK website to receive the Hay House
online newsletter and stay informed about what's going on with
your favourite authors. You'll receive bimonthly announcements
about discounts and offers, special events, product highlights,
free excerpts, giveaways, and more!
www.hayhouse.co.uk

D0263363

SHERARD COWPER-COLES is one of the most respected authorities on foreign affairs in the country. He has held a string of high-profile diplomatic posts, both in the UK and overseas, most recently as the British Ambassador to Kabul and as the Foreign Secretary's Special Representative for Afghanistan and Pakistan. He lives in London.

From the reviews of *Cables from Kabul*:

'Compulsory reading for students of Afghanistan ... Cowper-Coles won the respect and affection of all those who met him for his high intelligence and unabashed frankness ... his book vividly portrays the plight of an envoy who really cared about his brief, and felt unable to keep silent about looming failure in a vital region where Western intervention has been bungled'   MAX HASTINGS, *Sunday Times*

'The most insightful record yet published of the diplomatic wrangling that has accompanied the slow military encirclement of Western forces in the country. It is also the best account I have read of how post-colonial colonialism actually works'

WILLIAM DALRYMPLE, *Observer*, Books of the Year

'Lucid and sometimes devastating. A primer for a campaign that may finally be coming to an uncertain and dangerous close'

GIDEON RACHMAN, *Financial Times*, Books of the Year

'There have been plenty of bang-bang books about the Afghan campaign, but none has given as clear an insight into the politics of the war as this account. Cowper-Coles vividly evokes what it is like to work under siege, while describing the key figures he works with, notably the maddening Hamid Karzai'

STEPHEN ROBINSON, *Sunday Times*, Books of the Year

'Cowper-Coles is a sharp observer of diplomatic and political shenanigans ... terrific anecdotes and an incisive account of what went wrong in Afghanistan'   *Daily Mail*

'The clearest, best informed, and most honest account yet of why and how Britain was drawn deeper and deeper into the Afghan war, by the man who knows more about it than just about anyone else. If you want to understand what really happened, you absolutely have to read this book'   JOHN SIMPSON

'In my experience our former Ambassador in Afghanistan Sir Sherard Cowper-Coles is spot on in his book *Cables from Kabul*'
                                                    MATTHEW PARRIS, *The Times*

'Cowper-Coles is a diplomat who speaks truth to power. *Cables from Kabul* describes in deliciously indiscreet prose his journey from wary loyalist to hardened sceptic about the Afghan venture ... his concluding judgments are devastating'   LIONEL BARBER, *Financial Times*

'A highly readable and witty account of a crucial period in the Afghan conflict by one of our most dynamic and impressive diplomats'
                                                                    Daily Telegraph

'An important addition to those books already published on the Afghan war ... Cowper-Coles movingly describes the bravery and sacrifice of individual soldiers'   *Evening Standard*

" ANOTHER DAY, ANOTHER
    NEW AFGHAN STRATEGY "

SHERARD COWPER-COLES

Cables from Kabul

The Inside Story of the West's
Afghanistan Campaign

Harper
Press

Harper*Press*
An imprint of HarperCollins*Publishers*
77–85 Fulham Palace Road
Hammersmith, London W6 8JB

This Harper*Press* paperback edition published 2012

1

First published in Great Britain by Harper*Press* in 2011

A catalogue record for this book
is available from the British Library

ISBN 978-0-00-743204-2

Typeset in Minion with Giovanni display by
G&M Designs Ltd, Raunds, Northamptonshire
Printed and bound in Great Britain by
Clays Ltd, St Ives plc

MIX
Paper from
responsible sources
FSC™ C007454
www.fsc.org

FSC™ is a non-profit international organisation established to promote
the responsible management of the world's forests. Products carrying the
FSC label are independently certified to assure consumers that they come
from forests that are managed to meet the social, economic and
ecological needs of present and future generations,
and other controlled sources.

Find out more about HarperCollins and the environment at
www.harpercollins.co.uk/green

In memory of
Richard Holbrooke,
who gave his life for peace

British Embassy
Kabul

Sir Sherard Cowper-Coles KCMG
HM Ambassador

25 June 2007

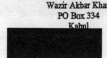

15th Street Roundabout
Wazir Akbar Khan
PO Box 334
Kabul

AFGHANISTAN: FIRST IMPRESSIONS

SUMMARY

A land of overpowering beauty, and seemingly unending violence. Extreme poverty, ███ Real progress since 2001, but much will be lost if we do not sustain our support.

DETAIL

1. After six weeks here, I am returning to London on 26 June for my first breather break, and for meetings on Afghanistan. These are my first impressions. Some suggestions for adjustments in our posture are in my separate letter of 25 June.

2. I have had time to make only the most superficial acquaintance with a country with a history and human geography as complicated as Afghanistan's. Every day I am reminded in so many different ways how little I know, and will probably every really know, about this land and its peoples.

3. But six weeks is time enough to start to understand why for thousands of years what has been Afghanistan for only two centuries has held such attraction

for outsiders of every kind and condition, from invading armies, arriving on horse or by helicopter, to individual travellers crossing the Khyber by lorry or Land Cruiser. First, the people, of truly extra-ordinary diversity, at ease with themselves, with their nationhood, and with foreigners, ▓▓▓▓▓▓▓▓▓▓▓▓▓▓▓▓▓▓▓▓▓▓

4. And then the overpowering physical beauty of the Afghan landscape. Even here, in the dirty dusty centre of Kabul, it is inescapable, and irresistible. Still, in late June, the snow on the peaks of the tributary ranges of the Hindu Kush can be clearly seen. Red dunes; yellow deserts; grey steppe; green valleys; khaki mountains; blue burqas; white, grey, green, brown and black shalwar kameezs: all produce a kaleidoscope of colour as rich and varied as any Afghan carpet, and just as alluring.

GENERAL

5. But such extraordinary beauty is set off against a darker truth: that this is one of the poorest countries on earth, a slice of sub-Saharan-style deprivation set down in Asia. A land broken by war, and drought, and extreme poverty, and neglect. Every journey, every meeting, is a reminder that most Afghans have somehow to exist on less than a dollar a day. In different ways, almost every Afghan you meet seems to be seeking help of one kind or another: the crippled woman begging in the dust as the foreigners sweep by, the policeman whose mislaid spectacles are a transparent alibi for his illiteracy, the shopkeeper seeking to offload his stock of soiled postcards, the student desperate for a visa, the official with no money or staff to do what his department is supposed to do, the Governor whose only means of reaching his province any time soon is a lift on an RAF Hercules, ▓▓▓▓▓▓▓▓▓▓▓▓▓▓▓▓▓▓▓▓▓▓

6. What makes this deprivation all the more poignant is the awful sense that the dark days of civil war, of unimaginable cruelty and suffering, could yet return. In Kabul and across the South there is a pervasive and growing sense of insecurity. The fear that the peace imposed nearly six years ago is starting to unravel. Anxiety does not stop people getting on with their lives – indeed it is often an incentive for hurrying faster – but it does divert energy and resources to preparing for the worst, instead of slowly consolidating the good. A chronic insurgency, with the rear areas necessary to sustain it, seems to have taken hold.

[...]

Contents

PART I:
BEGINNINGS

PART II:
HOPE OVER EXPERIENCE

PART III:
AGAINST AN EBBING TIDE

PART IV:
TACTICS WITHOUT STRATEGY:
ONE LAST HEAVE

PART V:
RECESSIONAL

List of Illustrations

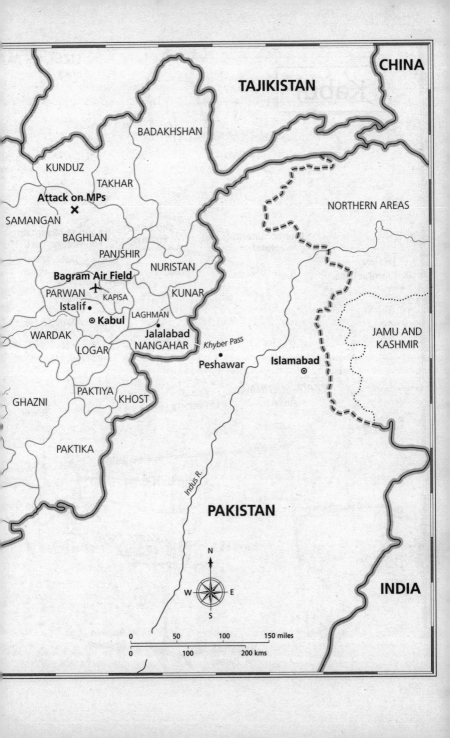

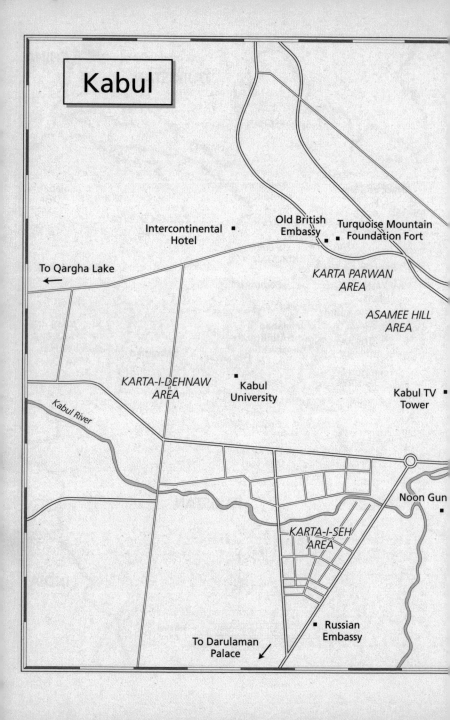

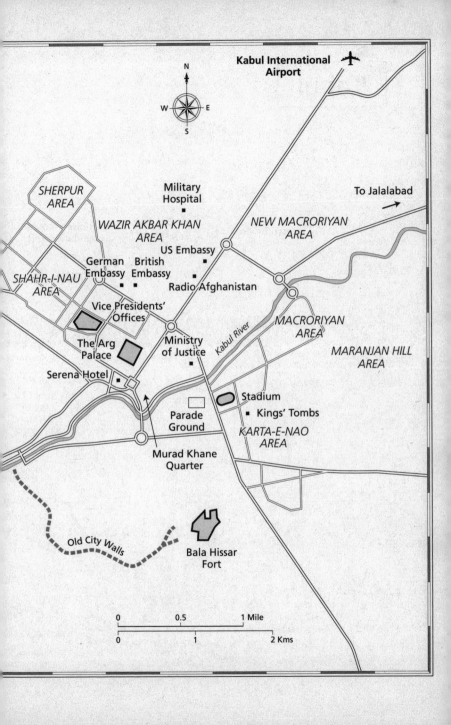

Kabul International Airport ✈

N
W E
S

SHERPUR AREA

Military Hospital

To Jalalabad →

NEW MACRORIYAN AREA

WAZIR AKBAR KHAN AREA

US Embassy ▪

German Embassy ▪ British Embassy ▪

SHAHR-I-NAU AREA

Radio Afghanistan ▪

Vice Presidents' Offices

MACRORIYAN AREA

The Arg Palace

Ministry of Justice ▪

Kabul River

MARANJAN HILL AREA

Serena Hotel ▪

Stadium

Parade Ground

Kings' Tombs ▪

KARTA-E-NAO AREA

Murad Khane Quarter

Old City Walls

Bala Hissar Fort

| 0 | | 0.5 | | 1 Mile |
| 0 | | 1 | | 2 Kms |

Tribute to the Fallen

Text of Diplomatic Telegram of 24 February 2008 from HM Ambassador Kabul to the Foreign Secretary in London:

1. On 23 February, thanks to a fortunate delay in obtaining a helicopter flight from Camp Bastion to Lashkar Gah, I was able to join Lt Gen Jonathon Riley (Deputy Commanding General, ISAF) and several hundred other British and allied troops at the Service of Repatriation for Corporal Damian Stephen Lawrence of the 2nd Battalion, The Yorkshire Regiment (The Green Howards). As this was the first British 'ramp ceremony' I had attended (I had once been to a much more elaborate Canadian ceremony at Kandahar), I cannot resist recording what I saw and heard, and felt.

2. Corporal Lawrence had died on 17 February, on operations with the Afghan National Army as part of an Operational Mentoring and Liaison Team. This difficult and dangerous work, performed with quiet distinction by the 2nd Yorks, is the keystone of our strategy in Afghanistan.

3. We gathered an hour before sunset. The troops – scores of Corporal Lawrence's regimental comrades, men and women of all ranks and regiments of the British Army, 40 Commando Royal Marines, the Royal Navy, the Royal Guards Hussars of the Danish Army, Estonians and Americans, were formed into a great three-sided square, facing west towards the new runway at Bastion, and the empty spaces stretching to Iran beyond.

4. In the centre of the square stood the Padre, wearing battledress beneath his bands, and the ramrod column of the Regimental

Sergeant Major, Mr Hind. Before us the sun was setting across the great southern desert, casting long shadows, illuminating the whole ceremony in shades of dusty gold. There was silence. The Chinooks and Sea Kings, Apaches and Lynxes, which usually buzz in and out of Bastion every few minutes from the helicopter lines behind us, had ceased flying, out of respect for the fallen.

5. And then, out of the sky to the north, appeared a single Hercules of the Royal Air Force. With a great roar it landed, perfectly, on the runway in front of us, and taxied out of sight, and sound.

6. Corporal Lawrence's Commanding Officer, Lt Col Simon Downey, marched stiffly out into the middle of the parade ground. The RSM called us to attention. A bearer party, found by the Green Howards, brought Corporal Lawrence's coffin, bound in the Union flag, out on to the centre of the square.

7. The service began, in the best traditions of lapidary Army Anglicanism. Plenty of dignity, not too much religion. The words of comfort for those who mourn from St Matthew; a few prayers, with responses; St John 14 ('In my Father's house there are many rooms'); Binyon's lines ('At the going down of the sun, And in the morning, We will remember them'), barked out, improbably, by the RSM; a lone bugler played Last Post, and Reveille; a well-judged eulogy, full of humanity and humour, by Colonel Downey; a deeply moving message of maternal pride, and affection for the regiment, from Corporal Lawrence's Mum, on the North Yorkshire coast; and finally the Collect of the Yorkshire Regiment ('Grant to the Yorkshire Regiment in its battalions and ranks, the strength that fears … no desperate endeavours and no foe bodily and spiritual; but advances in thy righteousness through all the rough places under the Captain of our salvation …'). The Lord's Prayer, said together, the Blessing, and the Service itself was over.

8. By now the evening wind was up, and it was growing cold. And out of the silence we heard again the gradually growing growling of the C-130's engines, as, with impeccable timing, it taxied back into sight. Then, in an extraordinary manoeuvre, it reversed thrust, and backed into the open side of the square, to take delivery of its sad cargo.

9. With the engines still turning, a loadmaster jumped down from the rear ramp, and stood to attention. A female RAF Corporal marched out, saluted smartly, and handed him the airwaybill. The Commanding Officer, and Mr Hind, formed up alongside the ramp. The bearer party shouldered the coffin, and, accompanied by the Padre, marched with perfect precision up into the hold of the Hercules. Colonel Downey mounted the ramp. Out of sight, he said his farewell to his fallen comrade. In short order, the bearers and accompanying party dismounted, the ramp closed, the Hercules taxied out, and took off. We stood in silence, listening to the fading murmur of its engines.

10. And then, in one of the most striking moments of the whole ceremony, from out of the setting sun came the roar of the Hercules, flying in fast and low. As the aircraft passed over, and started to climb, the starboard wing dipped, in impossibly eloquent tribute from the Royal Air Force to Corporal Lawrence and all those who had fallen here. As we watched, the aeroplane climbed in a great wheeling turn, up into a still blue north-eastern sky, taking Corporal Lawrence on back home, via Kandahar and Lyneham, to North Yorkshire.

11. The RSM dismissed the parade. The obsequies were over. It was now dusk. A great crush of men and vehicles pressed back into Britannia Lines, and the work of this war.

COWPER-COLES

Preface

Ah, love, let us be true
To one another! for the world, which seems
To lie before us like a land of dreams,
So various, so beautiful, so new,
Hath really neither joy, nor love, nor light,
Nor certitude, nor peace, nor help for pain;
And we are here as on a darkling plain
Swept with confused alarms of struggle and flight,
Where ignorant armies clash by night.

Matthew Arnold, 'Dover Beach'

Some 2,000 years ago, a Greek recorded a conflict which had convulsed the Hellenic lands for more than three decades. The writer wanted his work to be a possession for all time. He hoped that men would use it as a guide to avoid the mistakes that had precipitated the events through which he had lived. But he noted that human nature never really changed. Men probably would therefore ignore the lessons of his history, and repeat the errors he had reported. Nevertheless, he thought it worth setting down his account anyway, just in case expectation might for once be confounded by hope fulfilled.

The conflict in Afghanistan is no Peloponnesian War, although it has lasted even longer. And I am certainly no Thucydides. But for three and a half years, from May 2007, I experienced at first hand a struggle that was by the spring of 2011 swallowing each year some $125 billion of US taxpayers' money and getting on for £6 billion a year from the British Exchequer. This was a real war that had by then taken the lives of more than 2,000 coalition soldiers and of some 350 British servicemen and women, as well as those of tens of thousands of Afghans in and out of uniform. More than 10,000 American soldiers had been wounded in Afghanistan.

As British ambassador in Kabul from 2007 to 2009, and then as the Foreign Secretary's special representative for Afghanistan and Pakistan from February 2009 until September 2010, I saw politicians, generals, diplomats and officials struggling with successive strategies which never seemed to deliver what we wanted, and with military tactics which – we all knew – could not, without a credible political strategy, resolve Afghanistan's underlying problems.

In London, in the English shires, and in the border areas of Scotland and Wales which supply so many of our fighting men and women, as well as in Washington and the fifty states beyond, there was an uneasy sense that this war was misconceived. Many people shared the sentiment attributed to one of the wisest of British prime ministers, Harold Macmillan, that the first rule of politics is 'Don't invade Afghanistan.' For Britons especially, the unhappy history of earlier military expeditions into Afghanistan weighed heavily. Most press commentators were sceptical.

And yet we carried on, as part of a great US-led coalition, with a mainly military, and hugely expensive, campaign to stabilise a faraway country of which we truly knew little. We stuck at it because Britain couldn't and wouldn't let down its coalition partners, especially the Americans. We kept going because we wanted to support our troops. We stuck at it because we wanted to believe our generals. Each year they assured us that, at last, they had the strategy and the resources they needed to do the job. This year at last, they said every year, we were going to turn the corner. The Americans had a new plan, a new general, a fresh surge. 'Astronomical progress' was being made. The momentum of the insurgency was being reversed. There was reason for cautious optimism. Finally, it was safe to stroll (in body armour) in the bazaar of some fly-blown village in the Helmand Valley. Nobody, especially not politicians seeking votes in Middle England, wanted to be accused of not backing our boys.

But Middle England took a more nuanced view. The same people who were so fiercely loyal to the regiments woven into the fabric of British society had doubts about why those regiments were in Afghanistan at all, and about what lasting good they were doing there. Middle England, and Scotland and Wales and Ireland as well, had folk memories of what had happened to British battalions which had ventured too far, or stayed too long, west of the Indus. Among some of the armed forces' most loyal civilian supporters there was a consciousness about Afghanistan that combined *Carry On up the Khyber* and Flashman with ancestral memories of forebears who had fought and died on India's North West Frontier.

Most other books on the present conflict in Afghanistan have fallen into one of two categories. On the one hand, there have been dozens of breathlessly whizz-bang accounts of the fighting by journalists embedded with the troops. Each of those books is a potent and richly deserved tribute to the sacrifice and courage of our fighting men and women. But, precisely because such war stories focus so closely on combat, they sometimes miss the broader perspective of the war. Moreover, when a journalist has put his life, literally, in the hands of the men and women about whom he writes, it seems like bad manners or worse to ask what wider purpose is served by one's hosts' superhuman sacrifice. On the other hand, there have been some outstanding semi-academic descriptions of the conflict and of the lands, not just Afghanistan, in which it is taking place. But, by their nature, neither set of books has offered the picture of the strategic direction of this war which I hope here to provide. Thus this book tries, through the prism of my small part in the enterprise, to illuminate some of the political and diplomatic aspects of Britain's and America's mainly military engagement in Afghanistan.

I try to address some fundamental questions about the nature of the West's Afghanistan project. I explain how the doubts I had, even before I had left London, about the strategy we were supposed to be pursuing were confirmed by experience on the ground. I describe my growing admiration for the extraordinary courage and professionalism of our fighting men and women in Helmand. But I also explain how I came gradually to understand that the problems we faced went far beyond 'merely' countering the Taliban insurgency in the south and east. I tell how I came to see that the Taliban had never been defeated in 2001–2; that the Bonn settlement that had followed had been a victors' peace, from which the vanquished had been excluded; and that the constitution resulting from that settlement could last only as long as the West was prepared to stay in Afghanistan to prop up the present disposition.

More specifically, the book pays tribute to the tactical success our soldiers are undoubtedly having. But it also illustrates the deficiencies of a strategy focused on pacifying and garrisoning with Western troops selected areas of the country where the insurgency is strongest, in order to hand those areas over to the civil and military agencies of a half-formed central Afghan state. It suggests that, even if our military achieve local, tactical and temporary success in Helmand or Kandahar, that will be far from enough to achieve within three years our wider strategic goal of stabilising Afghanistan to the point where the Afghan authorities can secure and govern the country with only money and advice from outside. It points out that the 'Government' to which we plan gradually to transfer security responsibility, province by province, is far from being either able or willing to secure, let alone govern, such a legacy. And it shows how my then boss, the Foreign Secretary, David Miliband, and I became convinced that the only sensible strategic approach had to be a political one, drawing in all the internal and regional parties to a conflict with roots far deeper than the Western intervention of October 2001.

Finally, the book sets out my conviction that the Afghanistan project can be brought to a successful conclusion, but only once America is prepared to talk direct to its enemies, and then to devote unprecedented political and diplomatic resources to leading an international effort to devise and deliver an internal and regional political process. Whether the American Republic is confident enough to do that remains an open question. There must be doubts too about whether America will be willing properly to finish the job, now that the demon who first drew us into Afghanistan – Osama bin Laden – has finally been exorcised. And it may well be that the moment for negotiating a well-ordered exit from Afghanistan for NATO forces has passed, as the political pressure mounts for having our troops leave the battlefield by the end of 2014 more or less regardless of conditions on the ground.

None of this is to say that military success won't be achieved or proclaimed. Nor that a political framework for withdrawal won't in the end be negotiated, in something of a rush, to meet Western not Eastern timelines. But, without the West taking the initiative, it risks being sub-optimal and, in the great sweep of Afghan history, short lived. In time historians may point to the parallels with earlier imperial scuttles, with the baneful consequences of which the world is still living.

Inevitably, the book is written from the perspective of a diplomat, based in Kabul, and then in London, over three years from 2007. It does not cover the tragic diversion of attention and then resources from Afghanistan to Iraq from 2002, or the British Government's fateful decision to take on Helmand in 2006. It is not about the ground war in Helmand. It focuses on the means diplomats and their political bosses use to understand and influence. It describes the work of an embassy and an envoy, in circumstances that were highly unusual in many respects, but typical in many others. What made the Embassy in Kabul different was that we were operating in a war zone, alongside and in support of a massive military effort. But the work of reporting and analysis, of entertaining and influencing contacts, of international consultation and co-ordination, resembled normal diplomacy in other capitals around the world. In Kabul, however, it mattered more than it did in most places.

In putting this story into print, I have had no access to the extensive records I lodged in London of almost every significant official inter-action I had over more than three years. Instead, I have relied on memory, and on four daily lines of scribble in a rough and ready diary, telling me where I was, but not what I was really doing or thinking. The book does not therefore pretend to be a full or authoritative account of what happened: rather it is a reflection of my evolving understanding of what we were doing in and to Afghanistan, and of what Afghanistan was doing to us.

As a former official, I asked myself whether publishing an account of my experiences so soon after I had left the public service was consist-ent with my obligations to my former employer. But Diplomatic Service Regulations state that 'The FCO welcomes debate on foreign policy … The FCO recognises that there is a public interest in allowing former officials to write accounts of their time in government. These contributions can help public understanding and debate ... there is no ban on former members of the Diplomatic Service writing their memoirs ... but obligations of confidentiality remain ...'

What is at stake in Afghanistan is not trivial. It is not an issue of ideology. Nor is it a question of political allegiance. It goes deeper than diplomatic nicety, and beyond the pride of individuals or institutions. Few aspects of this story are truly confidential. It is a war in which the West has invested vast quantities of blood and treasure – and reputation. After nearly a decade of conflict, getting it as right as is now possible is a major national interest, for us, for America, for our allies and, above all, for millions of wretched Afghans who have suffered too much and for too long.

So if, in its small way, this book helps us correct some of the mistakes, of both strategy and tactics, that we may be making, it may do some good.

PART I

BEGINNINGS

If the task is arduous, the mission is noble.

President de Gaulle's sole instruction to the new
Government Delegate in Algiers, November 1960

Chapter 1

An Offer I Couldn't Refuse

Monday 30 October 2006 – the Ambassador's Office, British Embassy, Riyadh, Saudi Arabia: I was sitting sleepily at my desk after lunch, catching up on reading. I had returned only the night before from a family holiday in Egypt. My secretary came in: could I have an urgent word on the secure phone with a senior official in London?

Of course I could, I said, wondering with the usual mixture of excitement and dread what this could be about. The silky tones of the senior official soon cut to the chase. 'Ministers' had decided to upgrade Britain's civilian effort in Afghanistan, to try to keep pace with the huge increase in military resources being pumped into Helmand. They thought that I was the right person to take charge of what would become one of the largest and most unusual British diplomatic missions in the world. There had been pressure from the British military for a 'heavy hitter' to be sent as ambassador. I would be working on the standard terms of six weeks on, two weeks off. I would see more of my family than if I remained in Saudi Arabia to complete my tour there. I would go to Kabul for a year or so to start with, but, naturally, it was hoped I would stay for longer. The whole thing was still very secret (hence the secure line), not least because the incumbent in Kabul had not been told. Was I interested? Like the fool I am when flattered, I said of course I was interested. I would need to talk this over with my wife, but I knew this was just the sort of challenge I relished. The senior official sounded relieved. London would be back in touch in due course. In the meantime, not a word to anyone – apart of course from my immediate family.

Weeks, and then months, passed without my hearing anything more. I wondered if I had been dreaming, or if the senior official had changed

3

his mind – as he was prone to do on personnel matters. I managed to persuade a worried family that this early move made professional sense. I had already completed three of the four years I had been due to spend in Saudi Arabia. Privately, I thought, without being too pompous, that much of my career had helped prepare me for this. I had been opposed to the invasion of Iraq. But I had believed that we had had little alternative to joining the Americans in toppling the Taliban from power in Kabul in October 2001, when in the wake of 9/11 they had refused to hand over Osama bin Laden and his lieutenants. Like President Obama and many others, I had an instinctive sense that Afghanistan was the good campaign (in 2006 it was not yet evident that it was a full-scale war), in which much had been achieved for the long-suffering people of Afghanistan.

Moreover, I knew the job would involve working with the military. Ever since as a small boy I had manoeuvred my battalions of Britain's toy soldiers around the sandpit at home, I had been interested in matters military. I enjoyed dealing with soldiers. I knew their jargon, and admired their can-do style. I was in awe of their confidence and efficiency. And, at least since I had followed the great counter-insurgency campaigns of the 1950s and 1960s (Malaya, Algeria, Aden, Northern Ireland, Vietnam above all) through the pages of the *Illustrated London News* my grandmother had sent me each week, I had been interested in strategy and tactics. I had read widely about counter-insurgency. At Oxford, my best subject had been Roman military history. My favourite historians were those great chroniclers of ancient wars, Tacitus and Thucydides.

At least as important, my years in different parts of Arabia, and my fluent but flawed Arabic, had given me a sense of what mattered in the Muslim world and made it move. Working in a part of the Islamic world where people prayed in Arabic, but spoke or thought in other languages, had enormous attractions – especially one with as much history and geography as Afghanistan and the North West Frontier of Imperial India.

But what really decided me was a sense that, unlike so many British ambassadorships, this would be a real job. Success, or failure, in Kabul would matter to Ministers. It was a job for which I would be given the resources – both human and financial – I needed. Less flummery, more serious work. Vanity and ambition urged me on. I dismissed an American friend's earlier warning: Afghanistan was a morass; and there could be no good outcome to the present half-baked Western intervention, however well intentioned it had originally been.

Three weeks to the day after that call from London, personal tragedy struck, in the form of another wholly unexpected phone call from England. Out of the blue, my sister-in-law rang at nearly midnight Saudi time. My beloved middle brother, Philip, had been taken seriously ill. Every Monday evening in winter he and his friends in the Honourable Artillery Company Saddle Club used to exercise the gun-carriage horses of the King's Troop, Royal Horse Artillery. Philip had just taken a particularly difficult horse over the jumps in the covered school at the St John's Wood cavalry barracks and had collapsed. He was now at the Middlesex Hospital: could I ring and find out what was happening?

With a heavy heart, I got through eventually to the A&E department. A nurse answered. I told her who I was, and whom I was trying to track down. Trying to sound calm, she put her hand over the mouthpiece, but not well enough. I could hear her calling to a doctor. 'It's his brother,' she half whispered. 'Shall I tell him?' In a ghastly flash, I knew that my brother had suffered the same fate – sudden death by massive, unannounced heart attack – as our father had, on another Monday night, thirty-eight years earlier.

The weeks that followed passed like a rushing nightmare – working at long distance with my surviving brother to deal with all the awful consequences of sudden death, especially for a young family, all the while going through the motions of continuing with my work in Riyadh. Somehow, I summoned up the strength to preside and speak at a glittering Taranto Night dinner in the Residence Garden organised by my Naval Attaché. His enthusiasm for the Fleet Air Arm of which he was a member extended to inviting the Italian Ambassador to attend a celebration of the greatest defeat in the brief and inglorious history of Mussolini's Navy (luckily, the Ambassador had refused). And then, returning to England for a desperately sad funeral in Devon, I found myself summoned to London the next day for a meeting on policy towards Saudi Arabia.

And, through all of this, no one got back to me, as promised, on the Afghan job. A tentative enquiry to one senior official provoked surprise that I had even asked: it had all been agreed (even though I had heard nothing, still less any formal proposal, since the phone call out of the blue). My appointment would be a 'managed move', with no selection board or any of the usual procedures: it awaited only sorting out at the Kabul end, which I took to mean breaking the news to my predecessor. Alarm bells should have rung. The casual desperation with which the Foreign Office was moving to fill the post meant that the terms and conditions of the appointment were never put down in black and white, as a less credulous or ambitious officer might have insisted.

But, as I started to read and talk about Afghanistan, my enthusiasm grew. To those not in the know about my next job, I revealed only that one day I might be interested in working in and on that fascinating country. Rashly, I decided to try to learn Pashtu, the language of the great tribal confederation to which Afghanistan's President, Hamid Karzai, belonged. It was a choice between that and Dari, the Persian dialect spoken by the Afghans in the north, and the language of Afghan business and government. For an Arabist, the Pashtu alphabet was easy. But I soon discovered that neither the grammar nor the vocabulary was, especially when delivered to me in Riyadh down a video link of extreme fragility and fuzziness from the Diplomatic Service Language Centre in London.

By March 2007, my posting to Kabul was official, and I returned finally from Riyadh for eight weeks of unremitting preparations for the new job, from which the only relief was a ten-day family holiday in Syria. The pace and intensity of work were a foretaste of things to come.

What struck me most forcefully was the towering scale of British ambition in the troubled Afghan province for which Britain had assumed responsibility, Helmand, and across Afghanistan more generally. Then Lieutenant General David Richards had returned from Kabul only in February 2007, after nine months commanding NATO forces in Afghanistan. During a triumphant tour, he had displayed the charm and charisma, and aptitude for leading from the front, which would later take him right to the top of the military tree. Under David Richards, NATO had pushed into Helmand, the neighbouring province of Kandahar and across the south. When I visited the newly returned General and his staff at the headquarters of the NATO Rapid Reaction Corps at Rheindahlen in Germany, they briefed me, with PowerPoint displays, on Operation Medusa. This, they said, had been a significant victory over the Taliban before Kandahar, in which British and American troops had shored up underpowered Canadian forces in cleansing an area of the Taliban.

Back in London, I was given a stack of British plans and papers, including a 'United Kingdom' strategy for Afghanistan, and a 'United Kingdom' joint strategic plan for Helmand. In their enthusiasm no one seemed to notice the hubris of Britain drawing up, at great length and in extraordinary detail, its own semi-independent plans for stabilising a vast and violent province of Afghanistan, let alone the whole country.

Paddling furiously in the wake of this bow wave of military enthusiasm were Whitehall's civilians, notably the Foreign Office (FCO) and the much put-upon Department for International Development (DFID). My appointment was one of the main ways in which the FCO sought to show its support for the enterprise. But so was an elaborate and expensive (in FCO terms) plan to uplift both our Embassy in Kabul and our Provincial Reconstruction Team (PRT) in Lashkar Gah, the capital of Helmand. Occasional plaintive bleats from the Treasury about how much all this was costing were brushed aside. Our soldiers had to be supported with a proper civilian effort.

But it was not only those in government who spoke so persuasively of imminent success. Within days of my return from Saudi Arabia I was down at the Foreign Office's Wilton Park conference centre, in the lush downlands of Sussex, at a conference taking stock of progress on the 'Afghanistan Compact', between Afghanistan and the international community, signed at a great gathering in London in early February 2006. That Compact was a remarkably ambitious prospectus of commitments the Afghan Government had promised the international community it would fulfil over the following few years, covering almost every area of its national life. At Wilton Park, speaker after speaker took a line that was to become all too familiar in the months and years ahead: 'progress has been made, but challenges remain'.

Among the most persuasive of the optimists, and in many ways the golden boy of the international effort in Afghanistan, was Canada's former Ambassador to Afghanistan, and later Deputy Special Representative of the UN Secretary General, Chris Alexander. No Dr Pangloss, he was smart enough to acknowledge the warts on his vision of a slowly rising tide of security, governance and development. But, like so many other able and ambitious Westerners involved in the project, he saw no point in being anything other than optimistic.

In Wilton Park's ancient halls, and again several weeks later, at yet another conference, this time in the even more hallowed precincts of All Souls College, Oxford, my first doubts crept in. I was sure that progress had been made, and was being made. But I wondered how we would ever complete the enormous task we had set ourselves – of rebuilding the Afghan nation as well as the Afghan state – when none of the three main tools essential for success was yet fit for purpose: neither the Afghan Government in all its different manifestations, at national, provincial or district level; nor the international community, whether organised through the NATO-led International Security Assistance Force (ISAF) for Afghanistan, or through the UN, let alone the European Union; nor Afghanistan's neighbours, each of which needed to be committed to working in sustained and co-ordinated fashion towards the greater common good of a gradually stabilising Afghanistan, but all of whom were still competing in what amounted to another round of the Great Game.*

It was at Wilton Park too that I made my first acquaintance with a phenomenon of which I was to see much more in the years ahead: the Afghan conference industry. As with Ireland, or Palestine, or Sri Lanka, or most other conflicts, so Afghanistan's travails attract what can at times seem like a stage army of caring and committed local and international actors. They travel from conference to conference, endlessly re-examining the entrails of the problem. Such consultations, among governments, and between governments and non-governmental actors, can be valuable, in pooling knowledge and sharing best practice. But

---

* The nineteenth-century struggle between Britain's Indian Empire and the expanding Russian Empire for control over the lands which separated them, especially Afghanistan.

when the issues under debate are as intractable as those we face in Afghanistan, such meetings risk becoming ends in themselves, rather than means to the end of solving the problem. And, just occasionally, I have had a sneaking suspicion that some of those taking part – myself included – would feel a bit lost if the problem were actually solved and the conference circus ceased to rotate.

Not everyone to whom I spoke in London that spring was quite as upbeat as the British officers who briefed me. To his credit, one of the more senior Foreign Office officials responsible for South Asia told me, quietly, that he suspected that the Western military intervention in southern Afghanistan had provoked more violence than it had suppressed. His instinct was that the only approach capable of treating the problem would be a political one, involving both the internal and regional participants in the conflict. His quietly owlish demeanour belied a persuasive radicalism far removed from the conventional wisdom of the time.

Similarly worried were some of the more academic analysts in government, especially those more removed by temperament or geography from the pressure and pace of daily military and diplomatic activity in London. They warned me that, gradually, the insurgency in the Pashtun areas of the south and east of Afghanistan was spreading and deepening, and that NATO and its Afghan accomplices were not succeeding in creating stability that was either sustainable or replicable in the insurgency-infected areas where Western forces were not, or no longer, present.

Such gloomy thoughts were, however, far from my mind as I made my final preparations for a posting to which I was greatly looking forward. My team of three Pashtu teachers gradually brought me up to what the Foreign Office language experts call 'survival level'. They took enormous trouble to equip me as best they could for the linguistic and cultural challenges that lay ahead. One kindly invited me to stay with his family in north-west London for immersion training. All spoke of Afghanistan's recent history: the overthrow of King Zahir Shah in 1973 by his cousin, Daoud Khan, who established a republic; the Communist coup of April 1978, followed by the Soviet invasion in December 1979; the nationalist regime of the former Communist Dr Najibullah, which was established by the Russians and which survived their departure in February 1989 by three years; the appalling struggle between the warlords from 1992 until 1996; and, finally, the Taliban's beginnings as a movement of resistance to the depredations of the warlords, and their rule from 1996 until the Western intervention in October 2001. But my teachers played down the horrors which they and their families had experienced, in and out of prison. Each was a talent that would have been better employed back in his homeland rather than, for example, doing dry-cleaning in Shepherd's Bush.

My final week before departure was spent in the surreal surroundings of a former prep school in the Surrey heathlands, undergoing what is euphemistically called Hostile Environment Training. Over-enthusiastic ex-Special Forces instructors took a thinly disguised relish in putting us namby-pamby civilians through the meat grinder. They taught us how to wear a helmet and body armour; how to board helicopters and leave them in a hurry and in a dust storm; how to navigate across country with a compass; how to 'cross-deck' or, rather, be violently 'cross-decked' from a disabled vehicle to a rescue vehicle; how to apply a tourniquet and staunch a gaping chest wound; and, most terrifying of all, how to cope with kidnap and torture. My efforts to build a relationship in what I assumed was his native language with a very convincing-looking Al Qaeda operative were rudely rebuffed in unmistakable Geordie: 'Shut the fuck up, willya?'

And then it was time for my final calls in Whitehall before departure. The Permanent Secretaries of the three Whitehall departments directly engaged in the conflict had just returned from the first of several joint visits to Afghanistan. Their report to Ministers had struck an upbeat note. 'Overall, we are encouraged,' it had begun, before going on to celebrate the way in which all elements of the British presence in Afghanistan were working together, while noting that, of course, 'challenges remain'.

This was only the first of scores of reports back to Whitehall by visitors from London that I was to see over the next three years, only a few of which would address head on the scale of the mountain the allied effort in Afghanistan had to climb. Like the 'Three Tenors' (as the Permanent Secretaries had been dubbed, with that precious wit beloved of Whitehall), most such reports chose to accentuate the positive. Cautious optimism was the dominant theme. The civilian and military sides of the British effort in Helmand and Kabul were more 'joined up' than ever. We were at or approaching the turning point. There were no awkward questions about the credibility (or even existence) of a wider strategy for stabilising the whole country. Such was the pressure not to sound defeatist that all of us indulged from time to time in such self-congratulatory vacuities, as if the fact that most members of the UK team were facing in roughly the same direction, and talking to each other, was a matter for celebration.

At my last meeting in the Foreign Office before leaving for Heathrow, I mentioned to a senior official that my instinct was that we had made a strategic mistake in piling into Helmand the previous summer. He brushed my worry aside, assuring me: 'Well, we are there anyway, and there is nothing we can do about it now, so there is no point in worrying about it.'

Chapter 2

First Impressions

In 2007, the Foreign Office still felt it could afford to give VIP treatment to a new British ambassador travelling out from London to take up his or her appointment. An expensively hired limousine would convey him from home to Heathrow, he would use the VIP lounge once there, and the flight out would be in first class. And soon after he arrived he would send a telegram of First Impressions back to the Foreign Secretary in London.

Thus it was that on a May evening in 2007 I found myself climbing self-consciously into a large black Jaguar outside my home in Balham to begin the long journey to Kabul. As the chauffeur in an oddly anachronistic peaked cap negotiated the late rush-hour traffic, I reflected that the challenges in Kabul would be much greater, and much more real for Britain, than those I had faced in my two previous Embassies, Tel Aviv and Riyadh, each tough in its own way. How right that was to prove. I confess that I also wondered how, or whether, I would survive – literally. My posting had resulted in a huge leap in my life insurance premium, to which the Foreign Office was properly contributing.

An easy overnight ride to Dubai on Emirates, whose aircraft I would come to know so well over the next three years, brought my first surprise. Flights onward from Dubai to Kabul left not from the main terminal, but from one across the airfield, with decidedly inferior facilities. From here – dubbed the 'Axis of Evil' Terminal – the departures board announced flights to Baghdad, Tehran, Harare and a host of other exotic destinations.

And it was here that I first came across the civilian flotsam of the international conflict industry: Men In Beards, mostly, exotically tattooed, wearing sand-coloured cargo pants, military backpacks hoisted over their shoulders. Most looked like, and probably were, former soldiers, now making money as private security guards. Others were aid workers, journalists, spies or Special Forces types in thin disguise, or, just occasionally, diplomats trying to look more macho than they really were. Scattered along the line of male mercenaries checking in for the UN flight to Kabul were only a few women, of the confidently eccentric beauty which danger zones seem to attract.

The flight was terrifying. Service, from the South African crew of the ancient UN charter plane, was elementary. Apart from my fellow passengers, the landscape – the Straits of Hormuz, the mountains of southern Iran, then the dusty plains of Pakistani Baluchistan, followed by the great southern deserts of Afghanistan, divided by the grey-green valleys of the Helmand River and its tributaries – was the only entertainment. We moved north and east, and mountain ridges and then ranges rose out of the desert. As the ancient plane climbed laboriously up and over them towards Kabul, we ran into a series of violent summer storms. Circling around the great basin in the mountains in which the Afghan capital lies, we pitched and yawed for at least an hour, before the pilot told his relieved passengers that we would wait in Islamabad for the dust to settle, literally.

Three hours later than planned, we touched down in Kabul. From the window I could see a curious cocktail of aircraft. Ancient Antonovs and Ilyushins, and recently refurbished Mil helicopters, seemed to symbolise Afghanistan's past and perhaps its future. But the foreground – the present – was filled with Western military airframes: everywhere the C-130 Hercules, the utility truck of modern expeditionary warfare, bearing US, British, Canadian, Dutch, Danish and even Australian markings. Swarms of helicopters – American Black Hawks and Chinooks, a brace of French Eurocopters – covered the apron, plus a motley collection of civil aeroplanes: small propeller-driven aircraft in UN white; larger and older Boeings on charter, disgorging troops; and a rag-bag assortment of airliners of varying vintages, painted in the colours of airlines I had never heard of: Ariana, Kam Air, Pamir, Safi, among others.

My Deputy, Michael Ryder, an old Foreign Office friend and colleague, with the quizzical air of the Cambridge historian he once was, greeted me at the foot of the steps, along with my Royal Military Police Close Protection Team. I was hustled into a heavily armoured Land Cruiser and quickly briefed by the Team Leader: 'Never open the door yourself. If there's an incident, Sir, get down, and do exactly as we say. If we are incapacitated, this is the radio, and this our call sign. We are all medically trained, and there is a full first-aid kit in the back.'

We took the long, and supposedly safer, route to the Embassy. Only later did I learn that the direct route – Route White – was known as suicide alley. We wended our way through Kabul's north-western suburbs. I saw for the first time just how poor the place was, how squalid the conditions were in which most of the population somehow survived, how far the city had been wrecked, mostly in the savage intra-Afghan fighting which had followed the collapse of the Najibullah regime in 1992. That had been before the Taliban had ridden into town and restored order in 1996.

In my three years living in or visiting Afghanistan I would never tire of the rich panorama of Kabul street life: donkey carts, flocks of sheep and goats, bazaars for everything from printer cartridges to garden hoses, and low-tech engineering of the most creative kind, producing anything from axes to air compressors. Scattered around were the wrecked remnants of what had once been the garden city of South-west Asia, a city of tree-lined avenues and lush parks, to which the citizens of neighbouring countries had repaired for the 1960s equivalent of a mini-break. Now it was all laid waste. There was virtually nothing to show for five and a half years of Western engagement, apart from the narco-tecture of the drug lords' palaces on stolen land, and an encroaching tide of checkpoints, sandbags and earth-filled barriers of hessian and wire mesh. For me, the most poignant symbol of Kabul's desolation will always be the catenary poles for the Czech-made trolleybuses which once crisscrossed the city, now standing splayed against the sky, their torn wires flapping in the wind.

And then we reached the Residence. Smartly saluting Gurkha guards swung open two black metal gates in a nondescript side-street. We were in the garden of a neat suburban villa, an Afghan version of a Barratt home, with a narrow lawn, a small swimming pool, a terrace, three guest bedrooms, a one-bedroom flat for me, with an armoured keep – in fact my bathroom – in which I could (and would) take refuge, all hurriedly furnished by the Foreign Office estates team in a much mocked blend of IKEA and the Land of Leather. The only clues that this was the British Ambassador's Residence were the Royal Coat of Arms affixed, with a brass plate, to the wall by the front door; an idiosyncratic selection of gloomy British landscape paintings which my predecessor had persuaded the Government Art Collection in London to send out; and, hidden on the shelves of a pine-veneer sideboard, a small collection of battered silver rescued from Britain's grand old Embassy in Kabul.

In 1920, when the Foreign Secretary Lord Curzon ordered the construction of what was then known as the British Legation in Kabul, he decreed that the British Minister in Kabul should be the best-housed man in Asia. Ninety years later, Her Britannic Majesty's Representative in Kabul was not exactly the best-housed man in Kabul, let alone in Afghanistan, still less in Asia. Nevertheless, the Residence was warm in winter and cool in summer. A loyal and conscientious team of Afghans made it all work. The ability to offer British, international and Afghan guests food, drink and even a bed at almost any hour, with little or no notice, proved to be a powerful tool for the job – the kind of 'corporate entertainment facility' which every good ambassador's residence should be.

On that May evening, Michael Ryder had assembled well over a hundred members of the Embassy staff for a barbecue to meet the new Ambassador. It was only then, as I moved from group to group gathered in the dusk, that I realised just how diverse my new team would be. At least a third were women. There were people of many different ethnic backgrounds, and with disabilities (courageously, in Kabul).

But what was really striking was the range of institutional cultures represented on that Residence lawn. Only a small minority were 'straight' diplomats. Of course, there were spies, and members of the home civil service, from departments as different as HM Revenue and Customs (advising the Afghans on raising their tax take), the Ministry of Justice (which had sent out six prison officers), the Crown

Prosecution Service (including a Rumpole-esque representative of the English Bar), the Cabinet Office (a fast-streamer in search of excitement) and of course the Department for International Development (scores of enthusiastic development experts, known affectionately to the military as tree-huggers). But there were soldiers and sailors and Marines and airmen in desert uniform too, and British policemen, from the Met and the Northumbria Police, and customs men and women, and officers from the Serious Organised Crime Agency, technicians of every kind, and even builders from Britain, refurbishing the Embassy's secure zone. And, everywhere, the ubiquitous Men In Beards – some genuine Special Forces operatives, but mostly just pretending. Few of the home civil servants had ever worked in an embassy or dealt with the Diplomatic Service, let alone operated in an environment as difficult and dangerous as Afghanistan.

Turning such a mixed bag of officers, officials and civilian experts into a real team would be a never-ending challenge, especially as the working pattern for most civilian staff of six weeks on, two weeks off, with six- or twelve-month tours, meant that the turnover was unending. Every Thursday night (Friday was our only full day off) somebody would be holding leaving drinks of one kind or another, even if only to celebrate surviving another six weeks 'in theatre'. Sometimes, in despair, learning that some member of the team had just disappeared 'on breather', I would feel I was running a railway station rather than an embassy.

Mostly, however, it was more like being the headmaster of a run-down but generally happy and successful prep school, or the governor of an open prison whose inmates were repaying their debt to society handsomely and many times over. None of us doubted that, compared with our rivals – the overlarge and persistently unhappy American Embassy, the Canadians, the French, the Germans, the Danes and the Dutch, plus a UN mission almost always at war with itself – we were by far the most effective diplomatic operation in town. We knew more, did more, worked harder and had more fun than any of the other Embassies.

But, in May 2007, all that was still before me. In the gathering gloom, and with a distinct nip in the air encouraging brevity (Kabul is nearly 6,000 feet above sea level), Michael chinked on his glass, welcomed the new 'HMA' and asked me to 'say a few words'. I can't remember now exactly what I said then, or at meetings the next day for the British staff and then at a town-hall meeting for all the several hundred Embassy employees, of many nationalities. But I know that the messages I wanted to get across were as follows. First, and most important, we needed to be honest in our assessments of what was happening, and of what would and wouldn't work. Both the intervention in Iraq and the Afghan project had in my view been bedevilled by too much wishful thinking, an excess of over-eager-to-please officers and officials telling their masters, locally and back in capitals, what they thought those bosses wanted to hear. Second, I wanted us to work to high standards, everyone delivering to the best of his or her ability. Sloppy drafting, for example, meant sloppy thinking. Third, I wanted people to behave as though they were professionals: I had no objection, for instance, to casual dress, but visitors to the British Embassy needed to come away thinking we were an operation they could trust. 'More Goldman Sachs on dress-down Friday than Glastonbury' was the message I tried to convey. And, finally, I wanted us to have fun. We were in a tough place, doing a tough job. We needed to be able to chill out – within the proper boundaries.

How all this went down I don't know. But I do know that, in general, and despite the inevitable ups and downs, we were able over the next couple of years to build a team that really was a team, in the best sense of the term. It was much more than just the comradeship of adversity. It was because we all believed we had a real and important job to do, and we wanted to give it our best shot.

The next morning I started to get to grips with the Embassy's physical and human geography. The main offices were in a squat block of flats leased from the Bulgarian Embassy. The building was supposedly earthquake-proof, festooned with satellite dishes and wireless aerials, and still infested with builders brought out from London to upgrade it to match the Afghan ambitions of Her Majesty's Government (HMG). Most staff lived in converted cargo containers, or 'pods', in an area of the compound known, inevitably, as Poddington. But a growing proportion, including most of the DFID team, were transferring to a range of expensively leased and refurbished villas. Staff there lived student-style, sharing sitting rooms and kitchens. There was a canteen, serving subsidised food of varying quality from seven till seven, a small shop, a bar (of which more later), a gym and an asphalt sports pitch. A swimming pool was to come later, and in fits and starts. Almost all travel off this compound had to be authorised and, depending on the security situation, protected in varying degrees. About a hundred private guards from Britain, almost all ex-forces, plus over 300 Gurkhas, secured our operations, at a cost of tens of millions of pounds each year.

I took my first morning meeting, and my first weekly town-hall meeting. I ate my first canteen lunch – I would try always to lunch there when I did not have an official engagement – and drank my first drink at the bar. The officer in charge of my eight-man team of bodyguards from the Royal Military Police briefed me on the daily routine. And then it was down to business. At one of my first briefings, I told the Embassy's senior intelligence representative that my top priority would be building a relationship with President Karzai. 'Oh no it won't,' he retorted in the blunt northern fashion that I was to come to value. 'Your key relationship will be with the American Ambassador. He matters most to us.' In this he was not implying that my job wasn't to influence President Karzai and his Government, but that I would have a much better chance of doing so if I worked with the Ambassador of the predominant foreign power in Afghanistan.

So it was that on my second night in Kabul I found myself in the heavily fortified American Embassy compound, riding the lift up to the penthouse apartment of my new US colleague, William Wood. Bill was to become a valued colleague and a good friend. A highly intelligent and very senior member of the US Foreign Service, he had been person-ally selected by the Secretary of State, Condoleezza Rice, for this key job, having pleased the Bush Administration with his performance as ambassador in Bogotá. In effect, he was being transferred from the War on Drugs to the War on Terror. Bill was utterly professional and unfail-ingly loyal, despite often being saddled with impossible instructions from Washington. He never did more than hint at the doubts I suspected he had about some aspects of the Bush Administration's approach to Afghanistan. Behind a larger-than-life exterior, firing off one-liners and enjoying the occasional cigarette and Scotch on the rocks, lay a man of culture and discrimination, whose real loves were history and English literature, especially P. G. Wodehouse.

Bill, who had arrived only a few weeks before me, would often refer, somewhat nostalgically, to his Colombian experience, particularly of aerial spraying of the coca crop, which he believed to have been a huge success there. This had already led the Kabul diplomatic corps to christen him 'Chemical Bill'.

Little of that was obvious to me as we got to know each other over dinner and drinks on the vast terrace of the Ambassadorial apartment. As we looked over the parapet through the dust-filled night at the uncertain flickering of Kabul's lights, Bill revealed what was on his mind. He spoke of bringing over US Drug Enforcement Administration crop duster aircraft and helicopter gunships, and spraying the whole of the Helmand Valley with the weedkiller Roundup. C-130 transport aircraft could fly behind, dropping seed and shovels to the population. If it were done soon enough, there would be time for a second harvest in 2007.

As mildly as I dared at this first encounter with a key contact, I expressed doubts about whether this approach was practical. I wondered whether other green crops might be killed too. I asked what President Karzai and his Government (who were known to be strongly opposed to aerial spraying) would think, and how a population deprived overnight of much of their livelihood would react. I worried that such action might risk turning an insurgency into an insurrection. But Bill stuck to his guns. Aerial spraying had worked in Colombia. With British support, it could be made to work in Helmand. Bill would put US thinking down on paper and send it to me. He looked to me to swing HMG behind such an approach. I promised to think about it.

When I woke the next morning, I wondered if I had been dreaming. Or if Bill had been exaggerating for effect. But I realised how serious he was, and what difficulties we would face with the Bush Administration over poppy eradication, when an email from Bill popped into my home inbox, covering a one-page Word document in which was set down, in black and white, the US drug-eradication plan for Helmand.

Other first encounters were more straightforward. A week or so after arriving I was summoned to the old Palace in the centre of Kabul to present my credentials to President Karzai. Over the next three years I was to come to know well that Palace, in which so much of Afghanistan's bloody recent history had been played out. But for now my mind was on making a good impression on the man who was key to our whole strategy. I had met him only once before, at an economic conference in Jeddah. Like most of Hamid Karzai's foreign interlocutors encountering him for the first time, I had been immediately taken by his easy charm and obvious charisma, enhanced by perfect English and the stylish combination of Persian lamb cap and green and silver striped Afghan cloak.

As I was led by the Chief of Protocol through the dark hall and up the great stairs of the Arg Palace, I knew I was passing the spot where President Daoud and many other members of the royal family, including a dozen women and young children, had been gunned down in the Communist coup of April 1978. After a short delay, President Karzai came bustling in from a door in the corner of the audience chamber on the first floor. With my Deputy and Defence Attaché beside me, I marched up to the President, bowed and spluttered out a speech in broken Pashtu, which I had learned by heart. Karzai broke into a broad grin. The Ministers and courtiers ranged on the sofas at either side giggled. But I had made my point: my appointment signalled a step change in the relationship, and an effort by Britain to give Afghanistan in general, and President Karzai in particular, the political support and attention they deserved, given the scale of our military commitment.

We then retired immediately to the President's study just off the audience chamber. In a ritual we were to repeat scores of times over the next three years, Karzai took his seat in the chair on the right side of the fireplace, with his team ranged on the sofa to his left. I took mine in the chair to the left, with my team ranged on the sofa to my right, stretching back to the door. On the table between us were placed tea and coffee and cakes. I conveyed greetings from the Queen and from the Prime Minister (still Tony Blair). Karzai launched into rhapsodies about our royal family, about Blair and about a somewhat idealised vision of the British way of life. I spoke of my determination to work with the President, and to give him and his Ministers the support they needed.

I handed over the toy wooden railway I had brought out for Karzai's adored and long-awaited son, Mirwais.

All this sweetness and light was clouded by only one subject: narrowing his eyes, the President asked me what I thought of Pakistan. I confessed that, apart from my airport stopover, I had never been there and had no particular personal views. Karzai did not look convinced, but we moved on to other subjects. Here was a hint of trouble ahead.

In the days that followed, I paid my respects to all the other big players in Kabul. First and foremost was the Commanding General of ISAF, General Dan McNeill. A veteran of the fabled United States 82nd Airborne Division, Dan had served twice before in Afghanistan, and was proud never to have had a home tour north of the Mason–Dixon Line. He was a much wiser and more accomplished operator than those who criticised him from afar as too 'kinetic' ever really understood. His quiet, kindly manner concealed a depth of understanding and judgement we failed properly to appreciate or exploit.

Quite different from General McNeill was the Special Representative of the UN Secretary General, Tom Königs. As head of the UN Assistance Mission in Afghanistan (UNAMA), Königs was nominally in charge of all UN operations in Afghanistan, with well over a dozen different agencies represented. This was in theory only, however, as different baronies competed for turf and resources. Königs wasn't helped by his character or background: a gentle German public servant, with distinctly Greenish sympathies, he was said to have given most of his family fortune to the Sandinistas, the left-wing political party in Nicaragua. Following successful tours with the UN in the Balkans and elsewhere, he had been chosen to wind down the UN political presence in Afghanistan, in the belief, prevalent in 2005, that the mission was all but accomplished. Instead, he found himself facing a steadily worsening security and political situation, although still far less serious than that which confronted his successors. Königs's Deputy was the able Canadian diplomat Chris Alexander, whom I had met at Wilton Park; he was a formidable operator, who never let much check his unquenchable optimism.

The veteran European Union Special Representative in Kabul, Francesc Vendrell, had an even longer Afghan pedigree, having served variously as UN and EU representative for Afghan affairs since January 2000. Vendrell, who is Spanish by birth but British by upbringing, had forgotten more about Afghanistan than most of us would ever know. His family had sent him to England as a boy out of distaste for General Franco. He had ended up reading law at Cambridge and being called to the English Bar, before pursuing a long career as a UN diplomat. His wise understanding of the realities of Afghanistan was a refreshing contrast to the Panglossian pieties mouthed by others in the international community. Vendrell became a real soulmate. His one weakness was a passion for trams (or, more delicately, 'light rail'), to which most of his vacations seemed to be devoted. Sadly, his tram-spotting tendency was contagious, as I was to discover.

Vendrell's sceptical view of the Bush Administration's 'strategy' for Afghanistan was informed by the expertise he had built up in his office, starting with his remarkable Deputy, Michael Semple, a genial Irishman with twinkling eyes and a straggling beard, who spoke both Dari and Pashtu. Semple had an unrivalled understanding of the situation in the tribal areas on both sides of the Durand Line which separated Afghanistan from Pakistan. His eventual undoing was the fact that he knew too much about Afghanistan, even to the extent of dressing as an Afghan.

Michael was to become a good friend, and the source of much wise advice on what was really happening in Afghanistan. He represented the very best of Western commitment to Afghanistan, as did another remarkable Irishman (albeit from another part of the island), Mervyn Patterson. Mervyn was the chief political analyst at the UN Assistance Mission in Afghanistan, and was celebrated among Westerners in Kabul for the remarkable range of interesting Afghans he managed to assemble at his house. I was to have more to do with both men than I could possibly have imagined when I first met them.

On my first weekend in Kabul, Michael Ryder made sure that I became acquainted with three other key parts of the Kabul landscape: the old British Cemetery, dating back to 1840; the old British Embassy, an empty ruin which we were in 2007 planning to buy back and restore; and, next door to the old Embassy, the Turquoise Mountain Foundation, whose head, Rory Stewart, was in 2007 one of the leading lights of

Kabul expatriate society. As ambassador to Saudi Arabia, I had already come across the TMF, when the Prince of Wales (who, along with President Karzai, was a patron of the Foundation) had asked me to help persuade Saudis to donate to it. Seeing for myself the excellent work they were doing in gradually restoring the ancient Murad Khane quarter in the teeming heart of old Kabul, and the dedication with which they were promoting traditional crafts, such as calligraphy, ceramics, wood-carving and jewellery-making, at their base in the old fort alongside the former Embassy, I was filled with admiration. Nor could I fail to be won over by Rory's combination of courtesy, learning and intelligent ambition for his Foundation.

And they were only some of the characters with whom I would be working. Living and working in Kabul was indeed going to be interesting.

Chapter 3

Helmandshire

Within days of arriving in Kabul, I was travelling again: the soon-to-be-familiar high-speed dash through the crowded backstreets of Kabul out to the military side of the airport, then on to the RAF Hercules, for the ninety-minute night flight south to 'KAF' – Kandahar Air Field. On this, the first of countless such flights, I was accompanying the first of scores of Ministerial and military visitors from London, in this case the Minister of State at the Foreign Office, Kim Howells.

Dr Howells had spent the day in Kabul, on the Cook's Tour of Afghan Ministers and international actors the Embassy's hard-pressed visits team arranged for each of our senior official guests. As VIPs, the Minister and I were invited by the RAF to ride in the cockpit, rather than on the webbing seats slung the length of the cavernous cargo bay. Up front we had two advantages: first, we could see roughly where we were and what was going on, including awe-inspiring moonlight views as we flew south of the snow-covered peaks of the Hindu Kush and the Himalayas beyond; and, second, we were offered a 'brew', of instant coffee or builders' tea. I soon learned that, in the argot of the armed forces, milk and no sugar was a 'Julie Andrews' (white nun/none), whereas a 'Jordan' was white with two lumps, a 'Shirley Bassey' black with two lumps, and so on and even more politically incorrect and unrepeatable. Over the months that followed, I came to value what amounted to nocturnal confessionals with the RAF flight crew. Out on rotation to Afghanistan and Iraq, from the great RAF transport base at Lyneham in Wiltshire, the Hercules pilots had an intelligently detached perspective on both campaigns not always obvious to those of us caught in the toils of the ground war.

The approach to Kandahar was almost as spectacular as our spiralling ascent from Kabul. All lights extinguished, helmets and body armour back on, night-vision goggles for the pilots, radio silence, the groan of the landing gear being let down, and then the anxiously endless minutes of the final descent, before we hit the runway with a great shudder and were shaken by the roar of the engines going into reverse thrust. Once on the ground, we climbed out and were hustled into the building which now housed the RAF's headquarters in Afghanistan. The rocket holes in the roof were a reminder that this was where the Taliban had made their last stand against the forces from the north in December 2001.

We spent the night in the VIP accommodation at KAF: austere Portakabins at the centre of a sprawling military metropolis. Dust everywhere, the roads clogged with jeeps and trucks and armoured vehicles of every type and nationality. A bizarre palette of differing national desert camouflage patterns. Forests of aerials, cables festooned like some out-of-control vine from every hut, clusters of satellite dishes and national flags denoting the headquarters of the different contingents. Fat soldiers, thin soldiers, blonde soldiers, bespectacled soldiers, women soldiers. Earnest joggers, usually American, at every dark and daylight hour. And always and everywhere the whine and roar of jets and turboprops and helicopters, an aroma of kerosene on the breeze and the low hum of diesel generators producing more power than was consumed by all southern Afghanistan beyond the wire.

Early next morning we were up with the sun for a briefing breakfast in the headquarters of the British General then commanding in the south. The leitmotiv of the long war: we are making progress, but challenges remain. Then a dash to the apron, earplugs in, helmets and body armour back on, for the roller-coaster Chinook ride out over the great red southern desert, lo-hi-lo in RAF jargon, before dropping down to 100 feet for the final approach to the British Brigade Headquarters in its compound in the centre of Helmand's provincial capital, Lashkar Gah. In the back with us were British and American soldiers of every kind, listening to their iPods, reading dog-eared paperbacks, taking snaps with their digital cameras, showing their nerves. Piled high in the centre of the hold were Royal Mail sacks, and pallets of war cargo lashed down under nets. We flew in fast and low, across the fields and tributaries of the Helmand Valley, with sheep and goats running beneath and before us. Startled peasants stared up with a mixture of surprise and resentment, the women covering their faces and collecting their children.

Standing at the edge of the helipad in Lashkar Gah was the Brigadier, the first of eight I would come to know in my three and a half years working in and on Afghanistan. A calm quiet Parachute Regiment officer, with experience in Ireland and Iraq, he briefed the Minister on the progress the Brigade was making – but challenges remained. He spoke of the theory of 'Clear, Hold and Build'. British and NATO forces would clear an area of insurgents. They would then establish Forward Operating Bases and Patrol Bases and Combat Outposts across and around the cleared area. They would fill those islands of order with a judicious mixture of NATO and of Afghan forces, both Army and Police. And then they would start to build: security, governance, development – the three pillars of the new order in southern and eastern Afghanistan. Set out in PowerPoint, explained with enthusiasm, in neat counterpoint between civilian and military members of the British-led Helmand Provincial Reconstruction Team, the brief was utterly confident: to question it would have seemed ill-mannered.

We were shown around the compound. The military headquarters, with its cavernous operations room full of banks of computer screens on row after row of trestle tables, maps and charts and secure telephones everywhere, live feeds from Kabul, or London, or a drone circling over an operation under way somewhere up or down the Valley. The *Field* lay incongruously on the Brigadier's table. A young military assistant offered coffee and tea, and more coffee and tea. The base chapel, known as the Church of St Martin, Lashkar Gah, was in a tent to which the Padre had affixed his rather optimistic invitations to Sunday Eucharist and daily Bible study. Inside were stacks of the Armed Forces Operational Service and Prayer Book, bound in covers of desert camouflage. The book's last section contains, in case of need, Field Burial Services for Jews and Muslims, Hindus and Sikhs, and, most improbably, Buddhists ('there are no special ritual requirements regarding Buddhists and, since helping others is fundamental to Buddhism, there are no objections to transplant surgery').

The breezeblock and concrete offices of the Provincial Reconstruction Team were under a rocket-proof roof. In them, eager civil servants and contractors in jeans and tee-shirts pushed on with the business of stabilisation. The vehicle park was full of armoured personnel carriers of every kind, on wheels and tracks, each sprouting aerials and, usually, a machine gun or two. And then, most important, there was the canteen, producing some of the best food in Afghanistan, thanks, at that time, to the Royal Logistic Corps, but to contractors now: bacon and porridge for breakfast, bangers and mash for lunch, roast beef and Yorkshire pudding for supper – and a salad bar for those who don't have to lug 40 kilos of equipment on patrol along the lanes of Lashkar Gah.

We learned the liturgies, large and small, of the campaign: the commander's morning brief, the commander's evening brief, the ritual cleansing with Army-issue antiseptic gel before and after meals; the quick coffee under the pergola in the cottage garden cultivated by successive brigades in the centre of the compound; and the surreptitious evening cigarette with a senior officer whose thoughts too easily turn to a beloved family so far away, to a land of Volvos and Labradors and prep school playing fields.

And then, helmets and body armour back on, we were bundled into armoured Land Cruisers for the dash downtown, to meet real Afghans: the Governor, the leader of the Provincial Council, the Chief of Police and the head of the intelligence and security service. All are polite, and optimistic, appreciative of what Britain is doing for them, offering hot sweet tea in small glasses and trays of nuts.

A day in Helmand flashes by, in a whirlwind of briefings and inspections and high-speed moves by helicopter or protected vehicle. And then we are back on the Hercules to Kabul, for another round of calls on senior Afghans and internationals. We see President Karzai, Vice President Khalili, we brief the Minister over breakfast with the senior British General in Kabul. And, at the end of a very long day, we take a tired and thirsty Minister to the Embassy bar for a late-night encounter with the home team.

Two weeks later I am back in Helmand, for a proper visit in my own right: longer briefings, franker talking. I fly out to my first Forward Operating Base. I am struck by the contrast between the crude conditions there and those back in the headquarters compound in Lashkar Gah or in the several square miles of the great and growing British main base at Camp Bastion in the desert east of the Helmand Valley. The fighting soldiers spend six solid months – minus only a ten-day R&R break back in Britain – in the front line, crammed six or eight to a tent, or a mud hut, or a shelter built of giant sandbags and corrugated iron. In summer, the heat and flies are unremitting, in winter the cold is bone chilling. While the Grenadier Guards are whitewashing the stones (they really are) at the camp abutting Bastion where the Guards train the Afghan Army, an officer in the rather less refined (and newly named) Mercian Regiment tells me that he likes his squaddies' accommodation rough, because it makes them want to get up and get out on patrol. And, if the housing is rough, so can be the food in some outlying bases. Everything is airlifted in by helicopter, as, for security and sanitary reasons, locally bought food is not considered safe. The cooks perform wonders with the ten-man ration packs, coming up with scores of ways to present the modern equivalent of tinned spam and sweet corn swimming in brine. But I am not surprised, a year later, to hear rumours of scurvy in one of the outlying Patrol Bases.

The whole experience – of meeting troops engaged in combat in a real war, risking life and limb out on patrol every day – is utterly humbling. Kabul isn't comfortable, but compared with the FOBs on the front line it is close to paradise. I realise how lucky we civilians are; and how we should never forget the sacrifice our soldiers, most of them less than half my age, are making.

This time, Governor Wafa is in town, and I have my first meeting with an unlikely Afghan administrator who, with his long white beard, looks a bit like a cross between an Old Testament prophet and Father Christmas. He is of course all charm, especially when I greet him in rudimentary Pashtu. He speaks of the progress being made, of the good work being done by Task Force Helmand and the PRT, of his brotherly affection for the Brigadier and the PRT Head. I am reassured: even if Wafa means only 10 per cent of what he tells me, we must be doing some good.

I am shown around Camp Bastion, laid out in the western desert like a great legionary fortress. As with the Roman Army in Caledonia or

Cambria, so it is with the British Army in Afghanistan: a great ditch around the rectangular perimeter, to keep the natives out; a grid pattern of roads within the *limes* (as the Romans called their imperial boundary paths), at the centre of which is the headquarters, with the Union flag hanging limply in the hot desert air. Alongside, in tribute to the fallen, stands an eloquently simple memorial, of local stone, and brass from Britain. Its tablets listing the British dead are steadily filling up.

Accompanied by the Brigadier, I take a dusty ride across a short stretch of desert to the neighbouring Camp Shorabak, where the 1st Battalion Grenadier Guards are mentoring and training units of the Afghan National Army's 205 (Hero) Corps. I meet, for the first time, the exuberant General Mohayeddin, a brave and professional Tajik with a moustache to match. As one would expect with the Foot Guards, the camp is lickspittle tidy, the Guardsmen and officers bracketing every spoken sentence with a 'Sir' or two. Their account of the progress the Afghan Army is making is resolutely upbeat, and I come away encouraged.

Less encouraging is an event I attend later, at Kandahar Air Field, while waiting for the nightly Hercules back to Kabul. The Canadians are holding a 'ramp ceremony' to salute a fallen Canadian soldier, on his way back to a small town out on the prairie. Under a starry southern sky, hundreds of troops from all the different nations form up on the vast concrete apron. In what some might see as a typically Canadian touch, they are joined by scores of civilians working with Canadian forces. In pseudo-military fashion, an improbable army of cooks and clerks, of all shapes and many sizes, is marched out on the apron, arms and legs irretrievably out of step. Flags are paraded stiffly before us, a piper plays a haunting lament for the fallen, prayers are said and speeches made, at what seems like inordinate length. I feel strangely deflated as I climb up into the belly of the Hercules for the flight back north.

Chapter 4

'A Marathon Rather Than A Sprint'

Back in Kabul I got down to laying the foundations for all successful bilateral diplomacy: knowing your clients. At my request, my über-efficient Private Secretary, Alex Hill, had filled my first days as ambassador with calls on Afghanistan's two Vice Presidents, virtually the whole of the rest of the Cabinet, the Speakers of both Houses of Parliament, the great *jihadi* leaders from the struggle against the Soviet Union, every ambassador who counted (and some who didn't, but thought they should) and the heads of the main aid agencies.

The Embassy Press Section arranged an off-the-record session with the key British and American journalists in town, for me to get to know them, and for them to get to know me. I also made my first acquaintance with the Afghan written and electronic media, giving introductory interviews to radio and television. To my delight, I discovered that the most trusted, and popular, source of news for Afghans was the Dari/Pashtu stream of the BBC World Service: with more than thirty correspondents dotted round Afghanistan, its coverage was uniquely well informed, and balanced between sources and regions.

A large part of the fascination of working in and on Afghanistan is the astonishing range of international actors with an interest in the country, stretching far beyond the forty or so nations contributing to the NATO-led, American-dominated International Security Assistance Force, and including many non-governmental organisations (NGOs). One of the most effective of the latter is the group of charities run by the Aga Khan from his headquarters outside Paris. His Highness's representative in Kabul, a British Ismaili Muslim, is one of the wisest and best-informed members of the international community, with excellent access to senior Afghans, from President Karzai downwards.

The Aga Khan Foundation's development work covers the whole of Afghanistan. But it is also focused in part on the areas of Afghanistan where Ismaili Muslims – of whom the Aga Khan is the spiritual leader – are concentrated, notably in the vast province of Badakhshan in the mountains abutting the border with Tajikistan. The Aga Khan's people also undertake remarkable work restoring and preserving Afghanistan's cultural treasures, of which the sixteenth-century mausoleum and gardens in Kabul of the Moghul Emperor Babur are the most spectacular example. Almost equally impressive is the Foundation's work to promote music from Central Asia. One of my happiest memories of Kabul will always be the evening concerts of traditional music in the Babur Gardens organised by the Aga Khan's cultural foundation.

Alongside this development and cultural work, the Aga Khan is also a significant investor in Afghanistan. He is a major shareholder in the Roshan mobile telephone network – one of Afghanistan's greatest success stories of the past few years. For the international community in Kabul, however, his biggest contribution to their welfare, and that of their visitors, is the spectacular Serena Hotel – Afghanistan's only world-class international hotel. It was at the Serena that I was invited to a small private dinner with the Aga Khan shortly after my arrival. I was impressed by how well informed His Highness was, but also by his concern about what he and I saw as a deeply worrying outlook on both the security and political fronts: not for him the rosy platitudes of the NATO spokesmen.

Over my time in Kabul, as the conflict ramped up and the international military effort multiplied, several other countries followed Britain's lead and appointed a senior diplomat to lead their civilian effort in Afghanistan. But Russia had no such need, for its Ambassador to Afghanistan, Zamir Kabulov, had been working in and on Afghanistan since 1979. He used to joke that he had been in Kabul so long that the city had been named after him. Uzbek by ethnicity but deeply Russian in outlook, Zamir became a good friend and a source of wise counsel. He had lived through much of Afghanistan's recent history, including taking part in the evacuation under fire of his Embassy as the mujahideen bombarded the town. Since then the Embassy, on a huge compound in the west of the city, had been comprehensively trashed, and then restored. Just as the old British Embassy in Karte Parwan, now a smoke-blackened shell, symbolised one phase in Afghanistan's history, so too the 1960s Soviet architecture of Zamir's proconsular palace stood for another, more recent and even bloodier, era. One of Zamir's first comments to me was as amusing as it was chilling. 'I have a very varm feeling tovards you, Sheerard,' he volunteered, in his thick Russian accent. 'You are making all ze same mistakes as ve did.'

He and our American colleague, Bill Wood, kept their distance from each other during my first months in Kabul. But some time in the autumn of 2007 they met, for an exuberant exchange over dinner at the Chinese Embassy. A day or two later, Zamir commented to me: 'I like zis Bill Vood of yours. 'E smokes and drinks like me. Meeting 'im vas like a Russian vedding: ve started by fighting, but ended up making love.'

Like his successor, Karl Eikenberry, Bill Wood made a practice of taking regular trips outside Kabul to see the situation in the real Afghanistan for himself. The American Ambassador was able to call on the vast resources of the US military for such trips, and Bill was kind enough to invite me to accompany him on several. Without such a wealth of resources, my own visits to parts of Afghanistan other than Helmand and Kandahar had to be planned weeks in advance, and were often cancelled at short notice, given the pressures on the RAF air transport fleet. Only when, late in 2007, the Embassy obtained an aircraft of its own were we able to make such trips without almost insuperable difficulty.

But early on in my time we did manage an Embassy expedition to the city which dominates the western approaches to Afghanistan and forms the junction between Iran and its eastern neighbour: Herat. Thanks to expert planning by John Windham, the Embassy's Chief Security Officer, a distinguished former officer in the Irish Guards, we arranged to take our armoured Land Cruisers with us in the belly of a Hercules. John came along to help with the logistics for the trip, masquerading as my Agricultural Attaché (a role for which his farm in England just about qualified him).

In Herat, I called on the Governor, in his Soviet-era guesthouse occupying a small hill to the west. He had assembled most of the local dignitaries and offered a sumptuous lunch. Little real business was done, for Britain had little real business in that part of Afghanistan. The local ISAF troops were Italians, celebrated as much for the fine wine and pasta offered to visitors to their base at Herat airport as for their war-fighting abilities. But here, as almost everywhere in Afghanistan, the real war was being conducted by American Special Forces, whose shadowy presence was known but not much advertised – at least until the appalling massacre of civilians at Azizabad near Herat in August 2008 (of which more later).

Yet Herat did not feel as though it was really affected by war. The central bazaar was full and bustling. The streets were safe, and crowded. We visited the great Friday mosque. We saw and photographed the lofty minarets built in 1417 by Queen Gowhar Shah, who did more for Islamic art than almost any other woman. Now, only a lonely handful survived, thanks to dynamiting by British military engineers in 1885, earthquakes early in the twentieth century and then target practice by Soviet tank commanders. We ended the afternoon by climbing the citadel and surveying a city which showed what Afghanistan had been like before its present troubles, and could be once again.

Back in Kabul, a weekend or two later, I underwent one of the rites of passage for foreigners arriving in the city: an early-morning climb along the city walls, high above the western approaches of the metropolis. A small group of us assembled with our Close Protection Teams outside my house just after dawn on a Friday morning. We were taken to the disembarkation point, in a mostly Tajik shanty town on the upper slopes of one of the sharp ridges which surround the city. With our bodyguards fanning out through the houses, and chickens and children picking their way over the shoals of rubbish and streams of sewage which filled the alleys of the settlement, we started our ascent. Within minutes, I was rasping badly and feeling (or imagining) sharp pains in the left side of my chest: cardiac arrest seemed imminent. My CP Team looked alarmed. But somehow I staggered on. It was easy to forget that the Embassy was some 6,000 feet above sea level and that we were already another 1,000 feet higher than that. Moreover, Kabul's air, while thin, was also full of what was delicately described as 'solid matter': dung particles in summer, and the smoke from tens of thousands of wood stoves in winter.

Once up on the wall itself, we were rewarded with spectacular views. North, over the city centre, we could see the Presidential Palace guarded by ancient cedars and an oversize Afghan flag, but still surrounded by broken turrets and pockmarked roofs. Then the more modern Wazir Akbar Khan quarter, with the British Embassy's sprawling estate, and north and east of that the great fortress of the American Embassy. Further north still lay the vast and growing expanse of the airport, with an unending procession of civil and military aircraft dropping down over the mountains from the east, or climbing steeply up over the 18,000-foot wall of snow and rock just to the west. Beside and below them the helicopters: American Black Hawks, mostly, but Chinooks and Eurocopters too, and plenty of recycled Russian Mi-17s.

To the east we could see the long thin road to Jalalabad, and thence the Khyber, beyond which lay the Indus valley and the plains of the Punjab. The highway was always crowded with trucks carrying containers of supplies to feed the NATO beast, and cheap Chinese imports for an Afghan economy growing rapidly on a flood of foreign money. But it was also to become the setting for more suicide attacks than any other, as the terrorists made their way in from the sanctuaries across the other side of the border with Pakistan. To the west were the areas which had been laid waste in the fighting between the mujahideen factions in the mid-1990s: the parks of the university, and the polytechnic, the Soviet cultural centre, and then the Darul Aman Palace. The ill-fated President Hafizullah Amin had moved his office there, on Soviet advice, 'for his own safety', in 1979, just before the Spetsnaz, or Soviet Special Forces, had stormed the Tajbeg Palace next door (and killed Amin) on 27 December that year. The Palace still stood, a hollow-eyed shell, a reminder of past vanities and tragedies. To the south were the muddy marshlands and winter lakes abutting Highway One, leading to the Pashtun heartlands of the south and east and eventually to Kandahar.

After coffee and sandwiches in a derelict turret at the summit, and the obligatory photograph of a group looking as though they had just scaled Everest, we descended through another Tajik settlement on the western slope of the ridge. Waiting for us halfway down was our fleet of armoured Land Cruisers, surrounded by crowds of noisy Friday-morning children, flying kites, kicking footballs and hauling water. We met them on the stone terrace, recently restored by the Aga Khan, on which lay the two barrels of the cannon from which the noonday gun had fired its daily salute across Kabul until at least the early 1970s.

Within weeks of my arrival in Kabul we decided to celebrate the Queen's Birthday. We would do so in a style as close as possible to the traditional way in which Embassies in less exotic or dangerous locations mark Her Britannic Majesty's Official Birthday. As the Embassy did not have a garden large enough to take all our guests, the British Council representative kindly offered his grassy compound for the occasion. Behind high walls, in a district close to the abandoned former British Embassy, the lawns and rosebeds of the Council premises offered an ideal setting in which to relaunch the British presence in Kabul. The Commanding Officer of the 1st Battalion Grenadier Guards kindly sent up from Helmand a bugler and a drummer in bearskin and ceremonial dress.

We started with a minute's silence, for the fallen of all nations. The Irish Guards provided a piper, whom I asked to play the traditional plangent lament, 'The Flowers of the Forest'. As the sun went down behind the western hills, we held a flag-lowering ceremony. There were speeches by our guest of honour, the Afghan Foreign Minister, Dr Rangin Spanta, and by me. But best of all we had a wonderful turnout of guests, from the diplomatic corps and the international community, of course, but also Afghans from every walk of the local life with which our vast Embassy engaged: tribal chiefs in traditional dress, mullahs and men of religion more generally, Army and Police officers, administrators and academics, Members of both Houses of Parliament, and Afghan women as well as men. The home team wore roses in their lapels and worked hard to look after all our guests. It was one of the more optimistic and uplifting occasions of my first year in Kabul. The message was clear: Britain was Back, and meant Business.

As part of the mood of cautious optimism, the BBC announced it was planning an Afghan week, of coverage on radio and television, from Kabul as well as Helmand. Their veteran World Affairs Editor, John Simpson, had long experience of Afghanistan. His walk back into Kabul as the Taliban left in November 2001 had become part of television history. His judgements counted. In 2005, he had been able to proclaim that Afghanistan was 'a nation of shopkeepers once again'. Now he came back to Kabul, to chronicle the latest chapter in the never-ending story. He interviewed me on a Friday afternoon, walking round the gardens of the Emperor Babur. In the course of that extended conversation I said two things that attracted comment.

First, I described the work of rebuilding Afghanistan after decades of conflict as a thirty-year marathon rather than a sprint. Inevitably, the British media interpreted that as meaning that I expected British forces to remain in combat for three decades: something I believed to be neither possible nor desirable. More seriously, however, on the eve of my departure for my first breather break back in Britain, President Karzai took offence at my suggestion that the insurgency was largely a Pashtun insurgency. No one else had paid much attention to this statement of the obvious. But we received messages from the Palace reporting the President's distress: I decided that I could not leave for London without having first reassured Karzai. So I postponed my departure and managed eventually to see him. I explained that, while I believed almost all Taliban were Pashtuns, I did not believe that all Pashtuns were either Taliban or insurgents. Karzai seemed mollified.

By then, however, it would have been impossible for me to reach London on commercial flights via Dubai in time for my son's graduation ceremony at Edinburgh University. My excellent Defence Attaché, and the RAF Movements Officer assigned to the Embassy, managed to secure me a place in one of the Royal Air Force's giant Boeing C-17 transport aircraft, flying from Kandahar to Odiham in Hampshire, with a Chinook in the back.

It was a flight to remember. The view from the cockpit of the C-17, with its larger than usual windows, is spectacular: I was able to enjoy extraordinary panoramas of the mountains of Afghanistan and eastern Turkey, including Mount Ararat, before we changed crews at the vast American base at Inçirlik – a modern military caravanserai for troops and freight moving east to Iraq and Afghanistan.

AFGHANISTAN - 'IT'S A MARATHON RATHER THAN A SPRINT'

Putting the giant transporter down on the tiny runway in the green fields of rural Hampshire was a feat which both I and the personnel of the RAF Station could only admire. An excited Station Commander kindly came driving out to greet us in a car flying the RAF pennant from its bonnet. He brought me not only a note from my old prep school friend Vice Admiral Tim Laurence, who had just been visiting the base in his capacity as head of defence estates, but also the offer of an RAF car and driver to hurry me to Heathrow to catch a flight to Edinburgh in time for a celebratory dinner that evening. We duly raced off the airfield and up the M3, only to discover that all flights out of Heathrow had been delayed because of, improbably, a gas leak beside one of the runways.

I missed my son's graduation ceremony entirely: a trivial sacrifice by comparison with those our soldiers and their families were making, but this was not the first or smallest price my family were to pay for my service in Afghanistan.

Chapter 5

Breather Break

When I was originally approached about going to Afghanistan, I was told that the breather-break system – of six weeks on and two weeks off – would be one of the attractions of the job. But, in my experience, we never achieved the right balance between operational efficiency and giving individuals the time off they needed during tough postings such as Kabul or, even more so, Lashkar Gah and the outstations across Helmand. And, at least as far as the Foreign Office was concerned, we ended up with an expensive and inefficient system that gave us the worst of all worlds.

As with Iraq, so British diplomats and civil servants working in Afghanistan go there unaccompanied by their partners and families. Initially this was at least as much because of the shortage of accommodation as for security reasons. But, as the security situation steadily deteriorated, so security considerations became paramount. In my first eighteen months in Kabul, friends and family members were allowed to pay short visits to Kabul. But that privilege too was withdrawn.

No one seems to know where the 'six weeks on, two weeks off' rule originated: some British Government agencies in Kabul operated stricter regimes (eight weeks on, two weeks off, for example), whereas others were even more liberal, expecting their staff to spend only a month in theatre between breaks. And some departments, notably DFID, treated their staff even more generously, in terms of allowances and air fares. In part, this was the market at work: in general, diplomats were keener to serve in Kabul or Helmand than were home civil servants.

As a manager, I found the 'six weeks on, two weeks off' pattern hugely disruptive, with roughly a quarter of the Embassy away at any one time, and another quarter either just having returned from breather break or preparing to go on one. That, coupled with the standard tour length of only eighteen months, meant that generating a sense of sustained commitment was extremely difficult. But I think our practice was better than that of the US State Department, which rotated virtually the whole civilian staff of its Embassy more or less simultaneously every summer, while allowing those staff only a couple of breaks out of country during their year's tour.

In my first year in Kabul, I discussed with senior managers in London moving to a standard breather-break pattern for all staff of eight weeks on and two weeks off; but once again the sense that security was gradually deteriorating, with new restrictions on staff going out and about in and around Kabul for recreational purposes, meant that we could not move ahead. And it would have been difficult to deal with the sense of entitlement, on somewhat spurious health and safety grounds, that everyone developed. Nor was it obvious how we could have aligned all the different departments and agencies behind a single regime, without disproportionate effort.

This addiction to high allowances, and plenty of leave, has helped create a kind of post-conflict stabilisation industry. We would find the same staff, and contractors, who had served in Baghdad or Basra, turning up in Kabul and Lashkar Gah. Working in such an environment is adrenalin-inducing; and, especially for single people, or individuals with unhappy family situations, the rewards in terms of money and free time can also become dependency-inducing. In terms of productivity and operational creativity, this is not healthy: the constant recycling of staff from a limited pool risks promoting a mindset in which the problems staff are dealing with are contained or managed, rather than solved.

But such thoughts were far from my mind in June 2007, as I lugged home to Balham the helmet and body armour the RAF had insisted I take with me on the C-17 flight. What was on my mind were the meetings I was due to have with new Ministers, including a new foreign secretary, following Gordon Brown's appointment as prime minister.

My professional relationship with David Miliband began as it ended. In so many ways he was the ideal political boss: irrepressibly enthusiastic, insatiably curious, highly intelligent and open minded. He always encouraged my team and me to report honestly and to give him the best advice we could, however awkward it might be, if necessary on private channels. As was to happen time and again over the next three years, I was summoned in from my leave for a meeting with him, in the Foreign Secretary's magnificent office overlooking St James's Park and Horse Guards Parade. At that first briefing meeting, David made clear that Afghanistan and Pakistan would be his top priority as foreign secretary. His first overseas visit in that office, apart from day trips to Berlin and Paris, would be to Afghanistan and Pakistan the following month.

In an augury of how my whole posting was to turn out, many official demands on my time crowded in on that first breather break: a call on the Prime Minister, who listened carefully to my first impressions, and gave me a copy of his newly published book, *Courage: Eight Portraits*. He too would want to pay an early visit. I also met the Defence Secretary, Des Browne, and paid a brief courtesy call on the Leader of the Opposition, David Cameron. All would become familiar visitors to Afghanistan in the weeks and months ahead.

I also attended a debate on Afghanistan in the House of Lords during which the newly ennobled Mark Malloch Brown made his maiden speech as a minister. Mark knew Afghanistan from his time as a senior UN official: as head of the UN Development Programme, he told me how he had met the Afghan leader, Dr Najibullah, in his palace in Kabul while it was under fire. Mark's quiet scepticism about the whole Afghan project was founded on long experience: in the end, he was more right than David Miliband or I had been about the chances of persuading the US Administration to adopt the more political approach essential for stabilising the situation in a sustainable way. But he did not allow that to deter us from making the effort, especially once Barack Obama took office in January 2009.

That summer I saw another group of individuals with long experience of Afghanistan who were also worried about how things were going: over lunch Lord Salisbury (who had travelled regularly to Afghanistan during the anti-Soviet *jihad*) and his fellow peers expressed their concerns. Allowing hope to triumph over my still-limited experience, I was determined to be optimistic and to accentuate the positive in our current approach.

But it was difficult to be genuinely upbeat about the results of a conference in Rome in early July that year, at which, in the absence of a minister, I led the British delegation. This conference, on Justice and the Rule of Law in Afghanistan, was the fruit of a decision, at a G8 Donors' meeting, to split five ways the responsibility for Security Sector Reform (the phrase used by post-conflict reconstruction experts to cover the army, police, justice and the rule of law): thus Germany was to lead on police reform, Japan on demobilisation and disarmament, Britain on counter-narcotics, the United States on developing the Afghan National Army, and, somewhat improbably, Italy on reforming justice and the rule of law.

The Rome conference that summer was impeccably organised, with generous entertainment at the expense of the Italian taxpayer. Almost all the significant participants made solemn pledges to do, and give, more. In the margins of the meeting, the FCO South Asia Director and I sought a meeting with the US Assistant Secretary for Central and South Asia, Richard Boucher. I had known Richard from my time as head of the Foreign Office's Hong Kong Department: he had been a very successful and supportive US Consul General in Hong Kong in the run-up to the handover in June 1997. Later he had shown his consummate diplomatic skills as the State Department spokesman. I briefed Richard on my first impressions, including my worry that, without corrective action led by the United States, both the political and security situations in Afghanistan were on a gradual downward slope. To my consternation, Boucher took a different view – one he was to hold consistently through the rest of his time in office, under the Bush Administration. He was convinced, he said, that the reality was that progress was being made in Afghanistan: it just wasn't always obvious. There were no real grounds for concern.

Like almost every other international conference on Afghanistan I was to attend over the next three years, the Rome extravaganza produced a high-sounding declaration, and a work plan to be implemented by the Afghan Government and its international partners on the ground in Afghanistan. Most such pledges were honoured more in the breach than in the observance. But that did not stop us celebrating with a magnificent reception in the Villa Madama high on one of the hills overlooking Rome and the Tiber. Nor did it diminish my childish pleasure in the escort of Carabinieri on motorbikes and in patrol cars who accompanied me, as delegation leader, with much flashing of lights and screeching of sirens, on every move through Rome during the conference. There was after all something to be said for cutting a dash, Italian style.

PART II

HOPE OVER EXPERIENCE

The main cause of Britain's defeat in the first Anglo-Afghan War [of 1839–42] was that junior officers were afraid to tell their superiors just how bad the situation was.

British Brigadier, speaking at a dinner in Kabul in February 2010
to commemorate that defeat

Chapter 6

A King's Funeral

On returning to Kabul, my first priority was David Miliband's visit. This was his first significant overseas visit as foreign secretary, and the first of six he was to make to Afghanistan in three years in the job. It would be important in every way.

Visits to Afghanistan by a Cabinet minister need plenty of hard preparation, running down to the wire and beyond: fixing calls on senior Afghans and key members of the international community; drawing up guest lists for working breakfasts, lunches and dinners; liaising with the visits team back in London, and with the Embassy's own security people, as well as with the large Metropolitan Police Close Protection Team which always accompanied Ministers travelling to danger zones; and working with the RAF on flights into and out of Afghanistan, and around the country. Nothing was ever fixed until everything was fixed. Nor was anything fixed until the very last minute. Even then everything was subject to the security threat warnings which could derail the whole visit. But the overall shape of every such trip sets itself: a day in and around Kabul; a day in and around Helmand; calls on, and briefings from, key Afghan and international figures in both places; and, more important for politicians than anything else, meeting, and being seen to meet, our troops.

The final touch was always for me to draft a scene-setting telegram. I would send this just in time to go on top of the briefing pack the Minister would read on the way out, but not so far in advance that it would simply be plagiarised by the Department for the briefing they had had to prepare. I aimed in these telegrams to give the visitor a right-up-to-date feel for the mood in the capital and the country more widely, plus a sense of the issues likely to be at the forefront of his hosts' minds. In my view, and in my experience as Robin Cook's principal private secretary, a well-judged scene-setter carried more weight than the rest of the briefing put together. The latter would have been pulled together by a team of relatively junior officials in London, without a real feel for either the country or the visiting Minister. Moreover, senior officials in London had become lazy or diffident about editing work by more junior staff, and about making sure that it was in a state that Ministers would expect. The old Foreign Office culture of mentoring one's juniors had died away, though I tried in Kabul to do my best to teach and train the outstandingly talented, and committed, young diplomats in the Embassy. Both David Miliband and William Hague were to complain about the shoddy standard of the written briefing they received in London.

True to Afghan form, shortly before the Foreign Secretary and his party left London in late July 2007 a completely unexpected development threatened the whole visit. The news broke that Afghanistan's last King, Zahir Shah, had died. Zahir Shah had been deposed in 1973 by his cousin, Mohammed Daoud. He had been out of the country, in Italy, recuperating from eye surgery at the time. Daoud had established a republic, and had in turn been overthrown, and murdered, by the Communists in the Saur Revolution of April 1978. Zahir Shah and his court had stayed on in Rome, and the aged King had returned to his beloved country only in 2002. At the Loya Jirga (grand assembly) considering the Afghan constitution in December 2003, most of the Afghans present had wanted to restore the monarchy. But the Americans, led by the Afghan-American Zalmay Khalilzad, had over-ruled them: Afghanistan was to be a republic, with a highly centralised constitution focused on an elected executive president. Nevertheless, Zahir Shah had already come back home. He was granted the honorific title of 'Father of the Nation' (*Baba-e-Millat*). At President Karzai's request and invitation, Zahir Shah and several close members of the royal family had returned to their old apartments in the Arg Palace in central Kabul, where Karzai also lived (in a house in the grounds) and worked. The new President would call on the King every day, seeking the kindly old man's blessing for what he was trying to do.

Zahir Shah's main interest had been farming. As king, he had spent much time on his estates in various parts of Afghanistan. He had presided over what many Afghans had come to see as the *trente glorieuses* of their country's recent history. He had ruled with a light touch over what had been essentially a loose federation of Afghanistan's regions. His policies of gradual reform and democratisation had slowly brought Afghanistan into the modern era. It was Zahir Shah who had introduced the country's first democratic constitution, in 1964. And it was he who had allowed Khrushchev's Soviet Union and Eisenhower's America to compete in helping Afghanistan develop. The Russians had focused their efforts on the north, for example developing the gas fields there, and building the Salang Tunnel through the Hindu Kush.

The Americans meanwhile had concentrated on the south, particularly the Helmand Valley. It was there, in the 1950s, that American irrigation engineers had tried to replicate the success of the Depression-era Tennessee Valley Authority, with a vast system of canals and barrages intended to make the southern desert bloom. The present state of Helmand owed much to the civil and social engineering of the 1950s. Its fertility was due to the network of American-built waterways. The province had then been fertile enough to support dairy farming and the cultivation of cotton, and it was later to produce some of the world's bumper opium crops. But there had been problems too: the water table had risen, producing high salinity and areas of barren land that had previously been rich in crops. And the Afghan Government's efforts to settle groups from other parts of Afghanistan had produced a tribal mosaic of unmatched complexity – another source of future trouble. The neat US-style grid pattern of the streets of Lashkar Gah – itself a new creation – belied the darker realities underneath. Half a century later, British forces were to discover this to their cost.

In celebration of Afghan–American friendship, President Eisenhower had paid a state visit to Afghanistan in 1959, touring Kabul in a vast open American sedan – something unimaginable fifty years later. On his unannounced Thanksgiving visit to Afghanistan in December 2010, for example, President Obama did not even leave Bagram Air Base in northern Afghanistan: his only contact with the Afghan Government was a fifteen-minute phone call to President Karzai.

But the balmy days of Zahir Shah's reign were a distant memory when the world learned that Afghanistan's last King had died, on 23 July 2007. He had been sick for some time. I knew that, in line with Muslim tradition, the funeral would take place almost immediately, probably on the first day of the Foreign Secretary's first visit to Kabul. After a brief discussion with London, I recommended that the visit go ahead. My advice was that the interest, and prestige, of having the Foreign Secretary as the only senior foreigner present at the funeral would outweigh the disadvantages of the disruption to our carefully planned programme.

Thus it was that, after a briefing breakfast at my Residence, I found myself accompanying the Foreign Secretary to the ancient Arg Palace for the obsequies of Afghanistan's last monarch. Under the branches of the great plane tree beside the small mosque in the Palace quadrangle, we joined a throng of tribal leaders in turbans of all shapes and sizes. Ranged on one side were the Afghan royal family and the old royal court: princesses who knew the boulevards of Paris or Rome better than Kabul's mean streets; eccentric princes of various branches of the family, many of whom seemed to have been educated at Harrow School and still to live in north-west London; and courtiers, including several cousins, who had been brought back by President Karzai to senior jobs in his government. It was another world, another age, and one for which Karzai showed great deference and respect. He knew what most of his countrymen knew: that, compared with their country's present wretched state, Zahir Shah's Afghanistan had been a kind of Asian Arcadia, an obligatory staging post for young Westerners on gap-year voyages of self-discovery, at a time when Kabul had been a garden city, welcoming visitors from the subcontinent refreshing themselves away from the dust and heat of the plains.

Setting aside such dreams, we joined the line of those queuing to offer condolences to the senior members of the family, and then sat, on some hastily assembled chairs, on what had started as the front row of the mourning crowd. After a while the low boom of the bass drum and the somewhat cacophonous caterwauling of the band of the Presidential Guard announced the imminent arrival of the President, and of the King's coffin. With tasselled shakoes on their heads, high boots and red and black dress uniforms, the Guard goose-stepped out, in a surreal combination of comic opera and Soviet-style ceremonial.

Draped in the red, green and black Afghan flag, the King's coffin was lowered slowly on to the catafalque in front of us. The Koran was read, prayers said. And then the band started up again. The coffin was swung up high on the shoulders of the bearer party. The mourners, led by President Karzai, followed the band and the body on foot towards the city's vast parade ground. We formed a great rambling crowd, filling the street beside the rubbish-strewn dry bed of the Kabul River, walking in a silence punctuated only by the blowing and wailing and booming of the band.

After what seemed like an interminable wait on the parade ground, while further prayers were said, and lines of soldiers formed and re-formed, and marched and re-marched, in a rather ramshackle echo of Horse Guards, at last we moved up to the top of the low hill where Afghanistan's earlier kings had been interred. There, under the shell-punctured azure dome of his father King Nadir Shah's tomb, King Zahir Shah was finally laid to rest. In the July heat we milled around, as the Afghan Defence Minister, obviously feeling the heat, obeyed peremptory instructions from his President, personally shifting chairs and unrolling carpets to accommodate the swelling crowd. And then it was all over. Or so we thought.

Suddenly, there was the sound of a huge explosion. My Close Protection Team leader yelled 'Incoming!' He shouted at us all to take cover, as his colleagues did so, diving under our vehicles. Another loud boom followed, and then another. Only then did a rather shame-faced Royal Military Police captain realise that we were hearing the Afghan Army's twenty-one-gun salute, fired on one of their ancient Russian 130mm howitzers, not the first evidence of a terrorist attack. It was an incident we would not allow him to forget.

The rest of David Miliband's programme unfolded more or less as planned. Over the next three years the building blocks of such visits were to become all too familiar. For visiting politicians we always tried to include a meeting with representatives of Afghan 'civil society', as we liked to call it: NGOs, women MPs, religious leaders, activists of all kinds, people of courage and conviction, fighting to make their country a genuinely better place. Then there was the obligatory briefing lunch or dinner with 'internationals' – the ISAF Commander, the UN Special Representative, the US Ambassador, perhaps the Canadian Ambassador, the EU representatives (one from the Commission, one from the Council Secretariat), the NATO Senior Civilian Representative and one or two other prominent or persuasive internationals.

The choreography of such occasions varied only slightly: the visiting guest of honour would emphasise his government's support and admiration for all that those resident in Kabul were doing for Afghanistan, especially on the military side; he would ask a series of questions which purported to be penetrating, but which seldom cut through to the real issues; in response, there would be a table round, during which everyone expressed cautious optimism, stressing that the strategy was on the right lines, that the international (or national) effort was more joined up than ever, but that major challenges remained: the fault lay with the Afghans, who weren't responding in the ways that they should to massive international efforts to help them build democracy, prosperity and the rule of law. The meal would end with the visitor saying what a good discussion it had been, and everyone expressing mild satisfaction at the way things were going – despite the challenges that remained …

David Miliband was different. He didn't merely mouth platitudes. He was genuinely keen to learn. He said when he didn't understand, or wasn't persuaded. But however politely our local American guests listened to our concerns about the way they were running the war, all of us knew that the real decisions were taken in Washington, not in London or Kabul. And that what we on the front line thought or said or did counted for little back in the village beside the Potomac.

The next morning David Miliband had his first proper talk, over breakfast at the palace, with President Karzai. I confess that it did not go quite as well as I had hoped. The President was his usual charming and charismatic self. He conveyed his best wishes to the Queen and the Prince of Wales, and expressed his admiration for Britain in general and for the royal family in particular. He thanked us for what our troops were doing in Helmand. He moved on to explain why so many of Afghanistan's problems came from Pakistan, and alluded to his suspicion that the British Government was closer to Pakistan's rulers than it should be.

The Foreign Secretary tried to move off generalities to real and urgent issues: the state of security, the spread of the insurgency, government capacity, the training of the Afghan police and army. He got few substantive answers. And I learned later that President Karzai felt that the new young British Foreign Secretary hadn't been as respectful as perhaps he should have been.

We flew south to Camp Bastion and transferred to a Chinook for the fifteen-minute hop to Lashkar Gah. We were briefed by the British Task Force Chief of Staff and by the eager civilians of the Provincial Reconstruction Team. We met Governor Wafa of Helmand, with his long white beard, and old-fashioned manners and attitudes to match. From him we heard polite and wholly insincere courtesies about what British forces were doing, and promises about better government. It was a charade, and both sides knew it. And before we had had time properly to think or talk about what we had seen and heard, the Foreign Secretary was on the Royal Squadron's BAE 146 back to Bahrain, and I was on the C-130 to Kabul, wondering how I would frame the draft minute to the Prime Minister which the Foreign Secretary had asked me to prepare.

Sunday 26 July was not a good day. My diary tells me that I got up at six, and drafted a telegram reporting on the Foreign Secretary's visit, and the outline of the draft minute from the Foreign Secretary to the Prime Minister. Then it was the usual series of back-to-back meetings, ending with a dinner with internationals to discuss the Afghan National Development Strategy, a framework devised at the London Conference in February 2006, which was supposed to enfold all our efforts. But what spoilt everything that day was the news that the United States Government was planning to insist on going ahead with aerial spraying of the Afghan poppy crop, against our wishes and, much more important, against those of the Afghan Government. We had a fight on our hands, a fight which we would win only by telling the Afghan Government that HMG would support it in resisting US pressure to agree to spraying – to the fury of the US Government, or at least parts of it.

By the end of July, I had been in Kabul for only just over two months, and yet already I was behaving like an old hand. Such was the turnover of officials, and the pace of business, that everyone fell into the same trap: of substituting acquaintance for knowledge, activity for understanding, reporting for analysis, quantity of work for quality. I was determined to try to do better. So I did attempt in the months that followed to get to know as much as I could of the history and human geography of the country the West was trying to remake, or, as our forebears might have put it, prepare for self-government.

I also insisted that the Embassy staff should do the same. If we wanted, we could have spent all day, every day, in meetings with other members of the international community. But that was not why we were in Kabul. We were there mainly to understand and influence Afghanistan and the Afghans, and to report on both to London. We owed it to our troops to get out and about.

Chapter 7

The Spreading Virus

Within weeks of my arrival in Kabul, the team of diplomats and intelligence officers in the British Embassy came to realise that the outlook on the political and security fronts was trending downwards. None of us thought that things were going off a cliff. Nor did any of us judge that the situation was irreversible. But we did believe that, without 'course corrections' (the rather coy phrase I used when briefing visitors), the prospects for the Western effort to stabilise Afghanistan were not good.

I realised only much later that I had not understood in 2007 that in truth the underlying situation then was even more serious than I had been prepared to admit. That spring and summer I still thought that we would have a good chance of turning things round merely by adjusting our counter-insurgency tactics, reflecting lessons learned in Malaya, Algeria, Vietnam or Northern Ireland. I had not grasped the extent to which we lacked a coherent overarching political strategy. By nature an optimist, and eager to sound upbeat and constructive to London, I thus started work with the British Embassy team on two initiatives intended to raise our counter-insurgency game.

We did so against a steady drumbeat of indications that security was deteriorating across the country. It wasn't just the access maps provided by the UN, which showed fewer and fewer districts considered safe for operations by NGOs and other non-parties to the conflict. It was also anecdotal evidence from Afghans, who were no longer able, or at least willing, to visit their cousins in the provinces around Kabul or to travel by road to Kandahar. Added to this were the statistics of a steady rise in incidents, or SIGACTs (SIGnificant ACTions), recorded by NATO

53

forces, and by the reputable Afghan NGO Safety Office. We reported this to London, in a series of telegrams, as objectively as we could.

Although David Miliband and the Afghan team in the FCO, as well as civilian analysts across government, broadly accepted our judgements, the analysts in the Ministry of Defence's Defence Intelligence Service (DIS) were more doubtful. According to their analysis, security in Afghanistan had actually improved during the 2007 fighting season. What had not improved was the perception of security, which – the DIS conceded – was trending in the wrong direction. But the reality, they claimed, was that the insurgency was contracting.

Such problems were not unique to the British DIS, but affect, to a greater or lesser extent, all military intelligence services. The old joke about 'military intelligence' being a self-contradictory phrase is out of date: in my experience, nowadays most military intelligence officers are pretty able. But they are still serving officers, and part of a machine which understandably places a premium, especially in war, on optimism, loyalty and, to some extent, group think. In America as well as Britain, throughout the Afghan conflict we have seen distinct differences between the views of the military analysts and those of their civilian counterparts. For example, as the US media have reported, the analysts of the Central Intelligence Agency (CIA), deliberately kept quite separate from the Agency's operations wing, have been consistently gloomier than almost any other analysts, and more consistently right. In February 2011, the American press reported that the US intelligence community had refrained from revising upwards its estimate of Taliban numbers, in order not to upset senior US officers: one source reported that the intelligence community had accepted that issues bearing on the success of the US military effort in Afghanistan were 'outside [their] lane'.*

In three and a half years, I sat through scores of intelligence briefings on my regular visits to Helmand. Many were very good indeed. But too many showed little awareness of the situation beyond where the insurgency washed up against British forces, and thus no proper sense of the

* Gareth Porter, 'Deferring to Petraeus, NIE Failed to Register Taliban Growth', IPS Report, 14 February 2011.

underlying factors at work in Helmand. I remember in particular several excruciatingly simplistic descriptions of the tribal politics of Helmand (once it had become fashionable for us to 'understand the tribes').

Afghanistan has more than its fair share of geography, both human and physical, and of history. Understanding both as best one could was necessary, but never enough, for success. I had arrived in Kabul knowing only a little about Afghanistan's recent history, and was to leave knowing only slightly more. But that wasn't for want of reading and listening, whenever and wherever I could. Two periods interested me most: the Soviet intervention and the rise of the Taliban.

The story of the Soviet intervention has now been told in Rodric Braithwaite's authoritative account, *Afgantsy: The Russians in Afghanistan 1979–89*.* As he points out, the Soviet Union sent its forces into Afghanistan in December 1979 only reluctantly, and as a last resort, in response to repeated Afghan requests. They moved in, full of foreboding. Their motives were mixed, but certainly did not include access to a warm-water port on the Persian Gulf, as Western propaganda alleged at the time. The intervention was as much as anything to stop the Afghan Communist Party – the People's Democratic Party of Afghanistan – tearing itself apart. As with the Western intervention just over twenty years later, the Soviet move was meant to be temporary and limited. Inevitably, however, the Russians found that, once in, they could not easily leave, without destabilising even further a situation in which they had now become actors.

The story of the anti-Soviet *jihad* is relatively well known, thanks in part to films such as *Charlie Wilson's War* and books such as Steve Coll's remarkable *Ghost Wars*.† But much of the story is myth. The *jihad* was more chaotic and anarchic than many Western supporters of the resistance realised. The seven main *jihadi* groups were supported by Pakistan's Inter Services Intelligence directorate, and by the CIA and SIS (Britain's Secret Intelligence Service), using funds from Saudi

---

* London: Profile Books, 2011.

† London: Penguin, 2004.

Arabia and elsewhere in the Muslim world. Often they seemed to be fighting each other almost as much as the regime in Kabul.

And that regime was bad, but perhaps slightly less bad than Western propaganda suggested. The Russians had a deeper understanding of Afghanistan than many of their Western successors. Much of the trouble they encountered was the result of misguided efforts to modernise Afghan society. In this, they had some success with the urban populations, but less with the conservative rural people. When he became General Secretary of the Communist Party of the Soviet Union in 1985, Mikhail Gorbachev soon concluded that Afghanistan was a 'bleeding wound' (a sentiment echoed in 2009, by the then senior US General in Afghanistan, Stan McChrystal, in respect of the Marjah district of Helmand).

But it took the Soviet authorities another four years to extract themselves from the quagmire. They did it mainly by installing a strong Afghan leader, Dr Najibullah, and telling him to 'forget Communism, abandon socialism, embrace Islam and work with the tribes'. This he did, with some success. Out went the hammer and sickle, in came the crescent moon. Out went the People's Democratic Party of Afghanistan; in came the Watan or Nation movement. Najibullah's former viceroy in the south, General Olumi, was Deputy Chairman of the Defence Committee of the lower house of the Afghan parliament, the Wolesi Jirga, during my time in Kabul. He used to tell me how he had been responsible for the seven provinces radiating out from the southern metropolis of Kandahar, and how he had managed to stabilise them by working with, not against, the tribes.

As the commander of the Soviet Fortieth Army, General Boris Gromov, watched his son march across the bridge over the Oxus River on 20 February 1989, as the last member of the Limited Group of Soviet Forces in Afghanistan to leave, he little guessed that the regime the Russians had left behind would not only survive for three years, but defeat the Western-backed *jihad*, including in an epic battle later in 1989 during which the mujahideen tried and failed to take Jalalabad from the Afghan Government. What brought the Najibullah regime down, in 1992, was the collapse of the Soviet Union and Boris Yeltsin's decision to end all support, in money and kind (mostly arms and oil, but also food), to the Government in Kabul. No Afghan government in the last 250 years has survived without massive external subvention of one kind or another, and Dr Najibullah's government was no different.

When the Najibullah regime fell in 1992, there followed one of the darkest periods in Afghanistan's history: a bloody and bitter civil war between different regional warlords, many of whom are still active, and even in power, today. Most of west Kabul, and many other areas of the country, were devastated in the fighting.

As the last Taliban Ambassador to Pakistan, Mullah Abdul Salam Zaeef, has recorded in a remarkable memoir, *My Life with the Taliban*,* the movement began in the villages of Kandahar province in reaction to the depredations and anarchy of the warlords. The Taliban (from the Arabic for 'student') were religious zealots, who preached (and delivered) austerity, justice and a fundamentalist brand of Islam resembling the Wahhabi puritanism of the tribes of central Arabia.

Moving out from rural Kandahar, the new movement gradually took control of much of the south and east of Afghanistan. By 1996 the whole country, apart from the Panjshir Valley and one or two other pockets in the north, was in the hands of the Taliban. Given what the warlords had done to the country, it was perhaps not surprising that many Afghans, including Hamid Karzai, had at first welcomed the arrival of the Taliban in Kabul in 1996. The new authorities (if that is what they were) stood for law, of a sort, and order, and against chaos and corruption. They were ignorant and primitive and naive, but they could hardly be worse than the appalling anarchy which had preceded them. Only gradually did the cruelty and incompetence of Taliban rule sink in, particularly among urban populations with a more Westernised approach to life. For the educated and enlightened women of Afghanistan's cities and towns and villages, the new restrictions were especially appalling: a nightmare of medieval oppression, from which there seemed no escape.

One Afghan patriot, a Soviet-trained pilot who had reached a senior position in the Air Force under Communist rule, somehow stayed on

---

* London: Hurst, 2010.

through all this. He told me how much the Taliban disliked foreigners of all kinds. He saw the Taliban first and foremost as conservative religious nationalists, who stood for Islam, or at least an Afghan version thereof, and against outside influence of all kinds (except of course for that of their sponsors across the border in Pakistan). He spoke of the resentment the Taliban felt for the Arab 'guests' whose presence was known only to a few.

The extent to which the Taliban were aware of the horrors being plotted by Osama bin Laden and their other Arab and international guests has been much debated. For myself, I am persuaded that they were aware in general terms of bin Laden's interest in global *jihad* against the West. But I wonder how much they knew about the plans for the atrocities of 9/11. All of this has been analysed in detail in a new study by Alex Strick van Linschoten and Felix Kuehn,* the only two Westerners now living unprotected in Kandahar. They make the case for a sharp divide, in terms of both perceptions and operations, between the Taliban and Al Qaeda. It is a case which I and many others find close to conclusive, but it is an inconvenient one: as the US Special Representative for Afghanistan and Pakistan Richard Holbrooke once remarked to David Miliband and me, it suggests that, in the Western campaign against the Taliban, we may be fighting the wrong enemy in the wrong country – something the House of Commons Foreign Affairs Committee came close to saying outright in its report on Afghanistan, published on 2 March 2011.†

Plenty of contemporary accounts record the surprise and horror with which the Taliban and many Afghans greeted the news of the attacks on New York and Washington on 11 September 2001. Fewer witnesses report the turmoil which US and Western demands that the Taliban hand over Osama bin Laden and his lieutenants created among those then ruling most of Afghanistan. The same Afghan patriot who described to me life in the Afghan Defence Ministry under the Taliban also told me of the shuras (assemblies of elders) in Kandahar which

---

* http://www.cic.nyu.edu/afghanistan/docs/gregg_sep_tal_alqaeda.pdf

† http://www.publications.parliament.uk/pa/cm201011/cmselect/cmfaff/c514-ii/c51401. htm

debated the American demand. He was convinced that the tide in those discussions was moving in favour of expelling bin Laden, on grounds both of expediency (and survival of the Taliban government) and of justice (in that bin Laden had abused the precepts of *melmastia* or hospitality). But turning that tide into a majority would have taken more time than Western governments thirsting for violent revenge were prepared to give. After the humiliation of 9/11, America needed to kick some butt.

What happened after Western special forces, and intelligence agencies, helped the Northern Alliance (the anti-Taliban united Islamic front of ethnic groups mainly from the north) overthrow the Taliban regime, and drive the Taliban first from the north, and then from Kabul and Kandahar, is not for this book. But the key point is that the Taliban were not defeated then, or ever, but simply driven from power, and pushed out and down, south and east. The floodwaters had been pushed back, but they had not been drained. Worse still, at the hastily convened peace conference at the Hotel Petersberg on the Rhine outside Bonn in early December 2001 the vanquished were not represented: the resulting peace, and the political process that followed it, was a victors' peace, imposed without even the reluctant consent of those who had ruled most of Afghanistan for the preceding five years.

It was against that historical background that we in the British Embassy launched our two initiatives. The first stemmed from my early conviction (which grew the longer I spent in Afghanistan) that garrisoning the insurgency-infected areas of the Pashtun belt with troops from outside would deliver at best only temporary and local security. In many respects, it was immaterial whether those troops came from Peoria or Plymouth or the Panjshir Valley: American GIs, British squaddies and Tajik Afghan National Army soldiers (who did not speak Pashtu) were all aliens in the eyes of the Pashtun populations they were supposed to protect. Nor would we or any conceivable Afghan government ever have the force density to cover all areas in the south and east of Afghanistan then in the grip of the insurgents.

I remembered what a senior British officer had told me over lunch before I left for Afghanistan that spring. He said that, when coalition troops went into an Arab village to kill or capture members of Al Qaeda in Iraq, the inhabitants of the village would get out of the way, closing their doors and shutters and generally keeping a low profile: they had no wish to get involved in a fight. In Afghanistan, on the other hand, the risks were much higher. When a Chinook put down outside a Pashtun compound on a kill or capture operation, every male in the neighbourhood over the age of about ten would, rather than hiding, seize his Kalashnikov and come out to attack the intruders. In the British officer's view, Afghanistan was a much more dangerous operating environment than Iraq. In Afghanistan, or at least the Pashtun tribal areas, killing foreigners was a kind of national sport – a bit like village cricket in Sussex.

I also knew that in the nineteenth century Britain had discovered through long and bitter experience on the North West Frontier of the Indian Empire that the only way to pacify or stabilise the Pathan (or Pashtun) tribal areas beyond the Indus was to empower the tribes to secure and govern those areas for themselves. But we had taken more than half a century to learn this lesson. At first, in the 1830s and 1840s, and again in the 1870s and 1880s, the Victorian forerunners of today's neo-cons had advocated a forward policy, in which the British Indian Army and its auxiliary forces had themselves garrisoned the tribal areas. This policy, of trying to secure these areas ourselves, had resulted in the two disastrous Anglo-Afghan Wars of the nineteenth century. There had followed what was known as the modified forward policy, in which the garrisons from British India had been restricted to key towns and main supply routes. That hadn't worked either.

It had taken Lord Curzon, as viceroy of India from 1899 to 1905, to develop the policy which had kept the peace, more or less, on the North West Frontier for the first half of the twentieth century. Known as the closed-door policy, this had involved bringing British forces back east across the Indus and then using a network of political agents to get the tribes, or, more particularly, the tribal *maliks* (rulers) and elders, to take prime responsibility for security and governance. The political agents had been mostly officers from the Indian Army, who had transferred to the Indian Civil or Political Services and had spent an average of sixteen years on the Frontier between home leaves. One of them, Major (John) Gordon Lorimer, had produced what is still the best ever Pashtu grammar, published in 1902 by the Oxford University Press. A copy sits proudly on the shelves of the British Ambassador's office in Kabul. Lorimer's distinguished great-grandson, Major General John Lorimer, late of the Parachute Regiment, was the Commander of 12th Mechanised Brigade in Helmand for the six-month summer rotation in 2007 – and, almost as important, a lapsed classicist like me. John later became an outstanding MOD spokesman.

If, in those days, the tribes behaved, more or less, they were rewarded with bags of gold, or the equivalent. But, if they misbehaved, they were punished. At first, this was accomplished by columns of infantry and cavalry, such as the Malakand Field Force, so memorably described by Lieutenant W. L. S Churchill of the 4th Hussars in his book of the same name. Later, after the First World War, it was the Royal Air Force which was used to mete out the punishment, in what was described, in an Air Ministry pamphlet of the time, as Imperial Air Policing. (The American drone strikes in Pakistan are, of course, the modern equivalent of Imperial Air Policing.) The RAF, founded only in 1918, was in action more or less continuously on the North West Frontier between 1919 (when the Third Anglo-Afghan War ended) and the Partition of the Indian subcontinent in 1947.

With all that in mind, I recommended to London that we should encourage the Americans to look seriously at establishing a pilot scheme for what we called Community Defence Volunteers. The idea was simple: every male in the rural areas of the Pashtun belt had a Kalashnikov, or access to one. We should ensure that those guns were turned outwards against intruders, in the form of the Taliban, rather than inward, on whomever – if anyone – represented the Afghan Government locally, or on a rival tribe or drug mafia. The principle would be one of armed neighbourhood watch, or armed first response. The hope would be that such individuals, perhaps paid a small retainer, perhaps wearing a green armband or some other Islamically correct form of identification, would provide the first line of deterrence to intruders trying to intimidate the villagers. They would be provided with communications to enable them to call for help as soon as trouble appeared, but they would be expected to hold the line until that help arrived.

An essential condition was that any such local volunteers should be under the supervision of a tribally balanced assembly of local elders, as part of a wider political settlement, to be refereed by the UN and the international community more generally. Such volunteers would be there to keep the peace, once there was a peace to keep. Afghan forces of any kind, in or out of uniform, could not be expected to fight a full-blown counter-insurgency campaign.

I was keen to stress that we were not advocating the raising of militias, with uniforms and trucks and a formal structure. Instead, we were proposing something which went with the grain of tribal society in the areas where we trying, with very limited conventional forces, to protect the population. As one wag in the Embassy observed, it was not so much Dad's Army as Dadullah's Army: indeed the name harked back to the Home Guard, who had originally been known as Local Defence Volunteers. I also had in mind the system of *arbakai*, or tribal levies, which had protected Afghanistan's eastern border under the monarchy.

The other important point was that I was not suggesting that ISAF proceed full tilt with setting up such a scheme right across the insurgency-infected areas. Rather, I thought we should experiment with a pilot scheme which involved the Afghan authorities at least as much as ISAF forces. Such a test drive of the idea would require parallel political and economic progress. Only thus could one ensure that the volunteers were under proper political control.

This first idea received a generally positive reaction from London. Everyone could see the wisdom of at least trying something on those lines, and of how such an approach tracked with Britain's historical experience, in Afghanistan and elsewhere. An experiment made sense.

The same could not be said, however, of the second idea. Even before I had arrived in Afghanistan, I had been puzzled by the British Army's policy of rotating whole brigades through Helmand every six months. I knew that successful counter-insurgency needed experienced leadership, with detailed knowledge of the human as well as the physical terrain. It also needed leadership known to the local population, and known by them to be committed for the long haul. I was aware that Sir Gerald Templer had been asked to do a tour of at least two years in

Malaya, and that in Northern Ireland we had soon stopped rotating every six months the key brigade commanders in the province.

A further critical piece of background was that the standard US Army tour in Afghanistan at that time was fifteen months, *without* a break. The only exception to this was if a member of a GI's immediate family was dangerously ill. In my view, fifteen months without a break was far too long: many GIs, particularly those in some of the toughest bases in the eastern mountains, seemed to be sustained on their tours only by happy pills or the muscular brand of evangelical Christianity promoted by the US Army chaplains, or both. But there had to be a balance somewhere between the continual rotation of British forces and the excessive demands placed on American forces.

I therefore recommended to London, in the second of two telegrams, that we should look at the possibility of moving the senior British officers in Helmand, and other key officers, particularly those in intelligence, on to longer tours. They could do so on new terms, akin to those of the civilians in the field. Perhaps they could have the option of having their families quartered in the Gulf or Oman, or of a long weekend back in Britain every two months. The idea would be to establish a standing Helmand Brigade of the British Army. I also recommended that the fighting units, the battalions or battle groups, should continue to be rotated every six months, or perhaps at even shorter intervals, on a staggered basis, throughout the year, thus spreading the load on the RAF air bridge.

I gained some encouragement from learning that senior 'purple' officers in the Ministry of Defence (MOD) in Whitehall and at the Permanent Joint Headquarters at Northwood in Middlesex (PJHQ) – that is, those in tri-service jobs – were sympathetic to such an approach. But the top brass of the British Army did not favour such a change. The Army was organised on the basis of brigades, and fought on the basis of brigades. This was an Army matter, not one for civilians or the PJHQ to interfere in. This argument had a number of holes in it. One was that several brigades were formed specifically for the purpose of the Helmand tour, and dissolved shortly after returning to the UK. A second flaw was that operations which involved the whole brigade were few and far between.

But the main reason why I rather cheekily stuck my head above the parapet was my view that the six-month rotation system risked the British Army in Helmand continually reinventing the wheel. In three and a half years working in and on Afghanistan, I saw eight different brigadiers and their brigades in Helmand. Those officers were without doubt some of the brightest and best in the British Army and the Royal Marines. But, with important and laudable variations, I saw a pattern repeat itself.

Each brigade would spend months or even years preparing for deployment. Preparations complete, the brigade would be moved gradually out to theatre, under a procedure known as Relief in Place (or, more colloquially, as the RIP). As thousands of troops flew out from the air base at Brize Norton in Oxfordshire in one direction, so thousands flew back. The strain on the RAF's fleet of ageing Tristar troop transports was immense. Once in theatre, the brigadier and his team would work as closely as possible with the FCO and DFID teams in Helmand, as well as with the Afghans and, of course, the Americans. They clearly understood the importance of politics, particularly tribal politics, and of development. They grasped the need for strategic patience, and for consolidating the gains made by the previous brigade. They signed up to the 'comprehensive approach'.

And yet, in almost every case, each brigadier did what he could be only expected to do, as he enjoyed what had to be the highlight of his professional career as a soldier: commanding a brigade in war. He planned and launched a major kinetic operation. That is what soldiers do, with glory at the back of every half-decent warrior's mind. Each operation made local, tactical sense in Helmand. Each undoubtedly suppressed Taliban activity in its chosen area. Each might have happened even if there had been no six-month rotation system. Each was of course cleared through the ISAF machine. But, through no fault of the individual brigadiers, few of these operations were genuinely part of a serious overarching political strategy. None made more than a cursory nod in the direction of the US Army *Counterinsurgency Field Manual*'s reminder that counterinsurgency (or COIN) is mainly politics. Many consisted of little more than, in one Helmand brigade commander's memorable phrase, 'mowing the lawn'. If Ministers or officials in London questioned the need for a particular operation, they did so usually because they wanted to be assured that casualties would be kept to a minimum, not because they wondered how the operation fitted into a coherent national-level COIN strategy.

I was fortified in my conviction that longer tours for some officers made sense by an encounter during one visit to Helmand. A brave young officer who knew one of my sons came up to me and asked for a private word. He told a tale of disappointment. The efforts his battle group were making were just not producing lasting success. The strategy of training up the Afghan Army and Police to 'hold' areas 'cleared' by Task Force Helmand couldn't work in the timescales then envisaged. Much later, when he was back in England, he told me privately: 'many senior ... officers ... are covering up failings or trying to achieve short-term ... solutions which actually lead to longer term failings', adding, typically, that he would 'leap at the chance to go out again [to Afghanistan] tomorrow'.

Despite the initial rebuff, I kept up the pressure for a bit. But after a while I gave up, because, absent a coherent wider political strategy, the effort needed to make such a change hardly seemed worth the trouble. Yet, in January 2011, the *News of the World* reported what MOD sources were promising at last: 'TOP BRASS TO SPEND YEAR IN HELMAND'. We shall see.

The debate on CDVs or local defence forces ran on for years. The initial reaction from the Americans and the Afghans was sceptical. No one wanted a return to the bad old days of warlords and militias. Too many people had unpleasant memories of the way in which local private armies had terrorised Afghanistan between the fall of the Najibullah regime in 1992 and the arrival in Kabul of the Taliban in 1996. And there were more recent stories too, of how militias sponsored by Western agencies had driven the Taliban from power in 2001 and had had a free run of much of the country until NATO and the Afghan authorities had gradually asserted themselves. An Auxiliary Afghan Police Force had been raised in 2006, and then disbanded, for reasons which were never entirely clear to me. The US Embassy and the State Department were particularly hostile.

But, as the years passed, US forces started to experiment with rather more radical – and risky – ideas for raising local militia-type forces. So by 2011 this may have been an idea, invented this time in CentCom (US Central Command at Tampa in Florida) rather than in south London, whose time had come. But it will need careful handling. Back in 2007 we were probably too forward with our proposals. In the long run, however, Afghanistan will need some sort of armed neighbourhood watch scheme, but only as part of a wider political settlement which establishes representative local shuras of elders to whom such volunteers must be accountable.

Given that only 3 per cent of the soldiers in the Afghan National Army are Pashtuns from the south, some sort of more locally based recruitment for the Army has to make sense. Later in my time, I suggested that, in parallel with Community Defence Volunteers, we should look at experimenting with more territorial regiments in the Afghan Army, on the model of the British or Indian Armies. The principle would be unity through diversity, as any ceremonial gathering of British soldiers with all their different dress uniforms suggests. I always thought that the 1st Battalion The Helmandi Rangers, wearing some sort of local dress, might be more willing to garrison the Province than a mixed but predominantly Tajik unit of a homogenised Afghan National Army on a Soviet or American model. But, whatever shape the Afghan security forces take, the key point is that they can only help underpin a political settlement, they cannot deliver it – at least not an acceptable one.

The third area on which the British Embassy started to do some serious thinking in the summer of 2007 was what we then called reconciliation. By that we meant efforts to bring over at local or tactical level insurgents, either individually or in small groups. Our analysis made much of the different strands in the insurgency. Many of those we were fighting were said to be motivated more by greed than by ideology. There were the 'ten-dollar-a-day Taliban', paid to fight; the 'have-a-go Taliban', opportunistically joining the insurgency in order to secure material advantage for themselves; and the 'farmboy Taliban', who harvested their crops by day and fought by night. On the basis more of wishful thinking than of any detailed understanding of the insurgency, we expressed the view that, given the right carrots on offer from the Afghan authorities, many or even most of the insurgents would change sides.

The papers on this that we sent to London, and Lashkar Gah, and then to Washington, excited much interest. Everyone knew that all insurgencies that ended satisfactorily did so through a political deal of some kind. Patriotic Afghans knew this too, and, with our support, some of them started to put out feelers.

But we were naive in expecting reconciliation to occur on any significant scale in the absence of an overarching political process leading to a new political settlement. Just as the fighters of ZANU-PF would not have come in from the Rhodesian bush in 1980 without the political umbrella of a Lancaster House settlement, so large numbers of Afghan insurgents would not come in, and will not come in, until they can do so as part of a wider peace process. Of course, there may be local deals. And individuals, and individual groups, may change sides. But little will happen on the wholesale scale we need without the larger political framework.

Only later did we distinguish between what we later called reintegration (bringing over lower-level fighters) and reconciliation (deals with more senior Taliban commanders). And many of us underestimated the extent to which the insurgency was driven by ideas as opposed to more mercenary motives: much the same eclectic blend of fundamentalist Islam, conservatism, nationalism and xenophobia that had propelled the anti-Soviet insurgency. And ideas had to be fought with ideas. But our instinct – that the problem was in essence political, and needed to be treated politically – was right.

Chapter 8

The Great Game – Round Four

As I had already discovered, one subject always came up in every conversation with President Karzai: Pakistan. Like many of his fellow countrymen, Karzai was convinced that the source of many or most of his country's troubles was Pakistan in general, and the Inter Services Intelligence directorate (ISI) in particular. He believed that Pakistan had never accepted the removal of the Taliban – Pakistan's proxies – from power, and was striving by every means it could to restore the *status quo ante*. Karzai saw a Pakistani hand almost everywhere and in almost everything.

Worse than this, he believed that Britain was in league with Pakistan. Time and again he accused me of being too sympathetic to Pakistan, and of working for a government that was colluding secretly with Pakistan to control Afghanistan. He was convinced that SIS had especially close ties to Pakistan and operated in Afghanistan on Pakistan's behalf. The President's initially good relationship with General David Richards had been damaged when, towards the end of his nine-month tour as ISAF commander in 2006–7, Richards had travelled to Pakistan and returned seemingly more sympathetic to Pakistani views than Karzai had found acceptable. For President Karzai, Pakistan was a binary issue: either one was with Afghanistan, and against Pakistan, or vice versa: the middle was excluded.

Thus, in my first few meetings with President Karzai, he always steered the conversation round to Pakistan. His eyes narrowing, his voice lowering, he would ask me detailed questions about Pakistani politics – a subject which, thankfully, I understood even less then than I do today. As with many other visitors, I was being subjected to a thinly disguised *viva voce* examination on my soundness. Karzai's particular bête noire was President Musharraf. He had bad memories of the way President Bush had brought him and Musharraf together for what had apparently been a frosty trilateral dinner at the White House in September 2006. He never had much rapport with the Pakistani military. I suspect too that an element in his distaste for many Pakistani officers of the old school was his own rather ascetic Islamism (he neither smokes nor drinks, and his wife keeps purdah).

Sometimes President Karzai would become emotional about Pakistan, and about the need to reunite the Pashtuns/Pathans on both sides of the Durand Line. The Line was named after the senior official in the Foreign Department of the Government of India, a diplomat called Sir Mortimer Durand, who in 1893 had overseen the demarcation of what was supposed to be the border between Afghanistan and British India. The Line ran along the high peaks of the ranges separating the Indus Valley from the Afghan lands to the west. In doing so, it had cut in two the Pashtun tribal confederations in those mountains. Afghanistan has never recognised the Line as its eastern border.

Once, getting very excited, President Karzai told me that, if Musharraf did not accede to some particular demand (I forget what), he, Karzai, would personally head a Pashtun march on the Attock bridge across the Indus (the jumping-off point for many invasions in the other direction) and lead an attack into the Punjab itself. In this he was reverting, albeit briefly, to the Pashtunistan irredentism which Mohammed Daoud had adopted as prime minister and then president of Afghanistan. Like all his predecessors, Karzai believed that for him officially to recognise the border would amount to committing political suicide with his Pashtun base.

Despite this, I believed then, and believe now, that any serious effort to stabilise Afghanistan has to include a perspective or process leading to recognition of the Durand Line as Afghanistan's eastern border. As with the recognition of the inner Irish border, the aim should be to establish the Durand Line as the international frontier *de jure* just at the point when it had become *de facto* irrelevant, thanks to the creation of what I liked to call an economic Pashtunistan. There were, or should have been, parallels with post-war reconciliation between France and

Germany, and with the Schuman Plan for binding their two economies together.

With all that history in mind, I thought that there should be a massive international effort to connect the Pashtun tribal areas in the mountains on both sides of the Durand Line with each other and with the outside world, and to develop them economically, socially and politically. Infrastructure should be established to support and acknowledge the reality that the border was already an open one. The tribespeople of, say, the Afghan province of Khost were in most ways closer to their brethren in Pakistan's Federally Administered Tribal Areas than they were to their fellow countrymen in the urbanised areas of the Kabul River valley. As with Britain and Ireland, a Common Travel Area might be created, supported by a system of identity cards. Rather than trying to seal the border – which I had always thought was a quite impossible aim – we should be trying to keep it open, but in a controlled and benign fashion. That would enable both sides more easily to detect and deter the more nefarious cross-border traffic, in fighters and weapons and drugs.

Quite early on, stressing that I had no instructions from London on this point, I floated ideas on these lines with President Karzai. He looked suspicious but interested. I reminded him that Britain had negotiated for some three decades with an Irish Republic, Article One of whose constitution (amended only in 1999) had laid claim to British sovereign territory ('The national territory consists of the whole island of Ireland ...'). But that had not stopped us talking, in a mature fashion, about common-sense ways of addressing the double majority/minority problem. I was sure that, with goodwill, US and UN support and plenty of time, a similar approach was the only way of addressing the problems of the Pashtun areas. Months later I was delighted to discover that Bill Wood's predecessor in Afghanistan, US Ambassador Ron Neumann, and the American Institute for Afghan Studies (in a report published in November 2007) had separately reached similar conclusions. Karzai did not bite: his Government had neither the political strength nor, at that stage, the strategic vision to do so. Neither did the Americans, who listened politely but had other fish to fry.

In his approach to Pakistan, here was one of many examples of the President's Pashtun heart telling him one thing – authentically Pashtun – and his Afghan head telling him something else, rather more in the interests of the whole nation. While he remained distrustful of Pakistan, with distaste for that country, he knew in his head that he had to work with the Pakistanis in general, and with their leaders in particular.

Thus Karzai agreed to an idea which had somehow emerged from the awkward tripartite dinner in Washington: a joint Afghan–Pakistani grand peace *jirga*. This duly took place in the sprawling *jirga* tent on the western outskirts of Kabul in August 2007. Weeks of preparatory work by Ministers and officials from both sides, encouraged by quiet American diplomacy, produced an impressive gathering of the great, the good and the not so good from both sides of the Durand Line. An array of exotic headgear – every conceivable type of turban – and coats of many colours greeted the representatives of the Kabul diplomatic corps invited to observe the opening and the closing sessions. Useful conclusions were agreed, on further work by a series of sub-groups, and on holding more frequent smaller cross-border *jirga*s. Agreed, but never implemented.

President Musharraf turned up for the final session and spoke. Both sides then adjourned for a great celebratory lunch in the old *salamlik* or grand royal audience chamber of the Presidential Palace. At lunch I left the table reserved for ambassadors and seated myself among a mixed group of Afghan and Pakistani dignitaries – some of whom, on the Afghan side at least, had blood on their hands.

Two points stood out: first, how easily Afghans and Pakistanis got on. How much they had in common. How much history they shared, particularly those who had taken part in the anti-Soviet *jihad*, from either side of the Durand Line. Among the Pashtuns/Pakhtuns/Pathans, this familial intimacy was especially striking.

The embodiment of this was Pakistan's Ambassador to Kabul, Tariq Azizuddin, a blue-blooded Durrani Pashtun, from the same branch of the confederation as Karzai himself. Tariq had trained as a young officer with the Pakistani Chief of Army Staff, General Kayani, but had soon left the Army for the Pakistani Foreign Service. He was a man of high intelligence, great charm and real sophistication. Parties at his Residence were not to be missed, as they always achieved that critical mass of interesting Afghans and foreigners that, for a diplomat at least, is the point of entertaining, and being entertained.

Tariq had been part of the history of the troubled relationship between the two countries. At the Partition of India in 1947, Britain had gifted its former Embassy in Kabul to the new state of Pakistan and then promptly leased it back. In 1992, as the Communist regime fell and the warlords started to fight over Kabul, Britain had closed its Embassy and handed the premises back to Pakistan. In 1995, as Pakistani chargé d'affaires, Tariq had been inside the building when a Tajik mob from the surrounding neighbourhood had stormed the compound, killing his Defence Attaché. He never liked the former British Embassy, claiming that it was haunted: in 2007 he was one of those supporting the British Government's efforts to buy the compound back from Pakistan. In 2008, he was taken hostage by the Pakistani Taliban, driving back to Kabul from Peshawar: he later gave me an extraordinarily interesting and harrowing account of his ninety-six days in detention.

But the second striking point was how, alongside their Pakistani kinsmen, the Afghans came across as country cousins. The Pakistanis at the *jirga* seemed richer, better dressed, better educated, more sophisticated. Most spoke English with a curious mixture of exaggerated Oxford inflection and the more familiar soothing (and occasionally wheedling) tones of the subcontinent. Many spoke Pashtu, or Pakhtu, as the northern Pashtuns call it. Officious Pakistani officials were everywhere. President Musharraf was accompanied at every step by an impeccably turned-out military aide, carrying a briefcase containing, I suppose we were expected to imagine, the nuclear launch codes. The overall impression was of a government and a country rather more advanced than Afghanistan.

I knew everything was relative. But, as the Afghans struggled to put on a good show, and serve a decent meal in a cool room in a Kabul August, my heart went out to them. I could not help recalling that three decades earlier the boot might well have been on the other foot; or that in future the tide of fortune might turn again.

While Pakistan was, and is, the most important regional stakeholder in Afghanistan, it is far from being the only one. India is also a key factor in the conflict, and an essential ingredient for success and stability. And, while Karzai was viscerally anti-Pakistani, he was profoundly pro-Indian. He sometimes used to talk to me about his time as a student at Simla, the former imperial hill station. He claimed that it had been during his stay there that he had acquired his admiration for British imperialism and for all that Britain had done for India. He spoke of the Indian Civil Service, of the Grand Trunk Roads and of the railways. The railways in particular: Karzai loved railways, so much so that in 2008 I gave him, to the amusement of my staff, a slim volume, written by a railway enthusiast in Britain, entitled *A History of Afghan Railways*. In fact, there were no railways in Afghanistan in 2008. But there had been some in the past. They had included a British military narrow-gauge line crossing the border in the south, a Russian broad-gauge military line crossing the border (and thus the Oxus River) in the north, and, most memorably, a narrow-gauge railway running in from the Darul Aman Palace in west Kabul along the central reservation of the great tree-lined avenue there. And, in 2011, railways were once again starting to creep back into Afghanistan, from the north (being built or rebuilt by Turkmenistan and Uzbekistan), the west (Iran) and the east (Pakistan and China).

Warming to this nostalgic theme, Karzai once or twice said to me how much better he thought Afghanistan would have been for having had a period under British imperial rule. He had been fortified in this belief by the hours he said he had passed in Simla with an elderly Anglo-Indian gentleman who had retired there, but who had apparently seen service in New Delhi as Lord Mountbatten's valet when the latter had been viceroy in 1947. This old man had apparently imparted much wisdom to the young Afghan student.

Even if Karzai, like many Afghans, had not had such a positive view of India, the regional superpower would still have been a player in Afghanistan. Just as Pakistan feared encirclement by India promoting its own interests and proxies in Afghanistan, so India feared Pakistan once again in control of an extreme Islamic regime in Kabul that would export terrorism and fundamentalism across the subcontinent. For both sides, the conflict in Afghanistan was thus to some extent a proxy war. Pakistan alleged that India's intelligence service, the Research and Analysis Wing (known as the RAW), was up to no good in Afghanistan, and that there was a plethora of Indian consulates across Afghanistan whose sole or main purpose was to conduct intelligence operations against Pakistani interests. India's close ties with the Tajiks of the north were complemented by other links: the Pakistanis claimed that, alongside a generous programme of Indian aid to Afghanistan, focused on road-building and scholarships, Indian cash was being used for more nefarious – but generally unspecified – purposes.

Both the Indian Ambassadors whom I knew during my time in Kabul were Indian Foreign Service officers of the highest calibre, utterly professional representatives of the best of their country's public service. Both were very active, keeping in touch with politicians of all parties. Both had excellent access to President Karzai and his circle. Both were alleged to have distributed largesse, in cash and kind, to clients and potential clients, including in the Presidential Palace. Both oversaw generous aid programmes. Indeed, many of the other big players in Kabul were said to be doing similar things. Wherever the truth lay, it was clear to me that a stable Afghanistan would require India's consent and, probably, its active support.

The same applied to Afghanistan's western neighbour, Iran. Iran was and always will be a big shareholder in Afghanistan. It has close links to the Shia people of Afghanistan's central belt – the Hazaras – and also to the Tajiks and the other non-Pashtun peoples of the west and north, most of whom speak Dari, a dialect of Farsi (or Persian). Iran is a big investor in western Afghanistan, particularly the ancient city of Herat: the new railway line to Herat from the Iranian border is being funded by Iran.

Like most of Afghanistan's other neighbours, Iran has suffered collateral damage from the Afghan conflict: refugees, drugs, crime and violence have all flowed across the border. There are still about a million Afghan refugees in Iran, many of them there illegally, and often very badly treated. But the export of Afghan narcotics has done especial damage to Iran. Between 1979 and 2003, some 3,700 Iranian border guards and other officials are said to have lost their lives combating the traffickers. As a Shia state, Iran has always heartily detested the brand of Sunni fundamentalism represented by the Taliban. Relations between the two countries reached their nadir when, in 1998, the Taliban arrested and then murdered eight Iranian diplomats and an Iranian journalist who had been in the Iranian Consulate in Mazar-e-Sharif in northern Afghanistan.

Iran thus has no rational interest in continuing instability in Afghanistan, or in a Taliban victory. But pragmatic pursuit of national interest, and the divided nature of the Iranian state, has led Iran to pursue three parallel policies towards Karzai's Afghanistan. I discovered this for myself when, in late 2008, at the suggestion of our excellent Ambassador, I went to Tehran for talks on Afghanistan with the Iranian Foreign Ministry. It was striking how much our analyses had in common.

The first strand of Iran's Afghan policy, promoted by the Foreign Ministry and the Iranian Embassy in Kabul, is one of support for the Karzai Government and for the post-Bonn settlement. It is that policy that has led Iran to provide substantial sums of cash to Karzai and those around him, including his Chief of Staff, Umar Daudzai, a former Afghan Ambassador to Tehran who is widely regarded as Iran's man in the Palace.

The second leg of Iran's policy, promoted most directly by its intelligence ministry, is semi-covert support for its Shia co-religionists and for the Dari-speakers of the north and centre: this consists of cash for what was once known as the Northern Alliance, and for many of Karzai's political rivals. But it is said also to be reflected in great slices of Afghanistan's remarkably free media. Ironically, for a recipient of Iranian largesse, Karzai used regularly to complain to me about excessive Iranian influence in the Afghan press. He maintained that the style of many of the articles in the Dari media betrayed their Iranian authorship: sadly, I was in no position to judge.

The new Iranian-style blue mosque which adorns west Kabul, and is presided over by Ayatollah Mohseni, is also the fruit of Iranian largesse. But not quite all its support came from Iran: for reasons unknown to me, the British Council decided to offer some textbooks to the library of the small Shia university associated with the mosque.

The third, and most controversial, element in Iran's policy is that of covert support for the southern Taliban insurgency. Presumably, on the principle that my enemy's enemy is my friend, the Qods (or Jerusalem) Force of the Revolutionary Guard Corps is (or at least was) in touch from a base in south-eastern Iran with Taliban intermediaries. When we first decided to make these contacts public, in 2007, we were amused by the outraged reaction of, for example, the Iranian Foreign Ministry and the Iranian Embassy in Kabul. Their vehement denunciations probably reflected the fact that they had been blissfully unaware of a covert contact with the hated Sunni fundamentalists, a link that was deeply shocking to many Iranians.

The arrival of the US Marines in Helmand in 2009 must have provoked some puzzlement in Tehran: the Marines' policy of pushing as far forward as they could towards the border with Iran was not, as far as I could tell, authorised in Kabul, let alone Washington. I suspect that the exuberant US Marines were motivated at least as much by an interest in showing off the Marines' V-22 Osprey tilt-rotor aircraft as they were by geopolitics when they established, and then put down on, a landing strip virtually up against the Iranian border. A weary ISAF general complained that the US Marines in Helmand were out of control.

Iran's view of the situation in Afghanistan and of the American-led presence there mirrors that of many of the other neighbours and near neighbours. Iran does not want a great success for the United States or NATO in Afghanistan; nor does it want to see permanent American bases in the country, as some on the American right have advocated. But, equally and interestingly, Iran does not want us to fail and Afghanistan to succumb to a new round of civil war or to a Taliban takeover, at least in the south and east.

Russia took a similar approach, backing most horses in the race, except the Taliban. Like India and Iran, Russia is viscerally anti-Taliban. It fears the export of Islamic extremist violence from Afghanistan almost as much as it resents the flow of narcotics north and west across its territory. I was amused, in talks on Afghanistan, in Moscow, Tehran and New Delhi, to find myself in all three capitals agreeing in broad terms with almost all of my hosts' analyses, except when they each insisted that the only proper way to deal with the Taliban was to crush them by force. Gradually, as we promoted the idea of reconciliation and the need for a political solution, Russia moderated its tone. But elements in the Russian system, including the Ambassador in Kabul, Zamir Kabulov, continued to express great scepticism about the possibility of a political agreement incorporating elements of the Taliban. In this, they reflected the views of more reactionary Americans, and of hardliners both in Delhi and in Tehran (in the latter case, despite the covert programme of limited Iranian support for the southern Taliban).

China was more pragmatic. Its main interest was a stable and secure Afghanistan which was exporting minerals, particularly copper from the mine at Aynak on which China was proposing to spend some $3.5 billion, but not exporting drugs and Islamic fundamentalism to destabilise the Uighurs and the Muslim areas of western China. I remember the bright, fluently Anglophone Chinese Ambassador complaining mildly to me about NATO not being as successful as China had hoped in suppressing the insurgency. He was also, interestingly, enthusiastic about a British initiative to support small and medium enterprises in Afghanistan: not something one would necessarily associate with a member of the Communist Party.

Thanks to Lord Curzon and Britain's interest in establishing a bulwark between imperial India and Greater Russia, the Wakhan corridor – the finger of land which stretches up towards the high Himalaya between Pakistan and present-day Tajikistan – China is a direct neighbour of Afghanistan's. The three other direct neighbours – Tajikistan, Uzbekistan and Turkmenistan – were all engaged in different ways and in varying degrees, particularly with the areas of northern Afghanistan in which communities of similar ethnicity lived. But their lack of resources, their low diplomatic profile and their rather *ad hoc* national security apparatuses meant that they did not seem to us at the time to be serious players. But the long common border, and the shared economic interests in improved road, rail and pipeline links between Central Asia and South-west Asia, meant that they all needed to be engaged.

The same applied to two other near neighbours: Turkey and Saudi Arabia. Turkey had long regarded itself as a major actor in Afghanistan, mainly through its contribution to ISAF and through its sponsorship of the Turkic peoples, particularly the Uzbeks and their erratic leader, General Dostum. At least twice during my time in Kabul Turkey gave sanctuary to Dostum, a hard-drinking warlord with much blood on his hands. But its efforts to control and direct the wayward General seldom came to much. By late 2010 it was clear that Turkey was looking to back other, younger and less controversial horses in the Uzbek community.

Saudi Arabia's role was more potential than actual. I felt that, like us and the Americans, the Saudis had something of a conscience over their support for the anti-Soviet *jihad*, sowing the dragons' teeth from which Osama bin Laden and his monstrous terrorist engine had sprung. On my farewell call on King Abdullah of Saudi Arabia, he had expressed characteristically wise scepticism about the prospects for the Western military campaign in Afghanistan. But seeing the folly of a mainly military approach did not make it much easier to identify, let alone implement, an alternative. Saudi Arabia's genial Ambassador in Kabul distributed reasonably generous amounts of aid on behalf of the Saudi Development Fund, and he had good connections with many key players, particularly religious leaders. When, in 2009 and 2010, activity to promote talks with the Taliban got under way it was only natural that Saudi Arabia should offer to host such talks, under cover of the *hajj*, the pilgrimage to Mecca, or of an *iftar* or breakfast during Ramadan. But none of this amounted to an active role for the Saudi state.

Despite this, there were persistent allegations throughout my time in Kabul that the insurgency was being funded by wealthy individual donors from Saudi Arabia and its Gulf neighbours. At one stage, the Americans announced that they were launching an initiative to cut off such funding. But I never saw hard evidence of this. My instinct was always that the insurgency depended more on its own local sources of funding, including informal taxation of drugs and other traffic, and of course whatever came its way from its backers in Pakistan. But that is not to rule out the possibility that significant sums did occasionally find their way to the Taliban from rich sympathisers, or energetic collectors, in the Gulf. That was not, however, the financial foundation of the insurgency.

Thus, early in my time in Kabul it was clear to me that each of Afghanistan's neighbours was involved in the conflict there. More important, each had an interest in seeing Afghanistan stabilise and secure itself, thus gradually ending the export of terrorist violence, drugs, crime and refugees, all of which cost the neighbours and many of the near neighbours dearly. But, so far as I could see, neither the United States nor the United Nations had made any effort seriously or systematically to engage the neighbours in solving a problem which was, in the end, their problem. It was something which would have to await the arrival of a new administration in Washington.

Chapter 9

Hooked on Drugs

I have already (in Chapter 2) told the story of my bizarre first encounter with 'Chemical Bill' Wood, the US Ambassador who, apparently out of conviction as much as instruction, seemed sometimes to place almost as much emphasis on fighting drugs as on fighting terror in Afghanistan.

Thanks to Tony Blair's enthusiasm, Britain had landed itself with lead responsibility for counter-narcotics in Afghanistan. In London, and in Kabul, we assembled vast, multi-disciplinary teams of officials and agents and officers charged with working with the Americans and the Afghans on somehow collapsing the Afghan drug economy. In my first year in Kabul, I spent more time and effort on this subject than any other, almost all of it wasted. The energy and enthusiasm of our teams of young advisers knew no bounds. The funds we received from London seemed almost limitless. But in truth we made little headway in interfering with market forces far more powerful than the governments trying to counteract them.

Everyone knew two or three key 'facts' about the Afghan narcotics industry. First, and most important, that there was a symbiotic relationship between the insurgency and the illegal cultivation of, and trade in, opium poppy and its derivatives. In reality, money from the drugs business fuelled the narco-mafia who were in many ways the Taliban's most implacable enemies. In Helmand, for example, the Pashtun strongman, and ally of Karzai's, Sher Mohammed Akhundzada, who reputedly ran the province almost as a private fiefdom before the arrival of British forces in the summer of 2006, was widely believed to have been a kingpin of the drugs trade. The corruption associated with this trade, whether it was the vast sums of money allegedly siphoned off by certain Afghan Ministers and officials, or the much smaller sums appropriated by the wretched Afghan Police at their checkpoints, undermined the credibility and legitimacy of the Afghan state. In the eyes of many ordinary Pashtuns, Western military intervention was shoring up a state apparatus that was even more predatory and unjust than the only slightly less bad alternative offered by the Taliban. But it was true that, as the drugs trade spread, and as Western forces took a harder line against poppy cultivation, the Taliban quietly dropped their opposition to the trade. In many parts of Afghanistan, they did derive significant sums from 'informal' taxation of the trade, and political kudos from being seen to protect poppy farmers against the depredations of ISAF and what passed for the Afghan state.

The second 'fact' about the poppy business emerged only gradually during my time in Afghanistan: this was the belief that almost everyone in influential positions in public life was somehow tainted by the trade. Some were actively involved; others (probably the majority) were passive shareholders, or, more often and more likely, received a cut for not being involved, for turning a blind eye when the container-load of drugs passed through their province or district. How far the cancer had spread we never really knew. Throughout my time in Afghanistan, we believed that one of the main Afghan officials responsible for countering the drugs trade was himself actively involved in protecting the passage of drugs convoys through his home province. We believed that a senior official in the Interior Ministry, who had started 'clean', had within weeks of his arrival been seduced by promises of payments offshore in Dubai. We saw evidence of Ministers and officials living way beyond their means, in Kabul and, especially, in London, the Emirates or America.

The most persistent rumours surrounded President Karzai's half-brother, Ahmed Wali Karzai (AWK), in Kandahar. There was credible hearsay evidence to suggest that he allowed the drugs and other illicit trades to operate in areas where his militia exercised *de facto* control. And yet, for all our protestations of not tolerating involvement in the drugs trade, we allowed AWK to thrive, and continued to work with him. In late 2010, the British Commander in Kandahar, Major General Nick Carter, defended ISAF's engagement with him on the BBC, saying that ISAF dealt 'in facts, not rumours'. The Western press alleged that this was partly because certain Western agencies depended on AWK for intelligence and for co-operation in generating local militias.

For many ordinary Afghans, our engagement with people like AWK was proof of Western connivance in the drugs trade. But in reality the West lacked the will or the resources to remove and replace people like him. Insisting on AWK's departure would have shaken the West's relationship with President Karzai to its foundations, and might well have implied the latter's removal. And, at least as important, we just did not have the will or the resources to fill the vacuum of control and influence that would thus have been created. What applied to AWK applied in different ways and to different degrees to others occupying more senior, formal positions in the Afghan system. Indeed, almost the only person against whom there seemed to be no credible allegations of involvement in the drugs trade was the President himself. I never had the slightest reason to believe the suggestion put about in certain quarters that Karzai took narcotic drugs.

Ironically, however, Karzai's attitude to the drugs trade was rather more ambivalent – and authentically Afghan – than his personal lifestyle suggested. Over three years I had many conversations with him about the drugs trade, and about the corruption associated with it. I joined him in speaking at the launch of two anti-drugs campaigns, on national anti-drugs days. Here again there was a difference between what Karzai's head and his heart told him. On the one hand, he knew, intellectually and rationally, that drugs were bad, *haram* (forbidden by Islamic law) in fact, and that the drugs trade was rotting the Afghan state. On the other hand, his heart told him that this was really more of a Western than an Afghan problem: without the demand in the West for heroin, there would be much less of a headache for the Afghans. He also had a sneaking sympathy with Afghan farmers who earned their livelihood from growing poppy. He believed that, if they really wanted to, America and Britain were strong enough to eliminate the drugs industry, but that, for some hidden motive, they chose not to do so.

A final factor was that, for many poor Pashtuns, opium in various forms is the only anaesthetic to which they have ready access. There are no reliable figures, but often the easiest way of mitigating the symptoms of sickness in the remoter areas of rural Afghanistan is a dose of opium, particularly in the mountains in winter, when access is very restricted. And, for the miserably paid ordinary 'patrol men' (as they are called) of the Afghan National Police, the best way of making their unhappy lot more bearable may well be occasional consumption of opium. Thus it was not surprising that, in 2007, some 60 per cent of ANP officers from Helmand sent on ISAF training courses tested positive for consumption of opiates.

The third 'fact' about the poppy trade which everyone seemed to know was that the Taliban had successfully halted virtually all cultivation in 2001, but no one quite knew why. The optimists said it had been for religious reasons; the pessimists said that it had been in order to manipulate the market and keep prices high. The conclusion everyone drew from this was that the industry could be controlled, and that it was a market like any other. I believe that on both counts they were wrong. The Taliban were able to suppress the cultivation of poppy by using an apparatus of influence and control simply not available to a decrepit Afghan state present only patchily in the areas now dominated by the poppy industry. And the market was much less fluid, and less subject to the simple laws of economics, than many imagined. An example of the latter approach had occurred years before I had arrived in Afghanistan. Western officials had decided that they would simply buy up the crop in one Afghan province. Many were the times that I was asked in London, 'Why don't you just buy the damn stuff?' Well, one Western government tried, with disastrous results. The market grew rapidly, with producers ramping up output to meet rising demand fuelled by Western taxpayers' money. There was an analogy with what I had heard of America's weapons-purchase programme in Yemen: the result had been simply to raise the price of RPGs and Kalashnikovs and SAMs, with the Arabian Sea crisscrossed by dhows carrying weapons being turned out as fast as possible by Pakistan's artisanal arms factories to meet demand stimulated by American tax dollars. After one season, the Western opium-purchase programme was brought to an ignominious end.

Feeding the arguments in favour of legalised cultivation was the mysterious Senlis Council, allegedly funded by a Swiss pharmaceuticals billionaire and operating mainly through a courageous and colourful

Canadian QC, Norine MacDonald, who lived and worked in Lashkar Gah. Until the Senlis Council changed its name, to the International Council on Security and Development, and widened its focus, to the insurgency more generally, it campaigned incessantly for the legalised cultivation, under licence for medical purposes, of opium poppy in Afghanistan. In my view, the Senlis Council never explained satisfactorily how the economics of this would work, when countries such as Australia and Turkey could produce medicinal opium far more cheaply and with proper regulation. Nor did they explain how, absent security and governance, farmers would be prevented from producing illicit quantities of the crop, in addition to their licit production under licence. If the European Commission had difficulty policing the operation of the Common Agricultural Policy in certain Mediterranean member states, how much more difficult, not to say impossible, would it be for an Afghan government to enforce a licensing regime in the badlands of Helmand or Kandahar?

At the other end of the spectrum there were those who believed with ideological passion that the only way to deal with poppy cultivation was forcible eradication. President Bush told Tony Blair more than once that he was 'a sprayin' kinda guy', urging us to support aerial eradication. As on other Afghan issues, there were bitter divisions within the American system. The Drug Enforcement Administration was passionately committed to spraying. The State Department's Bureau of International Narcotics and Law Enforcement Affairs – known as INL – was more ambivalent. Paradoxically perhaps, the Pentagon and the US military were even more sceptical, fearing that forcible eradication, especially when conducted by aerial spraying, would jeopardise the counter-insurgency campaign. Those American senior officers and officials who really knew and cared about Afghanistan – the ISAF Commander, General McNeill, among them – realised that the Afghans associated aerial spraying of chemical agents with the Russians (however unfair the association might have been). An American attempt to do the same would have invited damaging comparisons between the two interventions.

As the debate raged back and forth, with pressure from 10 Downing Street for us to agree to some spraying, many of us either forgot, or did not know, that spraying had allegedly been already tried once since 2001. According to the *Guardian*, in a supposedly undercover operation in Nangahar Province in 2003, US aircraft had sprayed on a carefully selected area of poppy a chemical agent that was supposed to render the plants sterile or infertile, without changing their appearance. But word of the operation had leaked out, provoking furious Afghan reactions. The then US Ambassador, Zalmay Khalilzad, was alleged to have put out the word that this had been the work of the British – usually a foolproof escape strategy in Afghanistan.

Against that colourful background, it was clear to anyone who thought at all seriously about the drugs problem in Afghanistan that there was no silver bullet: neither of the extreme solutions would work – in fact, either carried out as its proponents wished would in the end have made the problem worse, not better. The boring reality was that the only sane approach was to tackle the cancer with a range of multiple therapies, designed to cut out the original tumour but also to treat both the causes and all the possible consequences of the disease. Diseased cells – illicit agriculture – needed to be replaced with healthy ones.

In this approach, there was a place for what we called targeted eradication. This meant eradication conducted either by the central Afghan authorities, using a small elite force of eradicators mentored by Western experts; or, less reliably, using governor-led eradication, in which local governors selected the target areas and used local resources to conduct the operation. Either way, spraying, from the ground as well as the air, was ruled out, as the Afghans were politically allergic to any use of chemicals in fighting poppy cultivation. So ground-based eradication tended to be pretty crude: small fleets of Massey Ferguson tractors drawing harrows, or, even worse, groups of soldiers or policemen flailing about with sticks or sickles and scythes, trying to beat the crop down. Such activity was very dangerous, with any or all of the local Taliban, narco-insurgents or angry poppy farmers itching to have a go at the lightly protected eradicators. Casualties among the latter were high, with desertion rates to match.

Despite these difficulties, in most experts' view there had to be *some* forcible eradication, targeted mainly at the kingpins who thought they could grow poppy with impunity. The purpose was simply to show key figures in the narco-insurgency that no one was immune from action by the legal authorities.

Much more important than eradication, however, were measures to encourage Afghan farmers to seek alternative livelihoods to poppy. This meant taking steps to ensure they could grow crops other than poppy, find buyers for those crops and then obtain a price for them that would make the whole thing worth while. Market access was critical. One of the advantages of choosing poppy was that the crop was collected by the dealers from the farm gate, and that loans – known as *salam* payments – were available from the dealers in advance, with which to meet living expenses and other costs. Intervening in the market to create the conditions in which farmers would choose alternatives to poppy was not easy. But various programmes did meet some success, including in 2008–9 a wheat-seed distribution programme in Helmand. I was, however, always instinctively uneasy about giving farmers free or heavily subsidised handouts. Something for nothing meant that the farmers were not really invested in the success of the programme, and that the risks were high of reversion to the *status quo ante* once the Western intervention ended.

What common sense, and figures and maps from the UN Office on Drugs and Crime, suggested was that, where there was security and governance, poppy cultivation came down. Where the Afghan Government was not present, or present only patchily, then the drugs trade flourished. Over my three and a half years working in and on Afghanistan, the geographical focus of the poppy industry narrowed to the provinces – mainly Helmand – where the insurgency was worst. Gradually, year by year, provinces in the north and east were declared poppy-free. Total cultivation came down. But I doubt whether the part the whole narcotics industry played in promoting instability, illegality and disorder was reduced.

In early 2009, the whole pack of cards was thrown up in the air by Richard Holbrooke's arrival as US special representative for Afghanistan and Pakistan. Encouraged by his adviser Professor Barney Rubin, Holbrooke was opposed to any eradication. He believed that the answer to the poppy industry was the aggressive promotion of licit Afghan agriculture. In this, neither he or nor Barney was wrong – it was just that they weren't right enough. After several months of debate, Holbrooke ended all US support for centrally directed eradication – the only form of eradication that could be relied upon to be reasonably impartial. Reluctantly, he conceded that he would not stand in the way of governor-led eradication, even though he acknowledged that such locally inspired measures were too often directed at the political rivals of the governor in question. Britain had reluctantly to go along with these virtually unilateral changes, which puzzled some Afghans almost as much as they delighted others.

The Bush Administration had seen forcible eradication, Colombia-style, as the best means of dealing with poppy cultivation. The Obama Administration took exactly the opposite view, wanting to end all eradication, thus depriving us of a secondary, but nevertheless important, tool for deterring the poppy cultivators. Here, in cameo, were the difficulties of working with a power whose policies could be driven as much by ideology as by informed understanding.

Chapter 10

Coping in Kabul

Life in Kabul soon settled into a routine. I came to feel at home in my small flat, and to enjoy the company of my books, my computer and my bodyguards. Even though the sense of danger from a terrorist attack was always present, and grew gradually worse, we civilians in Kabul were lucky compared with our colleagues in Helmand and our troops on the ground. We needed never to forget that: for most of us in the Embassy, regular visits to Helmand were an important means of keeping our life and work in Kabul in proper perspective. We had our diplomatic job to do: it was very hard work, and in the end it might have been more important in resolving Afghanistan's problems than the military campaign. But, on a daily basis, that campaign was far more difficult and dangerous than our regular lot.

My day began at 5 a.m. I would check the BBC News, Google News and *Guardian*, *Telegraph* and *Times* websites. I would answer emails. I would do the 'box': a locked briefcase full of papers for me to read, sign or comment on, prepared the previous evening by my Private Secretary, Alex Hill. There were folders for papers for action, for reading and for signature. The working day was so busy that I seldom had much time to process paper, let alone read, in the office: hence Alex would print off the key papers, and sort them, for comment by me overnight.

At six-thirty sharp I was off, with the bodyguard on duty, to the Embassy gym, in a couple of containers joined together, in the Poddington area of the compound. At that time there were always enough clients in the gym to make it feel used but not crowded: a few Special Forces types, showing off; some security guards trying to pretend they were Special Forces; a couple of blokes from the Serious

Organised Crime Agency, trying to reduce their paunches; plus a girl or two from DFID or the Embassy drugs team jogging in time to their iPods. Compared with the gym in Lashkar Gah, which was populated at all hours by soldiers pumping iron, the Embassy gym was less intimidating. Given the age and weight of some those working out in Kabul, I found it mildly reassuring.

At seven sharp, it was back to the Residence, for breakfast – always porridge, even in summer. The porridge had become a tradition, ever since on arrival I had asked if there was any – with cholesterol-reducing oats in mind – only to find that the Residence staff assumed that I meant porridge every day.

By 7.45 a.m. I was on my way across to the Embassy, where Alex and the Assistant Private Secretary (for most of my time, the outstanding Christine Carson, who had served with me in Riyadh) would have opened up the office, and the computers, before going to get their own breakfast in the Embassy canteen. Then it was an hour or so of catching up on the overnight classified email and telegram traffic from London, Washington, New York and so on. Occasionally a representative of one of the intelligence agencies would pop in to brief me on some development or other.

Then, at nine sharp, the Embassy daily meeting: a summary of the telegrams by someone in the Political Section, a security update from the Chief Overseas Security Manager, an update on military operations from the Defence Attaché, and a round-up of the British, international and Afghan media from the Press Section, followed by a table round of all the Embassy Sections represented at the meeting: Political (Internal and External), Politico-Military Affairs, Counter-Narcotics, Justice and Rule of Law, Defence, Development and so on, plus a video link to the team in Helmand. It was all over in theory by 9.30 a.m.

And then meetings, meetings, meetings, in and around the Embassy, in restricted areas and less restricted areas, keeping up with the work of a team that had grown to 150 by the time I ended my first tour as ambassador in February 2009. Plus calls on other ambassadors, on generals, on Afghan ministers and ministries. At least twice a week there would be meetings convened by the UN Special Representative, in what was known as Palace Seven. A restricted group would meet first, then a wider group, denominated by the somewhat precious ellipses beloved of diplomats: the Tea Club, the Coffee Club and so on. I tried to see the American Ambassador, alone, at least once a week.

And then there were the meetings at the Palace. I would seek private audiences with President Karzai only when I had serious business to transact, or an important visitor to accompany. I did not want to waste his time, or devalue the currency, especially as I was trying to encourage him to spend less time seeing visitors, and more time governing. But every Thursday morning, more or less, the US Ambassador, COMISAF (Commander, ISAF) and I would troop into the President's study for a meeting of what we called the war cabinet. Those attending on the Afghan side varied according to Karzai's mood, the subject matter and the efficiency of what passed for a Presidential secretariat. But those most often there were the National Security Adviser, the clever, quiet and kindly Dr Zalmay Rassoul (from 2010 Minister of Foreign Affairs); the Minister of Foreign Affairs, Dr Rangin Spanta (a decent German-educated former Maoist academic, who still spoke better German than English); the brave Pashtun Defence Minister, General Abdul Rahim Wardak, big in heart and body; the head of the Afghan intelligence and security service, the young Tajik from Panjshir, Amrullah Saleh; and the President's Chief of Staff, Umar Daudzai.

With the President and the American Ambassador seated in the armchairs on either side of the fireplace, the foreigners and Afghans ranged themselves on two sofas facing each other. Apart from the President, who talked almost non-stop, usually none of the Afghans would speak, unless spoken to. Among the foreigners, the American would speak most, with me intervening, usually in support: we tried never to disagree in front of Karzai. Neither of the ISAF commanders who attended while I was ambassador, General McNeill or General David McKiernan, was particularly at ease in what they saw – rightly – as a somewhat phoney setting. Preparations for, and follow-up from, the meetings directing the campaign in Afghanistan were rudimentary. Often President Karzai would be bending over his desk jotting down a list of subjects he wanted to discuss as we entered the room. As far as I could tell, no proper minutes were taken or records circulated. I would take notes, and dictate a record either in the car back to the Embassy or as soon as I returned. But I doubt that any of the other participants did the same.

At lower level, in my first year or so in Kabul there were weekly meetings at the Palace of a group invented by General David Richards when he had been the ISAF commander: the Policy Advisory Group. This had started as a meeting of representatives of the nations mainly concerned with the campaign in Regional Command (South) – the US, the UK, Canada and the Netherlands – but had gradually grown to include most of the major troop contributors, plus the UN and the EU. As membership widened, however, so the level of attendance on the Afghan side had fallen away. The meetings degenerated into stock occasions, with no real debate, no serious decisions taken. After a year or so, they became irregular, and eventually died altogether.

On the development side, there were also irregular meetings of various committees and groups set up to monitor how Afghanistan was getting on implementing a huge number of detailed commitments it had made to the international donor community in return for aid. Many of these had been enshrined in the Afghanistan Compact, signed in London on 1 February 2006: the Afghan National Development Strategy flowed from this. Through most of my first year in Kabul the Afghans were slaving away with their international mentors to finalise the strategy. Established under the Compact, the Joint Co-ordination and Monitoring Board was the development equivalent of a sung high mass, with the cardinals of the whole international and Afghan effort present. It met in full session every six months or so, and achieved little.

By far the most interesting of the international meetings I attended were the weekly private sessions I had with the American and Canadian Ambassadors. At these we would tell each other exactly – more or less – what we thought, and commiserate about the problems we faced in capitals as well as Kabul. But, for all the worries and all the confidences, both my American and Canadian colleagues remained utterly professional: if indiscretions were let slip, it was usually for good and carefully calculated reason. Our offices called these meetings the ABC Club – partly to put off other ambassadors who would want to join any group to which they did not belong.

For most Westerners, the Kabul working week ran from Sunday morning until Thursday evening. Fridays were almost always a day off – though, if senior visitors were around, they had to be entertained. Saturdays were more ambiguous: some international meetings were held then, but in the British Embassy at least we tried to discourage people from going into the office. Living on site meant that too many people spent too long in the office anyway: it was not uncommon to see the lights on in the Embassy at ten at night, as people returned to their desks after supper. Afghan Ministries did, however, work what was supposed to be a six-day week, although in practice for all but Ministers and the most senior officials working hours were patchy and variable. The military – especially the American military – worked the hardest of anyone. Or at least they spent the most hours in the office. At ISAF HQ, the first meetings of the day would start at 7 a.m., or sometimes earlier, and, because of the time difference with Washington and Tampa, continue late into the night.

The bane of our lives was the video conference with capitals. Usually convened at times to suit participants at home, one would find oneself sitting for hours on end alone in one of the Embassy rooms equipped with a video link, trying to follow, via a hazy screen and a fuzzy voice link, a debate among officials in Whitehall. For particular subjects, other posts, such as the UK Delegation to NATO in Brussels, or the British High Commission in Islamabad, or our Embassy in Washington, would be patched in. Almost everyone in the Embassy seemed to be caught up in such meetings at one time or another. They were necessary, and important. But they did seem to us on the ground to take up inordinate time. And, for all the improvements in technology, the participant at the wrong end of the video link still felt like an outsider, who should not speak unless spoken to.

To his credit, David Miliband was an enthusiast for involving Embassies and Ambassadors in helping formulate policy. I would speak to him regularly on the secure phone, and take part, by video link, in virtually all the Foreign Secretary's Office Meetings on Afghanistan. This had real benefits, for coherence and inclusivity. But there was a penalty to be paid, in terms of hours spent as a silent witness as officials in London, with more views than knowledge of what was really going on in Afghanistan, each took their turn to show off to the Foreign Secretary.

Back in London there was an alphabet soup of committees supposedly co-ordinating the British effort in Afghanistan: a Ministerial Committee, usually chaired by the Prime Minister; an informal trilateral meeting of the three Cabinet Ministers directly involved – the Foreign, Defence and Development Secretaries; an Afghan Strategy Group; an Afghan Senior Officials' Group; and others for specialised subjects such as media handling. All of these fed two illusions: first, that Britain could somehow have an independent strategy towards Afghanistan, and, second, that British Ministers could direct the military campaign in Afghanistan – in reality the military took their orders from the NATO command chain. But neither illusion stopped us spending many hours in often impassioned debate.

I soon realised that all this 'co-ordination' meant that one could easily spend the entire working week in Kabul doing little else but preparing for, attending or recording meetings with fellow Westerners, within the British system or outside it. 'Co-ordination' was little more than a long synonym for 'meetings'. To be a busy and reasonably successful player in the Western effort in Afghanistan, one didn't actually have to engage with Afghans, still less with the country in which they lived; one just had to 'co-ordinate' what one was doing. I suspected that many of my fellow Ambassadors, without the resources available to me, spent most of their time 'co-ordinating'. That was why we made such efforts to ensure that the British Embassy engaged with Afghans, in and out of government. We had constantly to remind ourselves that they were the primary reason for our being in Kabul.

Another major preoccupation was the unending stream of high-level visitors from London. Both the American Generals who commanded ISAF during my time as ambassador complained to me that they had to see more senior military visitors from Britain than from any other nation, including their own. But one could hardly blame the desk-bound generals back at home for longing to get out into the field, to see the men and women of their corps/branch/arm/division on the front line of the first proper war in a generation. And, we had to admit, it was fun, dressing up in desert camouflage, donning helmets

93

and body armour, and leaping in and out of helicopters and armoured personnel carriers.

Each senior international visitor, civilian or military, had to be given a programme of calls which accorded with his or her estimation of their own importance, each accommodated and transported securely. The handful of serious Ambassadors in Kabul found themselves endlessly attending briefing suppers arranged by their colleagues for visitors from their respective capitals, with the same routine at each event. Perhaps two or three evenings a week would be taken up with such occasions: security meant that invitations would be issued only a day or two before the visitor arrived. We all became used to being summoned at short notice to such events, often without knowing who the VIP in question was. All our tidy notions of the need for careful planning had to be set aside.

Getting me from event to event, from meeting to meeting, location to location, were the team of three outstanding Afghan drivers allocated to the Ambassador on a rota basis, and my Close Protection Team. The latter's professionalism, humour and common sense got me through the day, smoothing away the stresses of operating in a high-threat environment that could at times also be pretty chaotic.

Everyone in the Embassy worked extremely hard. But I tried to make sure they took time off too. Morale seemed generally high. Successive inspectors of different kinds from London confirmed this. In part, of course, this was the comradeship of adversity. Drawing on my experience of tough times in Israel and in Saudi Arabia, I decided that we should set up an Embassy magazine. Thanks to a group of talented and remarkably selfless volunteers, many of them improbable amateur journalists, the *Kabulletin* was born: full of useful information, news on arrivals and departures, competitions, gossip, jokes, articles on interesting things to do and places to visit. It was a powerful tool for building a sense of community in the Embassy and among and between teams from very different professional and personal backgrounds.

In an environment like Kabul drinking could be a problem. Under General Order Number One, American soldiers in theatre were not supposed to consume alcohol, and few if any did. But, until General McChrystal's arrival, the bars at ISAF headquarters and elsewhere served alcohol. So did the restaurants in Kabul, provided the purchaser was a foreigner. Many a thirsty British officer would welcome the chance of a quiet pint or an evening whisky at the Embassy.

The British Embassy bar, in a couple of Portakabins at the edge of our vehicle park, was an unending source of entertainment, and problems. As different groups cycled through the Embassy, the bar would reinvent itself. Regular refurbishments kept it looking reasonably smart. A competition produced the official name: the Inn Fidel. But too many Embassy staff spent too many evenings drinking late in the bar: we never achieved a completely satisfactory balance. The nadir came when an otherwise excellent Conflict Prevention Adviser sent out by DFID somehow became involved in conflict in the bar. I had to summon him to my office and ban him from the bar for three months, feeling more than ever like the headmaster of a bizarre boarding school.

For many of the women in the Embassy, most of whom were single, the bar could be an intimidating place. It was often populated by disproportionate numbers of expatriate security guards, giving it a Wild West feel. The ubiquitous dress – beard, safari jacket, combat trousers, boots – disguised a multitude of different occupations, from a host of agencies, civilian, military and paramilitary. It all added to the excitement of the place – the frontier atmosphere – but could also produce unhappiness: whenever the Australian Special Forces rotated out of town they seemed to leave behind more than a few broken hearts in the British Embassy. Too many believed the digger commandos when they claimed they were single. As one disappointed single girl remarked bitterly, in Kabul 'The odds are good, but the goods are odd.'

Perhaps rashly, and again drawing on my experience in Saudi Arabia, I thought we should institute a British Embassy Charity Ball, to raise money for Afghan charities, but also to bring together the wider Western community. Again, an enthusiastic group of volunteers, mainly from DFID, stepped up to the plate. The plan, which worked more or less, was to hold one ball in the summer and one in the winter. We made sure that any military who were able to come, including visitors from Helmand, received invitations.

The first British Embassy Charity Ball, in August 2007, was held in a great tent erected specially for the purpose on the Embassy sports pitch.

Some of the Afghans who attended said that it was the first such occasion since the early 1970s – and they were probably right. The tailors and seamstresses of Kabul certainly thought so, as they were deluged with orders to make dinner jackets and ballgowns not seen in the Afghan capital for more than three decades. After much drama, and a huge last-minute demand for tickets, the first ball was a big success – so much so that it was crashed by, predictably, a posse of Australians.

But large sums of money were raised for charity, and morale was given a boost. The relationship between the British Embassy and the wider international community was, I liked to think, pretty good. We were much more outward-facing and hospitable than our American colleagues. And I always took the view that we should aim to be as inclusive as possible, reaching out to other nationalities living and working in Kabul, and to all the other groups operating there, whether they were journalists, or aid workers, or the handful of expatriate professionals. We were all in the same boat, facing the same daily threats and challenges: if we could help build a wider sense of common purpose, that was all to the good.

Ever since I had served as press attaché in the British Embassy in Cairo in the early 1980s I had tried to implement the advice I had been given then: if we in government treated the press as grown-ups, they would behave like grown-ups. I remembered an SIS officer in Cairo telling me that he treated the outstanding BBC correspondent there, Bob Jobbins, as if he were 'Cleared up to CONFIDENTIAL' – meaning that he would tell Bob information classified as high as Confidential. He did so on the grounds that Bob was a responsible, and exceptionally scholarly and well-informed, journalist: if Bob was offered unambiguous ground rules for a briefing, he would stick to them. At least as important was the fact that we diplomats learned as much from good journalists as they learned from us.

With all that, and my experience working for Robin Cook and as ambassador in Israel and Saudi Arabia in mind, I was determined to treat the Kabul foreign press corps as adults. I was not going to give them 'happy talk' which neither they nor I would believe. Nor was I going to mislead them. The best among them knew far more about what was really going on, in the insurgency and across the country, than we diplomats did, sitting in our compounds, cocooned by close protection teams.

As it happened, one of the most impressive foreign journalists in Kabul, Carlotta Gall of the *New York Times*, had been known to my family as a girl. Carlotta's sisters had been in the Pony Club with my brothers in Kent. Her father, Sandy Gall, had travelled into the Panjshir as an ITN correspondent during the anti-Soviet *jihad* in the 1980s, and had written several books based on his experiences. He had also established back then a charity which still in 2007 provided prosthetic limbs for young Afghans disabled by landmines and other instruments of war, and was run by another of his daughters. It gave me great pleasure that Sandy received a second honour (he was already a CBE) in the 2011 New Year's Honours List.

Other journalists too had acquaintances in common with me. Tom Coghlan of *The Times* came from a street or two away from where I had lived in south London. His father could be spotted on Clapham Common wearing an Afghan *pakhol*. Tom reported on the conflict with enormous courage and perception, both as an 'embed' and, most dangerously, travelling independently. Another brave correspondent, Miles Amoore, knew one of my sons. Others included the exceptionally gifted Jon Boone, who migrated from the *Financial Times* to the *Guardian*, and the enterprising and courageous Jerome Starkey, who could turn out lapidary prose for the *Sun* just as easily as he could produce more thoughtful pieces of limpid clarity for the *Independent*.

Jon and Jerome shared a house in Kabul, where they entertained generously and amusingly. But I was not sure how amused I should show myself to be (in fact I *was* very amused) when they adopted a street dog who turned up during one of their dinners, at which I was present, and then named it after the British Ambassador. I found it slightly unnerving to read on their Facebook pages that they had taken Sherard for a walk, or that Sherard was off his food, or, worst of all, that they had had to take Sherard's temperature by inserting a thermometer up his bottom.

The BBC in Afghanistan were in a class of their own: with their network of correspondents across the country, they had better coverage than anyone else. Their bureau chief for my first two years, Alastair

Leithead, was an unfailing source of gossip, good food and clear-eyed analysis.

I liked all these journalists, and I trusted them. And that trust was never misplaced. They were working extremely hard to cover the story of their lives, a largely American war admittedly, but one in which there were many other players with proportionately at least as much at stake as the Americans had. And they faced much the same dilemmas and dangers as all war reporters have faced down the ages. War is ugly, and messy, and unjust, and cruel, fought for a mix of motives. But the home populations who send their sons and, increasingly, their daughters to fight and die in a far-off foreign land cannot bear too much reality. Understandably enough, the British red-top tabloids feel the need to back 'Our Boys', as the *Sun* has shown through its 'Millie' awards.

A particular difficulty for the journalists in Kabul is the physical danger of covering the fighting. Combat makes good, if somewhat repetitive, copy, and even better television. But the days are long gone when William Howard Russell of *The Times* could sit on a nearby hill-top and observe the fighting through his telescope: the modern journalist needs to be embedded with the fighting troops. And, in accepting an embed, he or she can be compromising, both implicitly as well as explicitly (in any agreement he signs), his objectivity. Morally it is difficult, having been under fire with extraordinarily courageous young men, to write negative things about what they have done, or call into question the point of it all. That is of course one reason why defence ministries are eager to embed journalists.

Defence correspondents are especially dependent on the military, and the MOD or the Pentagon, for access and information. But they can risk becoming little more than unofficial military spokesmen. Quite legitimately, the military news machines have their own agenda: to create the impression of unstoppable progress, and to boost support at home for the military in general and the campaign in particular. They also want the troops – all of whom are volunteers and have other options – to feel that their sacrifice is properly reported. Few things are worse for a soldier who has spent six months in Helmand fighting the most serious war in a generation than suspecting that his efforts are neither understood nor appreciated at home.

Just occasionally, an embedded journalist does write something less than complimentary about his military hosts, as when the British writer Stephen Grey, embedded with the US Marines, questioned the strategy behind their thrust down beyond the 'fish hook' in the Helmand River in the extreme south of the province.

The social centre of the foreign community in Kabul was the Gandamack Lodge: a bar, restaurant and hotel run by the former ITN cameraman Peter Jouvenal and his Afghan wife. Adorned with old silver, ancient guns and traditional rugs, the Lodge was a place of refreshment and respite from the frustrations of work. It was a meeting place, and, as with its equivalents in Beirut or Sarajevo or any city at the centre of conflict, an international crossroads and listening post. Other restaurants in Kabul, many of them run by foreigners, also played their part: L'Atmosphère and the Boccaccio, to name two. I remember meeting the veteran former BBC correspondent Martin Bell at 'L'Atmo': all he could say, again and again, was that it felt like Saigon in the 1960s. Nor will I forget the blunt advice, delivered in an exaggeratedly strong northern accent, from the head of my SIS team when I took him to dinner at Boccaccio soon after my arrival in Kabul: referring to the well-built Croatian waitresses working there, he said: 'When the waitresses 'ere start to look attractive, lad, you've been 'ere too long.'

It wasn't just the military who needed to explain to the folks back home what they were doing in Afghanistan: most people in Britain didn't have much idea of what diplomats actually did in Kabul. With that in mind, David Miliband asked me to produce a blog. This was part of a wider effort to update the Foreign Office's public diplomacy, on which David proved himself far ahead of his officials. At first, I was doubtful about self-publicity of this kind, and I wondered whether anyone would be interested. But, with the help and encouragement of the FCO's New Media team, I eventually produced a series, covering the work of the Embassy and some of our activities around Afghanistan. My Close Protection Team acted enthusiastically as producers, cameramen and stagehands, and we filmed in a wide variety of locations, using a small digital movie camera provided by the FCO. The first one was shot in Kabul, aimed at general orientation. Others covered a visit to

Helmand, a trip to the Panjshir Valley and life in Kabul more generally. To my surprise, the blogs became an almost instant hit: they were picked up in America and around the world. Originally I had said I would do it for no more than a month, but the blog was extended by popular demand. All the effort of editing them (not much) and then sending them down the link to London (a tremendous fiddle) became worth while.

The FCO was remarkably liberal in its editing: the only time I was told to suppress a scene was when I interviewed a DFID employee on her way to breakfast, and then pointed to the giant satellite dish on the roof of the Embassy and commented that that was how we communicated with London. Somebody in London who should have shown a bit more imagination told me that I was breaching security in naming an employee, and in revealing what time she went to breakfast, and the purpose of the dish atop the Embassy.

Only one viewer comment was suppressed by the FCO censors: when the head of security, the venerable and much loved Guards officer John Windham, and I were filmed dancing rather clumsily with the Gurkha guards at their annual party, one wit posted the following comment: 'Nice moves, John.' That was allowed by the FCO webmaster. But a second post – 'Strictly Come Mincing' – was suppressed by a killjoy in King Charles Street.

Living and working in Kabul meant switching from the serious to the sublime with amazing rapidity. The EU Deputy Special Representative, Michael Semple, was known not just for his knowledge of Afghanistan's political geography. He devoted much of his spare time to supporting the Afghan Water Sports Federation. Based at Lake Qargha in the foothills of the mountains to the west of Kabul, the Association was run by a local sheikh, Mullah Ezzatullah Atif, with a record of resistance to the Russians. He was the paramount chief of the tribes in Afghanistan who claimed descent from the Arab armies that had brought Islam to the Afghan lands in AD 672. From his time living and working in Islamabad, Michael had acted as unofficial coach to an Afghan national rowing team which had first got going in the years of exile during the anti-Soviet *jihad*. He had also trained up some expert kayakers. In the course of 2008 I paid several memorable visits to beautiful Lake Qargha, sitting behind a dam below which lay the parched fairways and sun-baked earth 'greens' of the Kabul Golf Club.

Qargha was a place of weekend refreshment and recreation for many Kabulis, who sat and smoked and drank tea and Coca Cola in little pastel-coloured metal pavilions – gazebos almost – along the lake shore. Early on in my time, Michael asked me if I could help Afghanistan's budding oarsmen: I did, thanks to an extremely generous offer from the bursar of Eton College, who made two 'eights' and the associated equipment available for the Afghans. The RAF rowing club followed suit. The boats were taken to the FCO transport depot in Buckinghamshire, and the blades were repainted. There they sat for many months, awaiting repair after a lorry had backed into them. But by then the Taliban had reinfiltrated Lake Qargha and the whole area was out of bounds to the Embassy and, I presume, to the Afghan oarsmen: another sad story of hope unfulfilled. Those balmy days at Lake Qargha, including a summer picnic for Embassy staff in a guesthouse amid the Mullah's orchards, had become a distant memory by the time I left Afghanistan for the last time in April 2010.

As the Embassy expanded, and our ambitions for the British presence in Kabul grew, it became clear that the temporary site of the British Embassy, spread across a hotch-potch of leased compounds and villas, would not be enough. Our grand plans required a grand embassy to match. We decided that we should try to buy back from Pakistan the old British Embassy in the Karte Parwan district of west Kabul. Architects were commissioned to draw up plans for a new embassy on the twenty-five-acre site. In what might have been a metaphor for British foreign policy in the early twenty-first century, they recommended keeping the grand imperial façade while putting a cheapjack new structure behind it. We talked to the Canadians and Australians about sharing the Embassy. We thought about holding the 2008 Queen's Birthday Party in the old compound. One Embassy wit even suggested that the press hacks be used to tread the areas of the gardens that had not been demined. Incredible as it may seem in these days of austerity, the Foreign Office's Estates Department came up with a budget of over £100 million for building Britain's new Embassy in the poorest country in Asia.

But there was one flaw in these cunning plans: the Pakistanis did not want to sell. Despite the enthusiastic support of the Pakistani Ambassador in Kabul, Tariq Azizuddin, the Pakistani bureaucracy would not budge. We lobbied at every level, from successive Pakistani Presidents down, over many months, but without success. Some of us thought this was a negotiating tactic, intended to extract a higher price from a government which sounded desperate. Eventually, however, it became clear that Pakistan's own imperial hubris was leading it to entertain hopes of restoring the past splendour of the Embassy. And by then anyway the money was no longer available from London, and we realised that our long-term commitment to Afghanistan was unlikely to be as long or as deep as it had seemed in the heady days of early 2007. The project was shelved: we would make do and mend with the existing leased properties, and we would cut the size of our vast Embassy better to suit our cloth.

Chapter 11

Highland Fling: Karzai in Scotland

One of President Karzai's more attractive traits was his love of walking. Every evening, he would take a lengthy constitutional round and round the grounds of the Palace in Kabul where he was effectively a prisoner. On learning of both these facts, the Prince of Wales generously invited Karzai to go walking with him in Scotland, staying at the Prince's house on the Balmoral estate, Birkhall, which had belonged to Prince Charles's beloved grandmother.

Somehow, over the summer of 2007, we settled on a date for President Karzai's visit to Scotland in late October. The Prince and President had already met several times, in London and elsewhere, but this would be the first time Karzai had stayed in a British royal residence or spent such an extended period with a member of the royal family, or indeed any senior Briton. Prince Charles kindly asked Rory Stewart (of whose Turquoise Mountain Foundation the Prince and President were joint patrons) and me to stay at Birkhall too.

The Government in London saw this as a chance to develop the better relationship between Britain and President Karzai which I had been tasked to build. In the latter part of 2006 and early 2007, there had been plenty of indications of worryingly anti-British views on his part. We wanted to put this behind us, and to introduce him to the new Prime Minister, Gordon Brown, who had taken over from Tony Blair at the end of June. We therefore turned the trip into what is known as a Guest of Government visit: just short of a state visit, with what the printed programme pompously describes as 'Her Majesty's Government *in* the United Kingdom' making all arrangements (and paying all reasonable bills), once the Guest and party have reached the shores of the UK. President Karzai, and his officials, gratefully accepted the invitation on the terms we explained to them.

But the course of true love between Britain and Afghanistan never ran entirely smooth. Only a couple of weeks before the President was due to land in London we in Kabul realised that we had a major problem. In the absence of any indication to the contrary from Karzai's protocol team, we had assumed that the President and his party would make their way to Britain in an aircraft of their own. But, in going over arrangements with the Afghans, it dawned on the British Embassy official charged with organising the visit from the Kabul end that our Afghan guests were assuming that the British Government would somehow get them to the UK. After all, that was what happened when President Karzai visited Washington or New York: the United States Air Force would take him all the way there and all the way back. But it turned out that there was no Afghan Presidential aircraft, and that the ancient Boeing 727 the Presidential Palace usually chartered or borrowed from the Afghan airline Ariana was not allowed to land in Western Europe, for safety reasons. Frantic further exchanges with the Palace revealed not only that there was no aircraft available, still less booked, but also that there was no Afghan money available to charter one, or even to pay for tickets on a regular airline.

Nor was there any budget in London for substantial unforeseen expenses of this kind. Nimble footwork by the Foreign Office's Afghan team found a Gulfstream jet available for charter, and established the (enormous) cost, including what looked like a quite exorbitant insurance premium for taking such an aircraft into and out of Kabul. But that was only the beginning of the battle. Just halfway through the financial year, nobody in London had available the tens of thousands of pounds needed to pay for a charter of this kind. Quite properly, the FCO Director responsible for Afghanistan insisted that we look at all other possibilities: RAF to Bahrain, or Muscat, followed by scheduled first-class flights on to London. Options were explored, alternatives costed: using the RAF and scheduled flights would be much, much cheaper. We tested the water with the Afghans: it was clear that President Karzai would be reluctant to travel by scheduled flight. And then the argument that always trumps everything was adduced: security. How could the President be protected in the cabin of a commercial airliner, when his bodyguards needed to carry guns?

I chipped in, arguing that the goodwill generated by the visit would be undone if HMG adopted a cheese-paring approach to what the Afghans would see as a minor logistical question. That also ruled out our appealing to the Americans for help: doing so would only complete HMG's humiliation in Afghan (and American) eyes. Somehow, at short notice, the British Government had to find the money for a charter flight, or dream up some good reason for postponing the visit. Perhaps the MOD could contribute to the cost: after all, they had more invested in Afghanistan, in both absolute and proportionate terms, than any other British Government player. DFID had far more money allocated to Afghanistan than it could sensibly spend. Could we not ask the Treasury for money from the Reserve, given the importance of a successful visit for wider British interests? If Ministers were enlisted, surely the Treasury would cave in.

The battle went on for the best part of a fortnight. There was the usual Whitehall shroud-waving: no one wanted to be the first to concede. No one doubted that the money would be found, but it was not clear from where, or whether it would be subject to conditions. Eventually, the teams in London and Kabul found some unspent Foreign Office funds that could – 'exceptionally and without creating a precedent', of course – be used to pay for the charter.

With Karzai blissfully unaware, I hoped, of what a close-run thing the whole exercise had been, the President and his party duly took off from Kabul early on Sunday 21 October 2007 in a large and luxurious Gulfstream executive jet, registered, embarrassingly, in Germany but chartered by the British Government. It had been decided that I would travel with the party, to use the nine hours of the journey to build my relationship with President Karzai and his Ministers. Apart from personal aides, the other members of the party were the Foreign Minister, Dr Spanta, and the National Security Adviser, Dr Rassoul.

We spent most of the flight looking out of the window, or gossiping about Afghan politics, with the President leading the discussion. The one point at which President Karzai became especially animated was when he spotted that I was reading Sir Olaf Caroe's classic work *The*

Pathans. Caroe had been the last British Governor of the North West Frontier Province before Partition, and had been asked by the new Government of Pakistan to stay on in that role. His mighty work on the tribes west of the Indus said, in suitably magisterial tones, all there was to be said about the Pashtuns. President Karzai sang the book's praises. He saw himself as a kind of Pashtun paramount chief. He believed that Britons in general, and Caroe in particular, understood his people better than any other foreigners.

Our reception at Heathrow's Royal Terminal made me proud: it was a reminder of just how good the Foreign Office's Inward Visits machine still is. At the foot of the steps, the President was greeted by representatives of the Queen and the Government. He was whisked into the main building, offered tea and biscuits by a black-coated butler, while his party were distributed among the vehicles in the motorcade by efficient FO ladies with clipboards. The President would ride in an enormous armoured BMW provided and driven by the Metropolitan Police. Drs Spanta and Rassoul had a limousine of their own. The rest of us were placed in couple of capacious people carriers, to reduce the length of the motorcade. Then it was off into London, accompanied by the motorcycle outriders of the Metropolitan Police's Special Escort Group.

The SEG is one of the unsung glories of official Britain. They move the Queen, VIP visitors and senior Ministers (if they so choose and have a real operational need) through traffic as a knife cuts through soft butter: quiet, efficient, undemonstrative, they use whistles, transponders to turn traffic lights the right colour and an extraordinary knowledge of London's byways to make British VIP motorcades a model to behold. In my two and a half years as principal private secretary to Robin Cook when he was Foreign Secretary, I experienced many motorcades around the world: the California Highway Patrol closing, quite outrageously, an entire freeway for the British Foreign Secretary; French motorcycle police banging hysterically on the roofs of cars to get them out of the way; Italian Carabinieri, sirens blaring, skidding out of control; and, most memorably, a sweetly inexperienced New Zealand motorcycle escort getting us lost in the suburbs of Auckland. Nothing beats the understated efficiency of the Met's SEG, as they race past in relays, holding traffic at side-roads and junctions, threading a way for the motorcade around traffic islands and obstacles of every kind, negotiating backstreets, bus lanes and routes through the Royal Parks. No noise, no fuss. Pure ballet.

The next morning, President Karzai flew on ahead to Aberdeen, on an RAF aircraft, in order to have time alone walking with the Prince of Wales. I followed on British Airways. From Dyce airport, a dark-green Land Rover from the Balmoral estate whisked me up the Dee valley. The views were breathtakingly beautiful, with the leaves turning every shade of dusky gold, against the darker blues and greens and greys of the moors behind and beyond. Birkhall could not have felt more comfortable or natural: a proper country house, without ostentation or extravagance, and full of family things, albeit from a rather special family. The staff were quietly courteous, showing me to my room, suggesting when I might like to join His Royal Highness and the President for tea. Hotfoot from Kabul, Rory Stewart arrived soon after me, equipped for his Highland stay with kilt and trews and tartan and tweeds. We chatted with Karzai's Private Secretary, who was still in disbelief about where he was and what his boss was doing.

After a while, the Prince and the President appeared, back from their walk. Hamid Karzai was beaming from ear to ear. Despite the difficulties of negotiating the heather in a shalwar kameez and black town shoes, he had had the time of his life. After tea, Rory gave him a gift from the Turquoise Mountain Foundation: a *sura* from the Koran inscribed in the most elaborate Arabic calligraphy. Then it was a bath, a quiet pre-supper chat with the Prince of Wales (who was longing to be allowed to visit Afghanistan) and the most delicious and healthy dinner *à quatre*, surrounded by nine grandfather clocks collected by the Queen Mother.

On the Tuesday morning the Royal Air Force flew President Karzai and me back to London. The Special Escort Group whisked us in from Northolt and on to Lancaster House for a full-dress luncheon in the President's honour, given by Her Majesty's Government.

Wednesday was another day out, this time in Oxford: the first stop was Magdalen College, whose beautiful tower stands guard over the approaches to Oxford and the bridge over the Cherwell of the same name as the college. President Karzai was greeted there by the President of Magdalen and by the President of the Oxford Union (an undergraduate): a summit of three Presidents. As we toured the President of Magdalen's magnificent lodgings, an impressed Afghan President commented ruefully that perhaps the President of Magdalen was better housed, and the President of the Union more powerful, than the President of Afghanistan.

Afterwards, we abandoned the motorcade and walked from Magdalen to President Karzai's next engagement, a speech at the Oxford Union. This, I knew, was what Hamid Karzai loved: striding out cheerfully, being greeted by startled American tourists and puzzled shoppers just off the bus from Blackbird Leys, a real politician connecting with real people. On the spur of the moment, I thought I would try to introduce the President to the Principal of my old college, Hertford, just opposite the Bodleian Library. The Hertford porter soon put me in my place: clearly thinking that I was a practical joker, and that the strangely dressed gentleman beside me was an impostor, he said firmly that the Principal was in a meeting and could not be disturbed, even for President Kampai.

In the Union's great debating hall, President Karzai delivered a *tour de force*, in front of a full house of students of every size, shape and background. It was in settings like this that one saw his skill as a speaker who could inspire and communicate fluently in three languages. He addressed questions, from smooth Indians, an angry American and worried Brits, with charm and conviction. We were on something of a high as we left the home of lost causes and forgotten dreams, for the President's audience of HM the Queen at Buckingham Palace.

The main event, on the last day of the visit, was talks with the Prime Minister over breakfast at Number 10, followed by a press conference. As I had hoped and expected, the President and the PM connected immediately. Hamid Karzai responded to Gordon Brown's seriousness, his mastery of detail and his willingness to listen. On a personal level, they had young sons in common, and exchanged gifts. Sarah Brown appeared with young John Brown, then aged four: Karzai was immediately charmed. Sensibly, the Prime Minister spent most of the time *tête-à-tête* with his guest. The press conference was a cakewalk.

As I made my own way back to Kabul, via Dubai, I reflected that the visit had been a success. The Afghan–British relationship was set on a new course. It felt good to be Ambassador to Afghanistan at such a time, making a difference. With the Prime Minister due to pay his first visit to Kabul in December, what could possibly go wrong?

Chapter 12

Mr Brown Comes to Town

As the Afghan autumn turns to winter, storm clouds gather over the high peaks of the Hindu Kush. Like a falling hem, the snow line creeps lower and lower. From the air, one sees mountain ridges dusted, then blanketed, in snow. Kabul feels more fenced in than ever, by weather as well as by geography. But, just as the showers of sleet and snow scurrying across the Shomali Plain north of Kabul are chased by shafts of bright sunlight, so every winter day of mist and cloud is only a brief break from clear blue skies and crisp luminosity. And, as so often in Kabul, mood and climate seem to march in step: long periods of bright optimism, interspersed with darker days of something close to despair.

One such day cast a shadow over my return to Kabul at the end of October. On Tuesday 6 November 2007, I was busy with the usual round of calls, culminating in a US–UK conference on the theory and practice of counter-insurgency, convened at my house that afternoon and evening. Our plan, hatched by a Royal Navy commodore on my staff who had made a study of such things, was to get our colleagues, especially the Americans, to see that successful COIN required more politics than force. But, as the day went on, I kept receiving increasingly distraught messages reporting a tragedy in the north.

It gradually emerged that some seventy people, including many children and six members of the Afghan Parliament, had been killed in a massive suicide bombing in Baghlan in the far north of Afghanistan. The MPs had been members of the Parliamentary Economics Committee, on a visit to a sugar factory as part of a tour of the north. The delegation's leader had been a former commerce minister, and the *de facto* spokesman of the former Northern Alliance (now known as the

110

National Front), the charismatic Sayed Kazemi: I had had breakfast with him at his home only a few weeks earlier. The attack had happened just as a group of schoolchildren had been welcoming the parliamentarians with flowers and songs. Ball-bearings packed in the suicide vest had mown down many of the victims. And, as so often happened, following the initial terrorist attack, many others had died or been wounded as a result of panicked fire by the security forces.

This was an Afghan tragedy, for the Afghans to deal with. All we could do was show solidarity, at a tough time. I decided that early the next day I had to go to the airport, with my Defence Attaché, in ceremonial uniform, to salute the return of the bodies of the MPs. We duly turned up and fought our way to the front of the crowd of Afghans of all backgrounds. We waited on the tarmac, first for President Karzai and then for the remains of the MPs, brought back in a line of Afghan Army helicopters. We were the only foreigners present. Later, I paid a condolence visit to the entire National Front leadership, gathered in mourning in their leader Professor Rabbani's house. On such occasions, being there is more important than what one actually does or says. But I was able to have quiet exchanges with some of the official mourners, including Amrullah Saleh, head of the Afghan intelligence and security service, the National Directorate for Security (NDS). Everyone to whom I spoke sounded in despair. If the trouble was spreading to the north, if children and parliamentarians were being cut down like this, where would it end? The recriminations about how the MPs' programme had become known had not begun.

A week or two later the black hand of terrorism made itself felt even closer to home. Early one morning, I was in my bathroom shaving, thinking about the breakfast I was about to have downstairs with the Chief of the Defence Staff, Air Chief Marshal Sir Jock Stirrup, on one of his regular visits to theatre. I was wondering what I was going to say to him: I knew that he and others in the MOD had been concerned about the downbeat tone of the political reporting from the Kabul Embassy. I wanted to sound cheerful, but stay honest. It would be tricky, but, like the then Chief of Joint Operations, my old friend General Nick Houghton, Jock Stirrup was less unthinkingly gung-ho than some of his colleagues.

And then, without any warning, the whole house shook, and there was a huge bang. I was squeezed by a sudden blast wave. Clad only in a towel, I felt exceptionally naked. My bodyguard came charging into the bathroom. 'Get down, Sir!' he yelled, handing me a helmet and body armour. I insisted on putting on a shirt and trousers first, and then sat glumly on the side of the bath, awaiting developments. My bodyguard's radio crackled, as he tried to find out what had happened. My dread was of an attack on the Embassy of the kind I had so often seen in Saudi Arabia: a bombing followed immediately by an armed assault. The Embassy tannoy broadcast John Windham's refined tones, telling everyone to stay calm and stay put.

Slowly, a picture of what had happened emerged. The attack, by a vehicle-borne improvised explosive device (or VBIED), had been not on the Embassy, but on an unmarked American military convoy which had been passing behind the Embassy on its way to ISAF headquarters. The explosion had been massive, blowing in all the windows in the dozen or so houses rented by the Embassy running along the road where the attack had taken place. Scores of staff, most of them young women, had still been in their beds when the windows had fallen in on them. Anti-shatter film had kept the glass from scattering, but had resulted in entire window frames being pushed in. Doors had been blown off their hinges, and metal gates and railings twisted. There was a pit in the road where the bomb had gone off. Bits of the bomber's vehicle were all around, including in the trees. Thanks to the armour on the American vehicles, none of the US soldiers had been killed, though their Land Cruiser had been wrecked. Most gruesomely of all, the bomber's body parts had been scattered over the Embassy houses and gardens and the neighbouring properties. I found part of his jaw bone. The Canadian Ambassador picked the bomber's scalp off his roof.

To the dismay of my bodyguards, I insisted on going straight to the scene of the explosion. Showing remarkable sangfroid, DFID staff who had been asleep in bed when the bomb had gone off were already starting to clear up the mess. American soldiers were everywhere, pointing their guns and shouting at everyone to keep away. A British ammunition technical officer was examining the site of the blast.

My next instinct was to call London. I wanted Ministers and senior officials to know, as they woke up and heard the news of a big suicide bombing just by the British Embassy, that everyone was safe. I spoke to the Permanent Secretary at DFID, to the Foreign Office's Response Centre and, later in the day, to the Foreign Secretary, who had called to express sympathy and solidarity.

We were all safe, but badly shaken. At times like this the support from London was unquestioning and unqualified. They sent out a security team, to start work on bomb-proof armoured windows that would not be dislodged by a blast. We began to think about other measures to guard against the possibility of armed terrorists entering our houses, gardens and compounds. With my support, the FCO sent out a team trained in trauma counselling to talk over with each of us the shocking events we had experienced. Any doubts I had had about the value of such counselling were soon dispelled, as some of the more anxious members of staff struggled to cope with delayed shock. It was then that I discovered that at least two of our team had not revealed to their worried mothers that they were in Afghanistan: one had managed to persuade her mum, even on Skype, that she was in Dubai. The other had said that she was in 'Central Asia'.

Despite the shock, the daily grind of Embassy work had to continue. In the weeks after the Karzai trip to Scotland there were two main preoccupations. One was a visit by the International Development Committee of the House of Commons, chaired by the Liberal Democrat MP Malcolm Bruce. They wanted to have a good look at the work DFID was doing in Afghanistan with getting on for £100 million a year of taxpayers' money, and they wanted to see President Karzai. They achieved both, though the cheerily general exchange in the Palace throne room with an upbeat President Karzai and a line up of his Ministers was not an occasion for talking turkey about aid effectiveness. But the Committee did at least see the sense of DFID's focus on putting money through Afghan institutions, in order to strengthen them. And they saw why DFID had sensibly resisted well-meant but misguided pressure from the Army to spend money on quick-impact projects that all too easily became quick-collapse projects.

The other theme of those weeks was more sensitive. We learned that, without consulting HMG, the respected Under Secretary for Political Affairs in the US State Department, Nick Burns, had asked Paddy Ashdown if he would be interested in succeeding Tom Königs as an upgunned UN special representative in Afghanistan, on the Bosnia model. As Lord Ashdown was the first to admit, he had never visited Afghanistan. But he had close-to-ideal credentials for the job: strong political and presentational skills, military as well as diplomatic experience, old family ties with the Raj of the kind locals loved, energy and enthusiasm, and a keen sense of priority. Back in London in mid-November, the FCO South Asia Director, Adam Thomson, and I went to see Paddy Ashdown in the House of Lords. He came across as very sceptical about the whole idea of going to Kabul: neither he nor his wife Jane wanted him to do another dangerous and demanding full-time job. At the same time, I could see that he was intrigued, and persuadable. I described the situation, stressing that things in Afghanistan were bad and getting slowly worse, but far from irretrievable. An Ashdown-like figure with the authority and vision to pull together the whole international effort, civil and military, was critical for success – or at least for avoiding failure. Speaking personally, I very much hoped that he would take up the challenge the Americans had offered him. But it had to be seen as an American plot, not a British one. Paddy said he would think about it – on condition that Adam and I produced a credible Mission Implementation Plan of the kind he had had in Bosnia.

We duly sent Paddy a draft Plan, but heard no more. The wires between London, Washington and New York were, however, buzzing: the Americans were determined to get the UN Secretary General to appoint their man. Without my being told until after the fact, my American colleague, Bill Wood, was instructed to sell the idea to a sceptical President Karzai, and then to negotiate Lord Ashdown's terms of reference with an even more doubtful Dr Spanta. Karzai was unhappy, and made this clear to Bill. Separately, he asked me what I knew about the idea: his tone and body language suggested that he suspected a British plot. He was wrong about that, but right to be worried that this English Lord was being sent out to act as some sort of quasi-imperial proconsul. He found my protestations that Afghan sovereignty would not be compromised singularly unconvincing.

But the Ashdown appointment was for others to manage: it was the Americans' idea, and they had to deliver. Britain had only a marginal role. I had another, more pressing preoccupation. With the Foreign Secretary's support, I had accepted a proposal from David Goodhart, the energetic editor of *Prospect* magazine, for a debate by correspondence between Rory Stewart and me. The January 2008 edition duly carried an exchange of three letters in each direction, from Rory to me and back again, entitled 'Are we failing in Afghanistan?'

My difficulty was that privately I agreed with much of Rory's diagnosis: we *did* risk failing in Afghanistan, we *were* pursuing 'a hubristic counter-insurgency campaign' (as he put it), and we *couldn't* defeat the Taliban militarily. But where I parted company with Rory was over the vague prescription he was offering at that time (and has subsequently improved): pulling British troops back and out of Helmand, apparently unilaterally, and abandoning the counter-narcotics campaign, while offering generous development aid, notably for a few 'prestige projects' (the Turquoise Mountain perhaps), and somehow preventing the Taliban becoming a conventional threat by leaving behind Special Forces. This was the Troops Out Movement in Tory tweed: as I pointed out in the debate, no responsible British prime minister could subscribe to such a strategy. Britain could not pull back from Helmand unilaterally without collapsing the whole international effort and damaging our relationship with the United States. If Britain left, there would be a rush to the exit by the other, weaker brethren in the coalition. Nor did I see how we could protect all that had been achieved in Afghanistan since 2001 by such a U-turn: we risked letting the Afghans down, badly, and doing great reputational harm to ourselves.

The weakness in my argument was explaining how we were going to succeed, if it wasn't by military means. We forget now how few people understood back in 2007 that the only sensible solution was some sort of negotiated settlement that would, inevitably, involve talking to the Taliban. Although a senior FCO official had told me, *sotto voce*, before I left London that spring that in the end the only solution would be talks of some kind, this notion was still toxic to the Bush Administration, and to the military on both sides of the Atlantic. Work on reconciliation and reintegration was only just beginning. None of us had yet developed the kind of thinking that David Miliband was to surface in 2009 on the need for a twin-track political process, addressing both the multiple internal sources of conflict (that is, about much more than 'talking to the Taliban') and the regional players, including Pakistan, India, China, Russia and Iran.

This tension between obligatory optimism and more prudent realism was highlighted in the run-up to Gordon Brown's first visit to Afghanistan in early December. He planned to fly straight back overnight from Kabul to London and to make a statement to the House of Commons, setting the course for his Administration's approach to Afghanistan. The statement had therefore to be prepared before the PM had even set foot in the country.

In its usual fashion, the Whitehall machine, led by the Cabinet Office, starting grinding away on preparations for the visit – which was supposed to be shrouded in secrecy – and for the statement to Parliament. The Defence Secretary, Des Browne, was sent to Kabul to play John the Baptist to the PM's Jesus.

It was in the weeks before the visit that a cloud not much bigger than a mullah's black turban started to appear. At a series of frantic meetings of the war cabinet, President Karzai had reported to the US Ambassador, General McNeill and me that he had received, apparently by mobile phone direct, frantic appeals for help from a Mullah Salam who, with his small militia, occupied a village to the east of Musa Qala. Unless ISAF intervened, Salam, himself a former Talib, would be overwhelmed by the Taliban. Something, said Karzai, had to be done. But if we *did* send help, Mullah Salam promised, the local population would rise up against the Taliban.

Musa Qala was a name carved on the heart of the British Army. The scrappy little town on the rim of a mostly dry river valley in northern Helmand had been taken in exuberant fashion by elements of Brigadier Ed Butler's 16 Air Assault Brigade in the summer of 2006. Butler had been responding to an Afghan request to garrison settlements across northern Helmand. But the British and Danish soldiers holed up in the platoon houses there had been outnumbered by the Taliban. Through no fault of their own, the Paras had had to withdraw. To the scorn of the Americans, their withdrawal had been negotiated, in return for the Taliban agreeing to stay away from Musa Qala too. But within a few weeks of the Parachute Regiment's departure the Taliban had broken the agreement and retaken the town. They were now exacting revenge on 'collaborators' in the neighbourhood, including Karzai's friend Mullah Salam.

Salam's request for help was therefore particularly opportune: ISAF could be seen to be responding to a direct request from President Karzai, the British Army could make up for its supposedly ignominious expulsion from Musa Qala the previous year, and the current Task Force Helmand commander, Brigadier Andrew Mackay, had the perfect vehicle for showing his own military mettle and that of his 52nd Infantry Brigade.

In his book *Operation Snakebite*, Stephen Grey* has documented the full story of the successful retaking of Musa Qala in December 2007, and the weeks of planning and debate which preceded it. We were all under pressure from President Karzai to move ahead as quickly as possible. He in turn seemed to be receiving continual phone calls and messages from Salam warning that, if the Afghan equivalent of the Seventh Cavalry didn't arrive soon, the Mullah would be done for.

Like many Afghans not used to reading maps, President Karzai's grasp of geography and of strategy could sometimes seem rather shaky. I remember one almost comical scene with General McNeill in the war cabinet, with the President complaining once again that ISAF were being too hesitant about moving on Musa Qala. He was forgetting that Mullah Salam had originally suggested that we didn't need so much to go to Musa Qala as let Musa Qala come to us. By that he had meant that the local tribespeople would rise against the Taliban without ISAF having to become directly involved.

We called for a map. But it turned out that the President's staff had no map of their country available. I therefore pulled out an RAF map of the country, which I always carried in my briefcase. The map was meant for aircrew to help them escape and survive if they were forced

---

* London: Viking, 2009.

down in hostile territory. It was printed on something like silk, so that it could be folded tight and concealed. It bore a legend, in six Central Asian languages and English, indicating that the bearer came in peace: help in returning him to friendly forces would be handsomely rewarded. We stood round, peering at the map, trying without success to find the hamlet, Shah Kariz, in which Mullah Salam had his compound. This was how the supreme command of the war operated.

Sensibly, both General McNeill and Brigadier Mackay were clear from the start that Afghan forces should have a leading role in the operation. Drawing on his long experience of working in Afghanistan, McNeill told Karzai that there had to be a guarantee that Afghan forces would hold Musa Qala once ISAF had retaken it; and he wanted better governance in the province – in other words, the replacement of Governor Wafa. Karzai seemed to agree; but he was not able to deliver on the first point, and took his time on the second.

It was only when I returned from my visit to London in mid-November that I realised that D-Day for the operation would coincide with the Prime Minister's visit. If the operation was a success, there was a risk that it would overshadow the announcement to Parliament of the Brown Administration's Afghan strategy. If there were significant casualties, we could face the nightmare scenario of the Prime Minister having to stand beside President Karzai in a joint press conference in Kabul at which Karzai would feel obliged to complain about civilian casualties. In a series of fraught video conferences with Whitehall, we discussed whether there was any scope for postponing the operation, but were told there was not. My instinct was that somehow it would be all right on the night – as turned out to be the case. But others, in London, were not so sanguine.

On the eve of the Prime Minister's visit, I flew down to Camp Bastion with the Defence Secretary, Des Browne, to await Gordon Brown's arrival. The good news was that Musa Qala had just been retaken by ISAF and Afghan forces, something which Brown celebrated in his comments to the troops and to the press.

Apart from that, the visit followed a pattern that was hardly to change at all for any of the half dozen or so visits Gordon Brown paid to Afghanistan as prime minister: the overnight flight from Bahrain or

Kuwait in a Hercules crammed with the PM's own party and the accompanying press, often including the Lobby of parliamentary journalists in search of some front-line action; military and, if we were lucky, political briefings at Bastion; a quick visit to one or two of the units based there; a speech to the troops; a flight up to Kabul and then straight on to the Presidential Palace by helicopter; a *tête-à-tête* with a President Karzai who genuinely got on with the Prime Minister; an awkward, and usually brief, plenary session with whichever British or Afghan Ministers happened to be around; a joint press conference; and then the helicopter flight back to Kabul airport and the onward flight to the Gulf, and then London. There were only two variations on this theme in my time as ambassador: a short side-trip to the British Embassy, during which the PM met the NATO Commander and the UN Special Representative, plus Embassy staff; and, later on, an excursion from Bastion to take the Prime Minister forward to one of the front-line bases.

On a whirlwind visit like this, there is time only for the briefest exchanges with the Prime Minister. Naturally enough, on this occasion, Gordon Brown was focused on his statement to Parliament, the draft of which he had in his hand, and on which he worked at every available opportunity, including on the flights within Afghanistan. He asked for my suggestions for the statement, and wanted also to talk about the Middle East. He had much on his mind, but was good humoured and came across as in command of the detail. He did not find at all easy the whole business of donning and removing body armour, and climbing in and out of helicopters, in the dark and freezing cold. Nor did I improve his confidence when he nervously asked, as we landed in pitch dark in a dusty field beside the Embassy, 'Where are we?' and I replied, trying to be humorous, 'In a minefield, Prime Minister.'

As he took off from Kabul to return to London, the Prime Minister asked me to send back overnight further thoughts for his statement to Parliament the day after his return. But what he told the House on the afternoon of 12 December 2007 was a mish-mash of high-flown rhetoric and unconvincing bureaucratese. It had been extensively rewritten in Number 10, with little consultation with others in Whitehall. It contained the usual tribute to the fighting men and women, and to their sacrifice. Sensible promises about Afghanisation and localisation were made. The Afghan Army and Police would be trained up. One hundred and fifty new armoured vehicles would be supplied to the British Task Force. The number of British troops in Afghanistan would remain at about 7,800. Thanks to sleight of hand by a reluctant DFID, there would be a big increase in British aid for Afghanistan, and a fund to attract investment and to support Afghan business.

But the most sensitive part had been influenced not by the visit to Kabul, or by advice from the ground, but by a headline in the *Daily Telegraph* that morning, claiming – wrongly, and as a result of over-enthusiastic briefing from the FCO Press Office – that Britain was planning to talk to the Taliban. As a result, the Prime Minister himself strengthened the passage on political reconciliation, by promising to 'defeat the insurgency by isolating and eliminating their leadership', and then adding the fateful phrase: 'I make it clear that we will not enter into any negotiations with these people.' Brown went on to proclaim that our objective was to 'root out those preaching and practising violence and murder'. But he added that President Karzai had told him that some 5,000 Taliban fighters had already laid down their arms.

These words about never talking to the Taliban were crafted in haste in response to perceived media pressure. They broke one of the first rules of politics: never say never. And they were to hinder the Brown Administration's efforts over the next two and a half years to produce, and then promote with the Americans, a sensible Afghan political strategy.

But none of that was obvious to us at the time. With a successful visit by the Prime Minister behind us, and the new Afghan strategy announced, we could relax in the run-up to Christmas. At the Embassy Christmas Ball at the Serena Hotel the day after the statement spirits were high. A senior DFID visitor from London had spent the day before the ball flying round in an American helicopter. So she chose to celebrate the dichotomy on the Department's intranet site. 'From Black Hawk to Black Tie' read the headline covering her enthusiastic report.

Soon afterwards I paid my first visit, with Brigadier Mackay, to Musa Qala, which had been 'liberated' only a week or so earlier. Despite the eerie feeling of emptiness in the town, there were signs of it starting to come back to life. The only sour note came when some shopkeepers complained that the Afghan soldiers brought in to protect the townspeople from the Taliban had seized their furniture for firewood.

Back in Lashkar Gah I had a series of private policy meetings with the Brigadier and his team. Despite what the Prime Minister had said at Westminster, in Helmand Mackay knew that the name of the game had to be reconciliation combined with military pressure. His staff briefed me on what sounded like exciting plans for bringing over several hundred former Taliban fighters, and retraining them, on a trial basis. I gave my enthusiastic support to the project, and returned to Kabul for pre-Christmas catch-ups with a cheerful President Karzai, grateful for the retaking of Musa Qala, and a relieved General McNeill.

As I boarded the plane to Dubai for my Christmas break, and settled down to reading Rory Stewart's book about Iraq, everything seemed set fair for a year in which at last we had reasonable hopes of turning the tide in Afghanistan. I could not have been more wrong.

PART III

AGAINST AN EBBING TIDE

We have been too often disappointed by the optimism of American leaders … To say that we are closer to victory today is to believe, in the face of the evidence, the optimists who have been wrong in the past … To say that we are mired in stalemate seems the only realistic, yet unsatisfactory, conclusion … it is increasingly clear to this reporter that the only rational way out will be to negotiate, not as victors, but as an honourable people who have lived up to their pledge to defend democracy, and did the best they could.

Walter Cronkite, CBS Evening News, *27 February 1968*

Chapter 13

Reversal of Fortune

Christmas Day 2007, just after breakfast, at my mother-in-law's house in north Nottinghamshire: the phone rang. I recognised immediately the deadpan tones of my longstanding friend and Diplomatic Service colleague Andrew Patrick, who was now my Deputy in Kabul. Andrew and I had first worked together in Robin Cook's Private Office. There Andrew's unflappable manner, dry humour and quietly infallible judgement had defused many a difficult moment with our irascible boss.

Andrew had kindly agreed to remain in charge of the Embassy over what we had expected to be a quiet Christmas and New Year. Now, he started the conversation by wishing me a Happy Christmas and asking after the family. He volunteered that he was just sitting down to turkey and trimmings in the Embassy canteen. I wondered what was coming. Even the infinitely courteous Andrew wouldn't have rung me up in England early on Christmas morning to offer me the compliments of the season.

And then, with quiet deliberation, Andrew dropped the bombshell. He had been summoned early that morning to what had turned out to be a difficult meeting with an emotional Dr Spanta. Spanta had told Andrew that the Afghan Government had declared both the EU Deputy Special Representative, Michael Semple, and the chief UNAMA political analyst, Mervyn Patterson, *personae non gratae*. President Karzai had given orders for them to leave Afghanistan by nightfall on Boxing Day.

Andrew had established that, just a day earlier, on Christmas Eve, Semple and Patterson had been detained in Helmand and flown back to Kabul. A retired Afghan Air Force general had been working with them. He had been thrown into prison in Lashkar Gah. But the full details of what had happened, and why, were unclear. All three had been working on the project to resettle and retrain several hundred former Taliban fighters on which I had been briefed during my visit to Helmand just before Christmas. The Afghan intelligence and security service (the NDS) and the Interior Ministry, as well as the Presidential Palace, had all authorised the programme, for which British officials were providing policy and financial support. But something seemed to have gone wrong, after the three had gone to see Governor Wafa to seek his views on possible sites in central Helmand for a resettlement camp. More than that Andrew could not tell me; but plainly there had been a serious misunderstanding.

We discussed what we should do. Clearly, our Ministers had to be told. But we needed to do what we could to prevent Semple and Patterson being expelled the next day: once they had gone, it would be much more difficult to get them back. I said I would try to speak to President Karzai, or at least to his Chief of Staff, Umar Daudzai. And I would look at options for returning to post as soon as possible.

My Christmas was ruined. I spent much of the rest of the day trying in vain to raise Karzai or Daudzai. I tried every number I had, and left messages everywhere. I attempted to reach the intelligence chief, Amrullah Saleh. He would surely know what was really going on; there were good reasons why neither Semple nor Patterson could ever have been a British spy. But no one returned my calls. Daudzai had switched his three mobiles off. Over a crackling line, Karzai's private secretaries were polite but firm: the President was in meetings and could not be interrupted. I was being given the brush-off. I knew I would have to return to Kabul as soon as possible and force my way into the Palace if necessary. Only President Karzai could resolve this. None of his minions would dare do so.

With a terrible sinking feeling in the pit of my stomach, five days after I had left Heathrow Terminal 3, I was back there again. En route, I had made a tiring excursion by coach and cross-country train to Devon, to see my mother and the other half of the family. Once again, my plans for a proper break back in England had been wrecked at the whim of the Afghan President.

I arrived back in Kabul on the morning of Friday 28 December. Afghans wouldn't attend official meetings on a Friday, so I had time to catch up, and to be briefed by the Embassy's political and intelligence teams. But, in the most important sense, it was too late. Semple and Patterson had already been shipped out of the country. Absent an order from the President, no one could have stopped this.

Bit by bit, we were getting a clearer picture of what had happened. As part of a low-level reconciliation project in Helmand, authorised in writing by the President's office and the Interior Ministry, HMG had been quietly supporting a proposal from a retired Afghan general to bring over several hundred insurgent fighters, and retrain and resettle them. The general had drawn up plans for a camp somewhere in central Helmand. He had even prepared a re-education syllabus covering the Afghan constitution, human rights and, bizarrely, hygiene. He had drafted this plan on his laptop, and put it on a flash drive. Michael Semple had been there to support the retired general. With the agreement of his boss, EU Representative Francesc Vendrell, Michael had been working in his spare time as a consultant to the project. Mervyn Patterson had had no official role. But, as UNAMA's chief expert on Afghan tribal politics, he had naturally been interested in the project. So he had offered to take his friend Michael down to Helmand and back again in one of the UN's ancient Russian helicopters, in return for sight of what was happening.

Everything had gone well until the trio had been to see Governor Wafa. They had wanted to brief him on the project and to seek his views on a site for the proposed camp. To their surprise and horror, Wafa had ended the meeting almost as soon as it had begun. Without any warning, he had summoned the local police to arrest the retired general. He had ordered Semple and Patterson to remain in their hotel until they had received further instructions. Wafa had then apparently telephoned the President. He had told Karzai that he had caught the British red-handed, plotting to train Taliban fighters. The President's reaction had been fast and furious: Semple and Patterson had to be thrown out of Afghanistan as soon as possible. The retired general had to be investigated and interrogated by the NDS and then punished.

Much of this had been put direct to Andrew by an extremely worked up Dr Spanta. It seemed to have occurred to none of them that Britain would have had no conceivable interest in training Taliban fighters to attack its own troops. It later emerged that Hamid Karzai had past form with Semple. He believed that Michael knew too much about the country and that he had been involved before in stirring up trouble and generally interfering in Afghan internal politics. In other words, he knew where many of the political bodies were buried – metaphorically only, in most cases.

As for the poor retired general, he was, as I discovered when I met him later, a truly noble Afghan patriot. He had trained as a pilot, in the Soviet Union, under the Communist regime and risen to a high rank in the Air Force. Uniquely, probably, for such a senior officer, he had stayed on through the period of warlord rule (from 1992 until 1996), and had been made chief of the Air Force when the Taliban took power. He had tragi-comic tales to tell of what it had been like to work for the Taliban. For example, he had been the only officer or official in the entire Defence Ministry to have a desk, because the Taliban regarded tables and chairs as infidel creations.

The retired general had had enough of the conflict which had laid Afghanistan waste for the past thirty years. Like most Afghans, he knew that the only answer was reconciliation between all the parties to the conflict. There had to be a new political settlement in which the Taliban, and the tribes and views which they represented, were included, not excluded. Trying to defeat the Taliban by military force would never produce lasting peace. He had being doing his best to help his beloved country. Now he was in prison, soon to be transferred to an NDS holding centre in Kabul. It was weeks before we saw him again.

Wafa's motives in all this were unclear. It was difficult to work out why he had reacted with such irrational fury and, quite unnecessarily, done such damage. The whole purpose of the meeting which the trio had sought with Wafa had been to brief and consult the Governor on the project. Perhaps he felt somehow shut out from what was going on. Perhaps it was simply because he was angry at hearing that the Brits and Americans were unhappy with his performance as Governor. I never found out.

The next day, Saturday 29 December, I re-engaged with the Afghan Government. In the morning, I saw the intelligence chief, Amrullah Saleh. He was in an awkward position, caught between his President's fury and his own understanding of the absurdity of the charge that Britain had been illegally sponsoring the training of Taliban fighters. He also knew that the project had been properly authorised by Afghan officials. Usually, Amrullah was frank and open, too intelligent to be anything else. But, on this occasion, he was cagey. He confined himself to advising me to tread carefully with his President and to saying that the investigation by his service had to be completed before anything could happen.

I went to see Bill Wood, the American Ambassador. He was sympathetic, but didn't really want to get involved. He had not known about this particular project and seemed to share many of the Bush Administration's doubts about the wisdom of trying to deal with the Taliban. Another factor was that, with all the problems of its own that America had with Karzai, it was quite helpful when somebody else was in the line of fire. Once, a friendly spy in the American Embassy had told me how, at the US Ambassador's morning meeting, the Press Attaché had read out a headline from the Afghan press: 'Britain blamed for Taliban upsurge'. Quick as a flash, the American Ambassador had quipped, 'At last, my work is done.' Typically, Bill was most amused when later I teased him about this.

That Saturday afternoon I went round to the Palace for what I hoped would be a frank heart-to-heart with the President. I had equipped myself with copies of the papers authorising the project. I thought I was on firm ground. No one could be so irrational as to believe that the British Government had any conceivable interest in helping the enemy improve his killing and wounding of its own troops. I was shown into the President's official study. To my consternation, half the Afghan Cabinet were already there. All the security Ministers and chiefs were standing in a loose semi-circle, plus some of President Karzai's closest political advisers and allies. They gave the impression that they were relishing the opportunity to put the British Ambassador on the rack. They looked righteously angry.

The President opened the batting, and spoke for some time. I cannot now remember exactly what he said: that will have to await the release of my reporting telegrams. But it was a litany of complaint about interference in Afghanistan by Britain in general, and by Michael Semple in particular. There were lurid stories, which I could not follow and did not therefore record, about Michael supposedly having been involved in rigging an election in the north and doing something with the Kuchi nomads. But Karzai's main charge was that Britain had had no business to be training the Taliban. Throughout this some of the more sycophantic of Karzai's Ministers nodded vigorously in support. Dr Spanta made one or two interjections, expressing outrage at British behaviour. Amrullah sat in embarrassed silence.

Nor can I remember exactly what I said in reply. But I do know that I explained in full what we had been trying to do and why. I pointed out that Karzai and I had always agreed that there could be no military solution to the insurgency. This project had been very much in the spirit of trying to find, at local level, political and peaceful approaches to stabilising Afghanistan. More important, it had been in support of activity by Afghans and authorised by Karzai's Government. To the President's mounting astonishment, I produced photocopies of papers signed by some of those present in the room, including the Deputy National Security Adviser, who happened also to be Karzai's brother-in-law. It was clear that none of those present had dared tell an enraged President that not only had they known about the project, but they had also authorised it. What they had imagined would happen when I appeared I cannot think: they must have been hoping against hope that I would simply fold in front of the assault from Karzai.

The President turned on his advisers. There were animated exchanges in Dari, and then in Pashtu. Karzai had been thrown off balance by my producing Afghan Government papers authorising the project. I said that, with hindsight, I was sorry that he had not been briefed personally on the project – although that should have been at least as much for his officials to do as for me. But I could assure him that the project had indeed been authorised and that it had, I believed, been very much in Afghanistan's interests. I hoped the patriotic Afghan general could be released as soon as possible: his only crime had been trying to end the conflict disfiguring the country he loved.

Karzai was non-committal. We would need to meet again to discuss this. He ordered Amrullah Saleh to speed up the investigation, including the interrogation of the old general. We left it at that. But I learned later that the Afghan side had been rocked by my ability to produce written proof that the whole project had been under Afghan authority. The President had complained bitterly that he had not been told, but, as the main culprit was his trusted brother-in-law, no further action was taken.

The saga dragged on for weeks. A depressed general was eventually released. He agreed to come to a discreet lunch at my house to talk things over: he was indeed the patriot of whom I had heard so much. But he had been broken by his experience and chose to emigrate with his family from his beloved homeland. A man who had stuck it out in Afghanistan under Communist rule, under the chaos of the warlords and under the dark shadow of the Taliban had finally been driven out. It was another small, but significant, setback to our efforts to help the Afghans rebuild themselves a functioning state.

All this took place against a darkening scene across the other side of the Durand Line. On 27 December 2007 had come the terrible news that the leading candidate for the Presidency of Pakistan in the elections due two weeks later, Benazir Bhutto of the Pakistan People's Party, had been assassinated at a rally in Rawalpindi. Hamid Karzai had always liked and admired Benazir and had been looking forward to working with her. He had warned her of the risks she was taking in returning to Pakistani politics. He told me that, in her last conversation with him, she had seemed to sense the evil about to befall her. He was deeply upset by her death, and that too must have affected his mood in the weeks that followed. I too had known Benazir pretty well from our time together at Oxford. I had risen up the ranks of the Oxford Union in her slipstream – she had fame and I had a funny name, both of which helped in Union elections. We had been in only occasional touch over the years. Our last meeting had been over dinner with friends in London a few years earlier.

After the whole affair was over, I raised the injustice done to Semple and Patterson several times with President Karzai. On Semple, he was beyond reason. On Patterson, he said that he had nothing against him personally and that time would probably allow a reconsideration of his case. But, understandably enough, neither of my immediate successors wanted to touch the case. Another expert on Afghanistan was lost to the cause, as Mervyn moved on to other work.

As if all this trouble were not enough, I had over the New Year period to deal with criticism and carping on counter-narcotics policy from two unexpected quarters. The excellent Brigadier in Helmand understood counter-insurgency better than anyone. He had produced an outstanding statement of commander's intent at the start of his six-month tour. But suddenly he started signalling his unhappiness with the Embassy's approach to counter-narcotics. He confessed that some of his views on drugs policy had been informed by his early career in the Drugs Squad of the Royal Hong Kong Police. And then there landed on my desk, or, rather, pinged into my Outlook inbox, a right hook from another, wholly unexpected direction: a long letter from HM Ambassador in Washington telling my Embassy and me what we were doing wrong on counter-narcotics policy. It was a bit demoralising for a team who were doing their best, in almost impossible circumstances, to produce a sensible mix of policies that worked. A private video conference, and a visit to Helmand, soon patched up our differences with the Brigadier. And the letter from Washington was allowed gradually to subside into oblivion.

But there were brighter aspects to the New Year. I had managed to persuade my old schoolfriend Kit Hesketh Harvey to bring out to Kabul his outrageously camp satirical cabaret act, 'Kit and the Widow'. Kit and his stage partner, the Widow, were nothing if not intrepid. They had been twice to Saudi Arabia when I had been ambassador there, and had done wonders for the morale of the expatriate community. Now they were on their way to Kabul, with me paying for their tickets out of my own pocket, and the Embassy meeting through ticket sales their generously reduced performance fees. Perhaps rather unenterprisingly, we arranged just two performances: one in the Embassy (*Cabaret in the Canteen*), and one (*Cabaret for the Coldstreamers*) at Camp Souter, the British base at Kabul airport, where elements of the 1st Battalion Coldstream Guards were providing the Kabul Patrol Company.

In his inimitable fashion, Kit took to the Embassy, and the Embassy took to him. He followed his usual practice in preparing for any private performance, whether at a house party or a palace. He went round, talking to '*simply* everyone', pulling as many skeletons out of cupboards as he could. He befriended my Private Secretary and, in two days, reached parts of the Kabul social scene that I had never penetrated. The social intelligence thus gathered was carefully distilled into his opening number, a wonderful satirical ballad of his own composition. Everyone who mattered in the British community and beyond seemed to feature, in teasing and often pointed caricature.

But the performance in the canteen was even more special. Somehow, Kit had learned that the American Ambassador, aka 'Chemical Bill', would be with us: I had asked Bill because I knew that, as a fan of P. G. Wodehouse, he appreciated the eccentricities of English humour. Latching on to this, Kit and the Widow performed their version of the Tom Lehrer song 'The Periodic Table' and dedicated the number to – guess who – 'Chemical Bill'. Afterwards, I nervously asked Bill to join us all in the Embassy bar. Bill could not have been more graceful: we English had a way with words that he loved.

Kit and the Widow's performance for the officers and men of the Coldstream Guards had been harder work. There had been no alcohol, for a start, to fuel the occasion. The electric keyboard had sounded tinny. But, most difficult, while the officers had appreciated the humour immensely and immediately, some of the soldiers had found it all a bit, well, poncey, and had taken longer to warm up. But once they did, Kit and the Widow brought the house (or rather the camp) down. One told Kit afterwards: 'You made me forget for an hour that I was in Afghanistan.'

Another bright spot in those dark days at the turn of the year was an early Burns Night celebration organised by an excellent Scottish woman officer in the Royal Air Force on attachment to the Embassy's counter-narcotics team. I shall never forget the sight of Ed Stourton, out in Kabul to anchor Radio 4's *Today* programme from my house, storming round my tiny drawing room as he took part in 'The Dashing White Sergeant'.

It was during this period that Andrew Patrick and I decided – I can't quite remember how or why – to engage in a sponsored beard-growing race. Towards the end of January 2008, the results were measured, and then removed, on the night of the first performance of the first ever

Embassy pantomime. I regret to say that Andrew won by at least a centimetre. In mitigation, I can plead only that I had lost ten days when I had had to shave on returning to see my family in England at Christmas.

But the best relief of all was the first ever Embassy pantomime, entitled *A Lad in Kabul*. The so-called organising principle of the show, brilliantly scripted by Chris Kealey from the Embassy political team, was an assault on the Taliban by a newly formed British regiment named 'The Queen's Own Penpushers'. This rather peculiar regiment was aiming to force the Taliban into submission by bombarding them with draft strategies – a parody that was, for some of us, painfully close to reality. Most of the Embassy personalities featured in the show, either as characters or as performers: I was dragged in as the wicked Sherard of Nottingham. A troupe of tree-huggers marched on stage in a pastiche entitled 'Day of the DFIDs'. Beneath the humour lay some darker truths.

One of those truths had been shown in sharp relief on the evening of Monday 14 January, when a group of terrorists had bombed and shot their way into Kabul's only five-star hotel. The Serena Hotel, owned and generously subsidised by the Aga Khan, stood in the very centre of the city, just beside the Presidential Palace. Using the classic tactic (which I had seen so often in Saudi Arabia) of vehicle-borne bombs to blast a way in, followed immediately by an infantry assault, the attackers had run amok in the hotel. The Norwegian Foreign Minister, Jonas Gahr Støre, and his delegation had been staying there and were on the premises when the attack took place. They were forced to take refuge in the basement. A Norwegian journalist accompanying Støre was among the six people killed. The attack on the Serena was a warning for the whole community of things to come. The stories of what had gone wrong, and right, that terrible night trickled out over many weeks. By far the most worrying were suggestions that the attack had been mounted by the Haqqani network, which was said in turn to be sponsored by Pakistan's Inter Services Intelligence directorate. Kabul would never feel quite the same again.

Meanwhile, the Americans were pressing ahead with their plans for inserting Paddy Ashdown to replace Tom Königs. With typical modesty, Tom had crept out of Kabul on New Year's Eve almost unnoticed. I had

had one last session with him, during which he had expressed disquiet at HMG trying to promote reconciliation in Helmand without officially involving the UN. He had a point.

In an extraordinary example of the law of unintended, or at least unexpected, consequences, the Serena Hotel bombing precipitated a chain of events which led to Paddy Ashdown withdrawing as a candidate to succeed Königs. On Wednesday 16 January, back in London *The Times* carried a leader on the situation in Afghanistan following the hotel attack. Sandwiched between the opening paragraphs of hand-wringing and the closing paragraphs of prescription (warning that the war would be lost unless all parties did as *The Times* suggested) came the following passage (emphasis added):

> President Karzai's precarious position only adds to the urgency. Even in Kabul he has little say in security matters … Nor is he in full control of his budget … *Ethnically, he is a lonely Pashtun in a government made up largely of Tajik veterans of the Northern Alliance.* And his fear of being cast as a puppet by his rivals has led to a dangerous strategy of promoting inept officials …

None of the British or American teams dealing with Afghanistan in Kabul or back in capitals took much notice of this when it appeared. Like most people, we didn't read *Times* leaders, or at least not very often. What we *had* noticed, however, on the front page of that day's paper, was a story headlined 'Ashdown to become "super envoy" in Afghanistan'. Similar stories, some datelined Brussels, appeared in several other British broadsheets the same morning: someone had been briefing the media, possibly on Paddy's behalf.

Before the arrival of the twenty-four-hour news cycle, two British Prime Ministers, Harold Wilson and John Major, had undermined their own premierships by reading the following day's papers before they went to bed, thus guaranteeing that they spent the night worrying about news management. President Karzai had a similar vice. Every morning he had a Palace official print off the internet everything about Afghanistan and about him in the British and American media. The official would then helpfully highlight passages of interest, particularly any critical of Hamid Karzai. The President would read through the pile of print-offs before and during breakfast. On the days when there was anything critical or damaging – something that happened with increasing frequency – he would often be upset for much of the day. Like many Eastern politicians, he was convinced that the British and American media were controlled or at least heavily influenced by the governments in London and Washington respectively. Bill Wood's and my efforts to convince him otherwise made little impact.

Thus, on a day when the Afghan Parliament rejected seventeen of the President's twenty-four nominees for Cabinet posts, he was also faced with an announcement in the Western media that a 'super envoy' was being sent to knock him and Afghanistan into shape. But what really tipped the President over the edge was the suggestion that he was a lonely Pashtun in a Tajik-dominated government. As a matter of fact, the assertion was wrong: if the *Times* leader writer had bothered to check, he (or perhaps she) would soon have discovered that there were more Pashtuns than Tajiks in the Afghan Cabinet. But, along with the inaccuracy, Karzai apparently found the references to ethnicity and to his loneliness deeply upsetting. Somehow this leading article combined with all the other pressures on him and caused the President to decide to retract his earlier agreement to Ashdown's appointment. This was despite the fact that he had apparently assured George Bush in one of his regular – too regular – video conferences with the American President that he would accept Lord Ashdown.

That acceptance had been based on a secret meeting between Karzai and Ashdown during an official visit to Kuwait by the Afghan President soon after the turn of the year. They had apparently got on well, with Ashdown giving Karzai a book of English poetry and speaking about his kinsfolk's lives on the North West Frontier. Neither the fact that Karzai had liked Paddy Ashdown nor the apparent promise he had given President Bush deterred the Afghan President from telling his Cabinet the following Sunday, 20 January, that he wanted clarification of Lord Ashdown's role before accepting him. Many of the Ministers urged the President to reject Ashdown out of hand.

The story now moved to the World Economic Forum in Davos, which President Karzai, the US Secretary of State (Condi Rice) and

David Miliband were all attending. If Ashdown's appointment was to survive, Dr Rice would have to tell Karzai to keep his word and accept Ashdown. But, as so often was the case with American diplomacy towards the erratic Afghan leader, Condi's discussion of the issue with Karzai was inconclusive. It was left to the British Prime Minister and Foreign Secretary to push for Ashdown – something that they were neither equipped nor especially willing to do. The idea that Ashdown should fly to Davos to clear up the misunderstandings in a meeting with President Karzai was dropped.

On the Saturday of the Davos meeting, 26 January, I flew to England, and spoke to Paddy Ashdown that evening. I told him that my instinct was that the Americans, having proposed him, were now going to drop him: in my view, he was better advised to jump before he was pushed. And that was exactly what Ashdown did, in a handsomely worded statement put out from his house in Somerset on the morning of Sunday the 27th. We were back to square one in the search for a high-octane successor to Tom Königs.

But the British part in the Paddy Ashdown saga was overshadowed by another, wholly unexpected public row about what Britain was doing in Helmand. Speaking to journalists in Davos on Thursday 24 January, Karzai had said what he believed: that the British military presence in Helmand had made matters there worse not better. Once again, *The Times*, of Friday the 25th, said it all, in a report that set the British–Afghan political agenda for weeks to follow:

Mr Karzai, Britain's key ally in Afghanistan, had little praise for the efforts of the 7,800 British troops deployed in his country. Most are in the restless southern Helmand province, where Britain has invested billions of pounds in trying to defeat the Taliban, bolster central government authority and begin reconstruction.

But Mr Karzai said that they had failed in the task, particularly the initial military mission launched nearly two years ago by 16 Air Assault Brigade – a unit that is returning for its second tour this year.

'There was one part of the country where we suffered after the arrival of the British forces,' Mr Karzai told a group of journalists at the Davos Economic Forum. 'Before that we were fully in charge of Helmand.

When our governor was there, we were fully in charge. They came and said, "Your governor is no good." I said "All right, do we have a replacement for this governor; do you have enough forces?" Both the American and the British forces guaranteed to me they knew what they were doing and I made the mistake of listening to them. And when they came in, the Taliban came.'

Asked if he was blaming British failure for the return of the Taliban, he added: 'I just described the situation of mistakes we made. The mistake was that we removed a local arrangement without having a replacement. We removed the police force. That was not good. The security forces were not in sufficient numbers or information about the province. That is why the Taliban came in. It took us a year and a half to take back Musa Qala. This was not failure but a mistake.'

That put the cat among the pigeons in decisive fashion. After the high hopes of just a month earlier, two of the major pillars of Western engagement with President Karzai had collapsed: the Ashdown appointment and the Afghan President's support for the Western military presence in Helmand, against a background of the most serious terrorist attack in Kabul for months and the rejection by the Afghan Parliament of most of Karzai's Cabinet.

Although we may not have realised it at the time, the worm had turned for ever in President Karzai's relationship with Britain, and with America. And, in a sense, it was *The Times* wot did it.

Chapter 14

'We Are Winning –
Only It Doesn't Feel Like It'

In early February 2008, I flew back to London, for what diplomats coyly call 'consultations'. I also wanted to take some of the leave I had been unable to take at Christmas, owing to the Semple–Patterson affair. But, as so often occurred when I was back in England on breather, David Miliband's Diary Secretary tracked me down and asked if I could come into the Office for a chat with the Foreign Secretary.

On this occasion, such a meeting made even more sense than usual. David Miliband had agreed with Condi Rice that the two of them would hold a joint seminar on Afghanistan and Pakistan at Lancaster House in London, before flying on together for a joint visit to Afghanistan. As was to happen almost exactly a year later with Mrs Clinton (see Chapter 21), David Miliband lined up his prize officials to perform in front of the US Secretary of State. David had asked me to give a short presentation on how I saw things in Afghanistan, and he wanted to go over the ground with me beforehand.

In the early spring of 2008, David Miliband and I had not yet thought through what was needed to deliver a political solution. Nor did we yet fully understand why the West's so-called strategy was so deficient. We still believed that it was more a question of improving the existing counter-insurgency strategy, and of supplementing it with programmes focused on politics, governance and development. We had not really absorbed that the 'Clear, Hold and Build' strategy wasn't really a strategy at all. In reality, 'Clear, Hold and Build' amounts to little more than a technique or tactic for suppressing, locally and temporarily, the symptoms of insurgency, rather than curing the underlying disease. Nor had I, at least, fully understood that the underlying political settlement within Afghanistan, and between Afghanistan and its neighbours, needed fundamental change if it was to be sustainable without a massive Western military presence.

When the two Secretaries of State sat down in one of the slightly smaller, but still vast, rooms at Lancaster House in February 2008, I told them that the overall political and security situations in Afghanistan were trending downwards. Neither was facing imminent collapse. But we needed to make 'course corrections', in order to halt and reverse those downward trends. With Paddy Ashdown out of the picture, we had urgently to find a suitable successor to Tom Königs. We needed better co-ordination of the international effort in Kabul. We needed a civilian surge to match the military presence. And we needed to adopt fresh approaches to giving Afghanistan's provinces and districts the confidence to secure and govern their own areas without relying too much on Kabul.

In front of Bush's Secretary of State, I would have been careful not to be critical of the Bush Administration's disastrously erratic handling of the Afghanistan dossier. It was all about working with what we had, rather than the radically different, heavily political approach that was really necessary. To my surprise and delight, in this meeting, and in discussions over the days that followed, on her aircraft and in Afghanistan, Condi Rice turned out to be much more open minded on Afghanistan than I had expected – and than most of her officials. When one US official told her that 'We are winning, Madam Secretary, only it doesn't feel like it,' Condi responded rather sharply that, in counter-insurgency, if you don't feel as though you are winning, then you are losing. It was as though we were briefing the practically minded, non-ideological academic Dr Rice really was, rather than an apostle of a neo-conservative foreign policy.

As well as a coterie of officials from her own office, the State Department regional bureau, the Pentagon and White House and the US Embassy in London, Dr Rice was accompanied by the State Department 'Counselor' (in other words, senior foreign policy guru to the Secretary of State), Professor Eliot Cohen of Johns Hopkins University. It was thoroughly refreshing to discover that he too was quite different from the neo-con my limited prior knowledge had him down as. He asked some searchingly honest questions. His rather owlish academic manner was lent added authority by the bow tie he seemed always to sport. Eliot is the only person I have ever known to wear a bow tie and a flak jacket at the same time. He was quietly dismissive of much of the 'happy talk' we sometimes had from the military briefers. It was only during our second meeting that I discovered that he was the author of the magisterial *Supreme Command*,* now sadly out of print. But in that great work he shows, by looking at Lincoln and his generals, Clemenceau and his generals, Churchill and his generals and Ben Gurion and his generals, that, left to themselves, military commanders risk losing great campaigns. Success in grand strategy lies in establishing a proper balance between political and strategic direction of the war and military command at theatre and field level. And it was only much later still that I discovered that *Supreme Command* had been one of Defense Secretary Donald Rumsfeld's favourite books, used by him to justify tilting the balance too far the other way, in favour of civilian micro-management of military campaigns.

After the seminar at Lancaster House, and an excellent lunch provided by the Government Hospitality Fund, the British and American delegations made their way separately to the Royal Suite out on the south-west side of Heathrow airport. There, waiting for us, in white and pale blue, with 'UNITED STATES OF AMERICA' emblazoned on its side, was a huge United States Air Force C-32A VIP transport aircraft, the military version of the Boeing 757. Aboard, green with envy, we were in another world from the cosy 1960s-style comfort of the much smaller aircraft of 32 (The Royal) Squadron of the Royal Air Force. This was an instrument of superpower power. A private cabin for the 'principal', in this case the Secretary of State, contained the bed which Jack Straw had once taken off Condi Rice: David Miliband was going to make no such mistake. There were kitchens and communications suites and offices, and rows of seats for the travelling officials, which seemed to recline further the more senior one was. David Miliband got the equivalent of a first-class seat; the rest of us were in the USAF equivalent of business class, but without the food or service.

---

* London: Simon & Schuster, 2002.

The folly of the Blair Government's repeated loss of nerve in failing to order two such aircraft for British Government business was obvious to all: in a twenty-four-hour world of news, and of action and reaction, secure in-flight communications – not available on the charters to which British Ministers are reduced – would alone have been enough to justify the cost. But the leaks from Gordon Brown's Treasury about the then Prime Minister's plans to commission 'Blair Force One' had twice killed the project; and now the age of austerity makes such expenditure politically impossible.

We flew from London to Inçirlik in eastern Turkey, working, resting, gossiping. Condi was everywhere, discussing, consulting, schmoozing: it was a privilege to have been one of the participants in her roadshow. Our landing in Kabul was delayed by snow and freezing fog, but eventually we were down. As soon as we were out on the military apron, we were walked straight across to a C-17 Globemaster of the USAF. With its engines running, the Boeing was waiting to take us down to Kandahar for a joint visit to the base there. Lashed to the floor of the vast hold was an enormous pallet. On it were rows of airline-style passenger seats (for the extras), a small cabin (for the Secretary) and what the USAF still calls a lavatory (for everyone).

We can't have been on the ground in Kandahar for more than an hour or so. The centrepiece of the visit was a briefing from, mainly, Canadians, about the progress they were making in pacifying Kandahar. Frankly, it was not an impressive performance, and Condi's irritation was obvious. The Canadians and others said all the right things, using the hopeful vocabulary of stabilisation and the eager-earnest syntax of counter-insurgency. Cautious optimism was the leitmotiv. But each of us knew that at least three essential components were missing: the West didn't have the military and civilian resources really necessary for the prodigious task in hand, or for long enough; the Afghans had neither the capacity nor the will eventually to take over from us, and wouldn't acquire either any time soon; and nothing was being done about the sanctuary areas across the Durand Line in Pakistan, which still provided a vast rear staging area for the insurgency. In Kandahar, Pakistan feels much closer than it does in Kabul, and its role, both passive and active, in the insurgency correspondingly greater.

After a brief pep talk to the troops from Condi, we flew back to Kabul, for a delayed lunch with President Karzai and his Ministers. Karzai was his usual charming self, with just a touch of the obsequiousness he reserved for the Americans. The two Foreign Ministers sat opposite him, at a long table along which were ranged much of the Afghan Cabinet and the senior members of the American and British delegations. There was only one conversation, a polite fencing match between the President and his two principal guests. As so often on such occasions, the rest of us just sat there, looking grave and attentive, some taking sporadic notes that were unlikely ever to be consulted again. The high point of the meal came when David Miliband reached for the salad and President Karzai cried out, 'Don't touch that, Mr Miliband, it's not safe to eat.'

At the end of the visit the two Secretaries of State concluded that the answer was more of the same: the US and UK should work together on fresh approaches to the challenges that all now agreed we faced. Condi was keen that we should do more joint thinking on the themes of Afghanisation, civilianisation and localisation: she placed great and proper emphasis on empowering local communities. So, less than a week after she and David Miliband had left, we had, on 14 February, the first of what was supposed to have been a series of joint secure video teleconferences (SVTCs), linking Bill Wood and me in Kabul with Washington and London.

But consultation and co-ordination of this kind were hard work. The good intentions from the joint visit were soon forgotten, in the face of more immediate diary and other pressures on both Ministers. Britain was always the junior partner. And, inevitably, the American Secretary of State found herself flying on to, and focusing on, the next trouble spot: she just could not give Afghanistan the high-level political attention it so badly needed. And, with the Presidential election approaching, the Bush White House was not in favour of anything which might imply that the President's Afghan policy had been other than a success.

Our first SVTC, or 'Sivits' as the Americans called it, was a stilted affair: there were just too many players, and too many differences in basic assumptions and in comparative knowledge and influence. The thing I mainly remember from that first electronic encounter was Bill

Wood looking at me rather sharply when I said, at the start (it must have been 7 a.m. Eastern Daylight Time), 'Happy Valentine's Day, Madam Secretary': that was not the way American officials spoke to their political bosses.

A week after that I was down in Helmand again, this time to review the latest British strategy for the province. This was known as the Helmand Roadmap, and involved carefully co-ordinated lines of activity. Security, governance and development were the three broad categories of work, each divided into dozens of sub-streams and then squeezed into a geographical matrix, district by district. The plan, as it emerged, was excellent; the problem came as always when the plan collided with Afghan realities on the ground. We could just about co-ordinate our own side – though the Americans were always reluctant to be co-ordinated by anyone, even their allies. But the Afghans were much less susceptible to this sort of guidance, however much we went through the motions of consulting them on our plans. I was given a briefing on the thinking emerging in Helmand, as one brigade handed over to the next, and was glad to give my general blessing.

Seeing the enthusiasm and expertise of the planners, the stabilisation 'experts' who had travelled from London, as apostles for this new cult, it was terribly difficult to pour cold water on their ideas. It sounded mean and disparaging, and in any case wasn't what anybody wanted to hear. Moreover, the latest strategy was always presented as the best ever, the *nec plus ultra* which would never be surpassed. Each plan was always more 'joined up' than the last, with plenty of 'cross-cutting' themes: the snake oil of stabilisation. But in time the Roadmap too passed on, to the great graveyard of Afghan strategies in, I suppose, southern Afghanistan's Dashti Margo – or Desert of Death. So, telling myself I was being kind rather than cowardly, I would offer words of encouragement and praise, for good work undoubtedly done, and try to keep most of my reservations to myself.

It was on that visit to Helmand that I found myself standing with the senior British officer in Afghanistan, Lieutenant General Jonathon Riley, on the edge of the windswept airstrip at Camp Bastion, as the Task Force bid farewell to the remains of Corporal Stephen Lawrence of the 2nd Battalion The Yorkshire Regiment (The Green Howards). It was a regiment I had long known and admired, for personal and family reasons: that only gave added poignancy to the ceremony, which I was moved to record in a telegram to London, reprinted at the start of this book. For all the doubts I had about the wisdom, or indeed the existence, of a political strategy worthy of the name, I never ceased to admire the extraordinary bravery and dedication of the men and women of all nationalities in uniform. Their sacrifice needed to be celebrated, with dignity.

Back in Kabul I paid my first visit to an infernal place that was the antithesis of dignity. Coming in to land at Kabul airport from the east, it is often possible to see on the drab and dusty plain below something resembling a giant concrete Catherine wheel. That edifice is the country's central prison, Pul-e-Charkhi, where over the four or so decades since it was built scores of thousands of Afghans have been incarcerated in the most appalling conditions, and tens of thousands put to death. More than anything else Pul-e-Charkhi symbolises for me the baneful legacy of Afghanistan's suffering in the three decades before the West intervened in 2001.

As part of our efforts to build a better Afghanistan, we had a team of six excellent officers from HM Prison Service attached to the Embassy. Their job, working with Americans and Canadians mainly, was to teach the Afghans how to run a half-decent prison, if possible using new facilities designed and built for them by the West. It was the final part of what my Canadian colleague used to call the 'Cops, Courts and Corrections' agenda for Afghanistan. None of the legs of the stool was much use without the other two. There was little point in having even a semi-effective police force unless those detained by the Police could be offered a fairish trial, and, if convicted, could be put in custody and be guaranteed to remain there, at least for a bit.

I had expected to be shocked by Pul-e-Charkhi and was not disappointed. Entering through the rusting gate was a descent into the darker parts of Dante's imagination. I was taken to see the prison governor, through a dank basement, with broken light fittings swinging from a ceiling through which water poured. The governor sat in his office, which felt more like a recess in the bowels of the great beast, and poured out his woes. At a time when DFID were telling me that an average

Afghan family needed $100 a month just to survive, the governor said that his official salary was $42 a month. His guards were paid $17 month. To live, he added, he and his staff had no option but to offer supplementary services to the prisoners in return for money: small sums by most standards, but enough to make the difference between a half-decent existence and half-starvation for the guards and their families. I was appalled that, seven years after the West had first invaded Afghanistan, the country's main penitentiary was in such a state.

Our prison officers were doing their best, against almost insuperable odds. They showed me a new, British-built facility, at the edge of the prison: it was a world away from the old cells along the spokes of the main wheel, each of which had at times contained as many as thirty prisoners. Beside the British facility was an even bigger American one, run by Americans, with higher walls and taller watchtowers.

To be fair, a series of disasters at Pul-e-Charkhi led to the Americans giving the issue the attention and resources it deserved. The situation there and in many but far from all Afghan prisons has much improved since then, despite the occasional break-out. Still, our prison officers found some of the American approaches a bit bizarre. For example, when it became necessary to move the prisoners from an old wing at Pul-e-Charkhi into a refurbished one, the US corrections personnel proposed pumping the old wing full of gas to knock out all the inmates, who would then be carried insensate to the new wing. To his great credit, a shocked veteran of HM Prisons Parkhurst and Albany strongly objected. He insisted that the move be done the hard, but humane, way, by having small groups of prisoners moved by prison officers wearing suitable protective clothing.

It was about this time that President Karzai decided to have a few of the scores of prisoners waiting on death row executed. He was under pressure to demonstrate the smack of firm government, and must have thought that a gesture like this would appeal to some of his supporters. About eight or so prisoners were selected, I never knew how. One bought his way out days before the execution date, allegedly driving out of the prison gates in a plush 4x4.

On the fateful day, the prisoners were taken out under cover of darkness, to the Afghan Army's main training grounds near Kabul, where the executions were due to take place. Unfortunately, the gate guards there said that they had had no orders to admit the prisoners or their executioners. Reportedly, the wretched party spent some time driving around, hoping to light on a suitable spot for the execution. Eventually they found one, and the guards removed the prisoners' manacles and shackles so that they could pray for the last time. But, in the darkness, the temptation to escape proved too great to resist. The prisoners made a dash for freedom, and ended up being mown down by machine-gun fire.

But the deed had been done, as President Karzai reported to the US Ambassador and me at a meeting of the war cabinet a day or so later. I was privately appalled at what had happened, but, rather ignobly, chose to say nothing. My American colleague was not so restrained: reflecting the views of the Republican Administration for which he worked, the US Ambassador told the President, without the slightest sense of irony, that the executions had been 'a beacon of hope for the future of Afghanistan'.

In the spring of 2008 I did something that lifted my spirits. The Commanding Officer of the detachment of the Coldstream Guards in Kabul invited me to go out on patrol with his men. The Coldstreamers were responsible for an area east of Kabul, either side of the Jalalabad road. Much of their parish was still remarkably rural, with many small farms and mud villages, crisscrossed with canals. It was there that we marched out, in Northern Ireland formation, as it were: a central column, with two flanking columns, each spread out. Soft hats, no helmets or sunglasses, hearts and minds in classic British fashion. I felt so proud of the squaddies as we walked quietly through the villages and along the tracks between the paddy fields: everyone we met was given a friendly greeting. We took great trouble to avoid damaging the crops, or anything remotely approaching threatening behaviour. It was a world away from the American style of patrolling: three heavily armoured Humvees, aerials waving, gun turrets swinging back and forth, the GIs yelling 'Keep back! Keep back!'

The whole experience gave me a warm feeling. We were invited to take tea with one of the village headmen. We distributed goodies to some of the children. We passed the massive footbridge over the

Jalalabad road, a proud gift to the people of Kabul from the oldest infantry regiment in the British Army. We were undoubtedly doing good, protecting the people, generating security within which the institutions of government could grow up, and the vehicles of development deliver. But, within a few weeks, the Coldstream were gone: other regiments had other priorities and fewer resources. And no other ISAF partner was much interested in foot patrols. In any case, the Afghans were due to take lead responsibility for security in Kabul – not such a radical step as it was meant to sound, since the Afghan lead would be underpinned by the presence of tens of thousands of ISAF troops. As that 'misunderestimated' (as George Dubya would have said) General Dan McNeill had once confided in me: 'I could do this, Sherard, if I had 500,000 men.' 'And fifty years,' I had been tempted to add.

My life, literally, depended on my Royal Military Police Close Protection Team. The whole team had turned out for the patrol with the Coldstream Guards, wearing, unusually for them, battledress (they normally wore civilian clothes). Later, I was often to meet former members of my team, similarly dressed, working for a senior officer. That spring, however, they were to face their greatest test.

In an uncanny echo of the bomb attack the previous November, one morning in late April, as I was shaving, the duty bodyguard burst into my bathroom. He shouted that bombs were going off all over Kabul. He rapidly squeezed me into a flak jacket and put a helmet on my head, and instructed me to sit tight on the bathroom floor. Once the 'boss' was safe, he used his radio to try to find out what was going on. The answer came back soon and embarrassingly enough: the booms had just been the Afghan Army, rehearsing its twenty-one-gun salute for the parade on 27 April to celebrate the sixteenth anniversary of the fall of Dr Najibullah's Communist Government to the mujahideen. The antique Russian howitzers which had fooled my first CPT in July 2007 had had the same effect on their successors, in April 2008.

In the weeks before the big parade, President Karzai discussed arrangements several times with the war cabinet. It was obvious that he was worried. He told the Afghan Defence Minister, General Wardak, that he wanted to spend as little time as possible in the open air. He suggested moving the ceremonies from the parade ground to the more confined space of the Olympic stadium near by. He quizzed General Wardak on how long he would have to spend inspecting the troops. He asked others to confirm that adequate security arrangements had been made.

The Embassy's security advice was that there was a risk of an attack at the parade. My new Close Protection Team had changed over only a day or two before. The new Team Leader, Captain Jim Devenney of the Royal Military Police, had long experience of these things. He made clear that he was worried about me attending the parade. Initially, I accepted their advice: I would stay away. But then I discovered that the American Ambassador and most of the rest of the diplomatic corps were going to be there. It would be noticed if the British Ambassador, alone of the more prominent ambassadors, stayed away. And, if an incident did occur, there would be Afghan conspiracy theories about the British having had advance warning, and perhaps even having been involved. So I concluded that I had no option but to attend. I reasoned that the Americans would have taken every possible precaution. Moreover, Karzai's 800-strong Presidential Protective Service was highly competent – and American mentored.

As was usual with events at which Karzai was present, the area was secured days in advance, and outside guests were expected to turn up hours early. Although my bodyguards tended to take such instructions literally, I knew from experience that one needed to be there only sixty minutes or so in advance. So that morning, of Sunday 27 April 2008, we arrived in the stand reserved for foreign VIPs at 8 a.m., and had to wait only until 9.15 a.m. before the President appeared.

I spent the hour gossiping in the sun with the other guests. The ISAF Commander, General McNeill, was there with a clutch of other senior officers, including the training mission commander, Major General Bob Cone. Among them were several British officers, including my Defence Attaché, Colonel Simon Newton, in dress uniform, wearing the dark-green beret of his regiment and a Sam Browne. Most ambassadors were there. Among those in the front row alongside me were the American, Bill Wood; the charming and able Canadian, Arif Lalani; and the immensely civilised Frenchman, Régis Koetschet, whom the French Foreign Minister Bernard Kouchner was shortly to move. I took photographs of my colleagues. My fellow amateur photographer, COMISAF's Executive Officer Trevor Bredenkamp, and I lazily took snaps of each other.

My mind flashed back to another parade ground, at another time: to Cairo, on 6 October 1981, the annual October War victory parade. With the world watching, Islamist terrorists dressed as soldiers had leapt from the military truck on which they were passing the saluting base, and pumped 40 Kalashnikov rounds into President Anwar Sadat. Many others had been killed or wounded. My first Ambassador, Sir Michael Weir, had narrowly escaped being hit. A great friend in the Australian Embassy had been badly injured. I had been watching the parade on television in the Embassy and had seen the screen suddenly go blank. I wondered whether, thirty years later, history was going to repeat itself.

In front of us the lines of Afghan soldiers stood in the sun, awaiting the arrival of their Commander-in-Chief. Their tasselled shakoes and high boots gave the whole assembly a slightly comic air. For security reasons, none of them carried a single bullet for their ancient rifles. The only fully armed personnel were those around the perimeter of the parade ground, including the Presidential Protective Service snipers.

Eventually, there was movement to the north. The Presidential motorcade rolled on to the parade ground and passed before us, with Karzai standing tall in the back of a camouflaged humvee. From the southern end of the ground the Defence Minister, my friend General Abdul Rahim Wardak, rolled forward in his humvee, to greet his Commander-in-Chief. General Wardak's uniform was a sight to behold: with a steeply raked Russian-style cap, his sunglasses and a chest-load of medals, he looked like a cross between a marshal of the Soviet Union and a Latin American dictator. He wheeled round and drove alongside the President as they passed in their humvees up and down the lines of soldiers. The motorcade stopped in front of the reviewing platform, fifty yards to the north of our stand. President Karzai and his party dismounted and took their places on the stand. The band struck up, we rose and stood to attention while the Afghan National Anthem was played.

As the dying bars of the Anthem faded away, I heard a faint crackling sound from across the parade ground: after a second or so I

Ambassador in action: every helicopter flight was a thrill.

Halcyon days: the old British Residence in Kabul, as it was in 1968. Curzon had said that the British Minister in Kabul should be 'the best housed man in Asia'.

The old British Embassy today, owned but not used by Pakistan.

Early morning exercise: in front of the Chancery, on my way to the gym, with my Royal Military Police duty bodyguard looking on watchfully.

Suicide bomb: the scene after the attack behind the Embassy in November 2007. We were lucky that none of our staff was killed or injured.

Those inside this Embassy Land Cruiser survived an attack by a suicide bomber, but with burst ear drums.

Addressing the 1st Battalion, the Grenadier Guards in Helmand, with the Task Force Commander, Brigadier John Lorimer, looking on.

Dusty ride: with the Commanding Officer of the Grenadier Guards, Lieutenant Colonel Carew Hatherley.

At work in my office in Kabul with, on the wall behind me, a portrait of the Queen and a map of Helmand showing the deployment of British forces.

Pretending to be friends: with Governor Wafa of Helmand on one of his visits to Kabul.

A hero's return: Lieutenant General Jonathon Riley and I pay our respects as Corporal Stephen Lawrence's remains begin the long journey home from Camp Bastion.

Brigadier Mark Carleton-Smith, who got it. He said that the Taliban could not be defeated.

Combat diplomacy: my first deputy, Michael Ryder, deployed in Helmand as head of the Provincial Reconstruction Team. He and Governor Mangal were nearly killed when their Chinook was hit by a rocket-propelled grenade.

Get-together in Garmsir: (*left to right*) me, the Chief of the Defence Staff Jock Stirrup and the International Development Secretary Douglas Alexander. Jock understood Afghanistan better than some of his colleagues, but still pushed Gordon Brown to send more troops to Helmand.

David Miliband, about to fly back to London after his first visit to Afghanistan.

The European team: EU Special Representative Francesc Vendrell (*left*) and his deputy, Michael Semple.

With President Karzai in his office in the Arg Palace.

Moments before the attack: President Karzai and
General Wardak pass the saluting base, April 2008.

Mullah Salam in Musa Qala with an Afghan police officer, shortly after the town's second 'liberation', in December 2008.

At the Af-Pak peace *jirga*, August 2007: (*left to right*) Hanif Atmar, then Education Minister, later Interior Minister, before he was fired; Abdul Karim Khurram, Minister of Culture; Abdul Jabar Sabet, the Attorney General; Abdul Rashid Dostum, the Uzbek warlord; and Hamed Gailani, Deputy Speaker of the Wolesi Jirga.

The Great Game is fun: the Iranian and Russian Ambassadors embrace outside the Arg Palace. Russian Ambassador Kabulov used to joke that he had been in Kabul so long that the city had been named after him.

Condi comes to Kabul: on the flight from London to Afghanistan, February 2008, with US Secretary of State Condoleezza Rice.

Always On: Richard Holbrooke seldom stopped working, usually via one of his three cellphones. On this occasion, as the 'R-R' on the headrest shows, he was hitching a lift to the White House in the British Ambassador's Rolls-Royce.

Speaking for Britain: at the Joint Co-ordination and Monitoring Board, sandwiched between the Turkish and US Ambassadors, with Major General Bob Cone, of the US training mission, looking on.

Sizzling Sangin: the CO of 2 Para, Lieutenant Colonel Joe O'Sullivan, briefs (*left to right*) Hugh Powell, head of the Provincial Reconstruction Team; me; then Leader of the Opposition David Cameron; and then Shadow Foreign Secretary William Hague in the blistering heat.

Friends united: with US Ambassador Bill Wood and General Dan McNeill at ISAF headquarters.

Rory Stewart, then head of the Turquoise Mountain Foundation, inspects the tile work in the great mosque in Mazar-e-Sharif.

Where Soviet tanks went to die: a Russian tank graveyard just south of the Panshir Valley.

Impossible embassy: Karl Eikenberry takes tea at Cliveden in May 2010 while we wait for Karzai to return from a meeting at Chequers with the new British Prime Minister, David Cameron, on his first weekend in office.

The finale of the beard-growing race between my deputy, Andrew Patrick, and me: he beat me by at least a centimetre.

The Special Rep takes the salute at the Edinburgh Tattoo, August 2009, with Major General Andrew Mackay, who had been my second brigadier in Helmand. Andrew understood COIN.

In the rank of General: Prince Charles visits the troops in Helmand on his long overdue trip to Afghanistan in March 2010. He gave the Armed Forces every possible support, but understood the importance of a political approach too.

Posers: up on swimming pool hill, with my bodyguards, for their team photograph on my last day as ambassador in Kabul.

realised it was gunfire. I assumed that some sort of rifle salute was being mounted and tried to see where it was coming from. It was then that I spotted the commandos of the Presidential Protective Service sprinting on to the parade ground, falling prone and starting shooting towards the south.

All hell broke loose. Screams, shouts, panic. The Afghan Army lined up on the parade ground broke ranks and fled, flinging their empty rifles to the ground, the tassels on their shakoes swinging up in the air. I spotted General McNeill taking cover. Others around me dropped on to their hands and knees and crawled forward behind the low concrete parapet that separated us from the parade ground proper. All around the Afghans guarding the perimeter were opening fire, with bullets whizzing through the air in every direction.

Suddenly, I felt a pair of hands on my shoulders, and a voice in my ear. 'Come with me, Sir,' said Jim Devenney, as he swung me round and frogmarched me up the steps and out of the back of the stand. There the position was if anything more dangerous than in front, as the Afghan perimeter guards seeming to be firing almost at random into and on to the parade ground. Jim gripped me to one side of him, saying that he had to put his body between me and the incoming fire.

We raced, or rather stumbled, towards the exit. Suddenly, I spotted the American Ambassador's armoured Land Cruiser inside the perimeter fence. I banged on the window. Bill Wood's bodyguard nearly shot me, but Bill levered open the door and told me to get in quickly. I did so, and was never more grateful to be inside an armoured vehicle. We sped off, scattering the crowds as we lurched and pitched over the rough ground to the gate. I had lost Jim and assumed he had got into the second American vehicle. But I owed my life to him, and to Bill Wood.

Once we were through the gate, I started phoning. The Embassy Ops Room first: they already knew that an incident was under way and confirmed that my CP Team were in hot pursuit of the American convoy. Next, I worried about my Defence Attaché, Simon Newton, whom I had not seen in the mêlée: no one knew where he was. It was an hour before we established that he had led several others to safety beneath the stand: there they had taken refuge while the bullets flew. I contacted the Foreign Office Response Centre in London, to ask them to alert Ministers and senior officials as they woke on the Sunday morning. As soon as my CP Team had recovered me from the American Embassy, I convened a meeting of senior staff back in our Embassy to take stock.

It was days before a full picture emerged of what had happened. President Karzai had been bundled to safety almost instantaneously by his bodyguards – so quickly in fact that his neighbours on the Presidential stand had not seen him going. General Wardak had rushed off to change into a somewhat more practical outfit, before returning to take charge – only to be accused of leaving the scene of an accident. Several people had been killed and wounded close to Karzai, including a Member of Parliament and a young girl. There had been six attackers, of whom three had been killed almost instantly by the Presidential snipers and three had escaped. They had been hiding in a run-down hotel some way south of the parade ground's perimeter for weeks, since before the first security sweeps. No one ever established why they had not been found when the hotel had been checked. But, once it had been checked, the six terrorists had been sealed inside the security bubble. The plot had all the hallmarks of the Haqqani network, or even Al Qaeda: it seemed too sophisticated for the Taliban. But that had not stopped the Taliban spokesman from phoning the BBC as the attack was under way – suggesting that they must have had some involvement.

The President's first reaction was fury that he had, as he saw it, been let down by his security advisers. They had, he claimed, assured him that the parade was safe – despite his premonitions of disaster. There was talk of dismissals, and resignations, and heated meetings at the Palace with no foreigners present. The Taliban maintained that they hadn't aimed actually to kill Karzai, merely to give everyone a nasty shock. I doubt that: they wanted maximum impact, and, if it could have been achieved, killing the Afghan President at the mujahideen parade would have been a huge coup. As it was, images of the Afghan Army running off the parade ground were worth thousands of words reporting that things in Afghanistan were not as good as they should have been.

I am not sure that there were any great lessons to be learned, but reviews were launched, scapegoats sought, resolutions made to do better next time. I had been more scared than I had ever been. But, as so often, Dan McNeill gave some comfort. As I was going to bed that night, an email from him pinged into my inbox. 'Sir SCC' (as he liked to call me), he began, followed by a crisp allusion to my coolness under fire. At least Dan hadn't seen how just how petrified I really had been.

Chapter 15

The Karzai Conundrum

Not surprisingly, the attack on the parade left President Karzai badly rattled. In future, he was to be much more cautious about appearing at setpiece public events. For example, in 2007 the August Independence Day parade had been held in Kabul's Olympic Stadium. A procession of groups ranging from disabled mujahideen to Afghanistan's cricket team had marched past. There had been displays of taekwondo and sword fighting, dancing and singing. But in August 2008 the whole thing was scaled down and held inside the Afghan Defence Ministry compound: a pale shadow of what it should have been, and a vote of little confidence in the security and safety of the city.

Throughout my first period as ambassador in Kabul I saw President Karzai on average once a week. But when I returned to Kabul in February 2010 for my second stint in charge of the Embassy, I found a President more reluctant to receive foreign Ambassadors without good reason. In this, he was not wrong: from the beginning I had encouraged him to spend less time seeing people and more time governing.

As the weeks turned into months, and the months into years, I became increasingly fond of President Karzai, and increasingly sympathetic to him. Someone once told me that the three things that mattered most to him were his beloved son, Mirwais, who was believed to have been born in 2006; his wider family, including his brothers and half-brothers; and his legacy. He really was conscious of his place in history and wanted to go down as the man who had brought his nation back again after the dark days of Communism, civil war and then Taliban rule.

In my view, Hamid Karzai's greatest strength is, and was, his political fluency: he has his finger on the pulse of his nation in the way few other leading Afghan politicians do, and is able to translate what he hears or sees into words that command attention, in Dari, Pashtu and English. He is able to work a foreign audience just as easily as he handles a domestic one. In my first year or so in Kabul, I was a bit sceptical about how well founded was his concern about civilian casualties inflicted by ISAF, and about how sincere were his doubts about the net effect of the Western military presence in the south. But increasingly I came to see that many of his instincts and judgements were in fact right: civilian casualties had done great damage to the credibility of ISAF; and it was true that Helmand had been less violent before British forces had blundered in, albeit under the domination of a particularly nasty narcolord, aligned with the President.

I remember in 2007 President Karzai starting to worry about the Presidential elections which were due to be held some time in 2009. He told me, almost plaintively, that there was no way parts of the south would be secure enough to hold credible elections two years later. He really didn't know what to do. He just didn't see how proper elections could be held. Later, under pressure from the Americans and from his own supporters, he gave up his opposition to holding elections in 2009. But in this, as on much else, his instincts were basically right: the south and east *were* too insecure to hold a credible election in 2007, and the situation there was even worse in 2009 – as the election fiasco showed.

Hamid Karzai would speak wistfully of being able to bring Mirwais up safely in his own country and of how that mattered more to him than almost anything else. He was a generous man too: once when I went to see him – I must have done something to please him – he had his tailor ambush me as I left and measure me for a shalwar kameez, the gift of the President. But he suffered from constant ill health, mainly colds and coughs, and seemed addicted to effervescent vitamin C tablets. I once brought him some nasal decongestant from England. Stress must have played a part in all this.

Karzai seemed to spend many hours watching television and surfing the internet, or at least the BBC News website. He was always up to date with the news from Pakistan, to which he would often refer. His favourite British television programme was *Last of the Summer Wine*, but he has a wide knowledge of English literature and of British history and culture.

But none of this made him the sort of strong leader Afghanistan perhaps needed. In September 2008 the French satirical weekly *Le Canard Enchaîné* carried a leaked telegram from the French Chargé d'Affaires in Kabul, Jean-François Fitou. In it he reported me as saying that the American strategy in Afghanistan was not working, that more troops would make things worse not better and that what the country needed was an acceptable dictator. I was not aware of having had such an exchange with Fitou, who had in fact had lunch with my Deputy, Andrew Patrick, the day before he drafted the cable which had appeared in *Le Canard*.

While the broad sentiments Fitou reported were ones with which I had much sympathy, the way in which they were set out was not my approach. And I was absolutely clear that Afghanistan did not need a dictator, since there was nothing to dictate with. Authors of diplomatic cables often cite others' views as cover for their own. But whatever the genesis of the cable, Fitou had certainly not written it intentionally to embarrass me or the British Government. Rather it was an entirely professional contribution to the debate then getting under way in Paris on whether France should send more troops to Afghanistan, for Atlanticist rather than Afghan reasons. Someone in Paris opposed to the troop uplift had leaked the cable to cause embarrassment for the French Government.

I happened to be in London, about to return to Kabul, when the story broke. I was pleased to learn from a senior official at the Foreign Office that his French opposite number had immediately rung to apologise and to promise a leak enquiry (which, as usual in such cases, never found the culprit). I returned to Kabul and went to see Karzai, with my heart in my boots.

To my surprise, the President greeted me with a beaming smile and outstretched arms. 'My dear Sherard,' he said, 'I agree with every word you said.' 'But, Mr President, I didn't say it, and those are not my views,' I replied. 'That doesn't matter at all,' Karzai replied. 'I still applaud you for saying it. Afghanistan does need some sort of dictator.' I protested again that this was not what I thought. But the President would still have none of it: discreetly taking the credit seemed the only option.

The 'acceptable dictator' remark was, however, never forgotten. Thanks to the internet, it comes up again and again, and was even cited by Tom Brokaw in the US Presidential debate on 8 October 2008. It will forever be associated with someone who had never made it, let alone thought it. As a louche English friend remarked drily, I had indeed been 'foutu par Fitou'.

Increasingly, as my time in Afghanistan went on, people began to ask whether President Karzai was the right man to lead his country through the next stage. In the eyes of many Americans, he went from the 'hero' who had been in the Senate Gallery during President Bush's State of the Union address in 2002 to a 'zero' who was involved in the drug trade and constantly criticising NATO for what it was doing in his country. There was much briefing against him, which inevitably had to be followed by private apology and appeasement. In my view, the only way to handle him was public respect and private tough love, with equal emphasis on toughness and on love.

George Bush gave Hamid Karzai plenty of love, but it was almost unconditional. I was told that the US President took the view that running any country was an almost impossible job, and he was not going to tell others how to do it. It was not the American President's role to second-guess how the Afghan President did his job. Thus, time and again Bill Wood or Dan McNeill would raise some point with President Karzai, and appeal to the White House for their President to back them up in one of his SVTC conversations with Karzai. But Bush seldom did. For example, although Karzai had promised Bush in one of these conversations that he would accept Paddy Ashdown, Bush never held him to account on this when Karzai backed away. To the near despair of American officials trying to manage the relationship and protect the vast US interests in Afghanistan, their President wasn't really willing to have a tough conversation with the Afghan President.

Karzai was sensitive about these conversations, for which originally he had to travel to the US Embassy: there were too many echoes of Najibullah and his predecessors taking their instructions from the Soviet leadership. The Americans therefore installed a secure video conferencing suite in the Palace, so that the President did not need to be seen entering the US Embassy. But even then, every time there was such a conversation, the following day the *New York Times* or the *Washington Post* carried a pretty full report of what had gone on – usually rather fuller than the account our Embassy in Washington was able to extract from the National Security Council.

Hamid Karzai knew that he had a special relationship with Bush. I often suspected that, in the hours they had once spent alone together at Camp David, George W. Bush had promised him that he would never seek to force him to do something he didn't want to do – or words to that effect. I have a clear memory of Karzai narrowing his eyes and, in referring to his 'friend' George Bush, implying that Bush would always in the end stick up for him. Or perhaps it was just my suspicious inference.

Of the other Western leaders, Karzai often used to tell me how much he liked Tony Blair. He said that he wanted to give Blair the Order of Wazir Akbar Khan – Afghanistan's highest decoration, named after the son of the Afghan leader Dost Mohammed, who had played such a part in resisting the British in the First Anglo-Afghan War. But somehow the President never got round to it.

I did believe, however, that he had a sincere and serious relationship with Gordon Brown. This was in part because the British Prime Minister was well briefed and interested in detail. But it was also because his quiet, almost diffident manner appealed to Karzai. So did the fact that they both had young sons and had come to fatherhood late. Somehow the Brown–Karzai relationship clicked, at least from my vantage point. But, for British policy-makers, the key point was that this was a real load-bearing relationship: the Prime Minister could and would raise points of concern to HMG and get a response from the Afghan President. Of course, the problem was that, while Karzai would promise Brown that he would, for example, send more Afghan Police to Sangin, he delivered on those promises only erratically. And he never really overcame a tendency to tell each interlocutor what he wanted to hear.

I have already described President Karzai's relationship with the Prince of Wales, which was a real asset, especially when times were tough. And, as I had seen in Saudi Arabia, the Prince would not shrink from raising difficult issues, if he was persuaded by advice that he should do so. But sometimes our enthusiasm for that relationship could backfire. After the rows over Semple and Patterson, over Ashdown and over British troops in Helmand, in late January 2008 my Deputy, Andrew Patrick, had the brilliant idea of getting the Prince of Wales to put in a New Year call to the Afghan President. After much toing and froing, the Prince, in Scotland I think, was eventually connected to Karzai. The conversation, of which we never had an official account, apparently went well. I set off for my next meeting with the Afghan President expecting things would now be a bit better between Afghanistan and Britain. Instead, I found Karzai rather downcast. When I asked him why, he explained that, even in terms of courtesy, we Brits always managed to outmatch him and put him on the back foot. The Prince of Wales had had Karzai to stay in Scotland, had written an exquisitely charming follow-up letter to him and had then telephoned him to wish him a Happy New Year. And in all that time Karzai hadn't got round to writing, let alone posting, the handwritten thank-you note he had intended to send Prince Charles: he felt badly overmatched and outclassed. Sometimes I felt we just couldn't win.

But however good the relationship between President Karzai and interlocutors back in Britain or America, the day-to-day relationship had to be managed by those on the ground. There was just too much business to transact. The key actor in this was, inevitably, the American Ambassador. In my first period in Kabul, Bill Wood saw more of Karzai than all other foreigners put together. He would be in and out of the Presidential Palace three or four times a week, on his own, with other senior Americans, at our Thursday-morning war cabinet meetings, and, too often for his comfort, accompanying Codels (Congressional delegations) and the unending stream of senior US civilian and military officials passing through Kabul.

But the weight of business, and the inevitable differences between US and Afghan interests, made it difficult for Bill. The only US Ambassador who had built a really functioning relationship, in very different circumstance, had been Zalmay Khalilzad – the conservative academic of Pashtun origin who had been Bill's predecessor but one, and who had gone on from Kabul to serve as Bush's ambassador to Iraq and then to the United Nations. As ambassador in Kabul, Khalilzad had had immense linguistic and cultural advantages, and, apparently, operated as something of a one-man band. But he did see the President for dinner several times a week, and was able to give Karzai the sustained support (and apply the necessary gentle pressure) he needed. It was almost as though the President's homework had to be set and marked on a daily basis as, to change metaphor, he was helped over hurdle after hurdle.

But Khalilzad had long gone from Kabul. Bill Wood's task wasn't eased by the fact that, during much of our time, Khalilzad, now that he was US Ambassador to the UN, seemed to be independently in touch with President Karzai and many of the other prominent political players in Afghanistan, and to be pursuing business and political interests of his own there. It was even rumoured that Khalilzad was actively exploring running for president of Afghanistan in 2009. The US Government's ban on spying on its own citizens, particularly those in prominent government jobs, made things very awkward for Bill Wood, who was not able to find out what was really going on.

General McNeill was far more political than he pretended, but, wisely, he insisted that politics was out of his lane and confined himself to speaking on security issues in our meetings with President Karzai. But his time in command in Afghanistan in 2002–3 had given him an excellent grounding in the realities of Afghanistan, and I found his judgement to be spot on. His mischievous sense of humour, accompanied by a twinkle in his clear blue eyes, was one of the joys of my time in Kabul. I remember Dan and his military assistant, Trevor Bredenkamp, coming to the farewell dinner I gave for him in identical, ill-fitting civilian suits made for them by the tailors of Kabul: the first and only time I saw the General out of uniform. Sometimes he would leave meetings of the war cabinet close to despair at the military folly of civilians with no grounding in either strategy or tactics, and little knowledge of the situation on the ground in Afghanistan. But he soon recovered his balance. All this earned Dan McNeill President Karzai's respect, but it meant that they did not have the kind of political relationship the US needed someone on the ground to have with Karzai.

Of the British generals whom Karzai knew, he was closest to David Richards, from the nine months David had spent in Kabul as ISAF commander. But Karzai was fondest of General Sir John McColl, who had been ISAF's first commander back in 2001. General McColl had brought Karzai into the Presidential Palace and given the Afghan leader reassurance when he most needed it. That led President Karzai to suggest that General McColl should be the UN Special Representative when Paddy Ashdown pulled out. Luckily, John McColl had the sense to turn the suggestion down flat. It would have been the end of a beautiful friendship.

In early March 2008, the UN Secretary General announced that he had appointed the veteran Norwegian diplomat Kai Eide as his special representative in Kabul, to succeed Tom Königs. I had seen quite a bit of Kai during my first year in Kabul: he had made a point of coming to visit me for breakfast whenever he was passing through town, in his capacity as a deputy secretary at the Norwegian Foreign Ministry. He claimed that he used to come to see me for the talk, not the porridge, but I know that he wanted the latter at least as much as the former.

What I liked about Kai was that he had a realistic assessment of the situation. But he also shared my belief – which I still hold – that, given the right measure of political will, in the right places, something can be done to turn the situation in Afghanistan round. I was therefore delighted by his appointment, and we pledged to work closely together.

After his arrival in Kabul in early May 2008, Kai got off to the best possible start, with the international community, and with President Karzai and the Afghans. He was political, he was fluent, he was focused and he was energetic. In particular, he built a good, almost affectionate relationship with President Karzai and began to have access to the Palace which only the Americans rivalled. All that was only as it should have been.

In three and a half years working in and on Afghanistan, however, I saw time and again the same phenomenon. A worried international community would place excessive hopes on a new appointee, in the hope or rather the wish that he or she could turn things round. And, inevitably, sooner or later the intractability of the situation and the absence of a serious American strategy would mean that the gilt came off the gingerbread.

Kai's honeymoon lasted longer than most. In my view, it was given an added boost by the exceptionally courageous stand he took over a massacre of civilians at a village called Azizabad in Shindand district in western Afghanistan in late August 2008. The details of what happened are still not completely clear. But it seems that US Special Forces working with Afghan troops went into Azizabad at night in search of, as they thought, some local Taliban. As they entered the village, they came under fire and eventually called in air support, in the form of an AC-130 Spectre gunship – a version of the Hercules transport aircraft which carries a 105mm artillery piece for ground bombardment. The Spectre duly flattened the village. When the US and Afghan forces went through it at daylight they found only half a dozen or so bodies among the rubble. They immediately proclaimed that six or so Taliban had been killed and that there had been few if any civilian casualties.

Within hours, however, it emerged that some ninety civilians had in fact been killed, with their bodies still under the rubble. Many had been in the village for a wedding party. Gradually the locals excavated the bodies and laid them out in a local mosque. From there images taken on a mobile phone of the entire prayer room of the mosque covered with the broken and dusty bodies of children as well as adults reached Kabul, where they caused outrage. Journalists were soon arriving in Azizabad, but only after, in Muslim tradition, most of the victims had been buried. Whatever the exact number of casualties, it was clear that it was many more than the half a dozen or so claimed by US forces.

Discreetly, Kai swung into action, presenting the evidence to Bill Wood, to the newly arrived ISAF Commander, General David McKiernan, and, separately, to me. It was shocking. But the Americans at first were in denial: an initial investigation backed up their Special Forces' account. It was only after weeks of tension and pressure that General McKiernan adopted a suggestion which I had made, and had a senior officer from CentCom fly out and review the evidence. That resulted in a big uplift in the number of civilian casualties conceded by the Americans. To Dave McKiernan's credit, he eventually went to

Azizabad in person to say sorry to a local shura, and to hand over compensation. It was a big gesture by a big man.

One worrying aspect of this incident was the suggestion that US Special Forces had unwittingly become involved in a dispute between two tribes over who had won the contracts for guarding the US base at Shindand near by. At least some of the dead had passes on them indicating that they worked for a British-owned private security company that was protecting the US base: being shelled by a Spectre gunship had been their reward.

Kai handled all this in exemplary fashion. He came under tremendous pressure to drop the whole thing, from some very angry and upset Americans, in denial about what their Special Forces had done. But with quiet persistence he steered the ship to port, without pointing too many fingers in public, in a way which enabled the Americans to correct – more or less – their own mistake.

The whole story showed how difficult it is to get armies in war, as with any institution, to mark their own homework. And it underlined a more serious problem about the three or more separate military command chains we had in Afghanistan for most of my time there. NATO forces and those of countries, such as Australia, allied with NATO reported to the ISAF Commanding General through four Regional Commands and one for the capital. COMISAF in turn reported to the NATO Supreme Allied Commander, Europe (SACEUR), a four-star American general (latterly an admiral) based at Mons in Belgium. In theory, he did so through the NATO Joint Force Commander (a four-star German general) at Brunssum in The Netherlands. In theory, SACEUR reported to the NATO Military Committee (of military representatives) and to the North Atlantic Council (of Ambassadors to NATO).

In parallel with this, the large proportion of US forces in Afghanistan who were not assigned to NATO had their own separate command chain for most of my time there. Beyond that, US Special Forces operated semi-independently across most of Afghanistan, and reported up a third, separate command chain to the Special Forces Command in Washington. Until General McChrystal got a grip on the problem, successive COMISAF and British brigade commanders in Helmand complained that US Special Forces did not liaise with local ground-holding forces as well as they should have done. Generals David Petraeus (at CentCom) and Stan McChrystal (as COMISAF) also had to deal with the tradition whereby the US Marine Corps had its own independent naval chain of command.

But these parallel command chains were far from the end of the story. Afghan forces had their own separate command chain. So did the paramilitary forces which operated, mainly in the east, under the auspices of agencies of the US Government. Overlaying all this was the fact that every national contingent also reported up its national command chain. Thus, British forces reported to our Chief of Joint Operations at Permanent Joint Headquarters at Northwood in Middlesex, and then on to the Chief of the Defence Staff in Whitehall. US forces had an even wider array of reporting requirements, including to CentCom at Tampa in Florida and on up to the Joint Chiefs of Staff in the Pentagon.

Even worse was the fact that most ISAF contingents were subject to formal national caveats of one kind or another, restricting the ways in which they could be used by ISAF commanders. Each had their own rules of engagement. Jokes about the Germans being forbidden from operating at night and being obliged to shout warnings in Pashtu and Dari before opening fire had a basis in truth. So did the fact that they weren't allowed to operate in the more dangerous areas of the country. When, during Condi Rice's joint visit to Afghanistan with David Miliband in February 2008, an American official complained to her that the Germans weren't pulling their weight in Afghanistan, she put the fact that they were there, fighting a war, in its proper perspective. 'We have spent fifty years getting the Germans *not* to fight,' she said, 'so we should now applaud the fact that they are fighting at all.' I remember once remarking to General McKiernan what a burden the coalition was. But he was sanguine. 'There is only one thing worse than fighting a war with allies,' he remarked, 'and that is fighting it without allies.'

But the Heath Robinson-like military command chains for Afghanistan were more than just a reflection of national politics: they also reflected the inability or unwillingness of senior commanders and their political masters to tackle all the vested interests involved. It made for a far less effective military machine than the challenge of the Afghan insurgency really required.

Chapter 16

Cracking On in Helmand

Once or twice during my posting to Kabul senior Foreign Office officials expressed concern that my reporting, on a very limited distribution, of US political and military concerns about the way the British Army was performing in Helmand would 'upset the MOD'. They stressed the need for the Foreign Office to have good relations with the MOD and urged me to report criticism from senior Americans in theatre either orally or not at all. It was ignoble advice, but probably wise.

With that in mind, I wrote in early 2008 a letter declaring that HMG should try to make 2008 the 'Year of Helmand'. I was aware that a number of factors were coming together that year which should enable us to show that a counter-insurgency strategy of the kind we had been pursuing in Helmand could be made to work, provided it was focused in a few key areas. I thought that credible progress in the comparatively tiny areas of the country where British forces were operating would have a demonstration effect: it wouldn't win the war, but it would show how, in theory, it might be done.

Perhaps the most important factor was that President Karzai had at last replaced the antediluvian and inadequate previous Governor of Helmand, Assadullah Wafa, with a competent Pashtun technocrat from central casting, Gulab Mangal. Like many of Afghanistan's best administrators, Mangal was Soviet trained. He had been a political commissar in the Afghan Army under the Communists. After the fall of the Taliban, he had served successively as governor of Paktika (on the eastern border with Pakistan) and of Laghman (just north of Kabul). He was everything Wafa wasn't, and even spoke some broken English. He became the mascot of successive commanders of Task Force Helmand and of successive heads of the PRT, and a figure in the British as well as the Afghan media. President Karzai made Wafa the Afghan equivalent of the ombudsman, based in the Presidential Palace, charged with handling Afghan citizens' complaints about maladministration.

As the Americans focused more of their military effort on Helmand, Mangal came to know senior Americans as he had come to know senior Brits. His greatest quality was that he always gave the impression of being serenely competent. He knew what to do and was never without an answer. He calmed worried visitors, whom Wafa had merely alarmed. Fighting and dying to prop up a provincial government run by Mangal somehow seemed more worth while than propping up Wafa's ramshackle operation.

A second important factor was the return to Helmand in April 2008 of 16 Air Assault Brigade, commanded by an officer, Mark Carleton-Smith, who seemed marked out for the top of the British Army. Few things fazed Mark. Under Andrew Mackay 52 Brigade had done a very good job, understanding COIN in ways that their predecessors hadn't always done. But 16 Air Assault had more resources, more coherence and more confidence.

In parallel with 16 Air Assault's arrival the Foreign Office accepted my recommendation to upgrade and upgun the Provincial Reconstruction Team. A new head was appointed, with the equivalent rank of major general, in the form of an able FCO official, Hugh Powell. The team was renamed the Civil Military Mission Helmand and was advertised as being more joined up than ever.

My original view had been that there should be one Briton in charge of all civil and military activity in Helmand. As most of the activity was military, I had favoured appointing a mini-Templer: a major general on a two-year tour, who would both command the Task Force and be in charge of all the stabilisation activity being mounted by what was formerly known as the PRT. He should have a civilian deputy. Only thus would we get the unity of command that the experts deemed essential for successful counter-insurgency. Sadly, however, the Army preferred to continue to rotate whole brigades and their commanders through Helmand every six months; and they were worried about how a major general in Helmand would relate to one in Kandahar. In 2010, the

Americans moved to the obvious answer: hiving off Helmand as a separate Regional Command (South-West), under a major general. The Army did, however, undertake a study to identify a few score posts which would be earmarked for continuity – meaning that the officers filling them would stay in Helmand for nine months rather than six. But putting this in place happened only gradually.

We therefore settled on having, on a tour of at least a year, a two-star civilian (the theoretical equivalent of a major general) alongside and slightly above, but not in charge of, a one-star military officer, a brigadier, commanding the Task Force, on a six-month tour. It was a compromise, which worked, in British fashion, thanks mainly to the exceptional individuals whom both the Army and the Foreign Office selected for the top jobs in Helmand. But it was less than optimal: institutional interests were still being put before the campaign.

In addition to the arrival in Helmand of Governor Mangal, Brigadier Carleton-Smith and Hugh Powell, the FCO and DFID found significant additional resources for stabilisation activity in Helmand, in support of the Helmand Roadmap. I did think that this was the year we could really make a difference in Helmand. If that didn't do it, then nothing could.

That year we had a stream of visitors from London eager to see the progress that was undoubtedly being made in Helmand. The Prime Minister was in Afghanistan twice in 2008, once in August and then again in December for the almost obligatory pre-Christmas visit to the troops. The formula for such visits was unchanging. I was not sure how much such senior visitors, who often seemed close to collapsing from exhaustion, really learned on such excursions.

Both the Conservative and the Liberal Democrat leaders also paid fact-finding visits: these were more useful, as the visitors were concerned not so much to obtain confirmation that the present policies were working as to find out whether the policies the next government might inherit were the right ones. Briefing them was a delicate balance between not underselling the tactical military campaign and setting out the scale of the strategic challenge. Even if the British were successful in Helmand, the Canadians in Kandahar, the Dutch and Australians in Uruzgan and the Americans in their provinces to the east, there were still vast areas of the country that would remain unstable. No one had a credible plan for what we were supposed to do about them.

Nor did any of us have a real answer as to what the Pakistanis were going to do. Or on how the Afghan authorities were supposed to acquire the capability and will to secure and govern the insurgency-infected areas of the country in the political timescales which applied to the Western troop-contributing democracies. Instead, I and others spoke hopefully of a demonstration effect, and concentrated on the minutiae of 'Clear, Hold, Build', rather than on the bigger picture.

One vignette was an incident during a visit to Sangin by David Cameron and William Hague. We were told of the progress that was being made there by the very brave Commanding Officer of the 2nd Battalion The Parachute Regiment. He took us on top of the District Centre (as the local town hall was known) to see the lie of the land, and began his briefing. The sun was hot and strong, and we were all starting to feel the heat. I noticed that William Hague – who was not wearing a cap or hat of any kind – seemed to be feeling the sun particularly badly. I was just plucking up courage to ask the colonel if we could move into the shade when we heard the rattle of small-arms fire and the crump of mortars responding. Spent rounds spun desultorily through the air in our direction. The colonel didn't even flinch and just carried on talking. When one of us asked rather timidly what was going on, he explained that a 'contact' was under way at an Afghan Police checkpoint about a kilometre to the south. My courage deserted me: I felt that to ask to move into the shade then would seem, especially to the Paras, like cowardice in the face of the enemy. So I kept quiet. But the briefing went on, and on, and on. With the Leader of the Opposition and the Shadow Foreign Secretary as his hostages, the colonel had moved on from the tactical situation in Helmand to volunteering his views on the United Kingdom's future defence posture. Under the scorching sun of Sangin, it was rather surreal to hear a lieutenant colonel in the Parachute Regiment explaining why the Royal Air Force didn't need Typhoon fighters and the Royal Navy didn't need carriers. I thought Messrs Cameron and Hague were remarkably good humoured in the circumstances.

That summer we had another visit by the Permanent Secretaries. But this time they brought the Cabinet Secretary with them. Two things seemed to make an impact on Sir Gus O'Donnell: the way in which the Embassy and the civilian effort in Helmand really were cross-government, with officials from such a wide range of Whitehall departments playing a real part in the effort; and the scale of the public expenditure needed to support HMG's efforts in Afghanistan, symbolised by the sprawling and ever-expanding Camp Bastion base.

The more amusing visitors were those who made their way to Afghanistan under their own steam. Prominent in this category were certain maverick Tory Members of Parliament, often with a military background, whose dissident views made the MOD reluctant to find places for them on the RAF flights; brave retired officers who were supporting charities of one kind or another; the widow of my first Ambassador, the enormously energetic, intelligent and enterprising Hilary, Lady Weir, out to see what the Brooke Trust (which she chaired) should be doing to help the working animals of Afghanistan; Dr Sarah Fane of the Afghan Connection, building links between British and Afghan schools, and supporting Afghan cricket on the side; military writers and commentators of every kind, from Sir Max Hastings to Sir Michael Rose, all eager to get close to the action and understand what the West's latest war was really about; and, early in 2009, the best war reporter of them all, Ross Kemp of Sky News, in Kabul to try to get a grip on the politics of the war.

But the visitor who gave me most pleasure in 2008 was Sandy Gall, and his band of gallant hikers, who came to Kabul and then went up to Bamiyan, the beautiful province in central Afghanistan where the Taliban had in early 2001 destroyed the statues of the Buddha, in order to stage a charity walk in aid of Sandy's Afghan charity. Sandy had been doing this every other year, and on each occasion assembled a band of doughty Brits of varying vintages to walk with him. Some were young, some were slightly older, many seemed to be Scottish dowagers: Evelyn Waugh couldn't have made it up.

Sandy had been dismissive of fussing about security from jobsworths in King Charles Street. The FCO had even instructed me to have as little as possible to do with the visitors in case I was held liable for any accident that might befall them. But, after a mine exploded uncomfortably close to Sandy's 4x4 on his reconnaissance of the land route from Kabul to Bamiyan, he did decide to move the party by air up to Bamiyan and back. I knew I had to give a dinner, and perhaps a dance, for such distinguished visitors. In my remarks at dinner, I told them – and I meant it – how proud they made me feel to be British Ambassador. I had rounded up all the reasonably respectable retired Army officers on my staff to come along, and dance with the dowagers – which they did with an enthusiasm which plucked an old heartstring or two.

Back in England that year interest in Afghanistan was at its height. In May, I was invited to give a lecture at the Hay-on-Wye literary festival, based on my written debate with Rory Stewart in *Prospect* magazine six months earlier. As the event approached, I was told that, instead of a lecture, the organisers would prefer a debate between Rory and me, to be chaired by, of all people, the Shadow Chancellor, George Osborne. I felt it would be cowardly to back out and so reluctantly agreed.

The debate was not my finest hour. Despite a substantial presence from Hereford and other West Country defence and security establishments, most of the audience shared Rory's scepticism about the whole Afghan venture. As in *Prospect*, my line was that, while Rory's diagnosis of the difficulties might be right, his prescription – a unilateral withdrawal of British troops from Helmand – was not remotely practical politics for any British prime minister who wanted to preserve his relationship with Washington. That somehow got lost, and I came across as defending an unwinnable war and an incredible policy. It was a relief when in 2010 Rory's election to Parliament, and my own departure from public service, brought our respective positions much closer together.

The other thing I did that summer, with help from my excellent outgoing Defence Attaché, Colonel Simon Newton, was to pay long-overdue visits to the ward in the old Selly Oak Hospital in Birmingham where most of our casualties were taken, and to the British forces' rehabilitation centre at Headley Court in the Surrey Hills. For logistical reasons, I visited them in the wrong order, starting with Headley Court. I left Surrey buoyed up by the determination of the severely disabled young servicemen to make the very best of the situation in which they found themselves. Their courage was truly humbling. One could only be impressed by the atmosphere of hope and renewal there, for people who had suffered the most appalling injuries. I laughed as a young

Marine proudly showed me the different speed settings on his Bluetooth-controlled artificial leg, which had cost about £17,000.

Selly Oak was rather different. The military casualties were mostly in one ward of an old Victorian hospital. But there were civilians in the same ward, and the place didn't seem quite right. I understood the logic of using the network of NHS hospitals in Birmingham, which could provide far better specialist treatment than any military hospital ever could. But it didn't seem right that the military patients, mostly soldiers in their early twenties, should be in the same ward as elderly NHS surgical cases: I am glad that that has now been put right.

Overall, however, the two visits left me a bit downcast. There was no doubt that our casualties were receiving the best possible medical treatment, both in theatre and on return to the United Kingdom. But how would it seem to these victims of the conflict ten or twenty years from now: what would a severely disabled ex-Marine, sitting in a pub in Liverpool, think it had all been for? I did not know then what I heard from one British officer when I was writing this book: that a collateral benefit of the injuries suffered by our forces in Afghanistan should be a massive improvement in the performance of our Paralympics team in 2012, boosted as it will be by the presence of many supremely fit disabled ex-servicemen. But that was not really the point.

I used to have the same, rather gloomy thoughts when writing to the next of kin of our war dead. The MOD's standard form for battle casualties gives little away. The tributes from colleagues say more. But one couldn't really get at the whole truth in circumstances like that. So, with a heavy heart, I would pen the best letter I could, always thinking back to sudden and premature deaths in my own family. A high proportion of the dead soldiers came from the poorer parts of the United Kingdom, and from broken homes. How many times did I read that Private (or Trooper or Fusilier or Rifleman or Aircraftman or Marine or Guardsman) Bloggs's mum or dad was his next of kin, but that he had a girlfriend who had a baby by a previous relationship and – too often and too sadly – was expecting, or had just had, his baby.

I also tried always to write to the Commanding Officer of the unit from which the dead soldier had come, though I never knew quite what to say. In general, the casualties seemed to upset the officers rather less than they did me. Mainly I think that was because they couldn't afford to be affected, even when the losses were staggeringly high, as in the case of the 3rd Battalion The Rifles, who had nearly one in four of a battle group of 600 killed or seriously injured during their bloody tour in Sangin in 2009–10.

The Rifles weren't alone in taking quite heavy casualties. Of fifteen officers deployed forward with the Welsh Guards during their tour in the summer of 2009, three were killed.* One of these was their Commanding Officer, Lieutenant Colonel Rupert Thorneloe, whom I had known as an able private secretary to Des Browne, as secretary of state for defence. His funeral, at the Guards Chapel, in Birdcage Walk, was a particularly poignant occasion, attended by the Prince of Wales and the Duchess of Cornwall. It was made worse for me by a senior officer, clearly upset at Rupert's death, telling me, in all sincerity, that the problem in Helmand was politicians' refusal to send yet more troops.

Ministers worried about casualties. In respect of Sangin in particular, there was constant pressure from London to keep losses to a minimum. Quite properly, all this led to massive, and urgent, investment in counter-IED measures of one kind or another. The courage of the counter-IED teams can never be overstated. But however good their efforts, somehow the bomber always gets through. It was the terrorist booby-trap (as the IED was then called) that had been largely responsible for causing Britain to give up fighting the Jewish insurgency in Palestine in 1946–8, even when we had had 100,000 men, including the 6th Airborne Division and a Guards brigade, under arms in a territory about the same size as Wales.

Rather courageously, at about this time the International Development Secretary, and later Shadow Foreign Secretary, Douglas Alexander, made a speech suggesting that a better formula than 'Clear, Hold and Build' might be 'Engage, Stabilise and Develop'. His thinking was that, since most of the Taliban were locals, the notion of Clearing an area of them was flawed. Similarly, Holding suggested garrisoning

---

* See Toby Harnden's excellent account of the Welsh Guards' tour: *Dead Men Risen*, London: Quercus, 2011.

an area with external forces against attack. In fact, the only sustainable way was to get the local population to take responsibility themselves for securing and governing, more or less, their own areas. And Building carried a notion of simply putting up schools and clinics, in the hope that such largesse would somehow win over a grateful population. In fact, time and again we saw that frightened Pashtun populations wanted security and certainty before they wanted anything else. As I have often said, they needed to know who would be in charge of their village or valley in five months' or five years' time, and they would back the winner. So what was needed was gradually getting stabilised areas to Develop themselves, rather than simply dishing out handouts.

Throughout my time in Afghanistan, different ISAF contributors claimed that an important reason why they were failing to stabilise the areas they were garrisoning was because their countries' respective development agencies were slow to engage on quick-impact projects in those areas. Sadly, as an important conference at Wilton Park in March 2010 concluded,* all the evidence was that quick-impact projects, and indeed development spending in general, were entirely secondary in stabilising insurgency-infected areas. Without a political settlement, such projects collapsed all too quickly. What people wanted was certainty about their political future. Development spending could underpin such a process but could not deliver it.

Afghanistan was littered with fraternal gifts from the Soviet Union which had simply been pocketed and had done nothing to win support for Afghanistan's Communist Government. Since the British had subsidised the 'Iron Amir', Abdurrahman, in the nineteenth century, no Afghan government had survived without external funding. But, as Britain, the Soviet Union and the United States all discovered in turn, the fact that Afghanistan was a rentier state did not make it an obedient client state.

Throughout Gordon Brown's time as prime minister, we went through agonies in the Afghan Strategy Group of senior officials, and in its subsidiary and superior bodies, about the right posture for Britain in Helmand. I was commissioned to study the American approach to

---

* http://www.wiltonpark.org.uk/en/reports/?view=Report&id=22580557

counter-insurgency in Regional Command (East). I paid two visits there, as well as talking to countless experts in Kabul. What I found was that the Americans were practising a form of military colonialism. The US Provincial Reconstruction Teams were mostly military run and manned. The personnel were mainly high-quality officers from the US Navy or Air Force or from the Reserves. Despite, or perhaps because of, the relatively small proportion of civilians in the American PRTs, they were often more effective than the British PRT was at making visible differences on the ground: schools got built, roads laid, in time spans that seemed wholly impossible in Helmand. To be fair, that was also because the Americans had more ready cash, notably through the Commanders' Emergency Response Program (or CERP). That money was Pentagon money, and was subject to only the most vestigial accounting procedures.

In all this, I discovered later, there were eerie parallels with the American experience in South Vietnam. In a recently declassified White House memo dated 1 December 1966, a young Foreign Service Officer just returned from Saigon had written: 'We are not trained or equipped to do what must be done in rebuilding government in the villages; moreover, it is an open-ended commitment in terms of both time and men, and could well lure us unwittingly into a strange sort of "revolutionary colonialism" – our ends are "revolutionary", our means quasi-colonial.' The author of the report was the twenty-five-year-old Richard Holbrooke.

So I concluded that the Americans were doing more, more quickly and more effectively, than we were, on the ground. But I suggested that the real question was how long any of this would last, and how far it would spread, once or where American forces were not present. To be worth doing, stabilisation has to be enduring and self-reproducing: in my submission, the massive American effort was neither.

But I had nothing but praise for the officers carrying it out: some of the finest talent from the US Navy and Air Force were working in the PRTs, in ways that civilians, British or American, could never do. That was in part due to what was called 'a duty of care': civilians could not lawfully be exposed to unreasonable or foreseeable danger without their employer risking huge liabilities. But it was also because the elite of the two sister services were better than the average reluctant State Department secondee to a PRT or civilian contractor.

All that left us rather smug about the slower, steadier British approach in Helmand. But that didn't stop the Army wanting to deploy more troops. As Dr Anthony Seldon has shown in his book *Brown at 10*,* as prime minister Gordon Brown was subject to continual pressure from the British military to be allowed to send more forces to Afghanistan, as they became available. There were a number of motives for this pressure. By far the most important was a genuine, but in my view misguided, belief that stabilising Helmand was mainly a matter of more troops. Once the numbers were right, security would follow, and then proper governance. Of course that had to be broadly right: if you put more policemen into a violent inner-city area, crime generally falls. But the real question is what happens when those policemen are withdrawn; and what is the effect in the areas where the policemen are not present. Is the presence of the policemen addressing the underlying problems of the area?

But there were other factors at work. Genuine, and laudable, military enthusiasm for a better war in Afghanistan after widespread criticism of its performance in Basra was an element in the Army's thinking at the time. Moreover, with units being pulled back from Ireland, Iraq and Germany, there was a perfectly understandable interest in fresh challenges for the Army. I got a flavour of this when a senior general told me, as I was sitting in his office in the MOD, that, if he didn't use in Afghanistan the battle groups then coming free from Iraq, he risked losing them in a future defence review. He summed up our talk with a simple phrase: 'It's use them or lose them, Sherard.' He does not now recall saying this.

In a similar vein, I was invited to breakfast, at the Sofitel at the bottom of Lower Regent Street, at the end of July 2008 by a senior general from the MOD's central staff. He made clear that there was concern in the MOD about alleged doubts in the FCO relating to a further troop increase, and wanted to talk things through with me. Having just secured agreement to one uplift, the MOD was planning to recommend to Ministers that they send several hundred more troops

---

* Anthony Seldon and Guy Lodge, *Brown at 10*, London: Biteback, 2010.

to Afghanistan. They were worried that FCO officials might argue against any such increase. I hedged my bets, saying we would want to see how exactly our team in Helmand were proposing to use them, and how the additional uplift would fit into a wider strategy.

It was about this time that the three Cabinet Ministers most involved in Afghanistan – the Secretaries of State for Foreign Affairs (David Miliband), for Defence (Des Browne) and for International Development (Douglas Alexander) – started meeting informally, without officials present, to discuss Afghanistan. All three were worried about where a heavily military strategy was leading us, but understood the pressure on the Prime Minister to be supportive of the military campaign. Each of them was well aware of the skill with which the Opposition, and sympathetic papers such as the *Daily Telegraph* and *Daily Mail*, had laid into the Government over alleged equipment shortages, whether of body armour or mine-resistant vehicles or helicopters.

In general, however, I felt that such criticism, some of it stirred up by leaks from the MOD or, in one case, open attacks on the Government, was a bit unfair. At almost every stage, the expansion of our military mission in Afghanistan, whether in terms of numbers of troops or of territory, had been agreed by often sceptical politicians on the basis of upbeat military advice. Whether it was the initial move into Helmand, or our moves south down the Helmand Valley to Garmsir, or north to Musa Qala and Kajaki, or west towards Marjah and Nad Ali, in the main it was the military who had recommended to Ministers that Britain take on each additional area.

Then, each time we moved into a new area, we seemed to find that we didn't have quite enough troops and/or equipment to hold it in an acceptable fashion. It was then that the criticism of Ministers would start, at first indirectly and then openly. How the politicians, with no military expertise at all, could have reasonably been expected to forecast exactly what equipment was likely to have been needed, or could be blamed for not having ordered Mine-Resistant Ambush-Proof (MRAP) vehicles five years earlier, was not clear. But blamed they were, and Gordon Brown found himself continually on the defensive, against pressure to do more and spend more.

The row over helicopters was an example of this unfairness. Gordon Brown and his Ministers were hardly responsible for the software failures in a Chinook fleet ordered years earlier. But that didn't stop one senior officer complaining that he had had to fly around Helmand in an American helicopter, even when sharing air transport is a natural corollary of alliance operations. In the summer of 2007, an RAF movements officer in Helmand had shown me a pie-chart of British helicopter usage in southern Afghanistan. According to his chart, 27 per cent of the movements had been for VIPs. And, though neither he nor I could prove it, we both suspected that most of those VIPs would have been senior military visitors from London.

All these questions should have been resolved through the Cabinet Office machinery for overseeing the British contribution in Afghanistan. In practice, however, the National Security, Intelligence and Defence Committee of the Cabinet was not the easiest place for serious discussion of such sensitive issues. As time went on, more issues seemed to be settled in private meetings between the Prime Minister and his senior military advisers. Sitting in the back of an official car with a colleague overseas, I remember pouring out my worries about how we were sending more and more men and equipment to Helmand without any real idea of the overall Western political strategy. His comment was brisk and to the point: 'When you are in a hole, the answer is not necessarily to send for more shovels.'

In May 2008 we had a nasty shock, which showed just how thin the dividing line between success and failure could be. Somehow, it had been decided that the new Governor of Helmand, Mangal, should hold a shura with the elders in the newly liberated Musa Qala. Several Chinook-loads of personnel were needed to mount this operation. The Governor was on the last inbound Chinook, accompanied by the acting Head of the PRT, my former Deputy Michael Ryder, and a woman first secretary from the Embassy in charge of politico-military affairs.

As the last helicopter was making its approach towards the town, somebody picked up 'chatter' which suggested that the Taliban had worked out that the Governor was likely to be on that helicopter. Quite properly, the pilot decided to divert and flew up a side-wadi towards Forward Operating Base Edinburgh, an outpost on the high ground above Musa Qala. As the helicopter moved up the wadi those inside heard a loud bang. The helicopter lost all its hydraulics. With great skill and courage (for which he was later awarded a well-earned Distinguished Flying Cross), the pilot managed to put the helicopter down with a bump close to FOB Edinburgh. Nobody on board was hurt. But the Chinook wasn't so lucky. A rocket-propelled grenade had passed through the helicopter's rear rotor housing and then taken a great bite out of one of the rear rotor blades. A millisecond earlier or later, or had the RPG's detonator worked, and the Chinook would have come down with an almighty crash. We would have lost the Governor of Helmand and two senior British civilians – plus many guards and other support personnel in the aircraft with them. The aftermath of such a catastrophe would of course have been Ministerial pledges not to be deterred and to carry on with renewed determination. But it would have been a serious blow. From the beginning, my nightmare was always losing a Chinook full of troops: the sturdy workhorse of the campaign could carry more than forty people.

Despite the commitment to making a success of Helmand in 2008, planners in London were keen that we should think, in a small and confidential group, about a Plan B, in case the current strategy didn't work. The trouble was that nobody knew what Plan B might be, or how Britain could possibly implement such a plan without the United States. We soon concluded that our best bet was to seek to influence the incoming US Administration, which seemed almost bound to be Democratic, and more open to reason on Afghanistan than Bush was.

In the meantime, we carried on cracking on. In November, I travelled down to Helmand with my Estonian colleague, Harri Tiido, to visit the brave Estonian infantry company which was part of the British Task Force. With his long lank hair and spectacles, Tiido looked like the dissident he had once been. But now he was double-hatted as the under secretary in the Estonian Foreign Ministry and as non-resident ambassador to Afghanistan. On our way down to Helmand, he revealed that he had been there before – as an unwilling conscript officer in the Soviet Fortieth Army. He was reluctant to talk about his experiences. But he did say that he had told his soldiers that the Afghans had every right to shoot at them, and that his reward had been time in a punishment camp for officers in the unbearable heat of Soviet Central Asia.

In 2008, the Estonians were stationed near Now Zad on the edge of the desert to the north-west of Lashkar Gah. Now Zad had been a town of some 30,000 inhabitants, but it was now deserted. The two sides were dug in, First World War style, in front lines of trenches and buildings some 300 yards apart. We were taken up to an observation post. At high noon, we could detect no movement in the Taliban lines. In the distant desert a lone motorcyclist made his way in a cloud of dust. He could have been a Talib spotter, or not: there was no way of telling. We moved to the Estonian headquarters, in a hill pockmarked with trench lines, dugouts and, endearingly, a DIY sauna and outside exercise area. We met a lone US Marine officer, who was preparing for the Marine Corps to take over from the Estonians in a few weeks' time. He noted, sardonically, that their role was as police mentors. But he couldn't find any police to mentor.

Finally, we were briefed on the tactical situation. An enthusiastic Estonian officer, with excellent English, unveiled the usual collection of maps and PowerPoint slides. As always, the theme was that we were making progress, but that challenges remained. At the end, the commanding officer turned to Harri and me, and asked if the two Ambassadors had any questions. I had none. 'I have only one question,' Harri began, portentously. 'What the fuck are we doing here?' I never discovered whether Harri meant Now Zad, Helmand or Afghanistan. But perhaps it didn't really matter.

Chapter 17

Afghan Attitudes

Sometimes life in Afghanistan seemed to be lived without Afghans. President Karzai and a few key Ministers and leading politicians, and Governor Mangal in Helmand, were the official Afghans of whom I saw most. But, apart from them, it was too easy to go for weeks without properly engaging with Afghans beyond the ramparts of earthen barriers and barbed wire which surrounded most of the places in which I lived and worked. Many of my fellow foreigners would spend their time in Afghanistan almost entirely in an international security bubble.

Even though I made a real effort to meet the people whose country we were trying to save, the only Afghans I saw every day (except Fridays) were the two very bright bearers in the Residence, Mohammed and Abdurrahman: they were my instant *vox populi*, as I asked them each morning how things were. Working for the British Embassy, they enjoyed incomes far greater than those earned by most of their families and friends. And yet, even for them, life was a struggle: each could afford to run a battered old car, but not to repair it. Neither could afford a computer. This inflation of wages and prices and expectations was caused mainly by American money, from US forces and from the US Embassy, and in particular by the US Government policy of always paying America's local employees at the top of the market. It meant that a cleaner in the British Embassy earned more than an under secretary in the Afghan civil service. One of our expert Afghan political officers, receiving the top British Embassy salary, could have earned more as a receptionist at the American Embassy. Too many Afghan public sector employees stayed in their jobs simply because they had nowhere else to go. The dedication and patriotism of those who did have a choice, but chose to serve their country's government, were truly admirable.

As elsewhere in the developing world, my main interest to many citizens of my host country was as a potential source of a visa to Britain. Wisely, the British Embassy in Kabul did not have a visa section. All applications were directed to our High Commission in Islamabad or to our Embassy in Dubai. That caused problems, especially with last-minute applications from bona-fide travellers, often visiting Britain on official business. But it was better than the alternative, of having the Embassy swamped by the whole business of issuing and, more often, refusing visas.

One member of my team spent his time working, with great sensitivity, on the distasteful business of repatriating Afghans who had entered the United Kingdom illegally. Every six weeks or so a Home Office charter aircraft would land at Kabul airport with the latest haul of Afghan illegals from Britain. Many had endured incredible hardship and expense in their journeys across Asia and Europe to England's Promised Land. But most had only economic motives for being there, and had to be returned, *pour décourager les autres*. To persuade them to go, HMG used a humane mix of soft sticks and generous carrots: the latter included resettlement grants and training and even temporary accommodation in a hostel built in Kabul by the British taxpayer.

In England, before leaving for Afghanistan, and on my visits back, I started to make some inroads into the extensive Afghan community, spread mostly across the leafy suburbs of north-west London. I discovered, partly through my team of Pashtu teachers, how the community or, really, communities mirrored the divisions back home in Afghanistan: there were Pashtun and Tajik and Uzbek and Hazara groups and associations. They were united by an obsessive interest, fed by satellite television, in what was happening back in their beloved but benighted homeland. Presiding over them all was the kindest and most gentlemanly of Ambassadors, Dr Rahim Sherzoi. He lived and worked in the wonderful old Afghan Embassy on Kensington Gore, overlooking Hyde Park in one direction and the Royal Geographical Society in the other. The building and the man seemed somehow made for each other: old, distinguished and redolent of Afghanistan's past glories and most profound values.

In London, interesting Afghans would pop up in the most unlikely places: driving a minicab, managing an authentically 'Italian' pizza restaurant, erecting television aerials, fixing broken computers, running dry-cleaning shops. I found myself speaking Pashtu in Balham as well as Brook Green. What they all wanted was a better future for their children. One particular vignette sticks with me: a white-knuckle minicab ride to Heathrow, driven by an old friend of the Karzai family, swerving to avoid at least two collisions, telling me proudly of the hope his children were acquiring in the schools and colleges of London's western suburbs.

Back in Afghanistan, I made every effort to meet as many Afghans as possible, and to get out beyond Kabul and the international goldfish bowl. I tried always to accept every invitation to visit Afghans in their own homes. Perhaps the most flattering was when, back in the summer of 2007, one of my drivers invited me to visit his father. The old man was suffering from cancer, at home in one of the Tajik shanty towns clinging to the hillside above the old British Embassy in the Karte Parwan district. There I found Zahoor Shah MBE, who had kept the Taliban out of our Embassy throughout the period of their rule, by claiming that it was the Italian Embassy. He had saved our Victorian silver (see Chapter 2) by burying it in the grounds. For his pains, he had received the MBE, which he drew proudly out of its small box from Spink. When he died only a few weeks later, he received a full obituary in the *Independent*, written with great sympathy by Terri Judd. Perhaps inevitably, the headline read simply 'The Caretaker of Kabul'.

Another occasion with strong British overtones was the funeral, on 3 July 2008, of General Abdul Wali Shah. Abdul Wali was King Zahir Shah's cousin and son-in-law, and a former senior commander in the Army. I was told that he had played an inadvertent role in precipitating the coup which had overthrown the monarchy in 1973, allegedly by having plotted to seize for himself a more prominent role in the running of the country. Whatever the truth of this, General Abdul Wali spent his last years sharing the King's apartments in the Arg Palace. I called on him at least twice. On both occasions he was wearing a perfectly cut Western suit and the blue-red-blue tie of the Household Division. In the accents of another age, he spoke of his time in Paris after the Second World War, when the British Ambassador, Sir Duff Cooper, had obtained for the noble young Afghan a commission in Sir Duff's old regiment, the Grenadier Guards.

As we had done almost exactly a year earlier, at the funeral of King Zahir Shah, in July 2008 we gathered under the great plane tree in the central court of the old Palace for General Abdul Wali's obsequies. We had first paid our condolences to the royal family, gathered in one of the Palace saloons, around an ancient fountain playing on the rust-stained marble. With me were my Defence Attaché, in uniform, and, wearing the right tie, a dashing Embassy first secretary who had himself held a commission in the Grenadier Guards. It was he who had obtained from Regimental Headquarters at Wellington Barracks a message from the Colonel of that distinguished regiment, celebrating one of its most unusual officers. He now handed the message over to a surprised and delighted Afghan princess. Somehow, we felt that, with General Abdul Wali's death, the old Afghanistan was slipping away.

But not quite. In most of the world's capitals, there is something that passes for 'society'. Often that world involves a few generous hostesses, the diplomatic corps, politicians and journalists, artists and creative people. It is a fluid and fickle world. But foreign diplomats, by becoming honorary members of it, and being able to entertain generously and thus be entertained, secure a fast-track route to the heart of the country that they are sent to understand and influence.

Every Afghan of a certain age and background told me that Kabul had once been like that, before 1978 and, especially, during the 1950s and 1960s. The old British Embassy, with its tennis courts and croquet lawns, and its sprung ballroom floor and bring-and-buy sales organised by the Embassy ladies, had been the centre of a bygone world of exchange and engagement between Afghan hosts and the foreign guests in their land. So many older Afghans spoke with nostalgic sighs of those happy times. Their tones were perhaps an echo of those in which our forebears, caught in the toils of the First World War, had spoken of the Edwardian age. But in 2008 a few pinnacles of talent and taste and ambition still poked above the dark sea of suffering and sadness which had engulfed Kabul.

One of these was the Gailani family, almost as much at home on the Old Brompton Road as they were in Old Kabul: an ancient family, originally from the holy places of the land of the two rivers, heirs to a potent blend of Sufism and saintliness. During the anti-Soviet *jihad*, the Gailanis had been known by some as the Gucci Muj (or mujahideen): one could see why, but also why it was less than the whole truth. Today, they remained a powerful clan in Afghan politics. Pir Sayid Gailani was still an *éminence grise* whom President Karzai always preferred to have with him rather than against him. One son was a deputy speaker of the lower house of the Afghan Parliament, the Wolesi Jirga; another was Afghan Ambassador to the Sultanate of Oman; a daughter, whom I used to describe as the uncrowned Queen of Kabul, was President of the Afghan Red Crescent – a serious welfare organisation if ever there was one; and a son-in-law was an economics professor from Chicago who served as Afghan finance minister through most of my time in Kabul. Lunch or dinner at one of the Gailani houses was always fun, with delicious Afghan dishes. But it was what one learned at those meals about the heart and soul of the country that made those occasions so precious, and the invitations such an honour.

Other pillars of the old Pashtun elite included the Defence Minister, General Wardak, who often entertained at home. His talented wife – Chatul (or 'Tulip' in Pashtu) – had a degree in, I think, law from Heidelberg University. With her formidable brains and beauty, she brooked no nonsense, especially from American generals. I always said she was worth to Afghanistan one of the armoured brigades her husband coveted.

Less socially prominent perhaps, but commercially and culturally active, was a younger generation of independent Pashtun businesswomen, producing some of modern Afghanistan's most exquisite exports. Their products were works of beauty and taste and originality, manufactured in and around Kabul by Afghan craftspeople, mainly women. They deserved the much wider markets that should come with peace. One of the foremost among this group of patriotic women was Mina Sherzoi, the daughter of the Afghan Ambassador in London, who had given up a life in California to be back in the land she loved.

The man who served as President Karzai's first minister throughout this time was another scion of the upper reaches of Afghan society. He would not have been miscast as a Roman senator, one of the immortals of the Académie Française or a member of the House of Lords. As a former foreign minister, Hedayat Amin Arsala made up in connections and judgement and experience for what his critics said he lacked in energy. I called on him, to hear about his plans to challenge President Karzai for the Afghan Presidency in 2009. As we took tea on the terrace of his villa, one of the First Minister's ornamental flock of guineafowl came up from the large lawn, strutted up and down before us and laid an enormous egg – apparently its first in many years. A Roman historian would have taken that egg as a certain augury of portentous events – wrongly, as Arsala's challenge to Karzai soon fizzled out, and he rejoined the Karzai camp.

Another prominent figure with an almost Roman appearance, manner and reputation was Ashraf Ghani, the post-Taliban Finance Minister and Chancellor of Kabul University who had moved to New York to set up his Institute of State Effectiveness. But Ashraf had never lost his deep affection for his native land and kept in close touch with developments there. He returned to run for president in 2009, and then stayed on, as an adviser to President Karzai. In many ways, Ashraf was the best Prime Minister Afghanistan never had: as finance minister, or, more accurately perhaps, as minister for the public finances, he had used his office in ways most finance ministers only dream of: to enforce fiscal and policy discipline, and delivery, across the public sector. That didn't make him popular. Nor did his inability to suffer fools at all gladly. But it had helped make for perhaps the most effective Afghan government since the fall of the Taliban.

A meeting with Ashraf, usually at his compound out in west Kabul within sight of the Darul Aman Palace, was never dull. Arriving or leaving one would cross other pilgrims to the ashram. In appearance and manner, often with a toga-like cloak cast over one shoulder, Ashraf resembled either the noblest Roman of them all, Cato, or (as I once told him) the Mahatma. An asceticism derived from past illness only added to the impression of otherworldliness.

Another world entirely, and one perhaps even more authentically Afghan, was that of the artistes formerly known as warlords, but now given more respectable titles. Each was widely regarded as having had an appalling record of human rights abuses, which meant we kept our distance. Of these perhaps the most prominent was another Panjshiri, the Tajik leader Mohammed Fahim Khan. During most of my time in Kabul, Fahim Khan (as everyone called him) had no official position. It was only after the Presidential election in 2009 that he became vice president, and was formally inaugurated in November of that year. But in or out of office he was always a key player in Afghan power politics, who was widely believed to have the muscle he needed to enforce his wishes, if it ever came to that. Certainly, I was surprised, on one holiday trip up the Panjshir, to have his private family compound pointed out to me, and to see, over the mud walls, what looked very like a squadron of Russian-made armoured personnel carriers.

But the most striking memory I have of Fahim Khan is of a *buzkashi* match he organised in April 2008. The excuse for the match was to say farewell to General Dan McNeill, who chose the foreign guests. But it was one of a regular series, with the contestants for this round being the Tajikistan national team and the team from the Panjshir valley. I say team. In fact, each side consisted of getting on for fifty assorted riders, operating alongside but far from in unison with each other. The match, when it got under way, wouldn't have provided the kind of sporting metaphor for team-building beloved of corporate coaches in Britain. In fact, it was much more a question of every man, and his pony (and the ponies were very tough), for himself. Neither side wore anything approaching team colours or a strip. But the Tajik national team seemed to have a preference for ribbed leather helmets – resembling a rugby scrumcap – of the kind worn by Soviet tank crew. The wisdom of this became obvious once the mêlée started.

Fahim Khan's *buzkashi* ground makes Smith's Lawn look positively pokey. At the far end was a single post. At the end closer to the spectators a circle about a yard across had been whitewashed in the dust. Fahim's guests were arrayed in a stand on one of the long sides of the vast rectangular dirt field. Most of the NATO Ambassadors were there, chosen by Dan McNeill. The variety of kit in which they had appeared showed that no one had the faintest idea what a fashionista wore for a *buzkashi* match. Some were in suits. Looking his *particules*, the Frenchman came dressed for the Arc, whereas the American seemed bound for a rodeo. The Dane had an obscenely long telephoto lens dangling from his belt, which became the source of some ribaldry.

And then the teams massed in front of the stand – lined up would be too exact a word – accompanied by a mounted referee with an electric megaphone. The assembled cavalry looked ready to sweep across the steppe to the gates of Constantinople. Instead, the disembowelled and headless carcase of a calf was dragged on, and dropped.

The game began. The ponies wheeled and reared, as their riders fought – literally – somehow to scoop the carcase up from the dirt, wedge it under one of their legs and then ride the length of the ground so as to circumnavigate the pole at the far end. The object of the team in possession was to drop the dead calf back in the white circle. The object of the team not in possession was to prevent that happening, by all means possible from horseback without weapons. The game was fast, and violent, and utterly thrilling. It was as if one had a ringside seat at one of the great cavalry battles of the past. Horsemanship of a very high order was evident everywhere. So was sheer courage. And amazing stamina.

Round after round was played, carcase after carcase was dragged on, with no intermission. At the end of every round the victor would scoop the carcase up from the circle where he had just deposited it and make for the stand in triumph. Like a Roman emperor, Fahim Khan would come down to the parapet to salute the winner. And then he would stuff handfuls of dollar bills into the hands of the winners. We watched for hours, enthralled and, also, appalled.

Another, and very different, former warlord alleged to have an execrable record was the Uzbek leader Abdul Rashid Dostum. I met him only once, when I found myself sitting on the same table as him at the Palace lunch to mark President Musharraf's visit, in August 2007. But his name, and his doings, were never far from my mind, or concerns. Repeated meetings of the war cabinet in 2008 were devoted to President

Karzai debating with us what he should 'do' about Dostum. The Uzbek leader was at that time holed up in his extraordinary palace complex in a district of Kabul renowned for its narco-tecture, just adjacent to the Wazir Akbar Khan quarter, and thus to the British and other Embassies. Dostum was wanted for questioning by the Afghan Attorney General in respect of what he and fifty of his fighters were said to have done in kidnapping his former ally, Akbar Bai.

Urged on by his Attorney General, President Karzai seemed determined to storm Dostum's citadel in order to enforce the law. But, when he realised that British or American forces weren't going to be available to help his own commandos, and in the face of somewhat equivocal advice from his own side, he changed his mind. I still feared an assault without notice, which could have caused problems for us in the Embassy, only a few hundred yards from where quite severe fighting would have taken place. The standoff ended only when Dostum backed down and left the country, apparently under Turkish sponsorship of some kind.

For much of my time in Kabul, Dostum was out of the country, allegedly receiving medical treatment in Turkey and visiting his wife and family there. Out of Turkic fraternal feeling, and perhaps a bit more, the Turkish Government took a close interest in the welfare of the Uzbeks in general and, until recently, Dostum in particular.

I marvelled at the tergiversations of Afghan politics when, in early 2010, Karzai appointed as chief of staff of the Army a man whom he had vowed to destroy, physically as well as politically, less than two years earlier. But Dostum had apparently delivered tens of thousands of Uzbek votes for Karzai in the Presidential election the previous August. Such payoffs are not unknown in other democracies, albeit in rather less dramatic circumstances.

If the variations in the treatment of Dostum left me feeling a bewildered outsider, another, quite different event did the same. In June 2008, Governor Mangal of Helmand was kind enough to ask me to attend the wedding party for his son, and to bring some colleagues from the Embassy. As ambassador in Saudi Arabia, I had often attended Saudi wedding parties, strictly separated into male-only celebrations (usually a sumptuous but staid banquet) and the women's party, with dancing and music and fun until the early hours. I imagined that an Afghan party would be similar.

In many ways it was. We gathered early one Friday afternoon in one of the large and garish multi-storey wedding halls that had sprung up in Kabul in the years since the fall of the Taliban. The men were assembled on a couple of floors at the top, the women lower down. Hundreds of tribespeople were there, predominantly from the Mangal clan, most of them – including the Governor himself – in traditional dress. We were the only foreigners present, and were shown to a table on the edge of a clear area in the centre of the room. We dined well, on lamb and rice and delicious Afghan vegetables. We took a few discreet photographs, but were more photographed (and filmed, at intrusive length) than photographing.

But then the real fun began. In the centre of the room a circle of young men wearing shalwar kameezes formed. Each had shoulder-length hair. As the music started, the youths started to whirl and twirl, shimmying around with their long locks blowing in the wind. If this wasn't homoerotic, nothing was. It was also physically taxing for the dancers as they swayed back and forth in time with the drums and pipes, their heads gyrating and their hair swirling in the air. My Political Counsellor leaned across and explained that this was the Attan – the traditional tribal dance of celebration, performed at Eid or in celebration or anticipation of victory in war. Any Wahhabi worthy of the name would turn in his grave at the sight of such a spectacle. The dance was said to date back to the Greeks and to have been learned from the Macedonians when Alexander's armies had marched this way. In my mind's eye, I saw the swaying circle of Afghan ephebes, hands joined, forming the decorative line on a piece of early Samian ware. We were told that the women downstairs weren't having half as much fun: no dancing for them. Nothing new under the sun doesn't mean that there's nothing surprising under the Afghan sun – it's just the context.

Weddings apart, I would try to see Governor Mangal whenever he was in Kabul, every couple of months or so. I would assure the Governor of HMG's support for what he was doing, and our admiration for his achievements – and his courage.

Unfortunately, Mangal didn't get quite the same unequivocal support from President Karzai. Usually, when in Kabul, he would be called to the Palace, although there were plenty of occasions when he needed to see the President and couldn't get in. The conversation with Karzai seemed generally to involve the President asking Mangal questions implicitly critical of what he chose to see as a British agenda in Helmand quite separate from that of his own Government. Mangal often came away from these encounters bemused and disheartened, particularly when we all knew that the President really wanted Sher Mohammed Akhundzada restored as governor. Sher Mohammed had run Helmand almost as a private fiefdom until he had been removed, at British request, in 2006 and made a senator. But he continued to hanker after returning to his old domain, and to lobby Karzai hard to that end. The President would promise Sher Mohammed one thing and us another, and end up leaving everyone disappointed and confused. Time and again visiting British Ministers or American Generals would extract from Karzai promises that he supported what ISAF was trying to do in Helmand, and that he backed Mangal. But we all knew his heart wasn't in it, and within weeks he would be back to his old ambiguous ways. Getting Karzai unequivocally to back the NATO campaign, not to mention his governor in Helmand, was a Sisyphean task.

Another, but more infrequent, Helmandi visitor to Kabul was Mullah Salam of Musa Qala fame. With his black turban, black beard and silver slippers with curled-up toes, he looked like a character out of the *Arabian Nights*. He had only one purpose in coming to see me: to complain. He complained, at length, and with passion, about everyone. But his main target was the British Army, and its failure to provide him with enough money/weapons/protection/respect. He spoke with feeling but good humour. And we always parted the best of friends: it was as though the meeting with me was for him catharsis enough. He didn't seem to expect me actually to do anything about his increasingly outrageous demands. He just wanted face time with the British Ambassador.

Such encounters made me realise how in Helmand we had somehow got ourselves into a position where we had responsibility for much of what happened (or went wrong) there. But in truth we had little power to direct the currents of alliance and antagonism roiling beneath the surface. Despite our relative impotence, I can't pretend it wasn't fun to sit with Salam, feeling rather as though one was the Governor General in the colonial capital, receiving a petition about the conduct of a provincial governor.

One of my best presents from my time as ambassador in Kabul came from Mullah Salam and arrived shortly before I left, in February 2009. The gift was never declared to the FCO's Conduct and Discipline Section. It was a pair of his über-bling curved slippers, which I treasure, for the time I am asked to play Aladdin in a village pantomime.

Helmand came to Kabul, but we also tried to take Kabul to Helmand. Throughout 2008 the British Army reported proudly on the good it was doing at Garmsir, the fly-blown town lying beside one of the few good road bridges over the southerly reaches of the Helmand River, in the valley about fifty miles south of Lashkar Gah.

When I first visited Garmsir, the Taliban were dug in along a line of poplars only about 150 yards south of the Combat Outpost from which we peered out at them. In the sky above, an Apache attack helicopter was using its chain gun to strafe the forward line of enemy troops. From time to time a mortar would be fired. With helmets on, we peered over the parapet. Beside and behind us were the Afghan Police whose outpost this nominally was. In filthy torn uniforms, glassy eyes staring vacantly, they lay around on flattened cardboard boxes, warming food over a messy fire. They reminded me most of similarly intoxicated vagrants under Charing Cross railway bridge. The promise that they would be the future bulwark against the return of the Taliban seemed somewhat improbable.

Nevertheless, thanks to the bravery of British forces, working with some of the first US Marines to arrive in Helmand, there had been progress in Garmsir. Over the summer of 2008, with strong support from 16 Air Assault Brigade, the 24th Marine Expeditionary Unit of the US Marine Corps cleared the Taliban out of the snake's-head area of the valley south of Garmsir. Lieutenant Harry Wales had been one of the forward air controllers for this operation. Visitors would be taken to see the mud shed in which His Royal Highness had slept, noting the hole made just opposite by a 107mm rocket. In a cameo echoing that at Iwo

Jima, the Marines raised the Afghan flag over the old Soviet fort at Jugroom, at the southern neck of the snake's head. The town's bazaar began to fill up. The Brigadier began to talk confidently of the 'Garmshire' farmers, almost as if he were referring to the Wiltshire branch of the National Farmers Union. We joked about Garmsir (pronounced Ga-ram-sear) meaning 'hot place or city' in Pashtu.

In celebration, VIPs started to flock south, rather like Churchill following British forces into Normandy and across the Rhine. The Development Secretary went, the Chief of the Defence Staff went, I went, and then we thought it would be a good idea if the British and Afghan Foreign Ministers went, together. Dr Spanta was one of the sceptics in Kabul about progress in Helmand, a province he had not seen since driving through it in the 1970s on his way from his home town of Herat to university in Kabul.

We were confident that Dr Spanta was in for a pleasant surprise. As well as the reopening of the bazaar, the school and clinic rebuilt by the Americans in 2006, smashed by the Taliban in 2007 and reopened by the British in 2008, were evidence of things turning for the better. David Miliband picked Dr Spanta up in Kabul, and we flew south to Bastion in an RAF jet. From there it was a short Chinook ride south to Garmsir. Dr Spanta was briefed, impressively. He inspected a troop of Afghan soldiers and, with David Miliband, undertook the obligatory stroll through the bazaar. In the wake of that year's Labour Party Conference, at which he had been photographed holding a banana in a rather unfortunate pose, David Miliband jokingly inspected a bunch of bananas, but, with the cameras watching, wisely bought a pomegranate instead.

Back at Bastion, the two Ministers went their separate ways. David Miliband went on to Bahrain and then Britain. Dr Spanta and I travelled back to Kabul in the darkened hold of the evening Hercules shuttle north. The Afghan Minister was not as communicative as I had hoped he would be about the progress he had been shown. I put it down to exhaustion and engine noise.

Not many days later we learned what Dr Spanta had really thought – and had told Karzai. He had been appalled at the destruction, at the fact that hundreds of British and American and Afghan troops were needed to garrison what had once been one of Afghanistan's richest agricultural areas, the fens of his homeland. The comparison he made was with the Helmand of his fondly remembered youth, not that of two or three years before. Unintentionally, we had succeeded only in re-inforcing his scepticism, and that of his political master, about the value of the military campaign.

With autumn, in those years, came Ramadan, or Ramazan as Afghans call the Muslim holy month. Borrowing a trick from my time in the Land of the Two Holy Mosques, I decided to offer *iftars* – evening break-fasts – for Muslim friends, for the Embassy staff above all, to whom we owed so much, but also for prominent Afghans, religious and less so. With the help of my political team, we brought together in my garden many of the most venerable figures in Afghan politics: the result was something like combining the Synod of the Church of England with the Conservative Party Conference. In my remarks of welcome, I remember jokingly asking anyone *not* intending to run in the following year's Presidential election to put his hand up. We had scooped the jackpot of diplomatic entertaining: achieving that critical mass whereby the guests come not to meet the host ambassador, interesting though he may be, but because they know his is a house at which they will find compatriots of interest.

That same Ramazan I asked to dinner alone a prominent Afghan minister. The Minister had fought bravely against the Russians, although he had at times been rumoured to drink like them. Over dinner, *à deux*, we gossiped and mused, and consumed a bottle of the Australian Shiraz that formed the sump of the cellar of Her Britannic Majesty's Ambassador at Kabul. After dinner, as we sat on the sofa, I ventured to ask my guest if he would like a glass of port. 'My dear Sheerard,' came the answer, 'I never drink port in Ramazan.'

Chapter 18

Waiting for Obama

It must have been in the spring of 2006 that I asked a liberal American friend whom she hoped and expected to win the Democratic nomination two years later. 'Well,' she said, 'everyone is talking about this first-term Senator from Chicago called Barack Obama. He sounds rather good.'

In 2008, as summer turned to autumn, the American Presidential election campaign made only occasional intrusions into our self-absorbed world in Kabul. We knew that candidate Obama had made clear that he wanted to withdraw from Iraq, but do more, militarily, in Afghanistan. The latter was for him the 'good war'. He was not against using America's military might, just against using it for the wrong ends.

Some of us wondered what he meant by that, and if he realised that Afghanistan was a far tougher challenge than Iraq. But I had been cheered by the talk I had had with Richard Holbrooke when he had passed through Kabul in the spring of 2008, preparing to serve as secretary of state in a second Clinton Administration or as something else in an Obama Administration: Holbrooke had seemed to get it, in ways that few Republicans did.

Earlier that year, in February, the man who was to become Obama's running mate, Senator Joe Biden, had also visited Kabul, in his capacity as chairman of the Senate Foreign Relations Committee. The Kabul rumour mill, and then the international press, soon reported on the Senator's dinner with the Afghan President. As the two sides had sat down to dinner at the long dining table in the Palace, the principal guest had invited his host to set out his thinking on dealing with the linked challenges of drugs and corruption. Almost exactly nine minutes later – one of those present claimed to have noted the time on his watch – the senior Senator from Delaware had risen from the table, mumbling something about having had enough – it wasn't immediately clear whether it was of food or talk. But press reports that Senator Biden had stormed out were denied: the US Embassy was clear that Senator Biden had been escorted out by President Karzai, anxious about his guest's health.

And, apart from a short visit by candidate Obama, during which he said little, that was about all we had to go on, as we moved towards the November election and the US Ambassador's carefully bipartisan election-night party in the Serena Hotel, complete with bumper stickers and campaign buttons – for both sides and all candidates.

The outgoing Administration had launched, at the last minute, a review of Afghan policy, which was intended more as handover notes for the transition team than as a real stock-take. Throughout those last months of Bush the message from Washington had been that nothing was to be done to suggest anything other than that the Afghan war was following that in Iraq on the path to success. As I went off to spend Christmas and the New Year (uninterrupted this time) with my family, I told myself that things could only get better under an Obama Administration.

PART IV

TACTICS WITHOUT STRATEGY: ONE LAST HEAVE

Tactics without Strategy are merely the noise before defeat.

Sun Tzu, The Art of War, *c.550BC*

Chapter 19

Biden and Beyond

In his *History of Rome*, Livy, like other contemporary writers, begins his chronicle of each year with an account of the strange happenings – auguries and portents – which presaged great changes in the affairs of mankind. Feeling a little superstitious, as I always did flying in or over Afghanistan, I landed back in Kabul from my Christmas break in a heavy snowstorm. At Dubai, I had joined a planeload mainly of Westerners returning to Afghanistan after time away. On the approach to Kabul, as we flew blind through a blizzard, some on board began praying aloud. Others adopted the brace position. Nothing was visible from the windows except driving snow and total blackness. The plane dipped and rose, and dipped again. After twenty minutes of this there was a great shuddering bump and a groan. We had landed, hard. But never have I been so glad to hit the ground.

That night, I was woken by an earthquake – 5.9 on the Richter scale – from somewhere deep in the Hindu Kush. The bed shook and swayed, and I leaped out, crouching in the doorway of my reinforced safe room. Later that morning I spent two hours with President Karzai, and another two hours with General McKiernan, catching up after two weeks away. Later I agreed that the Embassy security team should re-issue the Embassy's earthquake instructions: in essence, duck and cover, but never rush outside. Which was just as well, as an aftershock, almost as strong, followed the next night. We all learned to find the US Geological Survey's wonderful earthquake-monitoring website.

And then Pakistan's President Zardari arrived in Kabul, on a state visit postponed (by snow) but then hurriedly rearranged. Once again I found myself sitting in the great royal *salamlik*, reflecting on what brought these states together, and what drove them so far apart. But the only task that mattered in those first days of January was to get alongside another visitor. We heard that the Chairman of the Foreign Relations Committee of the United States Senate, who happened also to be Vice President-elect of the United States, Joe Biden, was going to be back in town. Having consulted London, I was given clear instructions to do whatever I could to brief him on HMG's perspective on the war, and on the need for a more political approach to Afghanistan from a new United States administration. We were in this with America, and could not succeed unless America did.

Thanks to Bill Wood, I somehow arranged to have lunch with Senator Biden, his colleague Lindsey Graham (North Carolina – Republican, and a Reservist in the US Air Force), General McKiernan and Bill – and no one else. The only snag was that the lunch would have to be in Camp Leatherneck in Helmand – the US Marines' vast cuckoo in the Camp Bastion nest. I rushed down to Bastion, reaching it in time thanks only to an exceptionally co-operative RAF officer at Kandahar, who diverted to Lashkar Gah a Chinook on the milk run round our outlying bases.

I had met Joe Biden two decades earlier, when I had been covering US politics in our Embassy in Washington. He didn't remember of course, but I did. Apart from thinner and greyer hair, he hadn't changed at all. He was as Irish as ever: charming, loquacious, combative when he chose. But he was also worried, and wanted to listen. And so I talked, as crisply and clearly as I could, about the need for the military effort to be complemented by a political approach, involving both the internal and the regional parties to the conflict; about the ineffectiveness of a military strategy focused on COIN unless it was complemented by a political strategy; and about the need to improve and focus our support for President Karzai and the institutions of government across Afghanistan. Bill Wood made an important observation. 'There is no military solution,' he said, 'but, equally, there is no non-military solution. The two go together.'

Senator Biden's scepticism about the feasibility – and affordability – of a serious counter-insurgency strategy in a country of the size and poverty of Afghanistan was clear. So I told him why I thought a strategy of the kind he had suggested – focused exclusively on counter-terrorism – probably wouldn't work, but could put at risk all that had been achieved in Afghanistan since 2001. There *had* been huge improvements in health, in education, in infrastructure and, amazingly, in prosperity. All these could be endangered if we pulled our ground-holding forces back unilaterally, and left southern and eastern Afghanistan to be fought over by the Taliban and the narco-mafia who opposed them.

The Senator took note but made few comments. Looking bored by my droning on, he gazed out across the southern desert stretching to the horizon. Like many American politicians meeting a British minister or official, he felt a need to quote Churchill coming on. 'You know, Mr Ambassador,' he began, 'Winston Churchill said that democracy is the worst form of government – except all the others.' I laughed, dutifully, and replied, 'Mr Senator, you know Mr Churchill also said that you could rely on America to do the right thing – once it had exhausted all the alternatives.'

Less than a week later, on a Saturday morning, I was working in my study at home. Suddenly the windows shook, seeming almost to flex inwards, and there was a mighty explosion. I ducked down. After a few seconds of total silence, the Embassy tannoy system crackled into life. We were all to stay where we were: we were on lockdown. Moments later, my bodyguard appeared, radio in hand. There had been a big explosion somewhere to the south of the Embassy, in the city centre.

Only later did we discover how big, and how close, the bomb had been. A suicide bomber had rammed his car – the inevitable Toyota Corolla – into a fuel truck in the narrow road between the German Embassy, our immediate southern neighbour, and the high Hesco barriers of the US training base at Camp Eggers, just to the south. An American soldier and five unlucky civilians had been killed. Despite the high wall round the German Embassy, the blast had flowed over the wall and smashed into the front of the Chancery building. Every single one of the armoured windows there had been blown, with its complete frame, out of its seating, into the building. Anyone who had been in the path of the falling windows would have been killed. The only diplomat in the office early on a weekend morning – the Deputy Ambassador – had for some reason bent down to pick something up milliseconds before the enormously heavy window of his office had come crashing down on his desk.

Up on the roof of our Embassy, some technicians from England had been examining our array of aerials. Some of them had never been to Afghanistan before. They had had the shock of their lives. First a vast fireball just to the south, and then the roar of the explosion and the pressure of a massive blast wave. They came hurtling back down the narrow access stairway to the roof, shaken and stirred. They hadn't fully recovered when I gave them dinner that night.

The German Embassy's offices had been wrecked. But, with Teutonic grit, they refused my offer of help and got on with dusting themselves off and starting repairs. As happens after every incident, the security measures escalator started moving again: greater distance between the outer and inner perimeters (known as 'standoff'), higher walls, better lighting and even greater separation between protectors and those they are seeking to protect.

A few days later I watched the grainy black-and-white CCTV footage of the early-Saturday-morning traffic outside the German Embassy that morning. It felt like watching *BBC Breakfast*'s traffic-camera footage of the Blackwall Tunnel approaches. And then the light-coloured Corolla comes slowly into view, the driver hesitating and swerving, before swinging into Camp Eggers. A silent puff of black smoke follows – the explosion itself was off camera. Perhaps ten seconds of nothing, then footage of some brave individuals sprinting towards the site of the explosion, while most are seen running or reversing away as fast as they can. After several long minutes, pickup-loads of Afghan Police appear: the men jump down and start running in all directions, waving their Kalashnikovs in the air. Another bomb, another day.

Security apart, all the talk in Kabul that spring was of the Presidential elections due later in the year. Thanks to ambiguities in the Afghan constitution, no one knew exactly when they had to be held, or when exactly President Karzai's five-year mandate ran out. More important, there were deeply divided views on whether security conditions in the south and the east would allow a credible election to be held. But money had been raised and a UN election team formed. After all, people reasoned, elections and democracy were what we were in

Afghanistan for. If, after seven years, we couldn't hold elections, what had we really achieved? The elections had somehow to go ahead. Once again Afghan 'good enough' would have to be good enough.

On 20 January – the day President Karzai opened the final session of the Afghan Parliament before the election – I held an unusual party. It had been some time in the making. A few months earlier I had realised that we were approaching, in December 2008, the eightieth anniversary of the first mass evacuation of civilians by military aircraft.

The story ran as follows. At the end of the Third Anglo-Afghan War, in 1919, full diplomatic relations were established between Kabul and the imperial capital in Delhi. At the expense of the Government of India, the magnificent new British Legation was built. But the Legation had only just been finished, and the new Minister, Colonel Sir Francis Humphrys, installed, when in late 1928 an Islamist uprising ignited by Shinwari tribesmen based in Jalalabad overthrew two Afghan monarchs in succession and put a Tajik bandit known to history as *bacha saqao* or 'son of a water carrier' on the throne. The origins of the problem were tribal, coupled with opposition to the Westernising ways of King Amanullah. Amanullah had returned from a European tour with some advanced ideas about modernising his country. His enemies distributed pictures of his Queen in a ballgown, with her head and shoulders uncovered.

The British Legation was besieged, and the decision was taken, in December 1928, to evacuate by air the entire foreign community from Kabul. The Royal Air Force was called upon to conduct the first ever mass aerial evacuation. And the Squadron which carried out the task was 70 Squadron, flying Vickers Victoria troop carriers in Mesopotamia and South-west Asia, just as the same Squadron flies Hercules troop carriers today in Iraq and Afghanistan. Nearly 600 civilians were taken to RAF Peshawar in eighty-four flights over the mountains by the Victoria troop carriers, accompanied by Westland Wapiti fighter aircraft. Hundreds of Afghans were recruited to clear the snow from the landing ground in the Wazir Akbar Khan area of Kabul – where the British Embassy is today. The evacuees included the new Afghan King (he had been on the throne for only a few days, following his predecessor's flight) and his harem, and, on the last plane, Sir Francis Humphrys.

An added twist to the story was the fact that an Aircraftman T. E. Shaw (aka T. E. Lawrence) was sitting at RAF Miramshah, spending his spare time preparing a new translation of Homer's *Odyssey*. But the word got out among the Waziri tribesmen that 'Al Urens' (as the Arabs called Lawrence) was among them, plotting. Telegrams from the Secretaries of State for Air and for India in London to the Viceroy in Delhi and the Air Office Commanding, India, soon ensured that T. E. Shaw/Lawrence was on his way as quickly as possible to Bombay, and then back home to England.

To mark this unusual anniversary, I held a party for as many guests from the Royal and other Air Forces as we could find in Kabul. Two RAF officers kindly prepared a series of display panels setting out the history. And the Afghan Defence Minister, General Wardak, generously came to the party and made a speech celebrating an exceptional moment in the history of the world's first air force.

Towards the end of January 2009 I flew back to London for the twice-annual meeting of the Foreign Office's Senior Leadership Forum. Every six months about twenty-five of the most senior Ambassadors – plus one or two carefully chosen representatives of small and medium Embassies – were flown back to London for a day of talks and presentations. The point of these meetings was not so much what was said as that it was said, in that Forum. The Ambassadors felt included and consulted. More important, Ambassadors from the more far-flung posts got a chance to see each other, and Ministers, and senior officials, and to catch up on shopping and family visits. It was a body that, once invented, was difficult to disinvent. But it was definitely one of the dignified rather than efficient parts of the FCO's constitution. In Kabul, we had plenty to do with Ministers and senior officials: if anything we needed less, not more, of them.

While in the Foreign Office, on a Friday afternoon, I bumped into the Foreign Secretary's Principal Private Secretary. He pulled me aside for a 'private word'. He wanted to warn me, in strictest confidence, that, when the Foreign Secretary saw me the following week, David Miliband was going to ask me to leave Kabul early and become HMG's Special Representative for Afghanistan and Pakistan. David wanted me to be the British Holbrooke.

My heart sank, and I know I looked uneasy. But, secretly, I was flattered too. Better always to quit while you are ahead: the best times in Kabul were probably behind me. Working from London with David Miliband, engaging with Holbrooke (whom I had met and liked) should be fun. And it was a real chance to help the Obama Administration deliver the political strategy capable of bringing sustainable success.

I confessed that I had wondered whether this might happen, on reading a record, from our UN Ambassador in New York, of a talk David Miliband had had in New York with the then private citizen Richard Holbrooke, while Holbrooke was still awaiting the formal call back to the public service he loved. Holbrooke had said that, much as he liked and respected the Foreign Secretary, he couldn't be bothering him continually on Af-Pak business. He needed in London a senior British interlocutor who knew the subjects and who could be his docking point in HMG. Seeing it put like that, I had half wondered whether to volunteer. But somehow I thought it better to wait and see.

The following Tuesday, as I perched on the edge of the red leather sofa in the Foreign Secretary's cavernous office overlooking Horse Guards, David Miliband duly made me the offer I had been told to sound surprised about. I accepted immediately. But I noted that this would mean my abandoning the plan for me to take up the Foreign Office's place at Harvard, for a sabbatical over the 2009–10 academic year, before running in the autumn of 2010 for the top jobs that would be coming free in 2011. I would give up the Harvard sabbatical, but wanted reassurance that taking this job would not affect my chances of one more worthwhile posting. After all, that was the basis on which I had agreed to go to Afghanistan. I was assured by David Miliband and by senior officials that I need have no worries on that score. They were grateful to me for responding to the call.

I also asked about how I would fit into the FCO hierarchy, and about how my role would relate to the other Ministers and departments engaged on Afghanistan. On neither front was I given clear answers – because there were none. We were making this up as we went along, in Holbrooke's slipstream.

So, even before I had started, it wasn't plain sailing. Gordon Brown's officials in Number 10 were suspicious of David Miliband having his own special representative. At Defence, John Hutton too had his doubts. There were arguments about my title. Number 10 didn't want me, based in the FCO, to be the United Kingdom special representative, still less the Prime Minister's special representative. So I ended up as the Foreign Secretary's special representative. My formal relationship to the Cabinet Office machinery and to the rest of government was Whitehall fudge of the best variety. So was my place in the FCO's policy-making machinery. That supposedly constructive ambiguity over my appointment was in time to prove rather destructive.

I had planned to be back in Kabul by early February. But we then heard that Holbrooke wanted to stop off in London on his way to 'the region'. It was too good an opportunity to miss: David Miliband asked me to stay on in London, for our first joint meeting with Richard Holbrooke.

On 22 January 2009, only two days after his inauguration, President Obama had travelled to the State Department. At a ceremony also attended by Vice President Biden, the new Secretary of State, Hillary Clinton, only just sworn in herself, had announced the appointment of Ambassador Richard C. Holbrooke as special representative for Afghanistan and Pakistan, alongside Senator George Mitchell's appointment as special envoy for Middle East peace. In brief remarks accepting the appointment, Holbrooke had noted that his was 'a very difficult assignment'. None of us then realised just how difficult. And less than twenty-three months later the man who was to become my dear friend as well as my sparring partner would be dead.

Heavy snow blanketed London early that February, virtually shutting down Whitehall. But I remember trudging in for a meeting with the Defence Secretary in a half-deserted MOD Main Building. I told John Hutton that, though I would be the Foreign Secretary's special representative, I hoped to work for all three of the Cabinet Ministers engaged on Afghanistan. It was likely that 2009 would be an even more difficult year for Afghanistan than 2008, with the uncertainties surrounding the prospective Presidential election overlaying a slowly worsening security situation.

Despite the weather, officials beavered away with preparations for Holbrooke's arrival. Meetings were held, papers drafted, lines to take cleared. But the only meeting which really mattered was the one-on-one breakfast David Miliband had with Richard Holbrooke. The Foreign Secretary told me later that he had set out his hopes and fears for the period ahead. He had taken broadly the same line as I had taken with Joe Biden. But he had focused on our worry that President Karzai, re-elected after a messy election, might not have the mandate needed to fight a serious counter-insurgency campaign.

We expanded on all this in a slightly larger meeting with Holbrooke. At David Miliband's invitation, I set out my thinking on alternative approaches, on a personal basis. I noted that, on the face of the Afghan constitution, and depending on how one counted, the country was due to have national elections of one kind or another in about fourteen of the next twenty years. Just ploughing on was not necessarily the best way to stabilise the country. I pointed to the need for a process of national reconciliation to complement the military campaign. And I wondered about encouraging the man who symbolised his country's rebirth – Hamid Karzai – not to step *down*, but to step *up* in order to preside over the coming together of all the Afghans: a sort of standing *loya jirga*, with Hamid Karzai assuming the role filled by Zahir Shah, 'Father of the Nation'. We should take time out from the remorseless electoral cycle to start trying to broker a new, and sustainable, Afghan political settlement.

Holbrooke listened, more or less, and sounded sympathetic. But he warned then, as he warned repeatedly later, that not everyone in the new US Administration saw things quite the way we did. Many in Washington agreed with the outgoing Bush Administration that things were broadly on the right track. In their view, the problem was not the strategy, but the lack of resources, especially for the military campaign. Holbrooke made clear that he did not agree with that analysis. But nor did he make any commitment to exploring an alternative approach.

Before I left London I had two meetings of significance. The first was a quiet chat, at his request, with the former Defence Secretary Des Browne. As ambassador in Saudi Arabia, I had seen Browne just after he had been appointed to a position for which he had little background.

But, from Kabul as well as Riyadh, I had seen him grow into the job and come to care deeply about the issues involved. On his visits to Afghanistan, I could see that, despite the upbeat briefings from his military advisers, he was worried, as a politician, by the way he sensed things were going. Now, once again a back-bencher, he could speak more frankly about just how concerned he really, and rightly, was.

My second meeting was long overdue. For more than two years I had been reading, and admiring, the writings on both Afghanistan and Pakistan of Ahmed Rashid. His sister and her husband were dear friends from Saudi Arabia. Ahmed's clear-headed realism made him a rare voice of reason, on Pakistan as well as Afghanistan. We clicked immediately, over tea at the Goring Hotel in Belgravia thoughtfully arranged by Elizabeth Winter of the British Agencies Afghanistan Group, the main British–Afghan NGO co-ordinating body. Seldom did Ahmed's views and mine differ significantly. But his point of view was all the more remarkable for coming from Lahore, not London.

I flew back to Kabul for the last time as ambassador full of hope for what 2009 would bring.

Chapter 20

Au Revoir Afghanistan

I landed at Kabul airport on 7 February 2009, and left Afghanistan again, for the last time as ambassador, on the 21st. It was to be one of the busiest fortnights of my life.

I started immediately on farewell calls, beginning with both of Karzai's Vice Presidents. One, Ahmed Zia Massoud, was the brother of the late mujahideen commander known as the Lion of the Panjshir, Ahmed Shah Massoud, and thus a prominent Tajik. The other, Abdul Karim Khalili, was a leading Hazara, and thus a Shia from the central belt. Karzai's style of government meant that neither was much involved in running the country. But each was deeply involved in politics and kept a watchful eye on what was really happening, and how that might affect the interests of the people he represented. Khalili remained for another term, after the 2009 election. Massoud was replaced, controversially, by the former Tajik warlord Mohammed Fahim. The balance of the coalition at the top of Afghan politics was thus maintained.

But three days after I got back unpleasant reality intruded. On 11 February the Taliban launched a series of violent attacks on government buildings across the heart of Kabul. At least twenty-seven people were killed in three separate but simultaneous assaults by suicide bombers accompanied by gunmen. The ensuing firefight with the security forces lasted more than three hours, shutting down the city. One of the Embassy staff, on official business at the Justice Ministry, was caught, almost literally, in the cross-fire. He and his personal bodyguard took refuge in a basement. After an agonising few hours, they eventually made their way out, but over the bodies of some of the victims. It was a shattering experience, a trauma to last a lifetime.

But such dramas could not be allowed to hold up the press of official business. Visiting British generals came to breakfast, visiting British journalists to tea. In between, I carried on trying to say goodbye – to Yunus Qanooni, for example, the smooth-talking Speaker of the Wolesi Jirga, the lower house. Qanooni was another Tajik from the Panjshir, and one of Karzai's most formidable political opponents. The Gailanis gave a family lunch, which left me sad to be going. At my farewell call, Karzai's outstanding Director (really Minister) of Local Governance, Jelani Popal, spoke as he always did: frankly but determinedly, with an air of amused resignation about some of the difficulties he faced in building systems and structures to govern Afghanistan outside Kabul.

And then Holbrooke arrived in town, on his first official visit as special representative. I was summoned to dinner at Bill Wood's apartment, hoping to carry on where we had left off in London. But there were at least a dozen other guests, and no chance to talk privately or seriously to Holbrooke. I did manage two minutes alone with his new deputy, Paul Jones. Jones was (and is) a serious State Department professional who had worked with Holbrooke on the Balkans fifteen years earlier. Now he flew in to Kabul from Manila, where he was serving as deputy chief of mission. He knew little about Afghanistan or Pakistan, but would learn fast.

Holbrooke phoned me the next day, on his way to Kabul airport and the next leg of his travels. I was staggered at how indiscreet he was on a mobile telephone that must have been the object of many hostile powers' interest. He gave me what turned out to be only a partial account of his meeting with President Karzai earlier that day. He said that he saw no alternative to pressing ahead with the election, difficult though that would be. The 'Cowper-Coles Plan' wouldn't work. It was only later that I discovered that Holbrooke had apparently gone in to see Karzai and told him something along the lines of 'Miliband and Cowper-Coles want to get rid of you.' How Karzai reacted is not recorded, not even in Wikileaks. But the President told me a few days later, during my farewell audience, that he hadn't believed Holbrooke. He then went on to press me to accept Afghanistan's highest honour, the Order of Wazir Akbar Khan, in recognition of what I had done as ambassador. In line with Queen Elizabeth I's injunction that her dogs should wear only her collars, I declined.

Now that Richard Holbrooke is dead, I shall never know exactly what he intended by apparently telling Karzai something that was as distorted as it was indiscreet. My guess is that it was his attempt to see how Hamid Karzai would react to an approach with which Holbrooke personally had much sympathy. But, instead of offering him an honourable path gradually up and out, Holbrooke had seemed to suggest that the idea was somehow to get the President to step down.

But with only a week left in Kabul I didn't have time to reflect. The next visitor was the Foreign Secretary himself, accompanied by my successor, Mark Sedwill. Mark had been due to take over from me in the autumn of 2009. Now, at great personal inconvenience, he had had to bring his arrival forward to May. Andrew Patrick nobly agreed to hold the fort until the new Ambassador arrived.

David Miliband had asked to see something of what the Americans were up to in Regional Command (East), to set against his exposure to the British experience in Helmand. So, early on the morning after his arrival late the night before, we set off, with the American Commanding General, in a pair of American Black Hawk helicopters for Kunar Province, in the mountains north-east of Jalalabad, up against the Pakistani border.

We flew first to the Afghan end of the Khyber Pass, inspecting from the air the long lines of trucks waiting to cross in each direction. We landed, and visited the Khyber Border Co-ordination Centre. Inside a windowless, American-built and -run bunker was a handful of Pakistani and Afghan officers sitting in what looked like a pale imitation of Mission Control, Houston. They were staring rather blankly at computer screens. A live feed from a drone was projected overhead. American officers fussed enthusiastically around. But one wondered what real use the Afghan officers on the ground would make of this. The officers present were too junior to have any executive authority; and their only means of raising GHQ in Kabul appeared to be an ancient field telephone. But, as with so much else, it was a start.

We flew on to Asadabad in the lower Kunar valley. I noticed that American helicopter gunships were now hovering above and behind us.

We met the local Mayor and were told of all that was being done by the PRT: new schools, new clinics, new roads, new businesses. Everything, it seemed, except security. When we left the American base to head for the Mayor's office, the whole of the high street was filled with American soldiers and their armoured vehicles, in front, behind and on either side of the MRAP carrying the Foreign Secretary.

No one could doubt that good had been done and was being done. But the old question remained: how long would it last once Western forces left, and what would happen in the many areas where there wasn't a Western presence, and wouldn't be one? As I had found in my research the year before, the American Reservists and Navy and Air Force personnel who made up the Asadabad PRT staff were second to none in their energy, their enthusiasm and, increasingly, their local understanding. But here too it seemed like a kind of military colonialism. To have a chance of making an enduring and positive impact on the host society, it would need to be done with much money and many men, for many years. And that was without even asking what the host society really wanted and might be willing to accept.

Back in Kabul, David Miliband plunged enthusiastically into a round of calls and meetings. Talks with the Foreign Minister, an audience of the President, a discussion of sub-national governance with Jelani Popal, frank exchanges with the exceptionally competent Interior Minister (Hanif Atmar) and one with the chief election commissioner. In between, questions, discussion, gossip and a working dinner. David was an exhausting guest, but a worthwhile one. He always made sure that he profited from being back in Afghanistan. And he seldom failed to make a positive impression on his hosts. I think it was during this visit that David asked Karzai about his manifesto for the forthcoming election: on what platform of fresh policies would he run? Without any apparent sense of irony, the President replied, 'More of the same.' David's jaw dropped.

Thirty hours after arriving in Kabul David Miliband was in the air again, travelling south. I prepared a draft of the Foreign Secretary's report to the Prime Minister on his visit, based on ideas David had given me before takeoff: it would be emailed to Dubai, for the Foreign Secretary to amend and approve on the flight back to London.

That night I held the second of two farewell parties: an open house for Embassy staff, ending in some exuberant dancing. An earlier one, for the Afghans and the international community, had been a quieter affair. But it had enabled me to put across a message of affection for Afghanistan. I had begun my speech by telling the Afghans that I had news for them: the British were still plotting (as every Afghan always believed they were), but plotting for a better and more peaceful future for a land and its people at once blessed and cursed by history as well as geography. I really meant it.

Earlier in the evening dear Dr Spanta had given a farewell dinner for me at the Foreign Ministry: the day that no ambassador ever thinks will come. The diplomatic corps was ranged round a series of great tables, with a troupe of Afghan musicians strumming sitars on a platform to the side. As I looked at my fellow Ambassadors, I realised that I would soon be parting from some good and distinguished friends, operating in one of the most difficult diplomatic environments in the world – and one where the stakes could hardly be higher.

The next morning I rose early, for the obligatory photograph with the current Close Protection Team. This one had chosen what we called 'swimming pool hill', above and behind the Embassy. There, carved out of the back of a long, flat, low hillock was an Olympic swimming pool, with a tower of diving platforms to match. But it was deserted and empty, and, allegedly, stained with the blood of the hundreds of Afghans whom the Taliban had executed in the empty belly of the pool. Surrounded by my team, their weapons at the ready, I posed self-consciously in the snow for photographs.

Then it was back to the Chancery, to draft my valedictory telegram, the redacted version of which forms the rear endpaper of this book. I had known for some months what I wanted to say, and the words flowed easily. It was all about a quasi-imperial recessional. Not about whether we would withdraw, but about how and under what conditions we were going to do so. All our efforts should be directed at persuading the Obama Administration to get a political grip on the whole enterprise. The promise Obama had made, in the heat of the Presidential election campaign, to send more troops to Afghanistan was secondary.

Then it was a final lunch with a very unJapanese Japanese Ambassador. Unusually, he was a Christian. He and I had been in Israel at the same time. Like me, he spoke Hebrew. Like me, he read ancient Greek (though he had taught himself). Like me, he had a passion for the Mediterranean, or what he called the Inner Sea. The reason for the lunch was not our mutual love of the Mediterranean, but the presence in Kabul of my friend Toshiro Suzuki, the Director General of the division in the Japanese Foreign Ministry responsible for Afghanistan. Suzuki had learned Arabic with us, at the British Foreign Office school above Beirut, and had been the best student in our year. Now, he made clear how worried he was about the outlook in Afghanistan. But Japan was in Afghanistan to show the United States what a good ally it was: whatever the Foreign Ministry's doubts, there could be no question of quitting. Japan's huge aid programme for Afghanistan was part of its subscription for its alliance with the United States.

That night I had a quiet supper at the Boccaccio restaurant with Andrew Patrick and the team from my office. It was a suitably low-key finale to the best and worst of diplomatic postings.

Chapter 21

Richard Holbrooke's Flying Circus

I landed in London on the evening of Sunday 22 February 2009. The following afternoon, I reported to the Foreign Office, to start work as special representative. The FCO's top management quietly forgot about enforcing the health and welfare rules on taking plenty of leave on return from a hardship posting. To be fair, so did I. I just wanted to get on with the new job. But it was a decision that I came to regret.

The first task was to find an office in the great Italianate palazzo on Whitehall in which the Foreign Office is housed. With a knowing grin, the Head of the Afghanistan Group played estate agent. The first property he took me to view was the office my old friend Lord Levy had persuaded a reluctant Permanent Secretary to provide for him as Tony Blair's Middle East envoy. Apart from history, it had two advantages: a plush red carpet, laid at Michael Levy's request, and a combination lock on the door. I was told that the latter had been installed after Michael had found a crisp packet in his office, suggesting that some official had used the vacant room in which to eat lunch. But the lock had apparently resulted in the office never being cleaned – which had apparently become another source of complaint. Sadly, someone had long ago removed the brass plate announcing Lord Levy's presence, which Foreign Office workmen had screwed to the door, allegedly in breach of English Heritage rules for a Grade I listed building.

I decided that I needed something less grand, but more practical: I would start by sharing an office with my team, still to be formed, and a fridge and a kettle. Later, I would move into an adjacent room, with interconnecting door, once the officials there had been relocated. It took several weeks, but, thanks to David Corlett of the Afghanistan

Group, and to Sarah Cowley, the superlative new Private Secretary whom I soon recruited, all went smoothly. Sarah even managed to extract from the FCO furniture store a Victorian bookcase in which to place part of the library of books on Afghanistan I had brought in.

As a senior official, I was also entitled to hang in my room one or two pictures from the Government Art Collection. We chose two. First, an ink drawing of what one Oxford don had once pompously told me was the most important tree in Europe: that which breaks the curve in Oxford High Street, overhanging the garden wall of the Warden of All Souls College. The second picture was a remarkable high-shutter-speed photograph of rose petals falling, almost exploding, into water, by the Israeli-British photographer Ori Gersht, one of whose works I had admired, and bought for the Residence in Tel Aviv when I had been ambassador there.

We completed the decoration with plenty of Afghan rugs, a beautiful illuminated example of Arabic calligraphy which the Turquoise Mountain Foundation had given me as a leaving present, and a set of coasters bearing cartoons of the warlords of Afghanistan. Only later did I hang some of my favourite cartoons, by Pont. The final touch, acquired a bit later, was an original print from *The Times*, depicting a man in pyjamas throwing open the curtains of the marital bedroom and proclaiming, 'Another day, another new Afghan strategy!'

As for what the Special Representative actually did, I had to make that up as I went along. Although I was the equivalent of a director general, I didn't have a management role or position in the Afghan hierarchy in the Foreign Office. I welcomed that, because I wanted to be free to travel and think and interact with Holbrooke. A formal role at home would have constrained that freedom. I had done plenty of managing, of money, people and policy advice, in Kabul. Moreover, I knew that an important part of my new role – though not in the job description – would be to act as David Miliband's informal *consigliere* on matters Af-Pak. I couldn't do that so easily if I was having constantly to put formal advice up to him through the policy chain. This *ad hoc* arrangement worked superbly with Adam Thomson as South Asia Director.

Within days of my appointment being announced, in late January, Germany and then France had followed suit, by appointing special representatives for Afghanistan and Pakistan (SRAPs) of their own. The Berlin Government brought back, for his last job in public service, their venerable Ambassador to India, Bernd Mützelburg. Bernd became a good friend and a congenial colleague. He was right at the top of the German Foreign Service, with experience, judgement and contacts to match. He made up for what he didn't know about Afghanistan and Pakistan by never being too proud to seek and accept advice from those less inexpert than him.

Our new French colleague, Pierre Lellouche, could not have been more different. Something of an intellectual, he was a politician of Gaullist tendencies, a member of the Assemblée Nationale and a Paris city councillor. He had plenty of form on politico-military and trans-atlantic issues. His relative ignorance of South-west Asia did not prevent him having, and enunciating, clear views, usually rather different from those of Richard Holbrooke. The brains and passion he brought to the job made Pierre always worth listening to – even if one couldn't agree with him. Sadly, the rules of French parliamentary democracy meant that he could do this second job only for six months. As it turned out, he was soon snatched away anyway, to a Ministerial position, as junior minister for Europe at the Quai d'Orsay.

But my first, and overriding, priority was to get alongside Richard Holbrooke, and to do all I could to help the Obama Administration devise and implement Afghan policies that would reverse the downward trends I had observed for two years on the ground. So after only four days back in London, having recruited a private secretary and found a desk, a computer and a telephone, I flew off to New York in pursuit of Holbrooke. Adam Thomson came with me.

We found Holbrooke in the offices of the investment bank Perseus, for which he had worked before returning to government. For the first time, I realised just how difficult it was going to be to get him to focus. He was late and had to go early, to the dentist. Throughout our meeting he checked his BlackBerry. When he wasn't doing that, he made and received calls, and yelled out orders to a laughingly tolerant secretary in the next office cubicle. At one point, only half-jokingly, I almost shouted: 'Listen, Richard!' But, as always with Holbrooke, it was clear that his heart was in the right place; and, good bureaucrats that we were, Adam and I leaped at his invitation to send him HMG's more detailed thoughts on paper.

Almost as important as meeting Holbrooke in New York was seeing his main academic guru on Afghanistan, Professor Barney Rubin of New York University. Barney had been in at the creation of post-9/11 Afghanistan. He was one of the leading Western academic experts on that country. He knew, as Adam and I did, that a military-focused approach would never bring lasting stability. Barney and I had got on well when we had met in Afghanistan. We continued to keep in close touch throughout my time as special representative. Barney was one of the most effective advocates in the US system for political dialogue. He took full advantage of his position, half in and half out of government. He seemed deliberately to cultivate the appearance and manner of a nutty professor. Perhaps this was in part designed to lull into a sense of false security many of those watching him, particularly in the US military.

After a good session with Barney, and a lunch with the senior UN officials dealing with Afghanistan, we went to the offices of the German Mission to the United Nations. There it had been agreed that Bernd and I would have a joint meeting with the Ambassadors of the Friends of Afghanistan Group – essentially the main troop-contributing nations, plus a few others. There was a real sense of hope that, at last, under Obama, we were going to develop a serious approach to Afghanistan.

I flew back to London from New York overnight on Friday/Saturday. I gave up that Saturday afternoon to take tea with a statesman whom I had long wanted to meet, the former Algerian Foreign Minister Lakhdar Brahimi. He was over from Paris to teach at the London School of Economics, and staying, modestly, in a hostel in Bloomsbury for academics. We had tea, and walked and talked. We connected, in an odd blend of English, French and occasional Arabic.

Brahimi was what I had hoped he would be: wise, witty and well informed about what was happening in and on Afghanistan. I knew that he was one of the few foreigners whom Karzai consulted. He had real influence over the President, dating back to his time, in 1997–9 and again in 2001–4, as UN special representative for Afghanistan, and as the godfather of the Bonn process. But Brahimi was big enough to admit that, in the haste to end the conflict then, mistakes, of omission and commission, had been made. His thinking on the necessary course corrections was very much in line with David Miliband's and mine. I hoped he could play a role, direct or indirect, in promoting the more political approach essential for success. In my report to David Miliband, I strongly recommended that he see Brahimi – which he did.

The next week I crossed the Atlantic again, this time to Washington, for a round of calls on Holbrooke and as many as possible of those involved in Obama's instant review of policy. I spoke to Karzai from Washington in the early morning, mainly as a device for showing the Americans whom I would see later that Britain too had access where it mattered.

Every official whom I met that day seemed sympathetic to the ideas I was peddling, on empowering communities, on building up the governors of Afghanistan's thirty-six provinces and 394 districts – the *wali*s and *uluswal*s – and on involving the neighbours in the search for a solution. We called this approach to governance 'The Golden 400'. The members of the new Administration listened politely and took notes. The one who mattered most – Bruce Riedel – was a softly spoken former CIA official who had been brought in from the Brookings Institution on a temporary assignment to conduct the review. Not surprisingly, he had the least time to listen. But I thought I made some impact on him, and on the Vice President's National Security Adviser, Tony Blinken.

My brief diary entries for the months that follow give the impression of perpetual motion. I soon lost count of the number of times I crossed the Atlantic, all in an ultimately fruitless effort to persuade an Obama Administration still finding its feet to adopt a more political approach to Afghanistan. Just plunging on with a strategy of pouring in more troops and more money, without doing something about governance and about the political offer to the Afghan people, and something to engage the regional players, was a recipe for eventual failure. I wrote papers for the Americans, drafted messages for David Miliband to send to them, worked up speaking notes for Ministers and senior officials to use. But seldom if ever did we get much by way of reaction or reply.

And when I wasn't in Washington, I was pursuing Holbrooke in Brussels or Paris, or enticing him to meetings in London, or trying to pin him down to a bilateral in the margins of one international conference or another. Chasing Holbrooke could be exhilarating, and humiliating: one day trip to Brussels got me ten minutes with him in a conference centre lobby, as he eyed the passing personalities and pretended to listen to me.

President Obama's statement of 27 March, announcing the results of the Riedel review, had said many of the right things – a clear focus on Al Qaeda, equal attention to the Pakistan side of the equation, 4,000 more American troops to train the Afghan Army and Police, more resources for the civilian side of the mission, proper measures of progress and no blind commitment, attention to corruption and governance, openness to reconciliation with the Taliban, the establishment of a Contact Group to bring together all those, including Iran, with a stake in Afghanistan, and a commitment to intensive regional diplomacy.

But the question was what all this meant. David Miliband and I knew that, without a real effort to build up Afghan government at all levels, but especially in the provinces and the districts where the fight against the insurgency was really being fought, none of the rest would mean much. Similarly, at national level, we needed a credible political product to offer the Afghan people caught between the insurgents and the narco-mafia broadly defined. Nor could Afghanistan be stabilised without engaging the neighbours, Pakistan above all, but also India, Iran, China and Russia, seriously and collectively. The serial bilateralism which had marked American diplomacy on Afghanistan would not be enough. We needed to get the regional stakeholders to believe that we actually wanted to work with them collectively in stabilising Afghanistan – something from which each would gain, as Afghan exports of refugees, violence and drugs came down.

As part of our efforts to help turn the President's words into a strategy that might actually work, David Miliband persuaded the new US Secretary of State, Hillary Clinton, to come into the Foreign Office for a seminar on Afghanistan (mainly) and Pakistan in the margins of the G20 economic summit in London in April 2009. It was only just over a year since we had had a similar exercise with Hillary's predecessor, Condi Rice.

What we found was an American team who believed that getting Afghanistan right was mainly a matter of pressing on with the Presidential elections – after all, we were in Afghanistan to deliver democracy – and of pouring in more resources, troops and money. They weren't really interested in our advice on strategy, since they thought they had a strategy. What they really wanted to know was what the Brits thought about the Afghan personalities with whom we were dealing, especially President Karzai.

It was clear that Mrs Clinton, from her time as a senator, had a soft spot for Hamid Karzai. At David Miliband's request, I told her what I knew and thought, including my conviction that he needed almost daily doses of tough love – with the emphasis on both words – from a sympathetic American on the ground. Public abuse and private appeasement were exactly the wrong ways to treat him – or indeed any other Eastern leader. So was management by remote control – video conference or telephone call – from Washington. She listened carefully, and seemed to agree.

I took Holbrooke off to lunch at my club, Brooks's in St James's Street, with my successor in Kabul, Mark Sedwill. Holbrooke spent much of the lunch telling Mark that he wanted him, when he arrived in Kabul as ambassador, to convene a group of ambassadors including the Iranian: despite the President's commitment to bringing Iran into a Contact Group, it would be difficult for America to do so direct. Holbrooke never let me forget that lunch – teasing me repeatedly about belonging to such a club. But he loved the experience, and was impressed by its Whig tradition. More important, he was flattered to have found himself at what he was convinced was the best table in the dining room. Richard never failed to combine work with pleasure. On arriving in London for that visit, his first request had been for me to get him a table at the Ivy. His second had been trickier. He wanted to know which was cooler for Saturday night dinner: the River Café or the refurbished restaurant at Brown's Hotel.

The following day – a Friday – I persuaded Holbrooke that he might benefit from a briefing on the state of the Taliban from Britain's Secret

Intelligence Service at their headquarters at Vauxhall Cross. Holbrooke agreed only reluctantly. He was going to the theatre with the financier George Soros that evening, and could spare an hour at most. He stayed for nearly three hours, asking for more, becoming totally absorbed in what the experts, led by the Service's Chief, 'C', had to say. Question followed question. His social life was temporarily forgotten. It was SIS at its very best. And then, as we got up to leave, Holbrooke remembered the outside world. Out came not one, but three, mobile phones, all switched on, in total breach of house rules. The Chief, Sir John Scarlett, looked his name. It was vintage Holbrooke.

As the weeks and months went by what had started as a quad of four serious Special Representatives for Afghanistan and Pakistan – Holbrooke, Mützelburg, Lellouche and I – grew and grew. Everyone wanted to join the club. Everyone Holbrooke met seemed to be invited to come along.

We had our inaugural meeting in Munich, on 1 April, appropriately enough. Holbrooke had had a soft spot for Germany ever since he had served there as ambassador. He had asked Mützelburg to act as the convenor of the collective. And so the twenty or so SRAPs who had then been appointed (the number later grew to nearly forty) gathered at the luxurious Bayerischer Hof hotel in the historic centre of the city. Holbrooke spoke in extravagant terms of his hopes for the group, now that Obama's new strategy had been announced, the week before. Mützelburg chaired, sensibly and quietly. Lellouche and I showed off, in different ways. With the date in mind, I managed to convince Holbrooke (and then Lellouche) that the Afghan Defence Minister was lobbying for the West to provide him with a navy.

In between all these meetings, I slipped back into Kabul, to catch up. It was striking how quickly one lost touch with the realities on the ground. In a whirlwind forty-eight hours, I saw a cross-section of key political and security players: President Karzai (alone), Speaker Qanooni, the Ministers of Defence and of the Interior, Fahim Khan (starting to come back into favour) and the Hazara leader Mohammed Mohaqiq. I had dinner with Bill Wood and Kai Eide. All the discussion was on the Presidential elections due later that year, and the question of when Karzai's mandate expired and of whether it could legitimately be extended until elections postponed from April until August. Passing through Dubai on my journey back to London, I saw, on his way to Kabul, Zalmay Khalilzad. Whatever the reality, he could not escape being seen as one of the *éminences grises* of Afghan politics. Many were asking whether he saw himself as a potential king, or king-maker. So it was worth hearing what he had to say.

In London that spring, I had another lunch at Brooks's. This time it was with, at their request, three acute observers of international affairs in general, and of our Afghan challenge in particular: the former Foreign Secretary, Douglas (Lord) Hurd; Professor Sir Michael Howard, a master of strategy who had once examined me for All Souls; and Sir Max Hastings, one of the finest contemporary historians of conflict. All were worried. All seemed to agree with the analysis that, however well resourced the military campaign, without politics it could be no more than tactics without strategy.

And all the time the Afghan roadshow rolled on, from capital to capital, and conference to conference. In late March it had been in Moscow, for a meeting on Afghanistan of the Shanghai Co-operation Organisation – a Central Asian security organisation founded by China and Russia.

Our Embassy in Moscow organised an excellent informal discussion over dinner with Russian academic and military experts on Afghanistan. I was struck by how much they seemed to agree with our broad analysis of the problem, and with the need for a political strategy. They spoke with great sadness of the mistakes which Russia, often against its better judgement, had made in Afghanistan, with terrible consequences both for the Red Army and for the Soviet Union itself. They took no pleasure in pointing out, as the Russian Ambassador in Kabul had done two years earlier, that we were making many of the same mistakes.

Perhaps even more significant was what Sergei Lavrov, the Russian Foreign Minister, said in his speech opening the conference: that, provided the Taliban broke with Al Qaeda, accepted the Afghan constitution and renounced violence, we could – and perhaps should – talk to them. Common sense at last, from one of the countries that had always maintained that the only way to deal with violent Islamic extremism was to crush it by force. His words were almost identical to those of Mrs Clinton two years later, in her Holbrooke Memorial Address in February 2011, making clear that the Taliban could come back into Afghan politics, on the same three conditions.

From Moscow, I travelled to The Hague, for a great conference on Afghanistan of all fifty or so nations and international organisations involved in the project. The Americans wanted the Hague event to align us all behind a new 'comprehensive' strategy, and to use the conference to extract pledges of more troops or money from allies eager to ingratiate themselves with the incoming Administration. In line with President Obama's speech three days earlier, Mrs Clinton spoke of the need for reconciliation and for a regional approach, involving Afghanistan's neighbours. And, in a sign of how high hopes then were, one of the essential regional players, Iran, was present.

The conference was opened by the Dutch Prime Minister and addressed by President Karzai, UN Secretary General Ban Ki-moon and Mrs Clinton, before an interminable table round in which every participating nation had to speak. But, as so often, the concrete results of the meeting fell short of the promise of the rhetoric. Cynics said that all the conference did was to enable the United States to maintain the moral pressure on its allies to stay the course. David Miliband sensibly stayed away, letting the Foreign Office Minister of State, Mark Malloch Brown, represent the United Kingdom. For me, the main benefit was a range of bilaterals with fellow SRAPs.

Afghanistan dominated everything I did in my eighteen months as special representative. That was as it should have been, given the size of the British investment of troops and cash in that country. And yet we knew that Pakistan was the bigger problem, and, if we were honest, the bigger threat to Britain's security. Gordon Brown's 'chain of terror' stretching to the streets of London came not from Afghanistan but from Pakistan. It was there that the remnants of Al Qaeda hung on, and it was there that young Britons of Pakistani origin went for indoctrination and training. Paradoxically, however, it was a problem about which we could do less, and to which we devoted less time, effort and money. But I knew that I needed to do more to build the Pakistan side of my dossier.

So, later in the spring, I embarked on an epic journey: to Tokyo, for a major Pakistan donors' conference advertised by President Obama in his speech on 27 March, to Canberra to brief and encourage the Australians (on Afghanistan), and then to Pakistan, for my first visit as special representative.

My main task in Tokyo was to represent Britain at a meeting of the Friends of Democratic Pakistan Conference. This preceded the donors' conference, but was supposedly not about aid to Pakistan. Instead, the focus was meant to be on political support for Pakistan's fragile democracy. Frankly, it was a distinction without a difference: President Zardari and his officials made little effort to disguise their belief that, without money, fine words buttered few Pakistani parsnips. But I made the best speech I could, quoting the Koran, and drawing on an excellent telegram from our High Commissioner in Islamabad, my friend Robert Brinkley. In that cable, Robert had reminded us that the Pakistani polity, for all its obvious defects, was three things: proud, Muslim and democratic. The last was meant in the sense that government had to respond to public opinion and was certainly not a functional autocracy.

In Tokyo, I was able to catch up with two friends: Toshiro Suzuki, the Foreign Ministry Director General responsible for Afghanistan, whom I had seen on my last day in Kabul; and our Ambassador, David Warren, who, as president of the Oxford Union, had helped launch both Benazir Bhutto and, in a minor key, me on our speaking careers in that place.

I then flew south to Canberra. My visit to Australia was Afghan-focused and was the idea of our High Commissioner there, Helen Liddell, the former Scottish Secretary. She wanted us to show the Australians just how much their contribution counted. I had no difficulty in doing that. In a round of calls on everyone from the Prime Minister's National Security Adviser to the Chief of the Australian Defence Force, I spoke of the courage and professionalism of the Australian forces deployed alongside the Dutch in Uruzgan, just north of Helmand. The Australian SAS were special heroes, even though, operating from their base in Kabul, they had broken many hearts in my Embassy.

As always with Australian officials, I found a degree of hard-nosed professionalism – an understanding of realpolitik – not always apparent in, for example, the softer-edged, more principled Canadians. It was a pleasure to talk. If my visit had one result, it encouraged the Australians to appoint a special representative of their own, though not necessarily on a full-time basis. I was delighted with their choice, Ric Smith, a retired senior diplomat who had served as permanent secretary in the Australian Department of National Defence. As well as his love, and expert knowledge, of cricket, Ric brought to the Special Representatives' group the judgement and courage to tell Richard Holbrooke – firmly but tactfully – that he might be wrong. Ric was a valuable addition to the collective, and one with whom I kept in close touch.

From Canberra, I travelled on to Islamabad, via Melbourne and Dubai – an epic journey involving a fourteen-hour flight across the Indian Ocean. I took time in Melbourne discreetly to snatch some photographs of the former EU Special Representative Francesc Vendrell's secret love: trams. Sure enough, he was able immediately to identify not only where my pictures had been taken, but also what line they showed.

The highlight of my first official visit to Pakistan as special representative was a day out in Lahore, the great Mughal capital of the Punjab which I had always longed to see. We started by calling on the Governor, Salman Taseer, who, less than two years later, was to be assassinated by one of his bodyguards for his opposition to the blasphemy law. Taseer was cool, calm and collected: the smooth, liberal businessman aligned with Benazir Bhutto's Pakistan People's Party whom my brief had led me to expect. He was not going to allow himself to be fazed by the challenges he faced.

From the city centre, I drove out to the farm of the 'leader of the opposition', the Pakistan Muslim League (Nawaz), Nawaz Sharif. Much about the exotically furnished house, and the gardens stocked with wild animals, reminded me of the wilder shores of wealth in Saudi Arabia – a country with which Nawaz, like me, had close connections. In our talk, during which he was surrounded by courtiers hanging on his every word, Nawaz gave little away. But it was clear that he was in no hurry to grapple with the challenges which President Zardari was facing. I thought of an edition of the satirical magazine *Private Eye* in the spring of 1976, when Prime Minister Harold Wilson had suddenly handed the reins of power to Jim Callaghan. The cover had consisted of a picture of the *Titanic* going down, with a voice bubble coming out proclaiming simply, 'You take over now, Jim.' The scale and complexity of Pakistan's problems seemed to mean that both the obvious alternative centres of power – the Army and Nawaz Sharif – were quite content to sit out Zardari's travails.

The visit to the farm full of exotic creatures, both human and animal, was followed by another surreal experience, a Hogwarts moment. Our High Commission had arranged for me to visit one of British India's great public schools, Aitchison College in Lahore. As we entered the gates, we could have been approaching one of Victorian Britain's great educational establishments: Cheltenham College sprang immediately to mind. And passing the cricket pitches and gothic classrooms, we came across the pupils – in British-style school uniforms. And, then, I was swept up by a kindly headmaster and, to my astonishment, asked to deliver an impromptu address to the school. I did so, with great pleasure: I remembered that I had to call for a half-holiday for the boys, but I also staged an impromptu quiz, including for some startled members of the British team, who were hauled up on stage too.

We rounded off the day in Lahore with two different experiences: a superb briefing from the senior political officer at the US Consulate General in Lahore, who was about to become political counsellor at the US Embassy in Islamabad; and a tour of some of the great historic sites of Lahore, including the ancient Fort – more a citadel than a simple fort – and the adjacent 'pearl' mosque of transcendent beauty. It was a reminder of how this bustling, chaotic metropolis was really part of a much older and deeper Indo-Muslim civilisation that had stretched across the subcontinent and back over the mountain ranges to the north-west.

Back in Islamabad I called on President Zardari for the first time. I was curious to meet Benazir Bhutto's widower, of whom I had heard so much, including from President Karzai. He was exactly as advertised: friendly, open, more worried than perhaps he let on, almost embarrassingly diffident about his own qualifications for high political office, with a keen commercial sense. More difficult was my meeting later with the Foreign Minister, in which he complained about Western bias against Pakistan. His was the zero-sum rhetoric of traditional Indo-Pak hostility and was not as constructive as it needed to be. On my first official meeting with him, he must have felt he had to give me the standard treatment.

But there was a special pleasure in store that evening: in the congenial surroundings which Robert and Mary Brinkley always provided at the High Commission, a meal and a gossip with one of Lahore's finest contemporary exports: Ahmed Rashid. As usual, Ahmed had his finger on the pulse of the best of the just slightly unconventional wisdom.

Not long after that, I was back in Pakistan again, for what was perhaps the low point of all the international meetings on Afghanistan I attended in three and a half years. The occasion was a meeting, in Islamabad's main conference centre, of the Regional Economic Co-operation Conference – Afghanistan, known as the RECC-A, which sounded about right. The international delegations sat around, and waited, and waited, and waited, for the meeting to begin. The reason for the delay was that the Afghan delegation had not arrived: they were, we were told, held up in meetings with President Zardari and Pakistani officials. Worse still, the official delegation never did appear. Some hapless deputy was sent to represent the Afghan ministers, and we began, some three hours late.

I was furious: here was an international meeting, focused entirely on providing economic support for one of the poorest nations on earth, and the beneficiaries did not bother to turn up. At that time, Afghanistan raised revenues of its own each year of about $800 million, while receiving at least forty times that in civil aid alone from the international community. It was almost a scandal – except the West was now in a position where it needed the Afghan Government almost as much as the Afghan Government needed its Western paymasters. Rather like the bank which cannot afford to let fail the customer who owes it a million rather than a hundred pounds, so our only hope of an honourable exit from Afghanistan was somehow getting the Afghan Government to fulfil its role.

But the visit to Pakistan for the RECC-A did have two collateral benefits. First, I was able to have a proper talk with America's

Ambassador to Pakistan, Anne Patterson. Her diminutive size belied her courage and her intellect, now open for all to see in those of her cables which have appeared in Wikileaks. She was one of the few career American diplomats not afraid to stand in the path of the Holbrooke bulldozer; and she got Pakistan like no other US official. The second benefit was more for my emotional than my intellectual education: I went to a camp on the outskirts of Islamabad to see some of the Internally Displaced Persons – refugees in real language – from the fighting in the Swat Valley and elsewhere in north-west Pakistan: it was an upsetting experience which put so much else of what diplomats did in proper perspective.

One week early that summer I was in Washington twice in five days. On the second occasion it was for the first off-site meeting on Afghanistan for the whole of the US Administration's vast combined civilian–military Af-Pak team. Although Holbrooke gradually widened the guest list for these events to include most of the key allies and, eventually, the Afghans themselves, the Brits were the only non-Americans at this first team-building spectacular.

The conference took what was to become the standard form: an early breakfast of military coffee and 'Danish', followed by a working day of presentations, mostly PowerPoint, by key members of the team, in a windowless room at the National Defence University at Fort McNair, in the District of Columbia. The sponsor of the event was really General David Petraeus and his team from the US Central Command based at Tampa. But Holbrooke was the co-star, and co-chair. Most of the senior members of the team were seated round a hollow square of desks, at which we each had assigned places, in rank order. At each seat was a fat briefing book, full of PowerPoint print-offs, put together by Holbrooke's shop and the team from CentCom. In the back of the room were rows of seats for other invited parties from around the Administration.

What followed was a cross between the Spanish Inquisition and the bureaucratic equivalent of gladiatorial combat. Speakers would step up in pairs to lecterns placed in the square on either side of a great screen. They would then 'present' on the area of Afghan policy or activity for which they were responsible: aid delivery, agricultural development, a surge of civilians into the PRTs, prison reform, strategic communications. Holbrooke and Petraeus would interrupt, ask questions, invite others to comment. One ill-prepared and unconvincing speaker was more or less fired on the spot. Brandishing one of his cellphones, Holbrooke constantly got up to receive calls, usually from (he would announce loudly) 'the Secretary', and to make them. Petraeus chaired, quietly but effectively, commenting, commissioning further work.

To an outsider, it was a bizarre way to work. Not a single speaker gave, or showed, any real sense of the strategy all this activity and expenditure, much actual but most prospective, was supposed to support. Despite the military majority in the room, little was said about the military campaign in Afghanistan, or about how exactly the extra 21,000 troops Obama had ordered to Afghanistan would be deployed. One had the sense of a great leviathan rolling forward, spending money, establishing programmes, but without really knowing what everything was for, and how it would deal with the real problem: an anti-foreigner insurgency then infecting most of Afghanistan's Pashtun belt, and spreading. Plans to develop Afghan agriculture and send scores of civilians to the PRTs were advertised, mainly by Holbrooke, as the key to almost everything.

Back in London the familiar pattern repeated itself: a few frantic days of meetings, talks and breakfasts, lunches and dinners, and then in the air again, this time to Istanbul, for the second meeting of SRAPs. I had managed to persuade Holbrooke to agree to a bilateral before the main meeting started, but he was late, and we had only ten rushed minutes. Richard rather threw me by asking me to guess what the most important issue for the SRAPs' meeting would be, as he was intending to speak on it. 'Reconciliation,' I guessed. 'Wrong,' he retorted. 'Governance,' I said. 'Wrong again,' Holbrooke replied. 'It's agriculture, Sherard. We must all put all our efforts to building up Afghan agriculture this year: that is how we are going to beat the insurgency.' I was, frankly, flabbergasted. All our efforts to persuade Holbrooke that the fundamental problem in Afghanistan was political seemed to have made no impact. But I suspect that in part he was playing games: he had political top cover for agriculture, but not yet for politics. We moved out on the terrace of the hotel, by the Bosphorus, for a session with Bernd Mützelburg and Pierre Lellouche. We then spent the afternoon and evening in plenary session: little of what we discussed or concluded made much difference to any Afghan reality.

The group was now bigger: Ric Smith, the Australian, had joined us for the first time. But so had many others, mainly Europeans. And the Indian Ambassador was there, scribbling furious notes whenever Pakistan was mentioned. But, curiously, neither Afghanistan nor Pakistan was yet part of the group. It was an odd and random international formation, reflecting more Holbrooke's operating methods than a coherent attempt to implement President Obama's commitment, six weeks earlier, to establishing a serious international Contact Group.

Once that summer I returned to Washington for talks with the Americans as part of a cross-Whitehall team. In two days there, I had only two brief encounters with Holbrooke, but he was too busy to attend the main talks with the British delegation. Again, however, it was the encounters in the margins that made the trip worth while – in this case, a dinner with Afghan experts arranged by our Embassy, and my first meeting with the French academic Gilles Dorronsoro, then at the Carnegie Endowment for International Peace.

Over breakfast at the magnificent Lutyens residence on Massachusetts Avenue, Gilles told me that he thought that ISAF had already lost the south. Our strategy, of fighting the enemy where he was strongest, was almost bound to fail. The insurgency was spreading, and we would be wise to consolidate our position in the north. Gilles sounded more gloomy and melodramatic than I ever was, and I was shocked. But he knew the insurgency better than any British or American intelligence analyst. And he had been one of the few to warn of the consequences of our insouciant intervention in Afghanistan in 2001. I had plenty to think about as I drove back out to Dulles that evening.

That Friday, back in London, the new Swedish Special Representative, Anna Karin Eneström, came for lunch and talks. Anna Karin was preparing for the Swedish EU Presidency in the second half of the year, starting on 1 July. She had the backing of a remarkable Foreign Minister, Carl Bildt. Over the next seven months she was to show what a small nation, with relatively limited interests in Afghanistan but a big interest in the Western alliance, could do, if it so chose, using professional diplomacy of a high order. She organised meeting after meeting, drafted papers and delivered, at the end of October, a strategy for strengthening EU activity in both Afghanistan and Pakistan. It would be foolish to pretend that any of this made much difference to the situation on the ground. But it did give greater coherence to the European input to the overall Western effort. It was a pity that America wasn't able to respond with active diplomacy of a similar kind, but on a larger and more significant scale.

And so, as spring turned to summer, the SRAP circus continued, substituting form for substance, discussion for delivery, activity for real achievement. With the ground war in Afghanistan steadily worsening, it was the kind of diplomacy for diplomacy's sake that gave diplomats and politicians a deservedly bad name.

The meeting which best summed up the whole charade was held in Trieste, in June 2009, to mark the mid-point of the Italian G8 Presidency. The full-dress meeting of Foreign Ministers and Special Representatives was pure *bella figura*. Thanks to the Italian taxpayer, we enjoyed lunches, dinners, drinks, beside the Adriatic, in the magnificent home port of the Austro-Hungarian Imperial Navy. As if to show what he really thought of it all, Richard Holbrooke failed to appear at all for his scheduled bilateral meeting with David Miliband – to the embarrassment of the US officials who had to keep the British Foreign Secretary waiting, and amused.

Meanwhile, in the country which was supposed to be the point of all these meetings, there was only one subject that really mattered: the Presidential elections on 20 August. Everyone was hoping against hope that the elections would be credible, more or less. But, at the height of the fighting season, violence was worse than ever. It wasn't a good omen.

Chapter 22

Where's Dick?

As with President Obama (according to Bob Woodward),* so with me, and no doubt many others. At one of our first encounters, Richard Holbrooke asked me, with only a hint of embarrassment, to stop calling him 'Dick'. His wife, Kati, he said, wanted him henceforth to be known as Richard: it was more dignified. Ever afterwards, I wondered whether those of Holbrooke's friends and colleagues who still called him 'Dick' did so out of ignorant over-familiarity (probably in most cases), by design (many older friends who couldn't or wouldn't change) or by invitation (the true inner circle). Thenceforth I stuck resolutely to 'Richard'.

Despite the injunctions from my family and, with less conviction, from the Foreign Office, that I should take some leave that summer, I had left for Scotland on the morning of Saturday 8 August and was back at work in London on the evening of Wednesday 19 August. There were two reasons for that.

The first was that, on the Wednesday evening, Obama's new Ambassador to London, Louis Susman, was giving his first official dinner, in honour of General Petraeus. I had to be there, especially as Petraeus was going where I had just been – Edinburgh. I had known the man who was now General Officer Commanding, Scotland, Major General Andrew Mackay, when he had been leading Task Force Helmand over the winter of 2007–8 (see Chapter 12). He now paid me the huge honour of asking me to take the salute at the Edinburgh Tattoo, which I did, with great pleasure. Andrew had asked General

---

* *Obama's Wars*, London: Simon & Schuster, 2010.

Petraeus to do the same, a few days later, with the King of Tonga (whose troops were performing at the Tattoo) sandwiched, metaphorically, between us. I took the opportunity to give General Petraeus a small present: Patrick Hennessey's *Junior Officers' Reading Club*,* describing, brilliantly, the author's time as a young Grenadier Guards officer in Helmand. Typically, I got an email back from Petraeus within three days, saying how much he had enjoyed the book. But the second reason for being back in London only ten days after I had left was the Afghan Presidential elections on Thursday 20 August. Holbrooke had tried several times to persuade me to be with him in Kabul on election day. I had told him, quite forcefully, that I thought that a bad idea. He, and therefore I, would be expected to offer a running commentary on the elections. Westerners would be accused of manipulating the results. I was sure this was a case of distance being wiser than proximity, in space as well as time. We would need to see what the elections produced, and then, taking our time, recommend to our political masters the right sort of response.

Holbrooke would have none of that. On 20 August the only place to be would be Kabul, visiting polling stations and taking (and being seen to take) a close and supportive interest in the Afghan democratic process. He was going to be there. It was up to me if I went. Having consulted David Miliband and Mark Sedwill, I decided to stay away.

Thanks, I think, to pressure from the Swedish EU Presidency, Holbrooke arranged a conference call with his fellow Special Representatives the morning after the Afghan elections. So, just before 7 a.m. on Friday 21 August I was in my room in the Foreign Office in London. The phone rang: 'State Department Operations here. Will you hold for Ambassador Holbrooke?' I did, and so did nearly thirty other SRAPs and substitutes around the world. While we were waiting for Holbrooke, in Kabul, to be patched in, I mucked around, pretending to be Hamid Karzai on the line. Anna Karin Eneström rumbled me first. Then Richard came on, getting straight to the point. The final electoral tally, certified by independent observers, would not be known for weeks. But already Karzai was claiming victory in the first

* London: Allen Lane, 2009.

round. Holbrooke was clear, however, that monstrous levels of fraud meant that there would have to be a second round. He and the new US Ambassador, Karl Eikenberry, were due to see Karzai for lunch that day and would tell him so. I chipped in, saying that a stolen election would be difficult to explain to the British people. We needed to wait for the full results. Others made similar points. We agreed to consult again.

What none of us knew, but what all of us should have realised, was that Karzai's people were listening in to our conference call. We had been speaking, across Afghanistan and around the world, on an open line. Holbrooke sounded as though he was on his mobile. However it happened, assiduous Afghan listeners reported our every word, or their version thereof, to Karzai in unusually quick time. Whether he exploded before, after or during his lunch with Holbrooke I don't know. But explode he did. To this day, Karzai is convinced that the West in general, and Holbrooke in particular, did not want him to win the Presidential election, and therefore conspired to steal it from him. Moreover, he sincerely believed, and still believes, that he won enough votes in the first round – well over the 50 per cent threshold – to make a second round unnecessary; but that the international community, led by the United States, deliberately massaged the numbers down to 49 per cent plus a fraction in order to force a second round.

To be fair to Karzai, this view wasn't entirely without justification. In the run-up to the election, Holbrooke had encouraged several other candidates to run against Karzai. In June, the US Ambassador had deliberately appeared at an election meeting with two of Karzai's rivals, Dr Abdullah Abdullah and Ashraf Ghani. In the event, however, the multitude of other candidates ended up running more against each other than against the incumbent.

The crisis over the Afghan election dragged on right through the autumn of 2009. Special Representatives met in Paris on 3 September to discuss the way forward. But at that stage we had only partial and provisional results, putting Karzai well in the lead, but not over the 50 per cent threshold. After several further announcements of partial results, the final certified figures did not emerge until late October, putting Karzai at 48 per cent. He reacted furiously, believing that the

West and the UN had manipulated the figures. He claimed there would be riots on the streets if a second round was forced through. Under continuous pressure, and thanks in large part to Senator John Kerry, Karzai eventually conceded a second round. Kerry had spent many hours with the President handling him in just the way he should be handled: with respect, especially in public, and firmness and affection in private.

The second round was duly set for early November, but then, allegedly under pressure, Abdullah pulled out. President Karzai was given a walkover. The election period had seen some of the highest levels of civilian casualties across Afghanistan in recent years. But the verbal violence, between Karzai and the international community, and within the international community, did more damage to the international credibility of the whole mission. Most spectacular was the public falling out between Kai Eide and his newly appointed political deputy, Peter Galbraith, a friend and former colleague of Richard Holbrooke's. It was a row that led eventually to Galbraith's dismissal.

In different ways, Eide and Galbraith had both been doing their best in almost impossible circumstances. Kai saw that Karzai was the only show in town, and was trying to keep that show on the road. But Galbraith, and many of the political team who worked for him, attached higher priority to the integrity and thus credibility of the electoral process. The real fault lay in the design of the whole project: a constitution drafted by a Frenchman and imposed by an American, that was (and is) out of sync with Afghan political realities. A constitution which imposes something like fourteen separate national elections in twenty years is not really sustainable, politically or economically.

The management of this unfolding drama fell mostly to Ambassadors on the ground. We Special Representatives watched from capitals with mounting concern as the process dragged on and on, and weeks turned into months. Holbrooke's relationship with Karzai was at its nadir. But he never lost his sense of humour or of perspective, pointing out that President Karzai's overenthusiastic supporters need not have gone to such trouble to fix (and thus spoil) an election that the President would probably have won anyway.

After the Paris meeting, the next gathering of SRAPs was in New York, in the margins of the UN General Assembly. Thanks to Anna Karin Eneström's enthusiasm and efficiency, EU Special Representatives now met in advance of the wider meetings: it was notable how much more businesslike the EU meetings were, compared with the wider ones. We really did think alike and have the same practical approach to the issues.

The full meeting lasted three and a half hours. Holbrooke was present for less than a third of the time. He announced that he had an important alternative engagement, although he later confided to me that the real reason for his absence was the opening of an exhibition of paintings by his son – to which he kindly invited me. It was difficult to see where the point of the whole exercise lay when the man around whom the whole Special Representatives' circus revolved felt able to attend only a fraction of a meeting he had described, with his usual hyperbole, as our most important yet.

That autumn and winter the SRAP roundabout slowed down. After the disaster of the Afghan Presidential election, it was as though Holbrooke's heart had, at least temporarily, gone out of the Afghan side of his work. Enemies in the Administration were circling. There were rumours that powerful figures in the Pentagon had been pressing for his dismissal. But, whatever the truth of those rumours, Mrs Clinton stuck by the man who had loyally stayed in her camp throughout the primary campaign, well beyond the point where it had been clear that Senator Obama would win the nomination. Certainly, Holbrooke had been unwise to pick three semi-public fights with Karzai: over Karzai running for election at all, over his choice of running mate (Holbrooke and others had, rightly, questioned the wisdom of choosing Fahim Khan, the former warlord) and over the second round. But, as so often with Richard, his motives had been basically right. And it seemed to me that the White House could have done more to direct and support him.

And as the SRAPs' gyrations slowed, so did the pace of work for my small team and me. I twice joined a cross-Whitehall team in Washington for consultations. General Stan McChrystal had replaced General McKiernan in June. By September he had produced his assessment of the seriousness of the situation, recommending a further surge of 40,000 troops (on top of the 21,000 extra Obama had ordered on coming into office that spring).

The elections, and the McChrystal surge, were the main issues on the agenda of a whole series of multilateral and bilateral consultations that autumn and winter. I went to Brussels for an EU Special Representatives' meeting to finalise the Swedish Presidency's EU plan for Afghanistan and Pakistan. Later, I was back in Brussels, accompanying David Miliband to North Atlantic Council meetings at which all the talk was of how many more troops the allies would send to support the surge (of a further 30,000 troops) which President Obama had announced in his speech at West Point on 1 December 2009. Meanwhile, I visited Berlin, Ottawa, Riyadh, Rome and Tallinn – as part of an effort by Britain to keep our allies engaged in the Afghan project. I never quite understood why Britain took it upon itself to act as principal cheerleader for the American-led effort in Afghanistan. But, given my experience on the ground in Kabul, I felt I was usually able to tell my hosts something they didn't know; and we had thought harder than most about the kind of strategy essential for success. I also went back to Pakistan, to keep that relationship going, as part of the UK's own strategic dialogue with the government in Islamabad.

And I spoke at conference after conference, lunch after lunch, dinner after dinner. In Geneva, to the annual meeting of the International Institute for Strategic Studies. In Sussex, at the Foreign Office conference centre Wilton Park, which I had visited on the first stages of my Afghan journey, two and a half years earlier. At Church House, Westminster, with Paddy Ashdown, General Richards and others. Always and everywhere I tried to strike a note of optimism founded in realism. For British audiences especially, family memories of forebears who had served on the North West Frontier, and the histories of British and Indian regiments who had fought and died there, meant that one had to overcome an innate scepticism. The paradox – the dilemma – for British audiences was that there was strong support for the troops, and for the armed forces, coupled with doubts about the mission. As one worried retired senior general put it privately, 'The mums don't like it.'

Of one speech I was particularly proud: at a meeting of the Global Strategy Forum, in the National Liberal Club in January 2010, I set out my dream of what success in Afghanistan might look like.* Two former Foreign Secretaries in the audience expressed polite scepticism. But I wanted to show, I had to show, that my worries about an overwhelmingly military campaign, focused on counter-insurgency, were not entirely negative. I had some constructive ideas too.

And throughout I pursued Holbrooke – by telephone, text and email, and, when I could find him, in person. In Paris, on private business, he invited me over from London to join him for dinner. We agreed that he would choose and book the restaurant, but that I (or rather HMG) would pay. I should have been more careful. Rushing from a delayed Eurostar, I missed an appointment with our Ambassador and headed straight to the restaurant, worried that I would have kept Holbrooke waiting. But he was even later. Neither that nor the fact that he had chosen one of Paris's best, and most expensive, restaurants should have surprised me. He hardly drank, but I watched with astonishment and dismay as he ordered an extra soufflé and then pudding. As usual, however, Richard's charm, his intelligence and his sympathetic understanding of the issues, coupled with a disarming frankness, made one forgive everything. What he told me over that dinner *valait le voyage*.

But the really memorable event of the autumn was David Miliband's visit to Afghanistan for President Karzai's inauguration on Thursday 19 November. Given the role that Karzai believed, wrongly, I had played in the election, I thought it best to let others accompany the Foreign Secretary to the inauguration itself, and on his call on the President.

One memory stands out from that visit. It is of a question which the Foreign Secretary put to two Afghan Ministers as we waited in the Residence for others to join us for dinner. David Miliband asked our guests, innocently enough, how long they expected the Afghan central government authorities, civilian and military, to stay on in Lashkar Gah after Western forces left. I don't know precisely what response David was expecting, but I imagine it was somewhere between decades and

---

* http://www.globalstrategyforum.org/newsshow.aspx?id=11&ref=79

infinity. So the answer we did get, delivered with an insouciant grin, was all the more shocking. 'Twenty-four hours,' came the reply. In three words, the whole object and purpose of our presence in Helmand were being called into question. I had always thought that the Afghan Government's will to secure and govern Helmand in the manner which we were proposing to them was at least as doubtful as their capacity. But here it was spelt out, in alarmingly stark terms.

We didn't have time to pursue the question, though later I recalled that I had been told by British officers at the Afghan National Army training establishments in Kabul that, if newly trained recruits were told that they were being posted to Helmand, 60 per cent went AWOL. As a result, they had to be put in locked buses and not told where they were going. That was not surprising, when we expected the Afghan Army and Police to ride around that IED-infested land in open and almost wholly unprotected Ford Ranger pickup trucks. Not for them the MRAPs and assorted armoured personnel carriers being sent out to our forces.

In January 2010, David Miliband went back to Afghanistan, for his fifth visit, and I went with him. I travelled to Kabul via the United Arab Emirates and India. In Abu Dhabi we had, early that month, what Holbrooke described, yet again, as the most important SRAP meeting ever – the first to be attended by Afghan and Pakistani Ministers. It took place in the surreal and sumptuous surroundings of the Emirates Palace Hotel. We conferred, we caucused, we consulted, and we then gathered around the usual great hollow square of tables.

With my excellent Japanese colleague Motohide Yoshikawa, I convened a dinner to discuss the topic of the hour: reintegration. In New York in September, Holbrooke had charged Moto and me with raising several hundred million dollars to fund a national reintegration effort, in time for a programme formally to be launched at the London Conference in January 2010. But, even before the money was raised, we needed the Afghan Government, working with ISAF and with the UN, to start designing and delivering a programme to turn promise into reality across the insurgency. A British retired general, hired by McChrystal the previous summer, turned up to brief the assembled SRAPs. The story was hopeful. Amid the encircling gloom of the

Presidential election and its aftermath, and higher than ever levels of violence, reintegration was everybody's favourite nostrum. Only a few wise voices urged caution, pointing to the difficulty of delivering anything in Afghanistan, even when the political will and the resources were there. Neither of these was properly present in this case, as we came slowly and sadly to realise in the months that followed.

In Delhi, my job, as always, was to show that we took India seriously as a key player in the game. It was difficult not to do so, when her Special Representative, the veteran diplomat S. K. Lambah, was a man of such quiet authority and experience. Each time I went to India I thought I had made progress in persuading my hosts that in the end there had to be some kind of political accommodation with the Taliban – as with all insurgencies, including those across the great Indian Republic. But each time I encountered new waves of worry and doubt: talking to the Taliban was appeasing Islamist terrorists. Firm security measures were the only answer. It was a question of India's worried heart overcoming its political brain. But there could be no question of denying that, for all sorts of reasons of history and geography, India had a large and legitimate stake in a stable Afghanistan.

Two memories stand out from that visit to Kabul by David Miliband in January 2010. The first was of a remarkable dinner which my successor as ambassador, Mark Sedwill, organised for the Foreign Secretary. Almost everyone who mattered on the US and UK sides in the project was there. Holbrooke and McChrystal were the main American guests. On our side, the senior guest was McChrystal's British deputy, Lieutenant General Sir Nicholas Parker. Nick Parker's mischievous intelligence was a breath of fresh air. Not for him, in private, the boilerplate clichés of counter-insurgency. He thought for himself, with an intellectual courage that didn't always endear him to the military machines back in Northwood and MOD Main Building. As always with David Miliband, debate flowed fast and furious. I am not sure we solved anything that evening. We didn't know then what Obama was going to decide. But we did know that McChrystal was worried, and wanted tens of thousands of troops. He was setting the pace, and I had the sensation that those of us arguing for a more political approach were left trailing in his slipstream. One of his most endearing qualities was the respect, and affection, he had for his brothers-in-arms in British Special Forces, some of whom had come out to work for him, to promote reconciliation and reintegration.

My second impression was of the extraordinary quality of the briefings the Foreign Secretary received when we left Kabul for the south. Major General Nick Carter had only just taken over as ISAF's regional commander for the south. But he treated the Foreign Secretary to a virtuoso performance, without notes, let alone PowerPoint, exhibiting plenty of enthusiasm and understanding, but also realism, grounded in a sense of the time needed to turn things round in ways that would last. In Lashkar Gah, too, we had a sense of being briefed by the A Team. The Brigade Commander, Brigadier James Cowan, did use PowerPoint, but in fresh and original ways that drew on medieval history as much as the latest iteration of the Helmand Roadmap. Accompanying him, the new Head of the Provincial Reconstruction Team, Lindy Cameron from DFID (who had served as head of DFID Afghanistan in Kabul during my first year there), orchestrated an outstanding team briefing, in which all the component parts of the civilian effort were given a voice.

The only jarring note was in the obvious tension with the US Marines, whose gung-ho style – one British officer publicly suggested – perhaps owed as much to their loyalty to the institution of the Corps as to the NATO campaign plan. The Marines' keenness to move as far and as fast south and west across and beyond Helmand was extremely impressive. But we had doubts about the strategic sense of much of the frenetic activity by a force in such a hurry.

More important than that was an uneasy sense that the fluency of the briefings, by some of the brightest and best in the British Army, was somehow beside the point. In our anxiety not to sound negative about the extraordinary efforts being made by some brave and dedicated servants of the Crown, we were at risk of confusing the medium with the message. Our worries about the latter led us to prefer to focus on the former.

On our way back to Kabul airport, we took time to do something that put much else in perspective. At his request, David Miliband paid a private visit to the old British Cemetery and quietly laid a wreath. He saw the old graves, civil and military, and the newer ones, mostly of young NGO workers killed in action, as it were. But he also stood before the tall panels of slate erected in memory of the British servicemen and women who had given their lives in this latest Afghan War.

Despite the darker spots, David Miliband and I flew back to London convinced that, on the ground in Kabul, Kandahar and Helmand, our best people were giving the job the best they had. One could not reasonably ask for more, with the London Conference only weeks away.

PART V

RECESSIONAL

La guerre, c'est une chose trop grave pour
la confier à des militaires.

President Georges Clemenceau quoted in Soixante Années
d'Histoire Française *(1932) by Georges Suarez*

Chapter 23

Embassy Encore

As with so many international meetings, the origins of the London Conference of January 2010 lay in a mixture of muddle, good intentions and political horse-trading. Throughout 2009 there had been pressure from the players on the ground in Afghanistan, particularly the American Ambassador, Karl Eikenberry, and the UN Special Representative, Kai Eide, for an international conference in Kabul. The idea was to hold a meeting to relaunch the whole Afghanistan project, under increasing Afghan ownership, once a new president had been elected, with a fresh mandate. Others in capitals, including me, had favoured international meetings outside Afghanistan to open and close a process of refurbishing the project by the time of the tenth anniversary of the Western intervention, in October 2011.

But the drawn-out Afghan Presidential election process, the inability of the Afghans to step up to the plate and some fast footwork by Gordon Brown meant that the first conference in the new series was held outside Afghanistan, and in London. During a visit to Berlin in September 2009, the Prime Minister agreed with the German Chancellor Angela Merkel that there would be a conference on Afghanistan in London or Berlin in early 2010. Downing Street officials followed this up very rapidly, by persuading the Germans to accept that London would host the first event, with a later one in Berlin, or Bonn, perhaps in the autumn of 2011. France's President Nicolas Sarkozy was presented with an Anglo-German *fait accompli*. But the French understood that, with a British general election looming, Gordon Brown's motives in wanting a conference in London then were at least in part political. They swallowed their doubts about whether the Afghans would have properly prepared for such an event. And the Foreign Office found itself having to pay for a huge gathering without any additional funding. But the Prime Minister had shown initiative. Whatever his motives, he had set the agenda in ways which could be put to good use.

The idea was that the London event would enable the international community to renew its pledges of support, civil and military, for a refreshed Afghan democracy. London was also about the international community getting its act together in Afghanistan and patching up its relationship with President Karzai. The appointment of the veteran UN diplomat Staffan de Mistura to replace Kai Eide was the most important single element of this. So were plans to find higher-powered NATO and EU diplomatic representatives in Kabul, with mandates to match. To its credit, the international community realised that, if it wanted the Afghans to raise their game, it had to do so too.

In response, the Afghan Government would set out its plans for honouring its commitments to its international supporters, at a second conference in Kabul, probably in the summer of 2010. Thereafter, there would be a peace *jirga* of some kind in Afghanistan, to launch the process of reconciliation, followed by the Afghan Parliamentary elections in September 2010 and the NATO Summit in Lisbon in mid-November 2010. Beyond that, a further international conference, perhaps in Berlin or Bonn, in the autumn or winter of 2011 could form the other bookend of the process.

Meanwhile, the withdrawal of US troops, which Obama had promised would start in July 2011, would get under way. As the Foreign Secretary pointed out privately, in what I came to call the Miliband paradox, the irony was that the more US troops were needed in Afghanistan in the long run, the greater the pressure for them to leave. The more stable the country, the easier it would be to keep them there for as long as necessary.

Thus did the politicians and diplomats set out the way markers for the Afghan project over the months and years ahead. But no Afghan plan survives contact with what the Russians call life itself. As Bob Woodward's book *Obama's Wars* has shown, this careful choreography of events disguised deep tensions in Washington and in the wider international community about the feasibility and direction of the whole project. The underlying reality was that the insurgency was continuing to spread and deepen, with violence at record levels. And, as many of us had feared, a flawed election had damaged, not repaired, the credibility of the Afghan Government's political offer to the mainly Pashtun populations in the south and east. They faced an unenviable choice between the cruel certainties of Taliban rule and the patchy and often predatory attentions of a government not seen as being on the side of ordinary people.

The world beyond the Afghan policy circuit did not pay much attention, or give these plans much credibility. The only facts that really mattered to outside observers were, first, that Karzai had somehow prevailed in an extraordinarily damaging electoral process, and, second, that Obama had decided to send more troops, and to start withdrawing them eighteen months later. It was not a convincing prescription.

But that didn't stop the London Conference being the success that all such events have to be. Amazing feats of organisation and preparation were performed by teams from the Foreign Office's Afghanistan, press and protocol departments. More than seventy delegations from governments and international organisations had to be looked after. The Prince of Wales kindly gave a reception for senior visitors, at which a delighted Karzai was the guest of honour. A communiqué was negotiated, agreed and promulgated. The central promise was of phased transition to Afghan ownership of the campaign, province by province, district by district (with the first candidates announced by President Karzai in March 2011). The world's press paid attention, for a day.

Apart from making sure that we were able to announce plenty of money for an Afghan reintegration fund, I played little part in any of this. I held a dinner for Special Representatives on the eve of the conference. I greeted President Karzai on behalf of the Government and bade him farewell. But I felt I was not really central to the whole effort.

In the margins of the conference there was much speculation that General McChrystal had finally succeeded in recruiting my successor as ambassador in Kabul, Mark Sedwill, as the new NATO senior civilian representative in Kabul. Like a Commons speaker being dragged to the chair, Mark appeared reluctant to accept the new job. After all, he had been Ambassador in Kabul for only eight months. But in the end he agreed. His successor as ambassador had already been designated, to take over in late 2010. It was to be William Patey, who had succeeded me in Riyadh in 2007. But William could not extract himself from Saudi Arabia before the spring or arrive in Kabul before May. So the Foreign Office, and the Foreign Secretary, began to think about sending someone senior out to take charge of the Embassy between Ambassadors.

As I was walking back across St James's Park to the Foreign Office one lunchtime in January 2010, my Private Secretary, Sarah Cowley, rang me: a senior official wanted to see me that afternoon. I had guessed what he wanted to ask: would I be prepared, exceptionally, to go back to Kabul, to lead the Embassy during the interregnum between Mark Sedwill and William Patey? Ambassadors almost never return to take charge of embassies they have once held, but this would be different. Once again, I was assured that making this further sacrifice would have no effect on my chances of securing one of the senior Diplomatic Service posts which had been dangled in front of me, both before I had gone to Kabul the first time round, and when I had given up the sabbatical at Harvard to serve as special representative. David Miliband was especially keen for me to go. And he was sincerely grateful when I agreed. Once again, Afghanistan and the Office had taken precedence over my personal life. I was the willing dupe, out of ambition, vanity and, perhaps most important this time, a growing sense that the SRAP job wasn't any longer a real one, whereas Ambassador in Kabul undoubtedly was.

Once the decision was taken, I was encouraged to leave at once. I spent the Monday after the London Conference, 1 February, making arrangements. Sarah Cowley and my outstanding PA, Catriona Gorry, had kindly agreed to come with me. With typical thoughtfulness, they had arranged, without my asking, to arrive in Kabul a day or two before I did, to set up our office and to familiarise themselves with how the place worked. It would be Catriona's first overseas posting: I felt a certain responsibility to her parents. But, as proved the case, I knew that working in the Embassy in Kabul at a time like this, in circumstances like that, would prove an unforgettable experience.

In deciding what title the new temporary ambassador should have, the Foreign Office lapsed into delicious self-parody – pure *Carlton-Browne of the FO*. The plan was for me to continue to act as special representative, but to be based in Kabul rather than London. As I was needed out there immediately, there was no time to arrange for me to be formally accredited as Ambassador. In any case, during my time back in charge of the Embassy I would have to seek *agrément* from the Afghan Government for William Patey's appointment as Her Majesty's Ambassador. So, to avoid confusion, the Foreign Office's protocol department ruled that I should be known as 'Minister and Chargé d'Affaires at Kabul', a delightfully dated title in which I revelled. (Though, to complete the archaism, 'Caboul' might have been even better.) Our first diplomatic representative after the end of the Third Afghan War, Sir Francis Humphrys, had been a minister, in charge of a legation, as almost all the heads of our diplomatic missions had been in those days. Luckily, no one suggested temporarily rebranding the Embassy as a legation.

Just over a week later I was on my way back to Afghanistan. I had spent the intervening weekend at the Munich Security Conference, where I had caught up with President Karzai, Holbrooke and a down-beat General Jim Jones, the US National Security Adviser. In a debate with Senator John McCain, Holbrooke had shown his true colours, disagreeing with the Senator's assertion that the Taliban had to be 'defeated' before a serious political process could begin.

Flying back into Kabul in early February 2010 I was given an easy snapshot of how much had changed, for better and for worse, since I had first been sent out as ambassador, nearly three years earlier. Somehow this return felt quite different from the visits I had paid as special representative. On the plus side, the civil side of Kabul airport was much busier, with more planes, more airlines and of course more passengers. The new terminal given by the Japanese Government was finished, even if the jetways (walkways) weren't yet working, and the terminal seemed largely unused. On the negative side, however, there was far more military activity at the airport than there had been in 2007. NATO had built itself a vast new apron and base area behind on the north side of the airfield.

For my personal security, the Embassy had made temporary arrangements. Mark Sedwill had taken the Ambassadorial Royal Military Police Close Protection Team with him to ISAF. So my team was civilian, provided, very professionally, by the Embassy's security contractors, ArmorGroup. The briefing the Team Leader gave me as I climbed into the armoured Land Cruiser was almost identical to the one I had had in 2007. And the high-speed drive through the crowded Kabul streets to the Residence showed that, although one or two roads had been asphalted, the impression of pervasive poverty and latent danger was as overwhelming as ever. Kabul felt less safe than it had done on my first drive in with Michael Ryder in May 2007. And of course it was.

With only three months in Kabul, I was determined to hit the ground running. We landed soon after 6.30 a.m., and by 7.30 a.m. I was giving breakfast in the Residence to Lieutenant General Parker, the Deputy Commanding General of ISAF. (The dear Residence team produced porridge, of course, without my even having to ask.) Then, and at a briefing Nick Parker gave me the following Sunday, this most modern General showed that he shared David Miliband's and my analysis of the importance of starting as soon as possible to harvest politically the gains ISAF was making militarily.

Then it was back to the old routine. The morning meeting. The town hall meeting. The gatherings at Palace 7 – the UN building – with concentric circles of international actors. But there were differences too. Mark had reorganised the Embassy by strands and themes, and by cross-cutting delivery teams, each of which had a manager and a leader. I decided to change nothing: it would be for William Patey to decide on how he wanted run the place, once he arrived. I was in Kabul only as a caretaker.

But the biggest difference was that we no longer had the kind of access to Karzai we had once had. There was no weekly war cabinet. The American Ambassador still saw the President several times a week, and occasionally, when he had visitors in town or urgent business to transact, more than once a day. General McChrystal had similar access. But no other foreigner was able to see the President on anything like a regular basis. Kai Eide was about to leave, but his relationship with President Karzai had not recovered from the election travails of the year before. There was a sense around town that the President was more distrustful than ever of his foreign, or at least his Western, 'friends'.

One thing, however, had not changed: the relentless pace of work, and life, in charge of the British Embassy in Kabul. Sarah, Catriona and I all realised just how lightly loaded the job of special representative had been compared with the demands now placed on all three of us. Every evening Sarah prepared a box of papers for me to work through. Every morning I rose at five or earlier and got down to my homework immediately. Any later, and I fell rapidly behind. Every evening there was at least one official engagement, but usually two or three. All day, every day, except, usually, Friday, there were meetings, visits, calls, video conferences with London. Almost every breakfast or lunch was a working meal.

But there were lighter moments too. On my first evening back, when I had been on the ground only twelve hours, I attended another eccentric event that made me proud to be British Ambassador: a dinner given by one of the senior British officers in Kabul to discuss and learn from the loss of the British Army of the Indus in the disastrous Retreat from Kabul in 1842. Only the British could mark such a setback (as they might have put it) by holding a dinner, in combat dress, but with candles and what passed in Kabul for mess silver. The Americans present were rightly impressed and, I think, rather awed.

In between the courses, and through the flickering candlelight, a bright young officer from the Rifles lectured us on the campaign of nearly two centuries earlier. In his concluding remarks, the Brigadier identified three main causes of the catastrophe. Of these the third was, I thought, still relevant: the reluctance of junior officers to tell their superiors what a mess they were in. I thought I could just make out Flashman, at the end of the table in the far corner. The spirit of Dr Brydon – who survived the massacre thanks to a magazine stuffed in his hat absorbing the blow from an Afghan sword, and who featured in Lady Butler's famous painting* – hovered over us.

---

* *The Remnants of an Army* (1879), displayed in the Tate Gallery. Brydon was believed, inaccurately, to be the be the sole survivor of the Army massacred during the retreat from Kabul in January 1842. He is shown on his exhausted horse arriving at the gates of Jalalabad. In 2007, the Royal Army Medical Corps named its field hospital at Camp Bastion 'Brydon Lines'.

On the Friday, I repeated what I had done on arriving three years earlier: a walk along the city walls, soon after dawn. This time, however, instead of searing heat and dust, we were struggling with thick snow and biting winds. But the views in deep winter were even more beautiful than those in high summer. And this time I did not feel as though I was about to suffer cardiac arrest. My Close Protection Team had, however, heard what had happened last time. So, determined not to lose their principal, they quietly lugged up the mountain a defibrillator and a collapsible stretcher. Trying to be kind, they attempted, unsuccessfully, to conceal from me their concern, and its consequences.

Over the days that followed I did the rounds. Breakfast with Karl Eikenberry, breakfast with Kai Eide, breakfast with the Head of DFID Afghanistan, dinner with some of the best NGO analysts on Afghanistan, dinner with the new (and strikingly realistic) head of the NATO Training Mission, Lieutenant General William Caldwell, and his very bright adviser, a US Navy captain who had been at the same Oxford college as me. The picture that emerged was strikingly consistent. Gains *were* being made, in all sorts of ways and places. On police training, on fiscal management, on local government capacity, even on security in certain areas. Extraordinary individuals were making heroic efforts, applying industrial quantities of will power, and money and men. Some things *were* getting better.

But. The fundamental questions remained. What would happen when and where we were not? How many of these improvements were either sustainable or replicable without long-term Western engagement? When would the Afghans really be ready and, at least as important, willing themselves to secure and govern their country in the ways that we expected them to?

A new and much trumpeted programme for improving local governance was a case in point: the District Development Programme. According to this, with Western support and cash, the Afghan Directorate of Local Governance was going to despatch to every one of Afghanistan's 350 or so districts, starting with those in the most dangerous areas, a cadre of committed and competent administrators. The numbers had been calculated, the budgets assigned, the contracts issued. It all sounded so good.

I hated to sound negative, to question the enthusiasm of others who, unlike me, had not seen something like this before. But I had to ask whether the scale and ambition of such a programme were remotely realistic. Even when, later on, our ambitions for the programme were cut back, it was just not realistic to imagine that the Afghan Government would be able to find enough capable officials to man, and keep manning, the district centres on the scale envisaged. I was worried that I had upset the briefers by asking such questions. I felt terrible. I seemed to be questioning the whole point of why these dedicated and sincere devotees of the stabilisation industry were in Afghanistan at all. But I had to ask: taxpayers' money was involved. This wasn't just marginal or ephemeral. It mattered, and, because it mattered, we had to be rigorous both in our points of departure and in our projections. I kicked myself afterwards. I should just have gone with the flow. Everyone else did. Even if we officials had doubts, it was for Ministers to reason why. But I drew some comfort from discovering a few days later that Karl Eikenberry had had similar concerns about the same programme.

Karl got Afghanistan. His quiet, almost diffident manner belied a steely intellect. And his military background concealed, or perhaps reinforced, an ability to put the uses of military force in their proper political perspective. The more I saw of him the more I admired him. But his approach made him enemies: the previous autumn, two cables, commissioned by the White House in the run-up to Obama's decision on the surge, had been leaked to the *New York Times* – secret NOFORN (NOT for FOReign nationals) cables marked personal, paper copies only. Despite an FBI investigation, the culprit was never publicly identified, but the circle of those who had seen the telegrams had been very small. In those telegrams, Karl had explained why he doubted – as anybody who knew anything about it had doubted – how surging a few thousand more Western troops into a problem on the scale of the one we faced in Afghanistan could work, unless and until some of the wider political issues essential for any counter-insurgency campaign were addressed.

But no such doubts seemed to have occurred to the American military strategists. Their plan had promised us that forty Afghan districts would be stabilised by December 2010, another forty by December

2011, with a final tranche in 2012. McChrystal's plan, first enunciated in August 2009, had survived the Obama review and became formal NATO policy that December, but with 30,000 rather than 40,000 extra troops. And Marjah in Helmand was to be one of the first districts to be thus pacified. As the US Marines' tee-shirts proclaimed, 'Marjah: Just Do It'. Privately, I was able to express some of my doubts about the feasibility of stabilising so many districts, so quickly, in various talks I had with American and other colleagues. We all wanted the plan – to which our political masters had signed up – to work. But it was very difficult to see how, given the scale of the challenges we faced, and the enduring shortages of Afghan capacity and will.

But Stan McChrystal was no fool. He had moved immediately to address one of the issues that most alienated ordinary Afghans, and thus President Karzai, from the NATO campaign: civilian casualties. He reduced the use of air strikes, except as a last resort, and made every ISAF soldier understand that protecting the population was front and centre of the new strategy. He changed the rules of engagement, putting the focus on what he called 'courageous restraint'. All this led to a real improvement in atmospherics, and to the best relationship between an ISAF commander and the Afghan President since General McColl.

A young British Apache attack helicopter pilot, on his second operational tour in Afghanistan, spoke to me that spring about the changes he noticed compared with his first tour, a couple of years earlier. He claimed that on his first tour young Pashtun males, many of them almost certainly Taliban fighters, had fled whenever an Apache had appeared in the skies overhead. On his second tour, however, the young men had seemed to believe that the new rules of engagement meant that they could be attacked only if they were bearing arms, and in a threatening fashion. So they would stand around, looking up at the helicopters, but would make no effort to flee or hide.

Sadly, the same pilot said that, from the air at least, he had detected no discernible improvement in the performance of the Afghan National Army over the two years between his tours. The ANA were still impossibly brave: often the problem was not getting them to fight, but getting them to stop fighting. Watching them going into action one always had the sinking feeling of seeing a rabble charging off, shooting in all directions, including at each other. It must have been a bit like having an aerial view of Wat Tyler taking his men into battle. The Army Air Corps officer added that it was striking to see how much more aggressive American forces were in pushing forward, more or less regardless, compared with any of their allies.

Holbrooke came through Kabul twice during my time back at the Embassy, and I was often in touch with him by other means. But one felt that, now that President Obama had committed himself to the surge, Holbrooke's wings had been somewhat clipped. As Bob Woodward reports, there was a strong feeling among the US civilians that Mrs Clinton had decided to back the US military approach, and General Petraeus in particular.

One especially important issue was whether it made sense to develop a political track in parallel with the surge, or in sequence with it. The Pentagon, Defence Secretary Bob Gates, Secretary of State Hillary Clinton, Chairman of the Joint Chiefs of Staff Admiral Mike Mullen and General Petraeus all apparently took the view that we should use the surge to gain the upper hand militarily – 'reverse the momentum of the insurgency' – and then negotiate from a position of strength. In the meantime, there was no objection to an Afghan-led peace process doing what it could with the Pakistanis and others. Nor could anyone shut down the non-governmental peace industry that was then sprouting up, on both sides of the Durand Line, in New York and London and Oslo and Geneva and elsewhere, in ways reminiscent of the Irish or Israel–Palestine peace industries. But the United States wasn't going to get serious about talking until it had defeated, or at least beaten back, the Taliban. Or until it had given the appearance of doing so.

But I was pleased to discover back in Kabul in the spring of 2010 that some of the most senior officers at ISAF headquarters took a more intelligent view. They realised that building a political track would be incredibly difficult and time consuming, and that waiting for military success would only make things more difficult. In addition, once the full surge was deployed, and all America's cards played, the Taliban would simply pull back and out and say, 'Is that it?' Just as the British Secret Intelligence Service had opened channels of communication to the IRA in the early 1970s, so America should be finding ways of at least communicating authoritatively with its enemies. The ISAF senior staff were arguing to Washington for the kind of parallel discreet pragmatism that David Miliband and I favoured. But they got nowhere. The 'fight first, talk later' approach prevailed. The olive branch could follow the gun, but not accompany it.

This was apparent during Holbrooke's second visit to Kabul that spring. He was there for the latest American off-site meeting on the campaign, held for the first time in Kabul, with Afghans and other allies present. It took place in the gigantic new headquarters complex on the north side of Kabul airport. Now known as a Rehearsal of Concept, or ROC, drill, it consisted as before of a series of PowerPoint presentations on different aspects of the campaign by those responsible for police training or agricultural development, for example. It was a sort of extended 'show 'n' tell' session, with little room for discussion. And missing from the whole show was any serious presentation on military strategy or on the overall political strategy. The poor Afghan Ministers present were each invited to speak, and did so, with varying degrees of embarrassment. Holbrooke and Petraeus presided, but it was clear who was really in charge. It wasn't a satisfying experience.

After the meeting, the American delegation went to see President Karzai. Later the Kabul rumour mill reported that Holbrooke had apologised profusely for the way in which the Obama Administration's unhappiness with the Afghan President had been reported in the US media. General Jones had criticised Karzai rather sharply in briefing the White House press corps in Air Force One, en route to Kabul at the end of March. Somebody in the Palace gleefully told friends that Mrs Clinton had then telephoned Karzai to express regret. After that call, diplomats in Kabul reported that Karzai had told his inner circle that Mrs Clinton was weak and that he had 'the foreigner by the throat'. After Holbrooke's apology, fellow diplomats reported that they had heard that the Afghan President had simply made a crude Pashtun gesture of sexual triumph over one's antagonist.

But however great Karzai's difficulties with the Americans he had somehow to get on with them. The same didn't really apply to us, or many others. On my second tour in Kabul there seemed to be a new edge, a certain froideur, in the President's dealings with the West. There were many sources of this, some justified and others less so. But the proximate cause was his absolute conviction that he had won the 2009 Afghan Presidential election fairly and squarely on the first round and that the Americans and their allies had conspired to take it away from him. My main impression from my first call on the President after my return was just how deep the wounds from the election went.

Despite this, certain Western individuals did build good relationships with the President. First among them was Stan McChrystal. As the American media have pointed out, his success may have been at the expense of Karl Eikenberry's own link with the President, but was pursued with remarkable imagination. McChrystal was even said to have invited the President, when he visited ISAF Headquarters, to see for himself the austerity of the General's own bedroom.

Another Westerner skilled in dealing with President Karzai was the new UN Special Representative, Staffan de Mistura. Although Kai Eide had left Kabul on something of a down note, I had no hesitation in paying tribute, at my farewell party for him, to the ways in which he had played an almost impossible hand with great skill and courage. I still thought his finest hour had been the guts he had shown in sticking quietly to his guns over the massacre of civilians by US forces at Azizabad in August 2008. But the high-wire act of making the elections happen at all was also a remarkable achievement.

Staffan was a different character from Kai, with none of the latter's propensity occasionally to succumb to bouts of Nordic gloom. With an Italian father and a Swedish mother, he combined Italian charm and cunning with a backbone of Swedish steel. His long years as a professional diplomat for the UN had given him resilience. He knew that successful diplomacy, particularly in as confined a theatre (in both senses) as Kabul, is in part show business; and that concentrating on a few things, and doing them well, is so much more important than trying to advance on a broad front. Staffan would under-promise, and aim to over-deliver. His arrival buoyed up the Kabul international community. My favourite memento from Kabul is still his: the tie he was wearing at my farewell party which he ripped off and presented to me.

Two senior Britons had similarly good relationships with President Karzai. But, entirely for logistical reasons, neither saw the Afghan

President when they visited Afghanistan in March 2010. First was the Prime Minister. Despite Opposition claims that the trip was a last-minute stunt to deflect a row over accusations that, as chancellor, Gordon Brown had blocked new equipment for the armed forces, the visit had in fact been planned for some time, as his last visit to the troops before the British general election. The visit followed the usual formula for such forays, but with differences. For the first time, the Prime Minister was dressed informally, in chinos and hiking boots instead of his customary dark suit. His staff said it had been quite a struggle to persuade him to dress down. And, for the first time, he went right forward, to operating bases in territory only just liberated from Taliban control: there was real danger in the air. But the address to the troops, full of repeated thanks, and the briefing tour of selected facilities at Bastion, were the same as ever, except more so.

I had one moment of comedy, and one of sadness, during the visit. At one of the Forward Operating Bases, in the middle of nowhere out to the east of Lashkar Gah, we found embedded with a British battalion of unremitting Welshness a section of French *paras*, with Gauloises and Ray-Bans, crewcuts and berets straight out of *La Bataille d'Alger*. The French detachment had been mentoring an Afghan commando unit elsewhere in Afghanistan when the commandos had been deployed south. Without batting an eyelid, their French mentors had come with them. It was as though they had swapped Warminster for West Belfast. And it was surreal to find in deepest Helmand a unit with a history of courage in counter-insurgency as fine as that of any British regiment.

The moment of sadness came as I stood talking to the doctors outside the amazing hospital at Camp Bastion. I asked about arrangements for collecting, preparing and repatriating the remains of our dead soldiers. With clinical detachment, they spoke of how it was done, not at all easily, in the heat and hurry of a summer campaign in Helmand. But my imagination caught, and choked, on the one point on which they were less than straightforward: the name they used for the mortuary was 'Rose Cottage'.

My final VVIP visit had been rather longer in preparation. With understandable impatience, the Prince of Wales had been lobbying for years to see Afghanistan: it had been the main theme of my audience of

His Royal Highness before I had left for Kabul in 2007. His impatience had grown when each of his sons had visited. Justifiably, he felt he had made a huge contribution to Britain's constructive engagement with President Karzai. He and the President were joint patrons of the Turquoise Mountain Foundation, for which the Prince of Wales had raised large sums of money. On a personal level, he wanted to see for himself the built and natural environment of a land about which he had first heard so much from contemporaries passing through on gap-year trips to India. And he wanted to visit our troops, and to see the campaign in which so many of the units and regiments with which he was connected were playing such a vital part.

My original idea had been to have the Prince of Wales lay the foundation stone for a new British embassy in Kabul, to be built to suitable ecological and aesthetic standards. But, with the new Embassy project set aside, we focused on just three objectives: to see the President, to inspect the work of the TMF and to visit the troops in the south.

My first task was to establish, as discreetly as I could, that President Karzai would be in Kabul in the very narrow window which the Prince of Wales, flying direct from Eastern Europe, had available. This I did, with Karzai's Chief of Protocol. Next, we had to sound out the Turquoise Mountain. They had already been briefed, in great secrecy, by Rory Stewart. And the southern leg of the visit ran itself: my only tweak was to remind the planners to make sure that the Prince saw something of the Afghan Army in training. After all, that was why we were supposed to be there.

So far, so good. Then, with just weeks to go, the Afghans dropped their bombshell. President Karzai would be out of Afghanistan on the date in question. It was utterly exasperating, not least for the President, who had long wanted to reciprocate in Kabul the kindness and hospitality he had received from Prince Charles in London and Scotland. But the constraints of Presidential and Princely diaries could not be circumvented, so we decided to go ahead anyway. In some ways, I thought to myself, this gave us more flexibility to plan the Kabul leg of the programme ourselves, securely. But it was less than ideal.

For most royal visits, especially one of this importance, there is a 'recce' by the visitor's Household and his protection officers, often months in advance. But, as usual, Afghanistan was different. Security and logistics meant that the reconnaissance took place only as the advance party of the equerry and detectives arrived.

There was one key question on which I needed to consult. The Prince, the Turquoise Mountain and I were all keen that our VVIP should see the quarter of old Kabul, Murad Khane, which the TMF was restoring, both economically and architecturally. But visiting such a poor and crowded part of town posed serious security risks, both from terrorist violence and from unhappy masses of people. Quite unexpectedly, both the Prince's equerry and his senior detective delighted me by agreeing, very sensibly, that we could mount such a visit, provided it was a total surprise and that the numbers were strictly limited. We therefore planned on a standard visit to the Foundation's base, in an ancient mud fort adjacent to the old British Embassy; there the Prince would see the workshops, inspect architectural models, see handicrafts being produced and meet staff (and the peacocks on the lawn). But en route to the fort we would build in a secret diversion, just for him and me, and a protection team, to drop by Murad Khane for less than half an hour.

On the day, the visit itself ran like clockwork. The Prince arrived in Kabul under cover of darkness, in the early hours of the morning, and rested at my house. President Karzai sent two Ministers to call on His Royal Highness, bringing greetings from the President. Rather quaintly, both the Ministers whom Karzai chose were of Pashtun royal descent. His respect for royalty ran deep. HRH toured the Embassy, meeting all manner and condition of staff and taking time to talk to everyone with his usual charm. We went to call on General McChrystal at his head-quarters. We invited a group of religious leaders, including, rather oddly, one of the Muslim chaplains to Cambridge University, to meet Prince Charles in my garden.

But the highlight of the day in Kabul was undoubtedly our dash into and out of Murad Khane, with the Prince in body armour and the market crowds pressing outside our armoured Land Cruiser. On arrival, we jumped down and walked smartly through the mud and rubbish under a medieval mud arch, there to be greeted by Rory Stewart. Of course, the Prince of Wales spent longer looking at the extraordinary transformation of the ancient buildings than a nervous security team thought ideal. But at last he had been able to see for himself the good that 'his' Foundation was undoubtedly doing.

My only difficulty was that, as we drove to the airport for the flight to Bastion, the Prince told me that he had been so impressed by what he had seen of the TMF that he wanted me to try to replicate in Helmand what Rory and the Foundation were doing in Kabul. Like a fool I said, 'Of course, Sir, I will see what I can do.' One day there *will* be a role for exactly that kind of craft activity, but only once a political process is starting seriously to kick in. This was the old truth: development can underpin a political settlement, but can't deliver it.

The Helmand leg of the Prince of Wales's visit was completely different in character. Before leaving Kabul, he changed into desert camouflage, with the rank slides of a full general. We spent the night in the VIP accommodation at Bastion and flew on by helicopter to Lashkar Gah and to two forward bases. This was the Prince of Wales in his almost mystical capacity as the embodiment of what HM Forces are for and about: everywhere we went he talked to the officers and men, Guardsmen and Gurkhas, cooks or counter-IED specialists with an easy familiarity born of long exposure to the military. But this was an army in a combat zone, up close to an invisible but dangerous enemy. It was all immensely impressive: enormously tiring though the day was for the Prince, he in turn drew some comfort from having offered so much comfort to so many.

On the Afghan side, we met Governor Mangal and members of the Provincial Council in an informal shura and, as I had hoped, HRH saw the Afghan Army learning new combat skills. As colonel-in-chief of the Army Air Corps, Prince Charles posed for a photograph with all ranks then serving in Helmand. But the most delicious moment was a photograph orchestrated by the Task Force Commander, Brigadier James Cowan, late of the Royal Highland Regiment – aka the Black Watch. James wore the Red Hackle of his parent regiment with pride, despite its amalgamation into the Royal Regiment of Scotland. As Prince Charles was Colonel of the Black Watch, we took a photograph of him with James Cowan and the members of the Black Watch then serving in Helmand, all wearing the Red Hackle. Just a few days after the Prince of Wales had left, James received a stuffy letter from Regimental Headquarters reminding him that the wearing of the Red Hackle was no longer authorised.

This was a visit to remember, and exhilarating for all involved. After most VIP visits, ambassadors send hackneyed reports to London, trumpeting the success of the visit. No cliché is usually left unturned. Every such visit is 'timely' and 'useful'. I sent such a telegram back to London, as the royal party were in the air on their way home. But there was a difference: I actually meant it, and anyway I wasn't in the habit of sending telegrams I didn't mean. To my disappointment, the whole thing was promptly leaked to the *Sunday Telegraph*, who wrote it up as a criticism of Karzai's staff for failing to fix the date. The reality of what was a truly historic visit had been rather more interesting, but less headline-worthy.

In my three months back in Kabul, I did two things to try to improve the coherence of the international effort there. I made great, but largely unsuccessful, efforts to get all President Karzai's different Western interlocutors to co-ordinate their dealings with him. And I made an ultimately fruitless attempt to establish regular meetings of the ambassadors of all Afghanistan's neighbours and near neighbours, as a first step to engaging them collectively and seriously in the management of the problem.

After the Prince of Wales's visit, I had a month left in Kabul. The imminent election in Britain meant that the flow of Ministerial visitors dried up. But still the generals and the senior officials came pouring through, each expecting to be briefed and entertained by the Ambassador. However burdensome such obligations, I knew that that was what I was there for. I actually enjoyed meeting most of the visitors in such a different context. Paradoxically, Kabul felt much more relaxed than Whitehall. One visitor who definitely wasn't official was Sandy Gall, out on family business, as it were, working on his book, promoting his charity, preparing for his next group excursion. He was always a pleasure to see; and he always reminded me how much I didn't know about Afghanistan.

One of our persistent worries throughout my time working in and on Afghanistan was the handling of Afghans detained by British forces.

A balance needed to be struck between holding them long enough to be able to extract as much intelligence as possible from them and the need to place them in Afghan custody as soon as reasonable. NATO rules generally allowed ISAF forces to hold Afghans for no more than ninety-six hours before either releasing or transferring them. Our military said that this was not long enough. They also claimed, with some justification, that, once Afghan prisoners were handed to the Afghans, they tended to be either released or abused. Neither we nor anybody else found the perfect solution to this series of dilemmas which, after the scandal of the abuse of prisoners by US personnel at the Abu Ghraib prison in Iraq, worried Ministers as much as any other Afghan issue.

But in my last few weeks in Kabul I thought the Americans had at last come up with a sensible approach: a modern detention facility, built by the Americans, that would be set up by the Americans, and gradually transferred, under careful supervision, to Afghan ownership. A team from the Embassy went to visit. The senior American officer present was a graduate of Balliol College, Oxford, as many of his nineteenth-century British predecessors in this part of the world would have been. The formula of co-management, with the Afghans gradually taking the lead, seemed to make much sense.

But I confess that I had doubts with a capital D in two or three important areas. First, I wondered how the Afghans were ever going to be able to maintain such a high-tech facility, in which the management of the custody arrangements and many of the services was electronic. Great quantities of technical skill and of electric power would be needed to keep the prison going: this was not a recipe for enduring Afghan success.

My second doubt, to which I confess I gave voice, was that some of the measures the Americans took in handling prisoners, supposedly for security reasons, seemed to me personally to be unnecessarily harsh. I stress that I saw no evidence of brutality. I urged the Americans to remember that detainees were essentially political: their release was likely to follow a peace settlement, and it was therefore worth treating them as well as humanly possible.

My third area of concern was one that applied generally to Western forces: although the prisoners were overwhelmingly Pashtun, the interpreters and proudly advertised 'Muslim chaplains' hired by US forces were predominantly Tajik. It would have been rather like providing Catholic prisoners in the Maze with Protestant pastors whose second language was English. It wasn't right, but, in the circumstances of our occupation, there may have been no alternative.

I was allowed one or two exeat weekends during my spring term back in Afghanistan. On one, Sarah, Catriona and I went to Dubai, where I spoke at a big charity dinner at the British Embassy to raise money for Help for Heroes. This was the brainchild of Nick Lunt, a former cavalry officer now living and working in Dubai; in my first year in Kabul he had brought to the job of ISAF spokesman the same élan he had shown as an armoured squadron commander. The event in Dubai made it a triple whammy of the main military charities, as in England I had already helped raise money for the Soldiers, Sailors, Airmen and Families Association (SSAFA) and for ABF The Soldiers' Charity, formerly known as the Army Benevolent Fund.

Away-days in other parts of Afghanistan were one of the things that made living and working in Kabul so enjoyable, and I managed two in the spring of 2010. The first, just a week after my return, was an extraordinary walk in deep snow and bright sun up one of the rocky river valleys above the village of Istalif. Istalif is perched in the foothills of the mountains that form the western edge of the Shomali plain north of Kabul. Since at least the time of Zahir Shah, it had been a place to which Kabulis repaired at weekends to relax and refresh themselves. Once there had been a royal guesthouse at Istalif, and a restaurant looking out across the plain.

Some believe that the original settlement of the hillsides dates back to Greek times, when the Macedonians (who farmed the plain below) may have cultivated its vines. The village has been laid waste at least twice: in the nineteenth century by a British punitive expedition, and in the twentieth century in the battles between the Taliban and the Northern Alliance. Nevertheless, Istalif has long been known for its handmade glazed pottery, and, nowadays, for an outstation of the Turquoise Mountain Foundation. All this and much more, including ancient firearms, is on sale in a bazaar running the length of a single high street. In 2008, my Deputy, Andrew Patrick, had bought there what he was assured was a 100 per cent genuine British Enfield rifle.

On this occasion, we passed up above and behind the village, and started walking and climbing, and climbing and walking, up what was essentially the bed of a mountain stream. We passed hamlets and villages clinging to the hillsides, and villagers walking down with donkeys laden with bales of textiles for sale. Our destination was the Remote Hydrolight Lodge, a guesthouse in the last hamlet beneath the tree line. For more than ten years, the lodge had been running a micro-hydro plant, supplying electricity to the surrounding areas. Established by an NGO, the International Assistance Mission, it had been destroyed during the period of Taliban rule, and then rehabilitated in 2002 with help from the US Agency for International Development. Now it was open for eco-tourism – though one could not help wondering how much business there was in a steadily worsening security climate.

A second excursion was to the Panjshir Valley, on my last weekend before returning to London. Two guests came along for the day. The first was the former Danish Special Representative, Carsten Damsgaard, with whom I had worked for nearly a year in the SRAPs' collective. He had just arrived in Kabul as his country's ambassador. A Danish battle group had operated for some two years in Helmand as part of the British Task Force. We greatly respected the Danes' bravery in one of the toughest parts of the province. We also found that we had much to learn from Danish approaches to stabilisation and development in conflict zones. So the opportunity to make a small gesture in Denmark's direction was too good to miss.

I owed my second guest nothing, but was keen that he understood the nature of the current Western occupation of Afghanistan as he wrote about the first. I knew William Dalrymple only indirectly, but admired his writing, particularly *From the Holy Mountain*,* about the Christian communities of the Levant. Willie was now engaged in writing a history of the First Anglo-Afghan War and was in Kabul for his research. It was a pleasure to talk with him, about so many things, including the parallels, obvious and obscure, between our present

---

* London: Flamingo, 1998.

predicament and those of our Victorian forebears. Shortly after our day in the Panjshir, Willie went to visit the site of the battle of Gandamack in 1842. Courageously using local guides, he was lucky to have escaped being kidnapped or worse by the local Taliban.

The high point of our day in the Panjshir, both literally and emotionally, was our departure from the valley over the pass that connected it to the Shomali Plain. Guided by the US Provincial Reconstruction Team responsible for the valley and the province of the same name, we decided not to return to Kabul via the narrow ravine that formed the entrance to the Panjshir. Instead, slightly to the east, we took winding dirt and rock roads up the southern wall of the valley, before finding ourselves on a high ridge, with breathtaking views south across the Shomali Plain almost as far as Kabul. To our left, on the valley floor, we could see the lights of the colossal American base at Bagram. It was easy to see why it was said to consume, and thus generate, more electricity than the whole city of Kabul. Bidding our American hosts farewell, our convoy plunged down the southern slope of the escarpment towards Kabul, and reality.

My last official engagement in Kabul was a pleasure not a duty. Working with the Aga Khan Trust for Culture, the British Library had assembled 150 digital copies of photographs of Afghanistan, mainly from the nineteenth century. The exhibition – 'Afghanistan Observed' – included some images taken by one of the first Western archaeologists to work in Afghanistan, Charles Masson, and striking watercolours by James Atkinson, a surgeon who had accompanied British forces during the First Afghan War. The pictures were beautifully displayed in the range of buildings known as the Queen's Palace in the grounds of the Babur Gardens in Kabul, under the exacting auspices of the Aga Khan's outstanding cultural representative in Afghanistan, Jolyon Leslie.

The British Embassy had contributed some funding, and I was asked to open the exhibition, along with the Afghan Culture Minister, Sayed Makhdum Rahin. Rahin had been one of the Ministers with royal connections who had greeted the Prince of Wales a month earlier. I pointed out that his antecedents and those of many Britons present in Afghanistan today were linked by these images of past encounters. The exhibition was a great success in Kabul, attracting many thousands of Afghan visitors, and then went on to Herat. It was an uplifting note on which to end.

Ten days earlier I had accepted an invitation from Major General Nick Carter to see for myself how ISAF's strategy for stabilising Kandahar was succeeding on the ground. A week or two after I had returned to Kabul in February, General McChrystal and Mark Sedwill had briefed Ambassadors from countries contributing troops in the south on their strategy for Kandahar. We had been invited to endorse the plan on the spot. I had expressed some scepticism about what was promised, and I knew that Ministers and senior officers in London shared my doubts. It had been very difficult to establish what the plan actually was. Mark had spoken of NATO 'shura-ing its way to success' in Kandahar, gradually squeezing the city from the outside, but not making a direct assault of the kind that the US Marines had spearheaded into Marjah. Over a video link, Nick had suggested that the British Ambassador should come to check things out for himself.

As the home of the Taliban, Kandahar was the key to pacifying southern Afghanistan. A stable Kandahar, reasonably well governed by representatives of the government in Kabul and its own people, would not be enough to turn the tide of the insurgency. But it was essential to the Western plan for the country. All through the spring of 2010 debate raged in NATO circles about how ISAF planned to tackle this, the biggest challenge, in a strategy that had promised that forty districts in southern and eastern Afghanistan would have been stabilised by the end of 2010.

Nick Carter is an outstandingly able officer. But what I saw and heard with him on that April evening strained credibility. In the twilight, we flew by helicopter low over the dusty half-urban, half-rural suburbs of Kandahar into the Canadian PRT. Then, it was into armoured vehicles for the short drive to the Governor's palace, once the King's main residence in southern Afghanistan. There we met the Governor, Tooryalai Wesa. Wesa was an agricultural expert, who had spent thirteen years studying and lecturing in Canada. His family came from a village in the Arghandab district of Kandahar Province and were linked by kinship with the Karzai family.

As governor since late 2008, Wesa was supposed somehow to build a causeway of good government between, on the one hand, the troubled waters of the Taliban insurgency and, on the other, the roiling sea of the narco-mafias, one of which was believed to be directed by the President's half-brother, Ahmed Wali Karzai. In April 2010, the Governor seemed to have plenty of bodyguards and domestic staff, but few, if any, serious administrative staff of his own. A photocopier was, however, due to be delivered by ISAF the following week. Over dinner, it seemed that the Governor really wanted to talk about the Holstein cows he had seen in Helmand as a young agricultural student.

But, as we sat beforehand in the grassy quadrangle of the palace, Nick Carter set out his hopes for what the Governor would contribute to ISAF's plan for Wesa's native province. Starting the following week, said the General, the Governor was to begin registering all motor vehicles, all guesthouses and, most improbably, all firearms in Kandahar. The Governor blenched. But he looked merely puzzled when the General handed over a paper copy of a PowerPoint presentation, in English and Pashtu, on the ISAF plan for Kandahar. The first slide was a 'to do' list for the Governor. The first bullet point read, in English, 'Develop a plan for Kandahar'. But in Pashtu it read 'A development plan for Kandahar', a rather different concept.

I could conclude only that we were deluding ourselves if we seriously thought that this mild-mannered agronomist was somehow going to bring, let alone enforce, even half-decent government for Kandahar. At best, with the Taliban suppressed or repelled, he would become the acceptable face of rule by some pretty dubious godfathers. It all underlined the Herculean task we had set ourselves in promising to rebuild the Afghan nation, and the state supposed to go with it.

Chapter 24

Untying the Knot

Sarah, Catriona and I flew back from Kabul together on Sunday 25 April 2010. We took the Emirates A380 from Dubai to London, and posed for a souvenir photograph in the bar on the upper deck. At least as far as Afghanistan was concerned, I would never have it so good again.

In London, I fell immediately into the pattern which had become so familiar in my first year as special representative. I received innumerable requests to give talks and briefings on Afghanistan. In fact, on my first day back, I was on my way to the Defence Academy at Shrivenham in Wiltshire, to give just such a talk to a vast audience of eager young officers.

On the Friday of that week, the new German Special Representative, Michael Steiner, came to London for an introductory chat. While I had been away in Kabul, Bernd Mützelburg had been allowed at last to take his delayed and deserved retirement. Steiner had come from being German Ambassador in Rome. He was known as a forceful and dynamic operator, who had spent many years working with the UN in the Balkans before serving as Chancellor Schröder's foreign policy adviser. I thought that, if anyone would understand the importance of a political approach, it would be Steiner, and so it proved. We got on famously.

But back in Whitehall there was an eerie sense of lack of interest or activity on Afghanistan. Ministers were away campaigning for the general election, on Thursday 6 May. David Miliband had signed off on Afghanistan, at least for the moment, with a thoughtful speech at the Massachusetts Institute of Technology entitled 'How to End the War in Afghanistan', which the *New York Review of Books* published on 29

April. He made a convincing case for a more political approach. But, with the British election a week away, no one seemed to notice or care. In Whitehall, the bureaucratic wheels were merely ticking over. Briefing had been prepared for alternative incoming administrations. The polls were suggesting that a hung parliament, and therefore perhaps a coalition government, was a definite possibility. But it was impossible to guess what that might mean for Afghanistan policy.

As it happened, it was on election day itself that I saw my line manager for the first time since my return. He was full of gratitude for what I had done. But the promises he had made to encourage me to take on Afghanistan turned out to be hollow. It was only in answer to my direct question that he confirmed what the rumour mill had for some time suggested, but what I had never quite believed: that he intended to take for himself the post that was the one I was best qualified for, and had most hoped for, after successive tough jobs working in and on Afghanistan, Saudi Arabia and Israel. He assured me that I would be the front-runner for another big overseas mission, even though he must have known that it had already been earmarked for somebody else.

But I tried not to let this get me down. The following week, as the coalition negotiations dragged on, I risked a trip to Lille, to brief the officers of the French Rapid Reaction Corps before their deployment to Afghanistan to supply much of the NATO HQ staff. As always, I tried to accentuate the positive, while remaining realistic: speaking to troops about to deploy on active service for their country, one has to strike a balance between encouragement and honesty.

I made it back to London just in time for William Hague's first Office Meeting, as Foreign Secretary, on Afghanistan. He listened politely and asked intelligent questions, as each of the officials in the room and those on the video links did his or her best to make a positive impression on the new Foreign Secretary. But he gave little away about what he thought.

The new Prime Minister had no intention of letting the Afghan grass grow under his feet. On David Cameron's first weekend in office, it turned out that President Karzai and most of his key Ministers would be overflying Britain in a US Air Force jet on their way back to Kabul from a visit to Washington. Cameron immediately invited Karzai to lunch at Chequers, on his first day there. Naturally, the President accepted.

Another prime minister had landed another daunting logistical problem on the Foreign Office without much notice or any obvious spare funds. With some twenty-four hours' warning, the FCO was faced with the problem of looking after the Afghan President and most of his Cabinet for the night and the day they would have to lay over in Britain, in order to land back in Kabul under cover of darkness. After some hurried debate, I suggested that we take over a suite or two, and a private dining room or two, at Cliveden, the luxury hotel high on a chalk escarpment overlooking the Thames as it snakes through the Berkshire lowlands on its way to London and the sea. It wasn't just Cliveden's beauty that made it an attractive choice. Its history, as the home of the Astors and the backdrop for the Profumo affair, gave it real cachet. On hearing that the house was to become a hotel, Harold Macmillan is said to have remarked, 'My dear boy, it always has been.' Moreover, as well as history, beauty and general sumptuousness, Cliveden also had geography on its side: it was en route both to Chequers and to RAF Brize Norton, where the USAF aircraft would land and take off.

With characteristic speed and efficiency, the Foreign Office protocol team set to work, booking overnight accommodation for the whole delegation at a rather drearier hotel near Heathrow (to the Afghans' disgust, Cliveden didn't have enough rooms for them all), and then much of Cliveden for much of the following day.

So, on Saturday 15 May 2010, the motorbikes of the Metropolitan Police Special Escort Group and those of the Thames Valley Constabulary found themselves shepherding motorcades back and forth along the highways of Berkshire and Oxfordshire, as President Karzai and the different elements in his delegation travelled to their various places of business and rest. The newly appointed FCO Minister, Alistair Burt, rose early to greet the Afghan President and kindly hosted a lunch at Cliveden for him. Along with the US Ambassador to Afghanistan, Karl Eikenberry, who was travelling back to Kabul with the Afghan delegation, they gathered on the terrace at Cliveden, and enjoyed the magnificent house and grounds. Perhaps the most bizarre encounter of the day was that between the head of Afghan intelligence and two National Trust 'character interpreters', wandering the grounds pretending to be William Waldorf Astor and his wife.

In the late afternoon, I bade farewell to the President and his party at Brize Norton. Last aboard the plane was Karl Eikenberry. As he turned to go, he looked and sounded as though he might almost ask for political asylum in Britain, rather than return to the maelstrom of life as ambassador in Kabul. But, patriot and public servant that he is, he carried on.

Back in the FCO that week, there was little or nothing for my team or me to do. I still had the usual round of meetings with visitors, and outside briefings and talks. But our time away in Kabul had meant that the waters of the Afghan official policy community had closed over us. I was, however, glad to hear that the new Prime Minister wanted to hold, at Chequers on 1 June, a seminar on Afghanistan, involving outside experts for an initial session, and then more private sessions for Ministers and officials to draw conclusions for policy. That was exactly how Mrs Thatcher had addressed serious foreign policy issues in her time. As a member of the Foreign Office's Policy Planning Staff in the 1980s, I had been involved in preparing papers for the then Prime Minister's seminars on policy towards Gorbachev's Soviet Union (conclusion: engage) and on the legality of armed intervention in other states (conclusion: illegal and, usually, unwise). It was good to hear that David Cameron was intending to adopt the same open-minded approach as his distinguished Conservative predecessor.

What was less good was that, as the official who knew more about Afghanistan than any other in the British Government, I was not consulted on the guest list or agenda for the seminar, nor was I invited to it. At a farewell drinks that Friday, a senior official explained that my successor but one in Kabul (who had been in post for five weeks) would be there, but not me. I decided I would make no fuss: if that was how new Ministers felt, so be it. But it soon turned out that that was not how new Ministers, or the Downing Street staff, felt. It was only officials who had decided to keep me away. As soon as William Hague spotted that I was not on the list, he asked for me to be there.

On the day, I duly appeared at Chequers. After the outsiders had left, the Prime Minister asked me to make a presentation on a political approach to resolving the problems of Afghanistan. He seemed to get it, in a way that his predecessor hadn't, or couldn't or wouldn't, perhaps for electoral reasons. But he also understood the impossibility of the United Kingdom doing anything serious without American cover. He grasped too the need to keep up support for the military effort, while pursuing the political track in parallel. As de Gaulle had once said, it was a question of signalling right but turning left. The Prime Minister duly resolved to discuss all this with President Obama, when he saw him at the G20 summit in Pittsburgh and again, bilaterally, in Washington DC.

But, despite the last-minute invitation to Chequers, I had concluded that I should seek to finish as special representative. There really wasn't a full-time job to do any longer. I had persuaded senior officials of this, asking them to make sure the new Foreign Secretary was content. They told me he was, so I briefed my key international colleagues on my decision at a meeting in Berlin on 27 May.

Holbrooke was furious: 'Just the wrong time to go, Sherard' was his reaction. For all his faults and foibles, Holbrooke understood as well as anyone what needed to be done to stabilise Afghanistan and to secure an honourable exit for our soldiers. He had been the best and worst of colleagues, but a man for whom I had come to feel great respect and affection. After I had gone, he sent me the nicest of private tributes. As Hillary Clinton suggested, in the first Richard Holbrooke Memorial Address to the Asia Society in New York in February 2011, he understood that in the end the only solution was political. His tragedy was that he died, on 13 December 2010, just as the Administration to which he belonged was beginning to find the courage to follow its first instincts, emphasising the primacy of politics and diplomacy in resolving Afghanistan's problems. As I had remarked to Richard shortly before his death, the hour of Holbrooke was about to come upon us. And then he was snatched away. Steiner too felt let down by my departure, as he had hoped to work with me in promoting a more political approach. But deep down I knew that, however painful, it was time to move on.

In early June, the whole SRAP flying circus convened in Madrid for a plenary meeting. I duly made my announcement, introduced the FCO official who would take on the role part-time in an acting capacity and flew back early to London for a delayed meeting with William Hague. I was surprised to learn from him that, despite what senior officials had told me, he did not think he had agreed to my moving on. After some toing and froing, he conceded that I could over the summer take some of the leave owed to me, but that he would want to reach a final decision in September, when the world returned to work. Only then, when I saw him on 8 September, did I manage finally to persuade him that there really wasn't a role for a full-time special representative.

But William Hague's decision in June that there should be no decision led to unfortunate press reports that the reason for my taking leave was 'clashes' over policy with the Americans and with NATO. It was too good a story to spoil with the prosaic truth that, after three and a half years working on Afghanistan, I had had enough work and far too little leave; and what was more, that I was too proud simply to hang around King Charles Street filling a dignified but wholly inefficient role. It was, as a friend remarked, always better to leave a party at its height.

Chapter 25

Three Lessons Learned

One of the greatest strengths of the modern American military is that it has the confidence to examine itself critically in the mirror of recent history. Conducting, after the event, a rigorous 'lessons learned' exercise is now firmly part of the US approach to military operations, and one which deserves admiration and emulation. I make no such claims for the rigour of the way in which I analysed, over the winter of 2010–11, my experiences of three and a half years' diplomatic work in and on Afghanistan. But, as the mists of oblivion start to roll in over the sea of consciousness of what I did, there are three main areas in which I would single out implications for wider policy.

The first is the theory and practice of counter-insurgency. The second is the difficulties of managing military campaigns in a modern democracy. And the third is the fitness of the American Republic successfully to prosecute quasi-imperial expeditionary activity of the kind in which it is engaged in Afghanistan.

Like its first cousin stabilisation, counter-insurgency, or COIN, has acquired some of the characteristics of a cult. Disciples speak of its properties with evangelical fervour. There are different routes for gaining admission to its mysteries, but most involve field experience in a conflict zone, recently Iraq or Afghanistan, and a period of postgraduate study of uneven rigour. Qualifying involves at least as much faith as works.

Associated with the cult is a vast literature of pseudo-academic tracts. Many refer back to historical experiences of counter-insurgency campaigns, in South-east Asia, Ireland and Algeria, to name only a few. For serious historians or political scientists, the revelations offered by the new apostles are seldom new, or far removed from common sense. The COIN cult's main contemporary source of revelation is US Army Field Manual No. 3-24, the *Counterinsurgency Field Manual*, the fruit of General Petraeus's tour at Fort Leavenworth in 2005–6.

By any standard, the *Manual* is a remarkable document. Beautifully written, it combines practical didacticism (where to position an interpreter when addressing the natives) with insights of almost metaphysical profundity (the primacy of politics in any successful counter-insurgency campaign). There is little in it for any serious student of strategy or contemporary history to disagree with. But, in relating all this doctrine to Afghanistan, I have two major concerns. The first is that we are not properly applying in Afghanistan the precepts in the *Manual* or in most other modern studies of COIN. The second is that, even if we were applying those lessons fully, we would still not prevail in Afghanistan.

Let me explain. On the first concern, the *Manual* rightly stresses a whole range of requirements that are simply not being met in Afghanistan. There is not, for example, proper unity of command. We just do not have the force densities we need. The political alternative offered to the insurgency-infected populations in the south and east is either incredible (the Government in Kabul, and its sub-national manifestations) or undesirable (rule by the narco-mafia as the only viable alternative to the Taliban). There is no serious plan for closing off the sanctuary areas within or alongside Afghanistan, into which the insurgents withdraw when put under pressure. The timescales envisaged by the leaders of the Western troop-contributing democracies are incredibly (literally) short. The present tactic of aggressively culling Taliban field commanders, and announcing a body count, is likely to hinder, rather than help, the delivery of a sustainable political solution (which is not to say that it might not encourage some frightened individuals to cease fighting). And so the list goes on. We are just not applying fully the theories we endorse.

In 2008, a Rand Corporation study of counter-insurgency in Afghanistan* pointed out that:

---

* www.rand.org/pubs/monographs/MG595

the analysis of 90 insurgencies since 1945 indicate[d] that three variables [were] correlated with the success (or failure) of counterinsurgency efforts:

- capability of indigenous security forces, especially police
- local governance
- external support for insurgents, including sanctuary.

In Afghanistan, none of those three variables is likely to swing definitively and enduringly in favour of the coalition for many years yet.

More important than such historical parallels is my sense that, even if we successfully pacified, in short order, all the geographical areas on which the NATO strategy is focused, we would still be far from solving the Afghan problem. Afghanistan's difficulties run much deeper and wider than the Taliban insurgency. Suppose that, incredibly, over the next three years, ISAF did successfully suppress the insurgency in all 120 districts promised by General McChrystal in December 2009. There would still be scores of other districts in Afghanistan, and others across the border in Pakistan, where the Taliban could operate with impunity. Nor in such short order could we possibly have addressed the defects in the national and sub-national political settlement, or the deficits of capacity and will, which need to be resolved before the legitimate Afghan authorities can secure and govern most of the national territory. Bringing down insurgency-related violence in the areas selected by NATO is far from stabilising Afghanistan in a sustainable fashion.

In short, implementing the precepts of the cult of COIN may be necessary for stabilising Afghanistan. But they are far from enough. At least in the Afghan context, COIN is tactics, not strategy.

Second, there are serious difficulties relating to the management of military campaigns, and perhaps also of the military itself, in a modern, especially American, democracy. One of my favourite films as a small boy was a ridiculous comedy called *The Square Peg* starring Norman Wisdom. Made just as National Service was coming to an end, it depicted the cheeky chappie as a road mender who during the last stages of the Second World War was mockingly disrespectful of the

Army. He dug up the road outside a military camp and generally caused mayhem for his Army neighbours. In revenge, the Army arranged for him and his municipal colleagues to be called up. Once in uniform, Norman ends up in the clutches of the Sergeant whom his antics as a council worker so annoyed. The plot, in so far as there is one, follows Norman's adventures in military service, first in England and then in France, where the Sergeant sends him as a punishment. The reason for mentioning the film here is that it mocks the supposed stupidity and self-importance of military figures in ways that would be almost inconceivable these days. When almost everyone had experience, direct or indirect, of the military, it was possible to treat the institution of the military in a more open-minded way.

In an age, however, where there is no National Service, and only a minority of politicians have any real military knowledge or experience (and then only through short-service commissions or time in the cadet corps at school), attitudes towards the military are much more deferential and less balanced. For obvious and proper reasons, the media, particularly the conservative media and the red-top tabloids, treat the men and women of the armed forces as heroes. This attitude is reinforced in a war by the media's need for copy, both visual and written, which can be obtained only by embedding with a military machine. As the row over Toby Harnden's book about the Welsh Guards showed, it then becomes awkward and unpatriotic to criticise that machine, and difficult to distinguish between the undoubted bravery of the troops on the front line and the quality of leadership at the top of the armed services.

As I suggested in my evidence on Afghanistan to the House of Commons Foreign Affairs Committee on 9 November 2010,* an army that is willing to fight and die must, almost by definition, be hugely optimistic, unquenchably enthusiastic, fiercely loyal to its own institutions, capable of group think and, ideally, not too imaginative. All those qualities make for an effective war-fighting machine abroad and a powerful institutional lobby at home. Britain's military tradition, the

---

* http://www.publications.parliament.uk/pa/cm201011/cmselect/cmfaff/c514-iii/c51401.htm

organisation of its regiments on a territorial basis, and our whole island story build strong bonds between the military vocation and the wider British polity.

But managing an institution, a lobby, as confident and vocal as the military in a democracy, particularly in a democracy at war, is not easy. The first line of management is the civilian officials, both in the Defence Ministry and elsewhere in Whitehall, whose job is to provide Ministers with objective advice. But, in my experience at least, the civilian officials in the MOD are treated by their military colleagues rather as second-class citizens. At senior policy levels, the civilians may have brains and education. But they don't always have the confidence that comes with a uniform. Moreover, sharing a building, an office and a career with the military can make it difficult for civilian officials to take too independent a view of their military colleagues' plans.

Thus, time and again over three and a half years I saw papers for Ministers from the MOD that fell short of the standards for clear and objective advice which the political leadership in a democracy is, in my view, entitled to expect. For one thing, MOD papers were often circulated late or in incomplete form. Too many times recommendations for additional activity in Helmand were submitted without costings, which were promised for later but seemed never to appear. Too many times Ministers were expected to decide on further deployments to Helmand without knowing how much they would cost the taxpayer. Perhaps understandably, with a war on, the figuring came last, and sometimes not at all.

An additional problem was the obscurity, for non-experts, of many of the MOD papers. Often, the use of jargon, and acronyms, buried in great slabs of indigestible prose, betrayed their authorship. Tired, busy and inexpert Ministers found the papers, often delivered late, difficult to absorb properly. Somehow, for a politician, preoccupied with other business, worried about leaks to the press suggesting that he was not backing our boys, it was easier to surrender to the can-do advice from the experts in uniform than ask a series of idiot civvie questions.

One example of this was a recommendation from the MOD that Tornado ground attack aircraft be sent to Afghanistan. At the time, the

NATO Joint Statement of Requirements (for troops or equipment needed in Afghanistan) indicated that the one weapons system which ISAF had more than enough of was ground attack aircraft. The first draft of the MOD paper argued that sending the Tornados would be important for the morale of British land forces, who would want to have the RAF in the skies above them. This was not a compelling argument for anyone familiar with the average British squaddie's view of the air force, and it was removed from later drafts of the paper. I suggested to one of the Cabinet Ministers considering the paper that he might want to question whether the deployment made sense, given that HMG would need to spend some £70 million on new taxiways at Kandahar to accommodate the Tornados. His reply illustrated all the difficulties of civilian politicians with no military expertise assessing military advice. 'Sherard', he said, 'I don't know the difference between a Tornado and a torpedo. I can't possibly question the Chief of the Defence Staff on this.' On another occasion, a Minister who had been dealing with Afghanistan for three years asked me quietly to remind him of the difference between a brigade and a battalion.

Despite doubts lower down the officer corps, few and far between were the senior officers who questioned the consensus that the answer in Helmand was more troops, regardless of whether there was in place a credible political strategy to harvest any tactical success the military might achieve. One honourable exception was Brigadier Mark Carleton-Smith, who told *The Times*, in a farewell interview, that a military victory over the Taliban was 'neither feasible nor supportable'.*

As Bob Woodward has shown, such problems are not unique to the United Kingdom. President Obama and his National Security Council seem to have had similar, but much larger and more significant, difficulties in managing the Pentagon's enthusiasm for the war in Afghanistan. But describing the problems faced by politicians in a modern democracy in managing an enthusiastic military is easier than prescribing a solution. All I can do is point to Professor Eliot Cohen's *Supreme Command*, in which he shows that wars are most likely to be won by a proper equilibrium between political direction and military

---

* *The Times*, 6 October 2008.

advice, enthusiastic or otherwise. As Clemenceau pointed out, it is a myth to suggest that wars should be left to the generals.

The third area in which I have drawn a lesson from my Afghan experience is one in which contemporary historians, from Paul Kennedy through Niall Ferguson to Bernard Porter, have taken much interest: that of the American Republic's ability to conduct this kind of expeditionary intervention. I am not equipped to theorise about America's alleged (and relative) decline. But close observation of America at work in and on Afghanistan over three and a half years did lead me to wonder whether the United States was fit for the quasi-imperial purpose it had assumed in that distant and still so foreign land. In doing so, I returned to ideas which had first occurred to me during the four years I spent in the British Embassy in Washington in the late 1980s, reporting on American politics.

I thought then, and think now, that the US constitution may well be a brake on America's ability to promote its interests overseas. The constitution is, after all, an eighteenth-century document to deal with an eighteenth-century problem, that of an over-mighty monarch (George III). The solutions adopted by the Founding Fathers – of the separation of powers, of creating a legislature almost continually seeking re-election and the funds with which to do so, of giving that legislature a role in foreign policy through providing fiscal oversight and authority – may bind together a fissiparous continental democracy. But the consequences of such conscious inefficiencies, including the eighteenth-century system of patronage needed to help the President fund his election, and the cult of amateurish short-termism in government, do serious damage to the Republic's ability to prosecute overseas wars.

There are various other disabilities too. One is the vigorous American tradition of inter-agency warfare, in Washington and in the field. No institution willingly takes orders from any other, and the State Department is somehow last among equals. Neither the Pentagon nor the CIA respects the State Department, or accepts its primacy in foreign affairs.

As Bob Woodward records, the turf war in Washington was replicated in the field. In Kabul, the US Embassy never succeeded in taking overall charge of the US effort in Afghanistan. One of the main principles of successful COIN, unity of command, is honoured more in the breach than in the observance. Worse still, as I have described, even within the US military command structure, US Special Forces and, most surprisingly, the US Marine Corps ran parallel chains of command and, at least until recently, weren't under the full control of the four-star American General commanding NATO forces across Afghanistan from Kabul.

Another is the way in which American tax dollars are scattered around. Sums which may seem quite small in Washington create powerful distortions, and feed much corruption, in economies as poor as Afghanistan's. This applies perhaps especially to the Commanders' Emergency Response Program funds available to field commanders to spend more or less at their own discretion. In 2008–9, the total Pentagon CERP budget for Afghanistan, of about $750 million, was roughly the same size as the total self-generated revenue of the Afghan state. A further aspect of this is that, thanks largely to the role of Congress, US aid funds are almost as much for Americans as for overseas beneficiaries. Thus, some 40 per cent of American aid moneys allocated to Afghanistan are said to find their way back to the United States, in the form of consultancy and security contracts, equipment orders, and so on. That is hardly a good way to win Afghan friends and influence Pashtun people. Here, as so often, President Karzai was not wrong in his criticisms.

And yet, while the Pentagon and the CIA would in some areas pay only lip service to Afghan sovereignty, in others America was surprisingly timorous about laying down the law. The United States was spending roughly $125 billion a year in and on a country that raised for itself rather less than one-hundredth of that. Occasionally, America was entitled to insist that the Government of Afghanistan should respect American interests. But the State Department would often take refuge in the conceit that Afghanistan was a fully sovereign country that could not be ordered around.

I remember telling my US colleague that, during the Second World War, Britain had certain interests at stake in another country that was supposedly sovereign, Egypt. When King Farouk had threatened, in 1942, to appoint a pro-Axis prime minister, the overbearing British

Ambassador, Sir Miles Lampson, had warned His Majesty against doing so. But Farouk had persisted, and the friend of Germany had become Prime Minister. A day later Lampson had had the Abdin Palace in Cairo surrounded by armoured cars, and a day after that the pro-Axis Prime Minister was gone. I wasn't suggesting that America surround the Arg Palace in Kabul with tanks, but I was suggesting that, just occasionally, the US Embassy and State Department could be a little firmer with their recalcitrant client.

Perhaps it is all because Americans don't believe they are imperialists anyway. And certainly they aren't interested in ruling other people, or for very long. But successful stabilisation requires strategic stamina, massive resources, lots of time and plenty of ambition. I wondered whether, in an entirely benevolent sense, America had any of these qualities for successful empire-building. As Donald Rumsfeld recognised, successful nation-building cannot be done quickly or on the cheap.

And yet, though America may lack the resources and will on the heroic scale necessary to stabilise Afghanistan, it is still by far the most powerful outside actor. No other ally comes close. As the head of the Embassy's intelligence team had pointed out when I first arrived in Kabul, if Britain wanted to make a real difference in Afghanistan it could do so only by working with the Americans. And, if we were to influence them, we had to show we were serious, about our military, political and developmental contributions. I believe we did that, above all on the military front. And yet, as this book shows explicitly, and Bob Woodward's implies, making that influence felt in Washington was hard work, not often rewarded. The net result of all our efforts to encourage a more political approach may only have been to get the United States to accept reconciliation and reintegration a bit sooner than it might otherwise have done. As Churchill had suggested, mostly America seemed to need to learn from its own mistakes, not take lessons from the Brits or anybody else.

Here again, my Afghan experience led me to diagnose problems without being able to prescribe solutions. But perhaps there aren't solutions. After all, Republican Rome had to turn itself into a centralised Principate, involving monarchical rule, in order properly to run its empire. I suspect, deep down, that Americans are just too democratic, and too nice, to be very good at ruling other people.

In April 1968, the *Atlantic* published an article entitled 'How Could Vietnam Happen? An Autopsy'. Among the factors shaping Vietnam policy were said to have been:

- a general perception of China-on-the-march, and a monolithic conception of the Communist bloc;
- a lack of real Vietnam or Indo-China expertise;
- the domestication of dissenters within the US Government;
- the 'effectiveness' trap, whereby those who had doubts about the wisdom of US policies feared that, if they spoke out, they would lose their traction inside the Government;
- a preoccupation with the presentation of the war rather than its substance;
- executive fatigue: worn-out ministers and officials simply gave up pushing for fresh approaches, even though it was obvious that the existing ones weren't working;
- a curator mentality: rapid turnover meant that officers and officials felt that their role was simply to keep the policy going until they handed over to their successors;
- confusion about the type of war the US was fighting;
- wishful thinking;
- bureaucratic detachment ('it's not our problem, it's the military's');
- the belief that an American 'victory' in Vietnam was essential, and that America could not afford 'defeat';
- human ego investment: those who had advocated sending more troops could not admit that they had been wrong;
- a steady giving in to pressures for a military solution; and
- repeated failure to exploit opportunities to seek a political solution.

The parallels need no elaboration.

Chapter 26

Back to the Future

'Tell me, how does this end?' then Major General Petraeus of the 101st Airborne Division is said to have asked a *Washington Post* reporter in Iraq in the summer of 2003. Now, since June 2010, when he succeeded his former subordinate, Stan McChrystal, as ISAF commander, General David Petraeus, more than any other individual, is in charge of deciding how this latest Afghan war ends.

Petraeus has made major changes in the pace and direction of the war. As the press have reported, he has authorised, indeed encouraged, more violence, lifting the limits McChrystal had placed on the use of airpower and on ISAF rules of engagement. He has ordered a quantum leap in the number of Special Forces strikes against Taliban commanders and has boasted regularly of a rising body count. He has launched a programme to establish local militias and has apparently set aside American qualms about working with some of Afghanistan's most unsavoury warlords. More positively, he has made more money available for reintegrating Taliban fighters. He has gone to great lengths to convince American politicians and press that ISAF is breaking the momentum of the insurgency and is therefore succeeding. He has also tried to lower expectations, by playing down the start of the withdrawal of American troops in July 2011, focusing instead on 2014.

In her Richard Holbrooke Memorial Address in February 2011, Mrs Clinton promised a new diplomatic surge to accompany the military and civilian surges launched by the Obama Administration two years earlier.

Linking the Taliban with Al Qaeda as part of a single 'syndicate of terror', the Secretary of State warned them that they could not wait

America out and could not defeat America. But, if they broke with Al Qaeda, renounced violence and agreed to abide by the Afghan constitution, then they could join an Afghan-led process of reconciliation and be allowed to take part in the political life of Afghanistan. The military surge had blunted the momentum of the insurgency. Province by province, between now and the end of 2014, NATO forces would withdraw, and Afghanistan would take responsibility for its own security, in a 'responsible' transition. The civilian surge had bolstered the government of Afghanistan, by tripling (to 1,100) the number of American development experts on the ground in Afghanistan; and it was giving the Taliban the economic and social incentives for participating in political life. The third leg – the diplomatic surge – would support an Afghan-led process of reconciliation within Afghanistan, and engage Pakistan and all Afghanistan's other neighbours and near neighbours behind that process. America would insist that the human rights of all Afghans, including women and minorities, were protected in this process.

Admirable though most of these sentiments are, three and a half years is not time enough to create across Afghanistan reasonably clean, credible and inclusive institutions with both the capacity and the will to secure and govern, on a sustainable basis, the vast areas of the country and of its national life in the grip of insurgency or criminal anarchy. Nor can one help asking whether Obama's America is up for the challenge of driving such a process forward with all the political and diplomatic resources such a strategy would require. In many respects, it was the speech Mrs Clinton should have made two years earlier. If only General McChrystal had been right when in February 2010 he promised the people of Marjah in Helmand that ISAF could deliver 'government in a box'.

Certainly, thanks to General Petraeus's new tactics, the Taliban are taking a hammering and have pulled back into their sanctuaries within Afghanistan and across the border in Pakistan. Undoubtedly, some of them are more willing to parley. But the chances of acceptable governance filling, in any lasting way, the spaces being created by those tactics are not good. Such a military-focused approach risks making Afghanistan safe not for better governance, but for the warlords and narco-mafias whom the Taliban originally targeted when they took power in the mid-1990s. Once again, the poor Afghan people – the population whom McChrystal rightly spoke of protecting – could be the losers.

Acts of anti-state terrorism, even on the obscene scale of 9/11, seldom in themselves do significant objective damage to the interests of their target state. But real harm can be done when, as the terrorists hope, the attacked state is provoked into an irrationally disproportion-ate reaction, doing in the longer run far more damage to that state's interests than the original terrorist attack. In the late 1940s, the US diplomat George Kennan devised the doctrine of containment, precisely because he feared such an irrational overreaction by the great democracy he served, to another perceived threat, that from Soviet Russia. I guess that Kennan would have been appalled by Bush's reac-tion to the 9/11 atrocities: he would, I am sure, have wondered how any sensible statesman could declare war on 'terror', any more than he could declare war on evil or on war itself.

When, in earlier centuries, empires, such as those of Rome, Russia or Britain, were attacked from ungoverned territory across the imperial frontier, they reacted generally in one of three ways: they launched a punitive expedition to deter and punish those responsible for the offence, and withdrew as quickly as possible; or they established a client kingdom in the offending territory; or, very much third best, they annexed the offending territory and brought it within the imperial *limes*.

For an America wounded and vengeful in the aftermath of the 9/11 attacks, Afghanistan was just such a troublesome territory, abutting the American empire's mental frontier. Somehow, the source of the attack had to be dealt with, and those directly and indirectly responsible punished, swiftly and violently. What followed has been an uneasy tran-sition from the first option – an in-and-out punitive expedition – to the second – trying to establish a reliable client state, by means of a dysfunc-tional multinational mandate. The enterprise has proved to be a model of how not to go about such things, breaking all the rules of grand strategy: getting in without having any real idea of how to get out; almost wilful misdiagnosis of the nature of the challenges; continually changing objectives, and no coherent or consistent plan; mission creep on an heroic scale; disunity of political and military command, also on an heroic scale; diversion of attention and resources (to Iraq) at a critical stage in the adventure; poor choice of local allies, who rapidly became more of a problem than a solution; unwillingness to co-opt the neighbours into the project, and thus address the mission-critical problem of external sanctuary and support; military advice, long on institutional self-interest, but woefully short on serious objective analysis of the problems of pacifying a broken country with largely non-existent institutions of government and security; weak political leadership, notably in subjecting to proper scrutiny militarily heavy approaches, and in explaining to the increasingly, and now decisively, sceptical domestic press and public the benefits of expending so much treasure and blood. As Rodric Braithwaite's book *Afgantsy* suggests, without ever saying so explicitly, the parallels with the tragedy of Soviet Russia's failed attempt to stabilise Afghanistan are too many and too close for comfort.

Most tragically of all, intervening in Afghanistan in such haste in 2001 may not have been necessary, any more than Britain should have attacked the Irish Republic in the wake of, say, the Birmingham pub bombings. As I have already said, in October 2001 the Taliban convened in Kandahar a great *jirga* to decide how to respond to American demands that Osama bin Laden and those responsible for the 9/11 attacks be handed over. Some of those present believe that, given a bit more patience and pressure, the majority would gradually have swung in favour of expelling those Arabs and other foreigners who had abused Pashtun hospitality by orchestrating the 9/11 attacks from Afghan territory.

Whatever the truth of that claim, it is unarguable that the West got into Afghanistan in October 2001 without a clear idea either of what it was getting into or of how it was going to get out. Without realising it, we have become involved in a multi-player, multi-dimensional, multi-decade civil conflict, the origins of which go back many years. It is an unresolved struggle, over the nature of the Afghan polity, between Islam and secularism, tradition and modernism, town and country, Sunni and Shia, farmer and nomad, Pashtun and Tajik, Uzbek and

Hazara. Unless and until those problems, and Afghanistan's relations with its neighbours and near neighbours, are addressed through an ambitious and continuing *jirga*-like process, internal and external, sponsored by the US and the UN, supported by the Permanent Five Members of the UN Security Council (the US, Russia, China, France and Britain), NATO and the EU, and engaging all regional players, conflict will continue. To have any chance of succeeding, such a process will need sustained and vigorous diplomatic engagement by the United States, from the President and Secretary of State down. In particular, America will need itself to talk to all the internal and external parties to the conflict, including the Taliban.

Better late than never, in late spring 2011, Lakhdar Brahimi and the distinguished retired US diplomat, Tom Pickering, recommended just such an approach: that the US should promote a negotiated political settlement, involving all the internal and external parties to the conflict.* And the Obama Administration brought back from retirement two of America's best diplomats – Marc Grossman and Ryan Croker – to succeed Holbrooke and Eikenberry respectively. In pursuing a peace settlement, we will need to accept, as we are already having to do, that often it may be better to let the Afghans themselves do a job badly than for us to do it for them. Even if the Afghan way may be less effective, and more corrupt and inefficient, than the Western way, it may be wiser to let the Afghans make their own mistakes, and learn from them. However imperfect the results of such a process, they may last longer than attempts by outsiders to buck the Afghan market.

If, as is quite likely, the results of the three American surges – military, civilian and diplomatic – are ambiguous, our troops will still leave the Afghan battlefield. Our taxes will still subsidise, and the civilian apostles of stabilisation still support, whatever Afghan state we leave behind. But, as the House of Commons Foreign Affairs Committee pointed out in its report of March 2011, calling for a political surge,†

---

* http://www.nytimes.com/2011/03/23/opinion/23brahimi.html?_r=1&scp=1&sq=brahimi%20pickering&st=cse

† http://www.publications.parliament.uk/pa/cm201011/cmselect/cmfaff/c514-ii/c51401.htm

unless we somehow in the next three years engineer a sustainable *Afghan* political settlement, we risk finding that we get out, militarily, only to have to get back in, perhaps several decades from now, and in another form. If that happens, our present sacrifice may have been largely in vain.

The killing of Osama bin Laden on 2 May 2011 by US Special Forces has changed everything and nothing. On the one hand, it has brought to an end a man-hunt that has lasted nearly a decade, caused America to invade and occupy two Muslim lands, and cost it some $2,000 billion. It has exposed, in compelling fashion, the dual nature of Pakistan's relationships: with America, with terrorism, and with the truth. Bin Laden's death has shown how the war in Afghanistan has indeed been, in Richard Holbrooke's words, against 'the wrong enemy in the wrong country'. And it gives Obama, running for re-election in 2012, the argument he needs to bring the boys back home faster than his generals would like. Most important, it offers an opportunity to begin healing the wounds of 9/11, and for a fresh start in the relationship between America and Islam.

And yet, in another sense, what many Muslims see as a revenge killing has changed little. The Arab Spring of 2011 has shown how irrelevant Al Qaeda and its leader already are. The reasons for Muslim antipathy towards America, focused mainly on its one-sided approach to Israel/Palestine, remain. Islamic terrorism will continue, some of it perhaps inspired by bin Laden's 'martyrdom', as part of what has become an AQ franchise. The difficulties of extracting Western forces from Afghanistan any time soon while leaving behind an acceptable and enduring state, able and willing to secure and govern its own territory, are as great as ever. The unremitting pressures of US domestic politics will still limit the American Republic's ability to do the right thing abroad, in this case pressing hard and from the highest level for political settlements in and around Afghanistan, and between Israel and all its neighbours.

But none of this means that, with his new diplomatic 'A' team in place, an American President who has always understood the realities better than most won't give it his best shot, within the limits of the politically possible. As Walter Cronkite pointed out, for another war in another century, only by pursuing a negotiated settlement can there be peace with honour. Only thus can we turn the temporary and local gains won at such cost by the military into long-term strategic success.

And only thus can we look in the eye the widows and orphans, the wounded, the eager recruits, and the sceptical veterans of several tours in the Pathan badlands, and, with a clear conscience, assure them that the sacrifice has been worthwhile, that in Afghanistan, '*Dulce et decorum est pro patria mori*'.

Afterword

Eyeless in Afghanistan

Veterans' Day in America, almost exactly six months after I wrote the last words of the first edition of this book, and I am thinking about what I should say in this Afterword.

As I walk in the whipping wind back up K Street to my Washington hotel, by Eastern Time it is now the eleventh hour of the eleventh day of the eleventh month of the eleventh year of the new century. Everywhere there are tributes to the brave men and women of America's fighting forces. For a Briton, the patriotism is overwhelming, and sometimes – free doughnuts for veterans – hard to digest. The *Post* carries the photographs of this year's war dead: by 11 November 2011, a total of 1,820 Americans have died in Operation Enduring Freedom in Afghanistan, including thirty US Navy SEALs, killed when their Chinook was brought down by a rocket-propelled grenade on 6 August.

Nowhere, though, is there much discussion of the war in which most of the recent dead have fallen. American politicians now speak only rarely about the cause for which our troops are fighting and dying in Afghanistan. Perhaps most significant, the eight Republicans contesting their party's nomination to run against Obama in the 2012 Presidential election cannot even agree if the war is still worth waging.

Back in England, for Remembrance Sunday, it is much the same. At the Cenotaph in Whitehall, and across the United Kingdom, wreaths are laid, flags flown, parades held. But, again, Afghanistan is strangely absent from the solemn commemorations.

Exactly two months earlier, on 11 September 2011, there was a similar silence. Naturally, every politician had something to say about the terrible attacks on New York and Washington a decade earlier. But few mentioned the distant war, now nearly ten years old, still being fought by some 150,000 Western soldiers on the dusty plains and in the dirt-brown hills of Afghanistan. If things were going well, the statesmen and the generals would not be backward in proclaiming imminent victory.

Instead, on Afghanistan everyone is quietly lowering expectations. In a magazine's special issue to mark ten years of war in Afghanistan, an article provided by the British government is headed 'We do not seek a perfect Afghanistan'. It asserts that '[Afghanistan] has made progress ... it is clear, however, that ... significant challenges remain'.* On television, our leading general redefines the strategy: Britain's role is not to 'extinguish the insurgency' but to reduce it to a level that Afghan security forces can take on, and to prevent the country being used as a base to train terrorists. 'We're on track to deliver that strategy,' he says.†

A week or two earlier, the US Secretary of State tells Congress that America is successfully pursuing 'a three-track strategy of fight, talk and build' in Afghanistan. She places the emphasis on fighting, and claims that, now the momentum of the insurgency has been halted, talks can begin.§

In the summer of 2011, I speak about Afghanistan to dozens of audiences, large and small, at literary festivals and book clubs, in church halls and town halls, in drawing rooms and assembly rooms, in clubs in Pall Mall and officers' messes across the land. I meet Middle England. In six months, I find no one who does not support our troops, who is not giving to the Soldiers' Charity or Help for Heroes, or who will not willingly put a bit more in the collecting box for his or her poppy this year.

But, in seas of worried faces, among audiences most of whom have sons or grandsons, cousins or more distant kinsmen, of their own or of their friends, in the forces, I find no one, literally no one, who believes that the war is going well. I find few who believe any longer that the war is worth fighting. Among the most anxious are those who know

---

* *New Statesman*, 7 November 2011.

† *BBC News*, 13 November 2011.

§ Hillary Rodham Clinton, Congressional Testimony, 27 October 2011.

South-west Asia. In Cheltenham, true to caricature, it is an ancient colonel, a veteran of the North West Frontier, who is most critical of the campaign. Those most doubtful of the wisdom of Operation Herrick often seem to be those with most experience of matters military.

As I describe my experiences of the mistakes the West has made in and on Afghanistan, I hear gruff cries of 'Hear, Hear' or 'Bravo' from older members of my audience. When I point out that the US Army's own *Counterinsurgency Field Manual* suggests that COIN is mostly politics, and argue that a more political approach to stabilising Afghanistan and its region might be wiser, I note vigorous nodding in many corners of the room.

On the ground, in Afghanistan, the rising level of violence speaks for itself. In part, of course, this is a result of General Petraeus's strategy of taking the fight to the Taliban enemy. In part, however, it is a result of the insurgents doing what insurgents have done throughout history: adapting their tactics, and avoiding direct confrontations with superior forces which they are bound to lose. ISAF has undoubtedly had success in beating back the insurgents. More Afghan police and army units have been prepared for battle, and put into the field. Provinces and districts have been 'transitioned' to Afghan primacy, and more will follow.

But the six months since I finished the first edition of this book have also seen a horrific series of assaults and assassinations across Afghanistan. Karzai's main peace negotiator, ex-President Rabbani, is only one of dozens of prominent Afghans to die in increasingly cruel and clever terrorist attacks. That oasis of civilisation, the British Council compound in Kabul, is attacked by terrorists. So too is what should be the most impregnable of Western outposts, the CIA station near the Presidential Palace. The UN declares 2011 the most violent year in Afghanistan's recent history. Still the ISAF spokesmen claim, as I suppose they must, that 'progress is being made, but challenges remain'.* Still we are told that the momentum of the insurgency has

---

* For example, Lieutenant General William B. Caldwell IV, 'Beyond the 10th Year', http://www.isaf.nato.int/article/focus/beyond-the-10th-year-in-afghanistan-security-force-assistance-and-international-security.html

been/is being/will shortly be reversed, thus opening the way for us to talk to the Taliban from a position of strength.

Sadly, the reality is more sobering, and more worrying. For all the hype about 'talking to the Taliban', we are still stumbling round in the foothills of serious political engagement with the parties to the Afghan conflict. By subcontracting the internal process to the Afghans, and the regional process to the Turks, we have been half-hearted about adopting a political approach. The ramping up of the violence over the past year, with a trebling in special forces strikes on the insurgents and of ordnance dropped on Afghanistan from the air, suggests that we are at best ambivalent about winding down the violence so as to create the conditions for a peace process. With at most three years to go before Western forces cease fighting, the insurgents have few incentives to engage with an outside power that still does not seem serious about cutting them into a new Afghan political settlement. Without a credible political strategy, handing over districts and provinces to be garrisoned by Afghans rather than Americans seems unlikely to stabilise the country. In these circumstances, 'transition' sounds most like a way of marketing Western withdrawal.

None of which should detract from what is being done by brave Americans and their allies across Afghanistan to secure and develop small patches of Afghan territory. In central Helmand, in parts of Kandahar and the east, progress *is* being made. Nor do I doubt that the Bonn Conference, due on the tenth anniversary of its predecessor, in December 2011, will produce a plan for restoring Afghan sovereignty.

The difficulty is that, for all the fine words, rather big challenges remain. Success, when it comes, is local and temporary. The military campaign may be suppressing, locally and temporarily, the symptoms of the sickness, but it is not curing the underlying disease. The 'strategy' is based on two hopes: first, that, absent a profound new political settlement of the kind Afghanistan needs, the Afghan security forces will somehow by themselves secure the country once Western forces cease fighting; and, second, that Afghan 'governance' will somehow take root in a sustainable way in the areas thus garrisoned, initially by NATO forces, and then gradually by Afghans.

For me at least, none of that is surprising. But what does rather take my breath away is General Stan McChrystal's admission, to the Council on Foreign Relations in New York on the tenth anniversary of the invasion of Afghanistan, that we did not know what we were doing there:

> We didn't know enough, and we still don't know enough. Most of us, me included, had a very superficial understanding of the situation and history, and we had a frighteningly simplistic view of recent history, the last 50 years, the personalities, the actions that occurred ... I think we were woefully under informed.*

As I reflect on the war, I can understand the errors of initial analysis, and see how so much of the execution went wrong, often for good reason and decent motives. But what upsets me is that, in the face of all the evidence, we carry on without trying to implement the kind of serious political strategy which everybody who knows Afghanistan believes to be essential – if not by itself enough – for success. We neither learn nor apply the lessons we claim to have learned.

Nearly forty years ago, analysing an earlier American land war in Asia of which he had once been an enthusiastic advocate, Dr Daniel Ellsberg wrote:

> The US Government, starting ignorant, did not, would not, learn. There was a whole set of what amounted to institutional 'anti-learning' mechanisms working to preserve or guarantee unadaptive and unsuccessful behavior: the fast turnover in personnel; the lack of institutional memory at any level; the failure to study history, to analyze or even record operational experience or mistakes; the effective pressures for optimistically false reporting at every level, for describing 'progress' rather than problems or failure, thus concealing the very need for change in approach or for learning.†

---

* General Stanley McChrystal, Council on Foreign Relations, New York, 6 October 2011.

† Dr Daniel Ellsberg, *Papers on the War*, New York: Simon & Schuster, 1972, p. 18.

Ellsberg had served as a US Marine Corps officer in South Vietnam and later worked as a civilian adviser on Vietnam for both the Kennedy and Johnson Administrations. He wanted America to succeed there, but became increasingly disillusioned, unpersuaded either that victory over the Viet Cong was possible or that America was capable of extracting itself with honour from the quagmire. Ellsberg later wrote that he saw the war in Vietnam 'first as a problem; then as a stalemate; then as a crime'.

To my surprise, similar sentiments were echoed by a young officer from one of Britain's more fashionable infantry regiments who came to see me in October 2011. Badly wounded by a booby-trap bomb, he had concluded that he had no future in his beloved Army. He wanted my help in finding a job. Everything he said about his experience of the war, in moments of rare frankness, underlined the sad central thesis of this book: that the West's campaign in Afghanistan had been tactics without strategy. The slogans of the statesmen – 'Fight, Talk and Build' – or of the generals – 'Clear, Hold and Build' – were no substitute for the kind of serious political engagement, from the outside in, needed to stabilise Afghanistan.

Unlike Ellsberg, neither that young officer nor I believed that the West's war in Afghanistan was a crime. As I awkwardly escorted the wounded warrior in his wheelchair to the front door of my office, I could not, however, help reflecting. It was bad, but understandable, that young men like him might be sent to fight and die for their country without the best body armour or the most modern of mine-proof vehicles. But it *was* close to a crime that men like him were still being sent into a battle without a strategy worthy of the name.

London
November 2011

Acknowledgements

This book was not my idea. For that, we have to thank the person who was later to become my agent, Caroline Michel. Several years ago we met at a dinner at the Irish Ambassador's house. Caroline told me that I had at least one book in me and that, if I ever wanted to write and publish, I should get in touch. Once I saw the light at the end of the Foreign Office tunnel, I did.

So first I must thank Caroline for her faith in me, and for the intelligent encouragement offered through some dark days by her and her team at Peters, Fraser and Dunlop, notably Alexandra Henderson and Tim Binding.

I am indebted also to the team at HarperPress: above all, my editor, Martin Redfern, and his colleagues, Annabel Wright and Kerry Chapple, who have worked so hard to knock this book into shape; but also to many others whose enthusiasm and interest have meant so much – Minna Fry, Helen Ellis and Arabella Pike, to name only a few of the HarperPress gang.

I am grateful too for the prompt and sensible way in which the Cabinet Office handled clearance of this book, and to the Foreign Office for releasing (albeit with heavy redactions) the telegrams from me in Kabul which form the tribute and the endpapers of this book.

My research assistant, Max Benitz, is an author, actor and Afghanophile in his own right: he has carried out countless checks and searches, and made many helpful suggestions with humour and efficiency.

But those to whom I owe most I prefer not to name here: my family (who put up with so much), and close friends, colleagues and companions on my bittersweet Afghan journey, without whose help and support I could not have managed. But they all know who they are. And of course any mistakes are my responsibility alone.

Shepherd's Bush
May 2011

20 February 2009

Subject ███████████████████ AU REVOIR AFGHANISTAN

Summary As the tide of outside engagement in Afghanistan starts to turn, we need to work with the Obama Administration develop policies that help the Afghans secure and govern their land for themselves, ████████████████████
████████████████

SIC

1. Five hundred years from now, when Chinese archaeologists excavate the great imperial ruins at Bagram, in the shadow of the Hindu Kush on the Shomali Plain north of Kabul, they will find first the remains of the American empire. They will marvel at the crude electric tablets on which the ancient Americans used long ago to type by hand. They will admire the extraordinary tangle of wires festooned round what once must have been the command post of the CI legion. They will marvel at the length of the runways needed by the flying machines of old. They will carefully collect the disgusting lumps of animal flesh and gristle still preserved in wrappers marked, oddly, Supreme█████████████████████
████████████████████████████████

2. But, as they dig a bit deeper, they will come across the detritus of an even older civilisation, which used an even stranger alphabet, known to none in the party. Those weapons and tools are fashioned in crudely cast iron, strong and simple, often bearing the mysterious legend CCCP. Deeper still they will come across coins - apparently nearly three thousand years old - on which the inscriptions are in an even earlier Cyrillic-style alphabet. Many of them are stamped with the head of a young man, wearing a laurel wreath, beneath whom the letters MAKEDON can be discerned through the dirt and dust

3. So, just as historians may one day see the fall of Baghdad in April 2003 as the high water mark of the American empire, they may come also to regard Obama's decision this week to send 17,000 more US troops to Afghanistan as the high point of the present phase of foreign engagement in this long-contested land. ████████████████████
████████████████████████████████████
████████████████████████████████████
████████████████████████████████

4. As every Afghan schoolboy knows, imperial Britain had difficulty making up its mind how to deal with the troublesome tribes across the mountains in Afghanistan. The neocons of the day, egged on by Disraeli, favoured a forward policy that twice ended in disaster. Realists and liberals fell back first on what was called the modified forward policy, of garrisoning key points in the tribal areas, but later settled on what Curzon described as the closed door policy: sitting back behind the Indus, while paying the tribes to behave themselves, and punishing them when they didn't.

5. Of course, history never repeats itself, exactly. Modern Democratic America is not Victorian Britain. Obama is not Gladstone. Afghanistan does not today abut the American frontier in the way it once sat between Imperial Russia and Britain's Indian Empire – ████████
████████████████████████████████████

6. In the great sweep of human history, however, my instinct is that the tide of Western engagement here is turning once again. █████████████████████████████████

7. That means that, whatever temporary military effect we seek ourselves to deliver in the years ahead, we must never lose sight of the overriding importance of creating security and governance arrangements capable in a few years from now of sustaining themselves without large numbers of foreign combat troops. ████████████████████████████████

But Al Qaeda and its malign associates will have all but left the land. ██ Instead, we will be implementing the strategy set out by the International Development Secretary in his speech at the IISS last year: helping the Afghan authorities, civil and military, to Engage with the populations of their land, to Stabilise the villages and valleys in which they live, and then to Develop them.

8. No-one should doubt, however, that in the short term the carefully calculated application of Western military force will be an essential part of reaching the point at which we can start gradually to pull back from combat. But, if it is to succeed in any meaningful way, such selective use of military power must be accompanied by serious programmes

9.

Sign Off   Cowper-Coles
Contact Name   COWPER-COLES

Attachments

Abbreviations

ANP	Afghan National Police
AQ	Al Qaeda
AWK	Ahmed Wali Karzai
CDV	Community Defence Volunteers
CentCom	US Central Command
CERP	Commanders' Emergency Response Program
CIA	Central Intelligence Agency (US)
COIN	counter-insurgency
COMISAF	Commander, ISAF
CPT	Close Protection Team
DFID	Department for International Development
DIS	Defence Intelligence Service (British)
EU	European Union
FCO	Foreign and Commonwealth Office
FOB	Forward Operating Base
GHQ	General Head Quarters
HMG	Her Majesty's Government
IED	Improvised explosive device
ISAF	International Security Assistance Force
ISI	Inter Services Intelligence (Pakistani)
KAF	Kandahar Air Field
MOD	Ministry of Defence
MRAP	Mine-Resistant Ambush-Proof (vehicle)
NATO	North Atlantic Treaty Organisation
NDS	National Directorate for Security (Afghan)
PRT	Provincial Reconstruction Team

RECC-A	Regional Economic Co-operation Conference – Afghanistan
RPG	Rocket-propelled grenade
SEG	Special Escort Group (Metropolitan Police)
SIS	Secret Intelligence Service (British)
SRAP	Special Representative for Afghanistan and Pakistan
SVTC	Secure video teleconference
TMF	Turquoise Mountain Foundation
UNAMA	UN Assistance Mission in Afghanistan
USAF	United States Air Force
VBIED	Vehicle-borne improvised explosive device

Index

SHERARD COWPER-COLES

Telegrams

Despatches from the Diplomatic Front-line

'When I joined the Diplomatic Service in 1977, we were told, only half-jokingly, that, like the fountains in Trafalgar Square, Foreign Office officials operated only from ten till six. We didn't need to arrive in King Charles Street before ten o'clock because that gave time for the distribution, around the Office and Whitehall, of the overnight telegram traffic. The first thing we did each morning was read a buff folder full of carefully sorted paper telegrams from different posts, held together by an India Tag.'

For over 30 years Sherard Cowper-Coles was on the diplomatic front-line in a distinguished Foreign Office career that took him from the corridors of power in Whitehall to posts in Cairo, Washington, Hong Kong, Paris, Tel Aviv, Riyadh and Kabul.

Filled with colourful anecdotes, *Telegrams* is the riveting memoir of life as a diplomat, to be published by Harper Press in November 2012.